AUDIO PRODUCTION WORKTEXT
Sixth Edition

AUDIO PRODUCTION WORKTEXT

Concepts, Techniques, and Equipment

Sixth Edition

DAVID E. REESE

LYNNE S. GROSS

BRIAN GROSS

ELSEVIER

AMSTERDAM • BOSTON • HEIDELBERG • LONDON • NEW YORK
OXFORD • PARIS • SAN DIEGO • SAN FRANCISCO • SINGAPORE
SYDNEY • TOKYO
Focal Press is an imprint of Elsevier

Focal Press is an imprint of Elsevier
30 Corporate Drive, Suite 400, Burlington, MA 01803, USA
Linacre House, Jordan Hill, Oxford OX2 8DP, UK

∞ Recognizing the importance of preserving what has been written, Elsevier prints its books on
acid-free paper whenever possible.

Library of Congress Cataloging-in-Publication Data
Reese, David E.
  Audio production worktext : concepts, techniques, and equipment / David E. Reese,
Lynne S. Gross, Brian Gross.
      p. cm.
  Rev. ed. of: Radio production worktext. 2006.
  Includes index.
  ISBN 978-0-240-81098-0 (pbk. : alk. paper) 1. Sound studios—Textbooks. 2. Radio stations—
Equipment and supplies—Textbooks. 3. Radio—Production and direction—Textbooks. 4. Sound—
Recording and reproducing—Equipment and supplies—Textbooks. I. Gross, Lynne S. II. Gross,
Brian, 1969- III. Reese, David E. Radio production worktext. IV. Title.
  TK6557.5.R44 2009
  791.4402'3—dc22

                                                                                    2008046889

British Library Cataloguing-in-Publication Data
A catalogue record for this book is available from the British Library.

ISBN: 978-0-240-81098-0

For information on all Focal Press publications
visit our website at www.books.elsevier.com

09 10 11 12 13 5 4 3 2

Printed in the United States of America

CONTENTS

CHAPTER 3   DIGITAL AUDIO PRODUCTION

CHAPTER 4   MICROPHONES

CHAPTER 5   THE AUDIO CONSOLE

CHAPTER 6   DIGITAL AUDIO PLAYERS/RECORDERS

CHAPTER 7   MONITOR SPEAKERS AND STUDIO ACCESSORIES

CHAPTER 8   SIGNAL PROCESSING EQUIPMENT

PREFACE

In its sixth edition, *Audio Production Worktext* sports a new title that reflects not only the changes that digital technology has brought to the equipment and the techniques of audio production, but also an admission that radio isn't necessarily the primary outlet for modern audio production work. Today, audio content is being produced for distribution in a wide variety of formats. Although radio still consumes a tremendous amount of audio production, the Internet also has its version of radio, along with podcasts, audio blogs, and other forms of audio content. Cable, broadcast television, and Internet video also include an audio production component. Audio content via satellite, cell phone, and other wireless links is another outlet for audio production work. And new delivery systems for audio content—not yet devised—may be lurking just around the corner.

Given this audio production environment, radio production seemed just too focused and this new text recognizes that. Furthermore, the scope of the text has expanded to include more of the thinking and planning that is part of the production process and production techniques that take place outside the traditional audio production studio. Of course, what hasn't changed is that this edition continues to offer a solid background about the audio production process in a simplified, straightforward text.

Audio production work is more competitive than ever, and those with a firm understanding of the basics of the digital audio production process will stand the best chance of succeeding in this field. Like much in life, what you get from this text is largely up to you. As the title implies, this isn't a book you just read, but rather a text that will become an integral part of your study and practice of audio production. The sixth edition continues to utilize this "worktext" approach, because it is our firm belief that this subject is best taught by a combination of theory and discussion and practical, hands-on use of audio equipment. Each chapter of the text is divided into the following sections: Information, Self-Study Questions and Answers, and Projects.

The Information sections for each chapter are divided into modular units so that all the primary concepts can be easily learned. These concepts are illustrated with drawings and images that help the student grasp the specific ideas being presented.

Self-Study Questions include multiple choice and true/false questions covering key material presented in the chapter. Answers, as well as suggested procedures for those who don't answer correctly, guide the student through this section. These questions are not really test questions, but rather are intended to be instructional, so that by the time the student has read the Information section and answered all the questions correctly, he or she will feel confident about knowing the information.

The Projects sections of the chapters contain practical projects that should give readers a degree of expertise in equipment manipulation and, we hope, lead them on to further creative audio production work. It is assumed that the reader will have completed both the Information section and Self-Study Questions before beginning the various projects. The importance of practical production experience cannot be overemphasized, and these projects should be viewed as a starting point for a developing production person. Additional hands-on work in the production studio is never wasted time and is strongly recommended.

The sixth edition still includes information about the equipment necessary for audio production work, but it doesn't deal strictly with a nuts-and-bolts approach. Other chapters deal with the planning and creative thought that should begin any production project. Additional production techniques, as well as mechanics, are included within most chapters. In fact, the book isn't intended to be that technical. It's written in an easy-to-read style that should enable people without technical training to understand the nature and makeup of the audio production process.

The book continues to refine its organization and content as some chapters have been combined and repositioned in the text to reflect the importance of their content for modern audio production.

This edition of *Audio Production Worktext* includes an easy-to-navigate CD-ROM that illustrates many of the important concepts discussed in the text. For example, when the terms "cross-fade" and "segue" are explained in Chapter 5, "The Audio Console," not only is there a definition of the terms and a diagram showing the concept, but there is also an audio clip that lets you readily hear the difference between these two basic sound transitions. There are also files on the CD-ROM that contain forms that you can download to help execute your audio productions. In addition, files provide material that you can use to create audio production projects. Some of these are for particular production projects in the text, but most of them are music and sound effects that can be used with a variety of projects. Those sections of the text that include an audio clip or other material on the CD-ROM are noted throughout the text with a small compact disc icon.

We've used the audio editing software program Adobe Audition to illustrate many digital production concepts in the text. To duplicate our demonstrations or create your own audio production projects, you can download a trial version of the program from www.adobe.com. Demo versions of similar programs may also be available. As noted in "Production Tip 3 A," you can also download Audacity, a free basic audio editing program.

Throughout the book, we have freshened and updated both the copy and artwork to reflect today's audio production world. Chapter 1, "Production Planning," opens the text and focuses on qualities that typify a good production person; a model production planning process; and working with the basic production elements of voice, music, and sound effects. Chapter 2, "The Studio Environment," introduces the reader to the layout and design of the audio production studio—the environment in which the reader will accomplish much of his or her production work—and describes briefly equipment that's detailed in subsequent chapters. This chapter also discusses some basic concepts regarding sound that will help the production person to understand the raw material being worked with.

The reader is quickly immersed in "Digital Audio Production" in Chapter 3. After a brief look at how audio is converted from analog to digital, this chapter introduces some of the equipment used for digital production and looks at the tools and techniques of digital editing. Essentially, all audio editing is now accomplished in this manner. Then, this chapter looks at the basics of multitrack production. Almost all digital-based production studios have multitrack capability, as do some analog-based studios, so it's important for the production person to learn the basic techniques of multitrack recording and the creative possibilities that they open up. Having mastered some basic production techniques, students should be ready to work with the sound sources that can serve as inputs or outputs for the console. One of these is covered in Chapter 4, "Microphones." Chapter 5, "The Audio Console," introduces one key component of audio

production work. Expanded material on digital interfaces and "virtual" consoles keeps this chapter firmly in the digital age. A solid understanding of the material is important because other audio equipment often operates through a console or mixer. Chapter 6, "Digital Audio Players/Recorders," deals with some of the players and recorders beyond those covered earlier in the text. Compact discs, MiniDiscs, DATs (digital audio tapes), Compact Flash, and hard disk players and recorders are all considered here.

Equipment that is often overlooked in audio production is included in Chapter 7, "Monitor Speakers and Studio Accessories." Monitor speakers and headphones are first discussed, and then the connectors, cables, and accessories that complement the major pieces of equipment in the production studio are surveyed. In this edition, Chapter 8, "Signal Processing Equipment," provides an introduction to the most popular signal processing equipment employed in audio production work. You will learn that digital equipment, especially audio editing software, can replicate most of the signal processing effects—usually faster and more easily.

Chapter 9, "Production Situations," considers several different production situations. The student will learn that many of the techniques and skills used for basic spot production are also employed for radio announcing, newscasting, interviewing, and sports play-by-play, to name a few. Chapter 10, "Location Sound Recording" is another new chapter in this edition. After surveying different types of field recording, this chapter discusses problems associated with location recording, the tools of field recording, and basic techniques used to capture sound in the field and get that sound back to the studio. Another new chapter is Chapter 11, "Sound Production for Video." After establishing the importance of sound to a video production, this chapter looks at techniques for recording dialogue, music, sound effects, and ambient sound. Microphone types and placement are discussed, as well as editing and postproduction considerations. The final chapter in the sixth edition, Chapter 12, "Internet Radio and Other Distribution Platforms," explains how to develop an Internet radio station and briefly looks at some of the other distribution methods for getting audio production work to the listener. Many new distribution platforms have provided an opportunity and an outlet for creative audio production. The appendix, "Analog Audio Equipment," is a historic survey of analog equipment, and some of the analog-based production techniques, as well as an admission that some facilities haven't completely abandoned the equipment and techniques of older technology.

Throughout the text, you'll also find Production Tips, which provide interesting notes that are relevant to various audio production topics. Also, key terms are listed in boldface when they appear in each chapter and are included in the Glossary. The sixth edition of *Audio Production Worktext* is available with an *Instructor's Manual*, which includes a sample syllabus, lesson plans, study questions, test questions, list of pertinent web sites, and more.

ACKNOWLEDGMENTS

We would like to thank the people who encouraged us while we put together this new edition of *Audio Production Worktext*. We are indebted to our colleagues at the University of Nevada, Las Vegas and California State University, Fullerton.

Many of our friends in broadcasting and related audio production industries provided us with valuable insight and "real world" anecdotes, which help to make our text as good as it is.

- Rick Baca, Traffic Reporter, KFI, Los Angeles
- Craig Breit, Professor, Mass Communications, Cerritos College, Norwalk, CA
- Dennis Clare, Freelance Radio Engineer
- Pete Demetriou, Reporter, KFWB, Los Angeles
- Mike Huffman, Program Director, GhostXM.com, Vancouver, Canada
- Phil Hulett, Anchor, KFWB, Los Angeles
- Andy Ludlum, News Director, KFWB, Los Angeles
- Mike Stark, Producer, Tom Joyner Morning Show
- Tammy Trujillo, Anchor, KFWB, Los Angeles
- Doug Watson, Chief Engineer, Motor Racing Network Radio

The authors have had the pleasure of working with Focal Press for a number of years on various book projects and readily acknowledge that each manuscript has become a polished, finished text because of the hard work, dedication, and expertise of the Focal Press team. We would like to thank all of our friends at Focal Press. For their guidance through the publication of *Audio Production Worktext*, we'd especially like to thank Elinor Actipis, Dennis McGonagle, Carlin Reagan, and Anais Wheeler.

1

PRODUCTION PLANNING

1.1 INTRODUCTION

Very little effective audio content is produced by accident; it usually involves fairly careful planning. Some of this can be done in your head, merely by thinking through what you want to do. Other planning involves putting something down on paper so that both you and those working with you understand the needs of the project. Still other planning involves making sure that you can actually gather the elements you need for your program and that you do so legally and ethically.

What follows in this chapter are a number of steps that are part of planning. They will differ from one project to another, but they are all concepts that you should consider as you start to put together an audio production.

1.2 THE IDEA

Ideas can come from anywhere—a book, a dream, a conversation with a friend, or an Internet site. One of the most common sources for ideas that end up on radio is the news of the day. It need not be the major news; it can be something tucked on the back page of a newspaper that appears to have an interesting back-story that you decide to explore. Depending on what your job position is, someone else may give you an idea and ask you to further develop it. This is particularly true for reporters who are assigned story ideas by their producers or others in the newsroom. But reporters also need to be on the lookout for ideas that will make meaningful stories (see Figure 1.1).

With the Internet and its ever-more-powerful search engines, instead of searching for stories, there are now ways to have stories come straight to you that might be of interest to you and your audience. On Google News (news.google.com), for example, you can personalize your own page with news stories from around the world that contain specific words or phrases. If your beat is health and wellness, for example, you might set up your Google News page to give you stories that

include the phrase "cancer treatment" or "antidepressant" or "avian flu." You can also set up Google News so that it automatically sends you an email whenever a new story with the words or phrases that you specify enters its system. Combined with a mobile PDA such as a Blackberry or iPhone, breaking news can search you out wherever you go.

In order to solidify an idea, you may need to undertake additional research. If you are preparing a story about the closing of a factory in a small town, you will want to find out when the factory was built, how many people it employed at its peak, what effect its closing will have on the town, and so on. Some of this information, such as when it was built, may be on the Internet. For other bits of information, you will need to search records in the city hall or interview people. As you do your research, verify your facts. A good rule of thumb is that you should get the same information from three sources before you use it. In other words, if one person tells you that the treasurer of the company embezzled money, don't include that information until you have verified it.

In today's information-overload society, being able to develop unique angles on stories can really make your career. Sometimes a printed news article might make passing mention of a person or organization that is related to an event. Radio, unlike print, lends itself more readily to somewhat lengthy interviews that provide perspectives on developing stories from individuals who are involved or affected by events. It's one thing to read about an off-duty police officer who was awakened by the sounds of someone trying to steal his car in the early morning—and who ran out of the house stark naked in hot pursuit. It's quite another if your audience can actually hear the story from the officer's perspective. If you are able to find willing interviewees who have strong opinions or personalities, all the better. But again, this approach can take some research and persistence. In the above-mentioned story, which occurred in New Zealand in early April 2008, the officer's name is not mentioned and there is only a quote from a nameless "police spokesman." But the officer's hometown is mentioned. Some searching on

FIGURE 1.1 Both the radio reporter in the foreground and the television reporters in the background who are covering this bank robbery story need to look for angles that will be of interest to their audience members.

the Internet and a few phone calls could yield an interesting and unique **sound bite**, if not a sizzling interview.

It is not always possible to research fast-breaking news, but you can prepare yourself for such situations by being well read and knowing the community from which you generate most of your ideas. Talk show hosts need to have, in their head, facts on a large number of issues. Disc jockeys should research the background of artists whose music they play (see Figure 1.2). Sportscasters need to have a source for statistics so that they can craft interesting background stories during the course of a sportscast.

1.3 GOALS AND OBJECTIVES

Before you embark on the production of an audio project, you need to decide in your own mind why you are producing

it. At a very basic level, is your goal to entertain, or inform, or a little of each? Knowing that motivation will affect how you put the piece together in terms of how you write it, how many facts you include, and even what type of music you use within it. At a more specific level, you can consider what action you want the listener to take. For example, let's assume that you are putting together a commercial for a new medicine that relieves tension. What do you want the person hearing it to do—buy the medicine, tell their friends about it, ask their doctor to prescribe it, or contribute money to further develop the medicine? If you are going to record a feature, how do you want the listener to feel during its broadcast— happy, proud, or angry?

As you think about goals and objectives, you may want to consider some specific qualities of audio. Radio is sometimes referred to as "theater of the mind." Lacking a visual image to point the way, people create their own visual

FIGURE 1.2   Disc jockeys should undertake research so that they are well versed about the music they play. (Image courtesy of Alan R. Stephenson.)

images, which often are more emotionally intense than what could be created with video. Also, although it is possible for millions of people to listen to one radio broadcast simultaneously, audio is really a one-to-one communication process, wherein each listener feels a personal tie to what they are hearing. Focusing on the intense, personal communication process of audio can help you create ways to reach your goals and objectives.

1.4 THE TARGET AUDIENCE

In the modern world, where many media programs are niche-oriented, it is important to determine who you expect will listen to your audio material. The most common way that such **target audiences** are defined is through **demographics**—statistical information such as age, sex, income, nationality, and marital status. At an obvious level, if your audience speaks Spanish, your piece should be produced in that language. Generally, if your target audience is young, you want to make your material more fast-paced than if your audience is older. Surprisingly, you can sometimes use the same information but package it

differently for different demographics. A feature about the Oscars might be equally interesting to young and old—all you need to do to get each group's attention is change the music you use in the background.

Your target audience may be defined by the audio entity you work for. For example, people who listen to National Public Radio (NPR) are more liberal than people who listen to Fox News. That doesn't mean you can't present conservative views on a program for NPR, but you might need to include more background information than you would for an audience that is going to share the point of view presented in the material.

Often people with common interests listen to the same material. If you are producing a story about surfing that is aimed at the general public, but your target audience is avid surfers, your program will probably not be well received because the avid surfers will be bored.

Consistency should also be a concern. Listeners who tune into a show for its frothy content might be turned off—for a day, or forever—if they one day encounter a lengthy segment about the weighty topic of self-esteem. Though listeners to a usually frothy program may have issues with or even a desire to improve their self-esteem, that was not the impulse that drove them to push that button on their radios. This concept holds as true for the so-called "free-for-all" world of the Internet as it does for commercial radio. A podcaster whose topics do not have an element of consistency will soon find listeners pointing their browsers elsewhere.

1.5 STYLE

Another element to consider is style. Do you want it to be serious, humorous, thought-provoking, etc? Style can radically alter the appeal and palatability of content to various audiences. The same content could be covered within an interview or banter between on-air personalities; it could be delivered in a dramatic skit, abetted by topical musical selections; or it could be an amalgamation of these and other forms.

What style you select will have a natural effect on the production—whether it ranges from serious to silly—and vice versa. Playing with style can create interesting and powerful effects for your audience. Delivering serious content in a lackadaisical manner or imbuing a trivial matter with gravitas can create dramatic tension on its own, even if your audience would be otherwise uninterested in the content. A quick and deliberate change in style can likewise create suspense. Of course, such dissonances between content and form ought to be carefully considered and are usually appropriate only for programs that aim to entertain, rather than inform. They can stir considerable controversy, especially if they catch an audience unaware.

For some programs, such dissonances become a trademark—arguably even their very reason for existence. NPR's *Le Show*, produced weekly by Harry Shearer, and the syndicated Phil Hendrie show are prime examples. Likewise, with shows such as AM radio's nighttime staple *Coast to Coast*, where topics can range from conspiracy theories to UFOs to a smorgasbord of metaphysical topics, it's hard to know when or whether the producers are aiming to entertain, educate, or possibly simply titillate their audiences.

Coming up with an idea, establishing goals and objectives, assessing the target audience, and determining style is a somewhat circular process (see Figure 1.3). Deciding that you want to make a program funny rather than serious may change your idea. Perhaps the first element you will consider is your target audience, and then you will search for an idea to appeal to that audience. The precise sequence of your thinking is not nearly as important as the need to make sure that you consider these elements before you get to the stages that cost money.

1.6 PRODUCTION PERSONNEL

The costliest part of audio production is often the salaries of the people involved. You definitely need to consider how many people it is going to take to produce the audio product. The answer may be "one"—yourself. Audio material,

FIGURE 1.3 Stare at this picture long enough to think of an idea that you could use for an audio project. Then think through these questions: What would you need to research? What would be your goal for your project? Who would constitute the target audience? What style would you use? How did your idea change as you thought through the various questions? (Photo courtesy of iStockphoto, Alex Grumerov, Image #2807197.)

because it is fairly simple and inexpensive to produce, can be completed by one person who comes up with the idea, hosts the program, engineers equipment, and edits.

If you possess the versatility to do it all, you will be more highly prized in the audio industry than if you can only perform or only edit. The trend in the industry is to give projects to people who can handle all facets of them. Reporters, for example, not only search out the elements of the story and conduct interviews, but they operate the recording equipment and edit the package together into a meaningful whole (see Figure 1.4). As **convergence** of the various media forms increases and media companies merge and buy each other, managers often look for people who can not only do all the jobs necessary to produce an audio product but who can then take the information and prepare it for other platforms such as newspapers, television, the Internet, and podcasting.

Many audio programs, however, are the result of teamwork. Quiz and variety shows on public radio employ more than 20 people. Although individual reporters contribute individual stories, a large team puts together an overall newscast. Therefore, in addition to versatility, people who

FIGURE 1.4 Radio news anchors undertake a multitude of tasks. Obviously, they read the news from a script, such as the one seen on the computer screen to the right of the anchor. They also do their own engineering, by operating an audio board and audio playback devices. They follow the list of items to be broadcast (seen on the screen to the left) and sign off that each element has in fact aired. They also look for new stories. The monitor to the far right can be used to check video feeds from television stations or news agencies and a monitor directly in front of the anchor can access databases and the Internet.

FIGURE 1.5 Brainstorming for an audio production project is a worthwhile experience that can yield beneficial improvements.

work in radio also need to have good interpersonal skills so that they can work cooperatively and brainstorm with others for the good of the overall project (see Figure 1.5).

They also need to be able to write—the main trait that professionals find lacking in their new hires. If you are a student wishing to get into audio, take every opportunity you can to improve your writing skills. If you can master the skill of writing a good **teaser** quickly, for example, you'll be in a position to wow a potential employer at a moment's notice. Radio lives and dies on teasers—they're what keep listeners tuned in through the all-important (at least in a financial sense) advertisements. Listen for teasers on your favorite radio show, then start reading news or feature stories in the newspaper or on the Internet and write some of your own. Read them out loud to yourself and your friends. Sometimes in programming that aims to entertain, the tease can become more important than the topic or than the topic deserves—like a pitcher's elaborate windup that delivers a simple fastball, low and inside, sending the batter walking lazily to first base. Of course this kind of dissonance between tease and topic, if used repeatedly, can become annoying and off-putting for audiences—akin to the boy who cried "wolf."

Computer skills and the ability to troubleshoot technical equipment problems are also high on the list of traits needed by audio people. They must also be curious and creative so that they can come up with infinite ideas, and they must be artistic enough to put the material together in a pleasing and often unique manner. Organizational skills are needed in order to proceed from idea to completion. A good sense of humor is also an asset—just as it is in most endeavors. There is some "hurry up and wait" in audio production, so people must balance their enthusiasm to get the job done with a temperament that includes patience. Another trait that has become important now that audio practitioners are expected to handle all aspects of production is a pleasant-sounding voice and an ability to speak extemporaneously. Those wishing to get into the field should avail themselves of as much public speaking experience as they can. Find a local chapter of Toastmasters International or make a video where you talk and post it on YouTube to test your chops.

Another characteristic that permeates most people who engage in sound production is passion. Be it radio, music recording, or some other form of audio endeavor, they love what they do. It's nice if some fame and fortune comes along, too, but the real motivator is a passion for audio.

1.7 PRODUCTION ELEMENTS

Once you settle on your idea, decide upon your goals and objectives, assess your target audience, determine your style, and gather together those who will be working on the project, you can get more serious about what you will need in order to put the audio piece together. There are three basic production elements that you have at your disposal: voices, music, and sound effects. Most productions mix several of these elements together.

Voices include the voice of the announcer or host of the program and sound bites from other sources. The announcer or host's voice is generally the most important element, because it conveys the basic information of the production (see Figure 1.6). Usually this is recorded first when putting a project together so that other elements can be recorded to fit with it. The voice will be discussed in more detail in Section 1.10.

Sound bites can come from a number of sources. You can find and interview people who have something to say relevant to your story and include their comments. Sometimes members of the general public come to you with newsworthy sound bites they were able to record by being in the right place at the right time. Often radio stations subscribe to services, such as the Associated Press (AP) or CNN Radio, and have rights to use sound bites collected by those agencies. More and more media organizations have set up phone lines and Internet portals where the general public can provide their input and submit photos, video, and recordings for use within their programs (having to agree to the unlimited use of the materials in the process, of course).

FIGURE 1.6   An announcer is an important part of many audio productions.

Music can be the subject of an audio production and in those cases it is very much in the foreground. Disc jockey shows are one example. At other times, music is in the background to help set the mood or convey additional information. For example, a sports show might feature a high-energy piece as its theme, and a Beatles track could be used for a program dealing with some phenomenon of the 1960s.

Radio stations and most other audio production facilities have **music libraries** that include CDs of entire songs that they regularly play (or have played) on air as well as CDs of shorter pieces of music that can be used as background on productions. There are many music library sites on the Internet from which you can download copyright-cleared music for a slight fee. Go to www.royaltyfreemusic.com for a list of music libraries. Production music, whether from a CD or an Internet site, is composed in a wide range of musical styles, including everything from symphonies to rap, and is often organized by its mood—suspense, romance, tragedy. Of course, if you are musically talented, you can compose music specifically for your production.

Sound effects also help set the scene of a production, but, in addition, they are often used to augment and punctuate a point. For example, the sound of a telephone ringing or door opening creates an instant mental image. Morning radio show hosts often use unusual sound effects to increase the aural elements of their shows or to accompany some zany feature that they air on a regular basis. One way to classify sound effects is as "atmospheres" or "stingers." **Atmosphere sounds** are employed to create a natural environment, such as using seagull cries and crashing waves to set the scene at the seashore. Sound effect **stingers** are individual, short, sharp sounds designed to capture immediate attention, such as glass crashing or a gunshot.

Like production music, there are libraries of sound effects both on CD and the Internet. In addition to using these "canned" sounds, there may be times when you record natural sound live as part of the overall production or simulate a sound yourself, such as crinkling cellophane near a microphone to create a "fire" sound.

Another element you can consider using in an audio production is silence or **dramatic pause**. If you're trying to highlight a specific copy point, don't be afraid to pause a little longer than normal before saying that phrase. Don't pause too long, however, or you will have **dead air**, which will be perceived by your listener as a technical problem rather than providing the effect that you're trying to achieve.

How you incorporate elements into your production depends on the type of production. A variety show may need live musicians, live sound effects, and people who can perform numerous voices for a mini-drama. A commercial might be composed of unusual sound effects never heard before. A sports show might have a stinger at the end of each segment. Tap into your creativity to use the elements at your disposal to increase the effectiveness of your production.

PRODUCTION TIP 1A
Pick Any Two

There is a saying: "You want it fast, cheap, and good. Pick any two."

This adage most definitely applies to audio production. If you do your program quickly and cheaply, it probably won't be very good. If you employ a large number of people so you can gather all the elements together quickly, you may get a good program, but it won't be cheap. If you settle for using equipment during brief periods of time when no one else is using it, you may be able to produce a good program cheaply, but it won't be fast.

The ideal, of course, is to have enough time and enough money to make the program as good as it can be. Such rarely happens in the real world, but you should at least be aware of which element you are not engaging fully so that your life will be more bearable. Often people just breaking into the business have to work cheap (or for free) just to get a foot in the door, but that shouldn't last forever. There will certainly be times in your career when you will need to work long hours, but that should not become a way of life. If you have it in you to create quality work, you should be able to endure the fast and the cheap, especially if you realize that is what you are doing and see a way for the situation to be rectified in the not-too-distant future.

1.8 THE SCRIPT

In all probability, you will be writing a **script** at the same time you are collecting other elements for the program. You may think of an idea for the script that necessitates revising the sound effects you were planning, or you may find that you can't create a specific sound and have to change the script. In fact, as you are writing the script you may even change a few facets of your basic idea.

Basically, however, a script is a blueprint for your program. Different types of scripts have different content, but most scripts have a beginning, a middle, and an end. For a work of a dramatic nature, the beginning is usually an introduction to the characters and the middle involves rising action and a climax; the end is a resolution to a story. A news story often starts with the voice of the reporter explaining the story, which then goes to a sound bite that elaborates and confirms major points and ends with a wrap-up by the reporter. News stories are also often organized around the five Ws and an H; in other words, somewhere within the story it answers the questions who, what, where, when, why, and how. To that, some people add "so what?"—the need to explain the importance of the story. There are many books that cover the intricacies of writing scripts. Those who are seriously interested in audio production should avail themselves of this material, which is easy to find on the Internet.

```
SLUG: FIRE                                         REPORTER: JENKINS
DATE: 3/8                                           PRODUCER: KAMINSKI
LENGTH: 47 SEC.                                     ANCHOR: SANCHEZ


FIRE CREWS ARE ASSESSING THE DAMAGE AT THE BRISTOL STREET
WAREHOUSE TODAY AFTER A FIRE RAVAGED THROUGH THE FACILITY
EARLY THIS MORNING. THE FIRE APPARENTLY STARTED IN THE BASEMENT
OF THE BUILDING EITHER IN THE FURNACE AREA OR THE KITCHEN.
ALTHOUGH TWO OTHER BUILDINGS BURNED IN THIS AREA DURING THE
PAST YEAR, THE FIRE CHIEF DOES NOT THINK THE FIRES ARE RELATED.

SOT: 17 SEC. FIRE CHIEF: IN: FROM THE LOOKS OF THE FIRE....OUT:
....WE'LL SEE TOMORROW.

ARSON HAS NOT BEEN RULED OUT AS A CAUSE. TOM JENKINS REPORTING
FOR KTTT FROM THE SCENE OF THE FIRE.
```

FIGURE 1.7   This is a sample script for a news story. Different news organizations use different forms, but most have something to keep their stories consistent.

There are standard forms for scripts in the industry. If you work in radio news, your news gathering organization will probably have a template that you can store in your computer and use for each story (see Figure 1.7). Although these differ from one facility to another, they generally include a **slug** (title of the story), the date, the length, and the names of the main people who need to work with the story in order to get it to air. These templates are usually set up in such a way that makes it easy for the writer to keep track of time—for example, each line equals approximately 5 seconds. Timing is very important in the radio business, and people who are on story assignments are usually given a length that their story should adhere to. Each story is typed on a separate sheet of paper or into its own computer file and that way the stories can be juggled when they are put together for an entire newscast.

A talk or variety show where some elements are prewritten word for word and others that are spontaneous may use a **rundown sheet**, which lists the items in the order they are supposed to occur and gives an approximate timing for each (see Figure 1.8). If you are producing audio used in conjunction with video, you will probably encounter a **two-column script** with one column for audio and the other for the video that is to be shown as the audio is heard (see Figure 1.9).

1.9 PAPERWORK

Some audio productions need very little in the way of paperwork. You can probably keep in your head all the details needed for something that is short and that you do all by yourself. But other people cannot read your mind, so you often need to put such things on paper so that they can accomplish their jobs effectively and efficiently. If a program is complicated and involves a number of recording sessions,

it is a good idea to prepare a schedule that lists what needs to be done and reminds you of any special needs the sessions may have (see Figure 1.10).

If you have guests on your show, you should have them sign **performance releases** that give you the right to use and edit their contributions (see Figure 1.11). The facility where you produce your work, including a university, may require you to fill out a form to reserve equipment, and the entity that is going to play whatever you produce may request a production order that gives them permission to distribute the work.

1.10 THE IMPORTANCE OF VOICE

As noted earlier, the voice or voices heard in your audio production play a key role in conveying both the basic information and style of the piece. Although you can't control the voice of someone in a sound bite, you should give careful consideration to how your program host, anchorperson, or announcer sounds. Voices that are generally considered to be "good" voices are strong in three areas. First, they tend to be in the lower pitch range and are full, resonant voices that are pleasing to hear. Second, your announcer should speak at a rate or pace that is easy to understand. And finally, the voice should have exceptional clarity, which usually means good articulation and pronunciation. Remember, *you* may very well be the "announcer" for your production and although a few people just have naturally good-sounding voices, almost everyone else can improve their vocal style. The most important vocal elements that you have a degree of control over include pitch, rate, tone, and volume.

Pitch is the highness or lowness of your voice and lower-pitched voices are more pleasant to listen to. Everyone has a natural pitch range, from low to high, and you should strive to be about one-quarter up from the lowest pitch at

TO YOUR HEALTH
"Honey and Cinnamon" – No. 35

No.	Talent	Slug	Source	Content	Segment Time	Total Time
1	Hannah	Tease	Studio	Are cinnamon and honey what you need to keep healthy? Some medical experts say "yes."	:05	:05
2	Jim Hogan recorded	Opening	Server	Music and VO	:30	:35
3	Hannah	Intro	Studio	Several new research studies have indicated that honey and cinnamon have healing and preventative powers. Today we have in our studio one of the doctors who conducted these studies, Dr. Haim Whetcome and one of the outspoken critics of this work, Dr. Theodore Axel. Welcome. Let me start with you Dr. Whetcome. What, specifically have your studies shown?	:25	1:00
4	Hannah & Dr. Whetcome	Pro discussion	Studio	Dr. Whetcome discusses studies.	2:00	3:00
5	Hannah, Dr. Axel & Dr. Whetcome	Anti discussion	Studio	Dr. Axel, how do you react to this? Dr. Axel discusses his points of view.	2:00	5:00
6	Hannah, doctors, & listeners	Call-in questions	Phone and Studio	Questions from callers and answers by doctors	5:00	10:00
7	Commercials	Commercial break	Server	DinoAid, Preparation Hope, Xetrol, Baskin-Willow	2:00	12:00
8	Network anchors	Hourly news	Network	News provided by the network	3:00	15:00

FIGURE 1.8 A sample rundown sheet.

which you can speak. Male announcers, of course, have an advantage here, as their voices are typically about an octave lower than a female's. The best announcers utilize their full pitch range while emphasizing the naturally lower end of their speaking voice.

Rate is the number of words you speak in a given period of time. Typical "out loud" delivery is about 160 words per minute. This is usually not as fast as your normal conversational rate, but is slightly faster than you are used to reading out loud. We're not normally an accurate judge of how fast we talk, so it's a good idea to record your speech and play it back to determine your rate as other people hear it. Of course, if you're dealing with a script, that may determine the speaking rate—a 60-second commercial must be read in 60 seconds, regardless of whether there are 140 words or 175 words.

A voice's **tone** is essentially the quality of sound that is made. You know that a guitar and piano can play the same notes, but you can easily tell the different tone quality between them because of the material that surrounds the strings that are vibrating to produce the sound. The human voice is similar and can take advantage of various resonators, such as the chest, larynx, or nasal cavity, to enhance the quality of sound. One of the best things an announcer can do is to relax and let his or her body produce a natural, full sound. Using a high-quality microphone will also help produce rich tonal quality.

DUI: THE CONSEQUENCES	
VIDEO	**AUDIO**
MARCIA	MARCIA: It's 2 AM. Do you know where your friends are?
SERVER: OPENING MONTAGE	MUSIC FROM SERVER: Runs :30. Ends with high note
MARCIA	MARCIA: DUIs are on the increase among teenagers. After a number of years of decline, they are once again rising. Arresting officers, who are on the front line, are in a position to have some explanations. We have two such officers with us today, Patrol Officer Wayne Polin and Patrol Officer Wendy Washington.
VARIOUS SHOTS OF MARCIA AND THE TWO OFFICERS	MARCIA AND TWO OFFICERS: Discussion of drinking and teenagers, ending with points about the importance of friends.
MARCIA	MARCIA: Let's take a look at a typical scene that demonstrates what the officers are talking about. SOUND EFFECT: Zing noise
RICHARD IN FOREGROUND WITH BAR SCENE IN BACKGROUND	RICHARD: Hey, it was Rachel's birthday. All we wanted to do was buy her a drink to help celebrate. It wasn't our fault.
ZOOM IN TO BAR SCENE	SOUND EFFECTS: Noisy bar talking MUSIC: "Revelry"
RACHEL, RICHARD, PHYLLIS, ALLEN AT TABLE	PHYLLIS (singing a little drunkenly): Happy birthday, dear Jennifer. SOUND EFFECTS: Noisy bar talking at softer level MUSIC: "Happy Birthday" at low level RACHEL (standing up unsteadily): Hey, thanks, guys, but I gotta go. I got another friend who thinks she's throwing me a surprise party. She'll be wiped out if I don't show up.
CU OF RICHARD	RICHARD: Rachel, are you sure you're OK to drive? MUSIC: "Happy Birthday" fades to "Ominous"
RACHEL	RACHEL: Sure, I've driven in far worse shape than this before. I'll be fine.

FIGURE 1.9 A sample two-column script, often used when audio is paired with video.

Volume is the loudness level of your voice and contributes to the energy or enthusiasm that your voice communicates to the listener. Another way to think of this is projection—pushing the sound out of your mouth. However, be careful of talking "at" the listener, rather than "to" the listener. If your voice is always "loud," you'll sound boring and uninterested. Good announcers use a variation in loudness and softness of their voice to help add to the interpretation of the copy they're reading. Also remember that a microphone and audio console cannot compensate for a soft or weak voice. Although you can electronically turn up the volume, it will still have a lifeless quality if the proper natural volume is not being produced.

Good announcers utilize all these vocal qualities to their advantage and work to develop a pleasant, energetic voice.

You will produce better audio if you look for just the right voice for your production or if you work to develop your own voice and announcing style.

PRODUCTION TIP 1B
Copy Marking

Copy marking means using a system of graphic symbols to help you interpret the copy; basically, it's adding supplementary punctuation to the script. There's no universal system and many announcers develop their own, but here are a few ideas for copy marking.

Underline words or phrases you want to give extra emphasis. Double underline means more emphasis. Use a forward slash to

SCHEDULE

Title: Video Game Sounds

Director: Tony Caprizi

Date	Time	Location	Talent	Operators	Equipment	Description	Comments
9/6	9:00 AM-11:00 AM	9th Street Arcade	Hector	Alex C. Shari K.	Shotgun mic Fishpole DAT Flash recorder	Hector's intro and outro General arcade sounds	Check with manager upon arrival
9/6	12:00 PM-2:00 PM	Electro-Arts Lab 1515 2nd St.	Hector Phil J.	Alex C. Shari K.	Shotgun mic Omni mic Fishpole DAT Flash recorder	Demonstration of latest sounds	Be sure to get oscillator
9/9	11:00 AM-4:00 PM	Arts Museum 1520 East Parkway	Hector Phil J. Mary T.	Shari K.	Flash recorder	Interviews about latest sounds	
9/10	5:00 PM-8:00 PM	Studio Edit Suite		Chris G.	Editing equipment Turntable	Edit open and close and some effects	Bring LP for "wow" effect
9/11	1:00 PM-3:00 PM	Nolan C.'s home 926 Lake Lane	Hector Nolan C.	Shari K.	Flash recorder Lav mic Cardioid mic Fishpole DAT	Interview about early sounds (and hopefully demo of equipment)	Keep mic/fishpole in car until get permission to use it

FIGURE 1.10 A sample of a schedule for an audio production.

PERFORMANCE RELEASE

Note: This is not intended as an authentic legal document. It is just a representation of a performance release. Check with your organization's lawyer before using.

In consideration of my being part of the program

_____ "The Philip Spear Hour" _____

(title or subject)
and for no subsequent remuneration, I do hereby on behalf of myself, my heirs, executors, and administrators authorize

_____ WZZZ Productions _____

(producer, station, or production company)
to use live or recorded my name, voice, likeness, biography, and performance for television or audio distribution throughout the world and for audiovisual and general education purposes in perpetuity.

I further agree on behalf of myself and others as above stated that my name, likeness, biography, and performance may be used for promotion purposes and other uses. Further, I agree to indemnify, defend, and hold the producer (or station or production company) harmless for any and all claims, suits, or liabilities arising from my appearance and the use of any of my materials, name, likeness, biography, or performance.

Signature_____ *Nedra Thomas* _____

Printed Name _____ Nedra Thomas _____

Email Address_____ Nedra@ozz.com _____

Date _____ 11/26/10 _____

FIGURE 1.11 A performance release.

indicate a pause. A double slash means a longer pause, with each slash being about a "one-thousand-one" count. Triple periods and triple dashes are also often used to indicate a pause. A two-headed arrow under a word or phrases means to vocally "stretch it out," and a squiggly line under a word or phrase means to read it more quickly. Bracket a group of words that you want to read as one complete thought.

Use an arrow over a word or phrase to indicate a pitch change; bend the arrow upwards to show you should raise your pitch and downwards to lower the pitch of your voice. Words that might be difficult to pronounce are often "flagged" by putting a box around them and writing correct or phonetic pronunciation above the flagged word. Exclamation and question marks give an indication of how to read a sentence, but because they come at the end of the sentence, they can be missed. Put upside down punctuation at the beginning of this type of sentence to indicate how it should be read at the start of the sentence. If words or phrases are changed, draw a single line through the old word and write the new one above it.

Use parentheses to indicate other directions to the announcer, such as "read with urgency." Of course, whatever is within the parentheses is never actually spoken. Along with regular punctuation, copy marking will help you interpret a script in your own unique style.

1.11 EQUIPMENT AND FACILITIES

You will definitely need some equipment in order to produce your audio material and you will need a place (or places) to do the recording and editing. You will also need the skills to use the equipment and facilities so that what you produce is aesthetically pleasing and technically clean. You must, for example, be able to record material at a consistent volume level and then mix and edit material together so that it moves smoothly from one element to another and so that one element (such as music) does not drown out another element (such as an announcer's voice).

The rest of this book is devoted primarily to facilities, equipment, and aesthetics. By the time you finish reading the text material, watching the CD-ROM, and undertaking the self-help projects, you should be ready to make your audio ideas become reality.

1.12 LAWS

There are many laws and regulations that govern the media. If you are working for a radio station, there will probably be someone with a law degree who has the overall responsibility for making sure the station abides by the law. However, everyone who produces material for radio or television should understand basic legal principles. One principle that allows the media to engage in investigative reporting and the broadcast of controversial ideas resides in the First Amendment of the Constitution, which guarantees freedom of speech. This does not mean that anyone can say anything, however.

There are other laws, for example, that prohibit **indecency** and **obscenity** on the airwaves. Indecency is defined as language that, in context, depicts or describes, in terms patently offensive as measured by contemporary community standards for the broadcast medium, sexual or excretory activities or organs. Obscenity, which is a more serious crime, is defined as material that contains the depiction of sexual acts in an offensive manner; appeals to prurient interests of the average person; and lacks serious artistic, literary, political, or scientific value. Neither are allowed to air on broadcast stations, and a number of radio broadcasters have been heavily fined for indecent comments made by program hosts and indecent lyrics in songs. Obscenity has been less of a problem, because—in their attempts to avoid indecency—most stations have avoided more serious obscenity. One of the problems with indecency is that the definition deals with "contemporary community standards," and those change over time and place. What was considered indecent in Missouri in 1980 may be commonplace in New York now. One of the jobs of the lawyers is to try to determine what constitutes indecency at any point in time.

Another legal principle that affects media is **libel**, which is saying something unfavorable and false about a person. Ordinary people are covered by a different standard than famous people who are considered **public figures**. An ordinary person can sue for libel if an unfavorable, false statement is made under any conditions, even if it was an innocent mistake. Public figures must prove that the reporter acted with **actual malice** in reporting the negative falsehood. For example, a public figure must prove that the reporter knew the report was false but broadcast it anyway.

Along the same line, there are **invasion of privacy** laws. These are state laws as opposed to national laws, so they differ from state to state. However, the laws usually allow for people to be left alone and stipulate ways that reporters cannot pursue them, such as not trespassing on their private property.

There also is a law against **payola**, which is the acceptance (usually by a disc jockey) of money or gifts in exchange for favoring certain records. The law states that if station employees receive money from individuals other than their employers for airing records, they must disclose that fact before they play the music under penalty of fine or imprisonment. The same principle holds true if a disc jockey promotes a business, such as a restaurant or car dealership. There are also laws against deceptive tricks, commonly called **hoaxes**, such as faking the report of a murder just for the fun of it.

Copyright is another legal issue that must be dealt with, particularly in relation to music. Most radio stations pay music licensing organizations for the right to use just about all the music that exists. If your audio production is going to be aired on radio, you probably do not need to worry about getting music copyright permission. You can also play the work within a classroom, but if you were to make a CD so that you could sell it, you would need to contact the copyright holder and secure permission—and probably pay a fee. If you use copyrighted material other than music, such as someone's poem, you need to secure copyright clearance for airing on radio.

There are numerous other laws that affect those producing audio material, but these are the ones you are most likely to encounter.

1.13 ETHICS

Whereas laws are codified and have set provisions and punishments that apply to everyone, ethics involves personal decisions regarding what is right and wrong. An ethical person, after considering the moral value of good and bad, will do what is good, even though there is no actual punishment for doing what is bad. Everyone pays lip service to being ethical. However, there are many temptations in life that lead to ethical misbehavior, in part because ethical behavior can be difficult to define. If there is a law about something (such as the payola law) then there are parameters and punishments that are clearly spelled out. But, from an ethics point of view, what if an old high school friend, who just happens to have released a record, buys you a hamburger?

Ethics boils down to decisions individuals make, but to aid individuals who work in the media, organizations develop codes or guidelines that outline principles that a committee of respected practitioners have decided represent ethical behavior. Sometimes individual stations or networks have guidelines for their employees and often trade organizations issue codes for people within certain professions. Figure 1.12 lists some of the provisions in the code of the Radio-Television News Directors Association, an organization for electronic journalists.

But codes cannot cover everything, and it is often up to individuals to make decisions—sometimes on the spur of the moment—regarding what is right and wrong. For example, if a man holding hostages calls a radio station and threatens to kill the hostages if he is not given immediate broadcast time to air his demands, what should you (as the person

---

SELECTED PROVISIONS FROM THE
RADIO-TELEVISION NEWS DIRECTORS ASSOCIATION
CODE OF ETHICS AND PROFESSIONAL CONDUCT

Professional electronic journalists should not:
- Manipulate images or sounds in any way that is misleading.
- Present images or sounds that are reenacted without informing the public.
- Pay news sources who have a vested interest in a story.
- Accept gifts, favors, or compensation from those who might seek to influence coverage.

Professional electronic journalists should:
- Clearly disclose the origin of information and label all material provided by outsiders.
- Treat all subjects of news coverage with respect and dignity, showing particular compassion to victims of crime or tragedy.
- Seek to understand the diversity of their community and inform the public without bias or stereotype.
- Present analytical reporting based on professional perspective, not personal bias.
- Respect the right to a fair trial.
- Clearly label opinion and commentary.
- Guard against extended coverage of events or individuals that fails to significantly advance a story, place the event in context, or add to the public knowledge.
- Refrain from contacting participants in violent situations while the situation is in progress.
- Gather and report news without fear or favor, and vigorously resist undue influence from any outside forces, including advertisers, sources, story subjects, powerful individuals, and special interest groups.
- Refuse to allow the interests of ownership or management to influence news judgment and content inappropriately.
- Investigate complaints and correct errors promptly and with as much prominence as the original report.

FIGURE 1.12 Selected provisions from the Code of Ethics and Professional Conduct of the Radio-Television News Directors Association. You might want to consider these while working on the ethics situations in Figure 1.13. The entire code can be accessed at www.rtnda.org/pages/media_items/code-of-ethics-and-professional-conduct48.php.

ETHICAL DECISION-MAKING

1. You and many other reporters are outside a hospital to which a famous celebrity has just been admitted for psychiatric care. A hospital employee comes over to you and confidentially tells you he has access to all patient files and can get you the complete medical records of this celebrity if you will pay him $100. In considering what you would do, you might want to think about the following options:
   - Pay him the $100 and await the files
   - Say you will pay him $100 after he delivers the files to you
   - Try to talk him down to $50
   - Suggest that he make his offer to a reporter from a competing station
   - Pay the money and get the file and then report the incident to the head of the hospital
   - Call your boss and ask what to do
   - Call the police
   - Scream
   - Pretend you don't hear him
   - Write a story about the fact that he approached you with the offer

2. You are putting together an audio production about automobile repairs and learn about a rather rare "ping" in a certain type of car that, if not fixed early, can lead to expensive damage. You manage to record this "ping" from a car that is in for repair, and plan to use the recording in the program. However, when you go to edit your program you cannot find the sound file that contains the "ping." You call the audio repair place to see if you can rerecord the sound, but the car with the "ping" has been fixed and returned to its owner. You go through a sound effects library and find a sound that is somewhat different but does sound like a "ping." Which of the following options, if any, would you consider?
   - Include the sound effects "ping"
   - Include the sound effect but give a disclaimer telling why you used a "ping" that was not authentic
   - Do the program without the "ping" sound
   - Put together the program without mentioning this "ping" problem at all
   - Accuse a co-worker of stealing the "ping" sound from your computer and tell her to find a way to rerecord it
   - Try to find another repair shop that happens to be working on a car with this "ping"

3. A committee of citizens is trying to recall the mayor from office. You don't like this mayor because he has not been at all accessible to the press, so you personally support the recall committee. You manage to catch the mayor before one of his rare news conferences and you ask him what he thinks of the recall effort. He says, "That recall committee is a bunch of thugs—I'm just kidding, of course. Don't broadcast that." What would you do under those circumstances? For example:
   - Follow the mayor's suggestion and do nothing—don't make it a story at all.
   - Broadcast the whole quote.
   - Broadcast just the first part of the quote, stopping with the word "thugs."
   - Broadcast the whole quote and mention in your report that anyone dumb enough to say such a thing to a reporter shouldn't be the mayor.
   - Give your recording to the recall committee and let them do with it as they will.

4. You are the producer for a commercial for a new restaurant in town and your station disc jockey has agreed to voice the commercial. During the recording of the commercial you overhear the restaurant manager asking the disc jockey to plug the restaurant when she is just chatting on the radio. He suggests that she particularly laud the roast beef special. The disc jockey seems somewhat reluctant, so the manager taps his wallet. What might you do at this point?
   - Nothing. This is a private matter between the disc jockey and the restaurant manager and is none of your business.
   - Nothing. No crime has been committed. Wait and see if you witness this being taken any further before acting.
   - Pull the disc jockey aside and remind her that plugging restaurants is considered payola.
   - Tell the restaurant manager that he should stop trying to get the d.j. to commit a crime.
   - Call the police.
   - Call the general manager of your station and tell him what is going on.

FIGURE 1.13 Read through these situations and decide what you think would be the ethical thing to do in each instance. In some instances, you might want to do nothing or do more than one thing. Some ideas are included, but you will no doubt come up with ideas that are more comfortable for you.

answering the phone) do? That's not the time to sit down and read the ethics manual or call for a meeting of top management. If you don't provide the airtime, the hostages may be killed, but if you do provide it, the demands may result in the death of more people and you will be encouraging other unbalanced people to demand airtime. It's a no-win situation and yet you must make an ethical decision.

The best preparation for making crucial ethical decisions is to have a set of values that you live by on a daily basis. When you hear about people who have had to make difficult ethical decisions, think through what you would have done and have a rationale for it. If you have a good feel for what you think is right and wrong, you will find that making ethical decisions is easier. Figure 1.13 outlines some situations in need of ethical decisions. Decide what you would do in each case and talk over your decision with others.

1.14 CONCLUSION

Regardless of the type of material you are producing or the media form that will deliver it, you must do some advance thinking in order for it to be effective. Content is the most important element of audio production. You can work in a state-of-the art facility or in your garage and, in all probability, your audience wouldn't know the difference. But they will know whether you have an effective idea that is well written, interestingly produced, clearly voiced, and legally and ethically based.

Self-Study

1. Where can ideas for audio projects come from?

   a) the news of the day
   b) conversations with a friend
   c) material in a book
   d) all of the above

2. In what way do ordinary people have different legal rights than public figures?

   a) Ordinary people do not have to prove actual malice in libel suits and public figures do.
   b) Ordinary people are subject to national invasion of privacy laws; public figures are subject to state invasion of privacy laws.
   c) Ordinary people don't have to obey copyright laws, and public figures do.
   d) Ordinary people are not allowed to perform hoaxes, and public figures are.

3. Which of the following is not a trait or skill that an audio production person should possess?

   a) convergence
   b) versatility
   c) equipment savvy
   d) sense of humor

4. What are short individual sounds intended to capture attention called?

   a) atmosphere sounds
   b) stingers
   c) sound bites
   d) dead air

5. Which type of script is most likely to include the five Ws and an H?

   a) news script
   b) rundown
   c) template
   d) slug

6. Which is a characteristic of a two-column script?

   a) It includes a pre-planning schedule.
   b) It gives a producer permission to use an interviewee's sound bites.
   c) It always has rising action and a climax.
   d) It is used when video and audio are recorded together.

7. Which term is defined as language that, in context, depicts or describes, in terms patently offensive as measured by contemporary community standards for the broadcast medium, sexual or excretory activities or organs?

   a) obscenity
   b) indecency
   c) libel
   d) payola

8. Which of the following would be considered a target audience?

   a) the radio network NPR

b) people who do not fit any demographic

c) a style that relates to theater of the mind

d) married women in their thirties

9. Which of the following does ethical behavior involve?

   a) succumbing to life's temptations

   b) consideration of the moral value of good and bad

   c) using equipment in such a way that music does not drown out an announcer's voice

   d) codified laws

10. Which of the following refers to the number of words spoken in a given time period?

    a) pitch

    b) rate

    c) tone

    d) volume

ANSWERS

If you answered A to any of the questions:

1a. This answer is correct, but there is a better answer. (Reread 1.2.)

2a. Right. Only public figures must prove actual malice.

3a. Yes, this is the correct answer. Convergence involves media forms melding together and is not a personality trait or skill.

4a. No. Atmosphere sounds are not short or individual. (Reread 1.7.)

5a. Correct. A news script would answer who, what, when, why, and how.

6a. No. A schedule is not part of a script. (Reread 1.8 and 1.9.)

7a. No, but you are close. (Reread 1.12.)

8a. No. NPR might have a target audience, but NPR, itself, is not one. (Reread 1.4.)

9a. No, quite the opposite. (Reread 1.13.)

10a. No. Pitch refers to highness and lowness. (Reread 1.10.)

If you answered B to any of the questions:

1b. This answer is correct, but there is a better answer. (Reread 1.2.)

2b. No. One form of these laws does not exist. (Reread 1.12.)

3b. Wrong. Radio production people who can do many different things are prized. (Reread 1.6.)

4b. Yes. "Stingers" is the correct term.

5b. No. A rundown is a script form and may contain the five Ws and an H, but it is not the form most likely to contain them. (Reread 1.8.)

6b. No. A script is not a performance release. (Reread 1.8 and 1.9.)

7b. Correct. This is the definition for indecency.

8b. No. This is impossible. (Reread 1.4.)

9b. Yes, this is the correct answer.

10b. Yes, this is the right answer.

If you answered C to any of the questions:

1c. This answer is correct, but there is a better answer. (Reread 1.2.)

2c. No. Everyone should obey copyright laws. (Reread 1.12.)

3c. No. You need to be able to operate and troubleshoot equipment if you are involved with audio production. (Reread 1.6.)

4c. Wrong. Sound bites can capture attention, but they aren't individual sounds. (Reread 1.7.)

5c. No. A template is part of a script, but not a script. (Reread 1.8.)

6c. Wrong. Two-column scripts don't just deal with drama. (Reread 1.8.)

7c. No. You are not on the right track. (Reread 1.12.)

8c. No. This is totally unrelated. (Reread 1.3, 1.4, and 1.5.)

9c. No. This is something you should do, but it is a technical point, not an ethical one. (Reread 1.11 and 1.13.)

10c. No. Tone refers to quality. (Reread 1.10.)

If you answered D to any of the questions:

1d. Correct. Ideas can come from just about anywhere, including all of the options listed in a, b, and c.

2d. No. Hoaxes are out of bounds for anyone. (Reread 1.12.)

3d. No. A sense of humor is a good trait in most occupations. (Reread 1.6.)

4d. Wrong. Dead air is no sound at all. (Reread 1.7.)

5d. No. A slug is part of a script form but not a script itself. (Reread 1.8.)

6d. Yes. This is the correct answer.

7d. Wrong. You are not on the right track. (Reread 1.12.)

8d. Correct. This would be an example of a demographic you might use as a target audience.

9d. No. Laws are codified, but ethics aren't. (Reread 1.13.)

10d. Wrong. "Volume" refers to loudness. (Reread 1.10.)

Projects

PROJECT 1

Undertake Production Planning for a 15-minute Interview Show.

Purpose

To help you walk through the steps of preplanning with a project that is fairly simple.

Notes

1. You may not need to consider all things for your particular show. For example, it is possible that you won't need any sound effects, so you do not need to mention them.
2. You can write all your points continuously on the same sheet of paper. In other words, you do not need to write your idea on one sheet of paper and your goals on another sheet.
3. Some of what you write will be full sentences and some will be lists or clauses. Use whatever seems most appropriate.

How to Do the Project

1. Come up with an idea for your show and write it down in 25 words or fewer. Do research, if needed, to solidify your idea.
2. Decide on at least three goals or objectives for the program and write those underneath your show idea.
3. Write one sentence describing the target audience for your show.
4. Jot down the style of your show.
5. List the people, by job title, that you think you will need to help complete your show. Don't forget to list all the people who will be on the program. After each person, list one skill or personality trait that you think that person must definitely have.
6. List the elements you will need for your program—voices, music, and sound effects, as appropriate. Be as specific as you can; for example, don't just list "opening music." Indicate with a few adjectives the type of music you want.
7. Write a rundown sheet for your program. Be sure to include timing information.
8. Make a theoretical schedule for recording and editing your program.
9. List several elements of voice that will be important to your show and tell why they will be important.
10. If you think there are any legal or ethical issues that may arise given the content of your program, list these.
11. Give your paper with all this information to your instructor to receive credit for this project.

PROJECT 2

Assess Your Skills.

Purpose

To help you decide whether you have the skills needed for audio work and to indicate ways you might improve on your skills.

Notes

1. Answer this honestly. Perhaps your instructor will not collect this assignment, so that all students can be honest with themselves without worrying about their grades.
2. If you think of other traits that are important, feel free to add them.
3. Reread Section 1.6 if you need to refresh your mind on what each trait involves.

How to Do the Project

1. Make a chart and write at the top of it "Trait" and "Score."
2. Under "Trait," list the following:
   Versatility
   Interpersonal skills
   Writing skills
   Computer skills
   Troubleshooting ability
   Curiosity
   Creativity
   Artistic ability
   Organizational skills
   Sense of humor
   Patience
   Pleasant-sounding voice
   Ability to speak extemporaneously
   Passion
3. Under "Score," give yourself a rating on each trait from 1 to 10, with 1 being the lowest and 10 being the highest.
4. Consider your two lowest scores and write a short paragraph discussing how you could improve in each of those areas. Also, look at your two highest scores and write a short paragraph about why those are your strengths.
5. Give the paper with your scores and paragraphs to your teacher, if instructed to do so, to complete this project.

2

THE STUDIO ENVIRONMENT

2.1 INTRODUCTION

As you'll learn as you read through this book, audio production can be accomplished in a variety of situations and in a number of different environments. Recording "in the field" may simply entail using a single microphone and portable recorder or perhaps a setup consisting of a laptop, audio software, and a microphone. On the other hand, recording in the studio may entail multiple microphones and other sound sources feeding into a large audio mixer or just a basic editing suite. This chapter takes a look at the more formal setting of the traditional audio studio.

The room that houses the equipment necessary for audio production work and in which the finished product is assembled is known as the **production studio**. What may initially appear to be merely a roomful of electronic equipment will become a comfortable environment once you've become familiar with the space and components that make up the production facility. If your facility has several studios, they may be labeled "Production 1" or "Prod. B" or identified with another abbreviation for the production studio, "PDX." Today, a streamlined digital "studio" may merely be a workstation desk set up in the corner of a room with a mix of computer and audio equipment, as shown in Figure 2.1.

FIGURE 2.1 An audio production environment can be a small editing suite that combines computer and audio equipment. (Image courtesy of Motor Racing Network Radio.)

Most radio stations utilize at least two studios. One is usually delegated as the **on-air studio** and is used for live, day-to-day broadcasting. The others are audio production studios, used for putting together programming material that is recorded for playback at a later time. This includes such items as commercials, features, **public service announcements (PSAs)**, and station promotional or image spots (**promos**). Regardless of the actual physical size or shape, the production facility is the creative center for a radio station or audio production house. Often the production studio mirrors the on-air studio with the same or very similar equipment configuration and serves as a backup for the on-air room. Some facilities also have a studio that is considered a **performance studio** or **announce booth**. It usually is smaller than the other studios and houses nothing more than microphones, a table, and chairs. The output is normally sent to a production studio to be recorded, although sometimes it's sent directly to the on-air studio for live broadcast. A performance studio can be used for voice-over work, for taping interviews, for discussions involving several guests, or for recording a small musical group.

Two of the biggest concerns for studio design looked at in this chapter are acoustics and ergonomics. **Acoustics** refers to how sound "behaves" within an enclosed space, and **ergonomics** refers to design considerations that help reduce operator fatigue and discomfort. Acoustical considerations have become increasingly important because of the high-quality recordings that can be obtained within a digital environment. Although you may never build or remodel an audio studio, an understanding of the characteristics of the production room can help you assess your facility and suggest ways in which you can improve the surroundings that you'll be working in.

2.2 THE AUDIO CHAIN

Figure 2.2 shows a simplified "map" of a typical audio production studio and how a series of audio equipment is interconnected. Starting with various sound sources, such as a microphone or an audio recorder, it shows the route or signal path that sound takes to ultimately be broadcast or recorded. This path is often called an **audio chain**, because the various pieces of equipment are literally linked together. The trip can be complicated, because the sound can go through several changes along the way. For example, it can be dubbed, or copied, from CD to MiniDisc; or it can be **equalized**, which is a form of signal processing. The solid lines show sound being sent to the audio console from an audio source. Then it goes through **signal processing** equipment and finally to the transmitting system, which would be normal for an on-air studio. The broken line shows the sound being sent back to an audio recorder after signal processing, which would be common for an audio production studio. In both cases, the sound can be heard in the studio through monitor speakers or

headphones. You'll learn more about all of this as you work your way through this text, but for now the diagram in Figure 2.2 provides a look at where you are headed.

The equipment shown is also representative of what could be found in the typical audio production studio. A **microphone** transforms the talent's voice into an audio signal. It is not uncommon for a production facility to have one or more auxiliary microphones for production work that requires several voices. Most production rooms also have two **CD players**, enabling different CDs to be played back-to-back or simultaneously. Besides CD players, many production studios utilize various digital record and playback gear, such as the **MiniDisc** recorder, personal audio editor, **CD-R** (compact disc recorder), or computer-controlled **digital audio workstation**. How many recorders or players are found in the production room depends on the complexity of the studio and the budget of the facility. All of this equipment feeds into the **audio console**, which allows the operator to manipulate the sound sources in various ways. Signal processing equipment, such as an **equalizer**, **noise-reduction** system, or **reverb** unit, is usually put into the audio chain between the audio console and the

FIGURE 2.2 The audio chain shows how equipment is interconnected and how sound moves through that equipment in an audio studio.

transmitting or recording equipment; however, most signal processing is now done in postproduction using specialized audio software. Monitoring the sound during production work is accomplished with studio **speakers** or **headphones**. Compare Figure 2.2 with Figures 2.4 and 2.8 to see how the audio chain translates into the actual production studio.

2.3 THE STUDIO LAYOUT

Many audio production studios use a U-shaped layout (see Figure 2.3) or some variation of it, because this allows the operator to reach all the equipment control surfaces, and puts the operator immediately in front of the audio console. With the use of remote start/stop switches for any equipment that's out of the operator's reach, all equipment manipulation can occur at the audio console once everything has been set up and cued. Today most radio work is done **combo**; that is, the announcer is also the equipment operator. Because of this setup, the equipment and operator are in a single studio, be it a production or on-air room. This type of studio layout facilitates working combo. In earlier radio days, the announcer was often located in a separate room or announce booth adjacent to the studio that housed the actual broadcast equipment. Visual contact and communication were maintained via a window between the two rooms. An engineer was required to manipulate the equipment, and the announcer merely provided the voice. Many larger-market radio stations still use a similar announcer/engineer arrangement, popularly known as **"engineer-assist" broadcasting**.

One of the basic ergonomic considerations in putting the studio together is whether it should be a sit-down or stand-up design. Sit-down studios would have countertops at desk height and would include a chair or stool for the announcer. As the name implies, stand-up operations have counter height set for the announcer to be standing while doing production work. If you're designing a stand-up studio, make sure that even the shortest person can reach the equipment, especially equipment in turrets or countertop modules. One approach isn't really better than the other, so it is a personal choice of the individual facility.

2.4 PRODUCTION STUDIO FURNITURE

Studio furniture provides the foundation for the production studio, because all the equipment in the room sets on it, mounts in it, or is wired through it. Studio equipment is often installed on and in custom-built cabinets and counters. Although the cost can be high, such furniture can be built to the exact dimensions of the studio and for the exact equipment that will be housed in that studio. A less expensive but equally functional approach is to lay out the studio using modular stock components (review Figure 2.3). Audio studio furniture has been designed expressly for recorders, audio consoles, and other pieces of studio equipment. Using modular furniture and racks often makes it easier to reconfigure the studio or add additional equipment if the studio needs to expand.

Today's studio furniture systems also include space and cabinet modules for computer monitors and other computer equipment that's being integrated with traditional equipment in the audio studio, as shown in Figures 2.4 and 2.8. A computer monitor should be about 2 feet away from the announcer and the topmost screen line should fall slightly below eye level. Monitors that are placed too high, such

FIGURE 2.3 Many audio studios use modular furniture components arranged in a U-shaped design that allows the operator to see and reach all the equipment easily. (Image courtesy of Graham Studios.)

as on top of a studio module, can cause neck strain. Some monitors can be kept off the studio furniture by using a special wall-mounted or ceiling-mounted TV boom. Flat-screen monitors offer more mounting options, take up less space, are aesthetically pleasing in the audio studio, and have become the standard in most audio studios. If possible, the computer keyboard should be placed in line with the monitor rather than off to the side. Sometimes the keyboard can be placed on an under-counter drawer to accomplish this, but you have to watch the operator's knee space in such a setup. If possible, avoid putting a keyboard near hard counter edges that can cause a painful problem if the operator's wrist strikes the counter edge, and make sure that the computer mouse can be reached without stretching the operator's arm.

Most studio furniture is manufactured of plywood or particleboard with a laminate surface; however, a few modern counters are employing a solid-surface countertop of Corian or similar kitchen-counter type material, as shown in Figure 2.4. Both custom-built and modular cabinets and counters are also designed to provide easy access to the myriad cables necessary to wire all the studio equipment together yet maintain an attractive image for the look of the studio. Digital equipment offers the advantage of better cable management, as linking equipment via digital inputs/outputs requires less cable than analog wiring. Other cabinets or storage modules are also available for CDs and other material that may be kept in the production studio. Furniture housing equipment may require cooling, but most digital equipment will operate fine with a passive air flow provided by back panel vents in the furniture. If a forced-air fan is required, be aware of the noise problem it could present.

Does stylish furniture make a studio sound better? Although that notion would be hard to quantify, a positive studio image does imply a commitment to high-quality professional production, and this often translates into more creativity, more productivity, and a better "sound" produced from that studio.

2.5 STUDIO SOUND CONSIDERATIONS

The audio production studio is a unique space, in that the physical room will have an impact on the sound produced in it. Because of this, several characteristics of sound should be considered in designing the studio, including sound isolation, noise and vibration control, and room acoustics. When sound strikes a surface (such as a studio wall), some of that sound is reflected, while some is absorbed within or transmitted through the material of the surface. Most of the sound that hits a hard, flat surface will be reflected. However, if the surface is irregular, it will break up the sound wave and disperse the reflections—a phenomenon known as **diffusion**. Sound that's absorbed into the surface is dissipated within it, but **penetration** occurs when sound goes through a surface and is transmitted into the space on the other side. Figure 2.5 illustrates that penetration, absorption, reflection, and diffusion are all characteristics that help determine the sound that is both produced and reproduced in the studio.

FIGURE 2.4   A solid-surface countertop on studio furniture provides the audio studio with a sleek, modern look. (Image courtesy of Mager Systems, Inc.)

When a sound (such as a talent's voice) is produced, the **direct sound** is the main sound that you hear. In a production situation, it is sound that goes from the sound source straight to the microphone. On the other hand, **indirect** or **reflected sound** reaches the microphone fractions of a

second after the direct sound does because it has traveled a circuitous route. Reflected sound consists of **echo** and **reverberation**. This indirect sound has bounced off or been reflected from one surface (echo) or two or more surfaces (reverb) before reaching the microphone (see Figure 2.6). Because it's an early reflection, echo provides a distinct repetition of the sound, such as "hello—hello—hello." On the other hand, a reverb's repeated later reflections provide a continuous decay of the sound, such as "hello—oo—oo." The components of direct and indirect sound make up what is commonly called the sound's **life cycle**.

In designing the audio studio, the goal is to manipulate these sound characteristics to create a proper sound environment for production work. When considering reflected sound, we think in terms of reverb ring and reverb route, with the same concepts applying for echo but to a lesser extent. **Reverb ring** (or **reverb time**) is the time that it takes for a sound to die out or go from full volume to silence. **Reverb route** is the path that sound takes from its source to a reflective surface and back to the original source (or a microphone, if recording). Excessive reflected sound tends to accent high and midrange frequencies, which produces a "harsh" sound; to blur the stereo image, which produces a "muddy" sound; or to cause standing waves (see Section 2.7), which produces an "uneven" sound. Reflected sound can also be **reinforced sound**, which causes objects or surfaces within the studio to vibrate at the same frequencies as the original sound in a sympathetic fashion.

Both **absorption** and diffusion are used to control reflected sound. Part of the reflected sound can be absorbed within the carpeting, curtains, and walls of the studio. Absorption soaks up sound and shortens reverb time to prevent excessive reflection. Absorption provides a **dead studio**, which has a very short reverb ring (sound dies out quickly) and a long reverb route that produces a softer

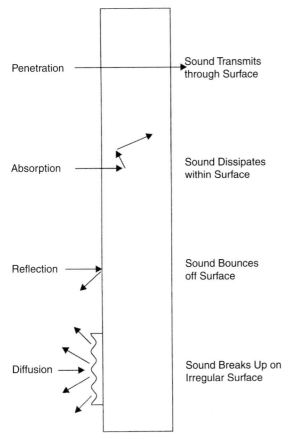

FIGURE 2.5 Sound striking an audio studio wall will reflect off, penetrate through, be diffused by, or be absorbed by that surface.

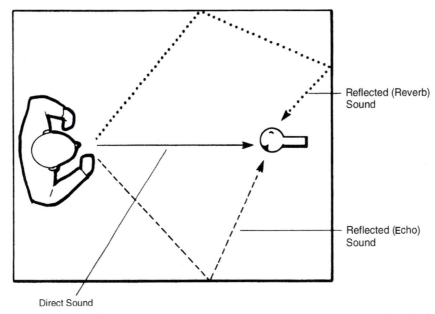

FIGURE 2.6 Direct sound takes a straight path from the talent to the microphone, but reflected sound is also produced in the audio studio.

sound. Excessive absorption produces a totally dead studio, which provides a "dry" sound that is unlike any normal acoustic space and isn't really desirable. In contrast, a **live studio** has a longer reverb ring and a shorter reverb route that produces a harder or more "brilliant" sound. Diffusion uses irregular room surfaces to break up sound reflections. This decreases the intensity of the reflections, making them less noticeable, but doesn't deaden the sound as much, because the sound reflections are redirected rather than soaked up. Most studio designs control reflections by a combination of absorption and diffusion techniques.

One common audio studio design is a **live end/dead end (LEDE)** approach. The front of the studio (where the operator and equipment are located) is designed to absorb and diffuse sounds. This dead end quiets some of the equipment operation noise, picks up the direct sound of the talent's voice, and absorbs the excess reflections that pass by the microphone from the live end. The live end, or back, of the studio adds a desirable sharpness to the sound by providing some reflected sound so the studio isn't totally dry. Other acoustic designs include early sound scattering (ESS), which uses a great deal of diffusion, and reflection-free zone (RFZ), which uses a great deal of absorption to control unwanted reflected sound in the studio.

2.6 STUDIO CONSTRUCTION MATERIALS

Another design consideration involves the actual construction materials used for the studio. Ideally, you want to keep penetration to a minimum by keeping outside (unwanted)

sound from entering the studio and inside sound from escaping from the studio, except via the audio console. Audio studios utilize **soundproofing** to accomplish this sound isolation. Doors are heavy-duty and tightly sealed; windows are often double-glassed with the interior pane slanted downward to minimize reflected sounds; and walls, ceiling, and flooring covered with special sound-treatment materials. For example, studio walls may be covered with acoustically treated and designed panels that both absorb and trap reflected sounds (see Figure 2.7). Some stations use carpeting on the studio walls, but this type of soundproofing doesn't absorb low frequencies very well. Some production studios have actually used egg cartons on the walls as a sound treatment. If you compare the design of an egg carton with the design of the acoustic panel shown in Figure 2.7, you'll see why the inexpensive egg carton route works—to a degree.

All materials absorb sound to some degree, but each material will have a different **absorption coefficient**, which is the proportion of sound that it can absorb. A coefficient value of 1.00 indicates that all sound is absorbed in the material. On the other hand, a coefficient value of 0.00 means that no absorption occurs and that all the sound is reflected back. Hard, smooth surfaces like plaster or panel walls and hardwood floors have low absorption coefficients. Heavy, plush carpets, drape-covered windows, and specially designed acoustic tiles have higher coefficients. For example, using a 1,000 Hz tone as the sound source, the absorption coefficient of a sheet rock wall is 0.04, and a 2-inch Sonex foam tile is 0.81; a glass window is 0.12, and a window curtain is 0.75; a painted concrete block wall is 0.07, and a carpeted concrete wall is 0.37. The purpose of any

FIGURE 2.7 Acoustic panels and tiles help control reflected sound through both absorption (by the foam material) and diffusion (by the irregular surfaces). (Image courtesy of Auralex Acoustics, Inc. Photo by Erikk D. Lee.)

soundproofing material is to help give the studio a dead sound. Soundproofing absorbs and controls excess reverb and echo and helps produce a softer sound.

2.7 STUDIO SIZE AND SHAPE

The size and shape of a production studio can also determine how reflective the studio is. As noted, the audio production studio shouldn't be overly reflective, because sound produced or recorded would be too bright and even harsh. Unfortunately, standard room construction often counters good studio design. For example, studios with parallel walls (the normal box-shaped room) produce more reflected sound than irregularly shaped studios. Sound waves that are reflected back and forth within a limited area, such as between studio walls that are parallel, can produce standing waves. In basic terms, a **standing wave** is a combination of a sound wave going in one direction and its reflected wave going in the opposite direction. If the distance between the walls is the same as the wave length (or a multiple of it), the waves interact and produce an undesirable combined sound that tends to be uneven, as previously mentioned. To help prevent standing waves, adjacent studio walls can be splayed (joined at an angle of more than 90 degrees) to help break up reflected sound and control excessive reverb and echo.

The actual size of the production facility is partially determined by the equipment that must be housed in it. However, in constructing the audio production room, consideration should be given to the fact that when rooms are built with height, width, and length dimensions that are equal or exact multiples of each other, certain sound frequencies tend to be boosted, and other sound frequencies tend to be canceled. As this "peaks and valleys" sound is not desirable in the audio production room, cubic construction should be avoided when possible.

2.8 STUDIO AESTHETICS

There are some studio design considerations that can be categorized as the "aesthetics" of the production room. In general, any studio should be pleasant to work in; after all, the operator may be confined to a rather small room for long stretches of time. For example, fluorescent lighting should be avoided when possible. Not only does it tend to introduce "hum" into the audio chain, but it's also harsher and more glaring than incandescent light. If possible, the studio lights should be on dimmers so that an appropriate level of light can be set for each individual operator. If the lighting causes glare on a computer monitor, use an antiglare shield or screen to diminish this problem or use track lighting that can be directed away from the screen.

Stools or chairs used in the audio studio should be comfortable and functional. User-friendly adjustments should allow the user to set the seat height so that the entire sole of the foot rests on either the floor or a footrest. Chairs must move easily, because even though most of the equipment is situated close to the operator, he or she may have to move around to cue CDs or speak directly into the microphone. The production stool must also be well constructed so that it doesn't squeak if the operator moves slightly while the microphone is open. This may not be a factor for production studios designed for a stand-up operation in which there is no stool, and with counters at a height appropriate for the operator to be standing while announcing. This stand-up operation allows the operator to be more animated in his or her vocal delivery and actually provides a better posture for speaking than a sitting position.

Many radio production rooms are decorated with music posters or radio station bumper stickers and paraphernalia. Not only does this feature keep the studio from being a cold, stark room, but it also gives the studio a radio atmosphere. Figure 2.8 shows the interior of a typical radio production studio. An audio production facility may decorate with paintings or art posters to give the facility a more business-like, professional feel.

PRODUCTION TIP 2A
Static Electricity

Static electricity can be a problem in production studios, because of the heavy use of carpeting. Most people don't enjoy getting shocked every time they touch the metal control surface of an audio console. Also, some modern audio equipment and computer systems have electronic circuits that can be disrupted by static discharges. There have been instances where audio recorders have switched into "play" mode when an operator just "sparked" the faceplate of the machine. If design factors can't keep the studio free from static, commercial sprays can be put on the carpeting or spray fabric softener can be used to provide an antistatic treatment at a modest cost. Dilute the fabric softener a bit or you'll build up a dangerous, slippery gloss on your carpets. A static touch pad can also be used in the studio—the operator merely places a finger on the pad to harmlessly discharge static buildup. Some studios have even been built with conductive laminate countertops connected to the studio's ground system to help minimize static.

2.9 ON-AIR/RECORDING LIGHTS

On-air lights (see Figure 2.9) are usually located outside the audio production room or studio. Normally they are wired so that whenever the microphone in that studio is turned on, the on-air light comes on. A light outside an audio production studio will often read "recording" instead of "on air." In either case, a lit light indicates a live microphone.

FIGURE 2.8 Any audio studio should be a comfortable and functional environment. (Image courtesy of Arrakis Systems, Inc. www.Arrakis-Systems.com.)

Good production practice dictates that when an on-air light is on, you never enter that studio, and if you're in the vicinity of the studio, you are quiet. Inside the studio, another alert light may come on when the microphone is turned on and the announcer often says "Standby" to alert others in the studio that he or she is preparing to turn on the microphone.

2.10 HAND SIGNALS

Hand signals don't play a major role in modern audio production; however, there are situations when vocal communication isn't possible and hand signals are necessary. For example, if a voice-over talent and engineer are recording from adjacent studios with a window between them, as mentioned earlier in this chapter, they must be able to communicate with each other. There are also times when two announcers must communicate in a studio, but an open or live microphone prevents them from doing so verbally. Because of situations like these, hand signals have evolved over the years to communicate some basic production information. Figure 2.10 shows some of the basic hand signals.

Often hand signals concern getting a program started or stopped. A **standby** signal is given just prior to going on air and is immediately followed by the **cue talent** signal. To convey "You're on," this cue is given by pointing your index finger (using the same hand that gave the standby signal) at the person who's supposed to go on air. The common signal for stopping a program is the hand across the throat gesture or **cut** signal. This signal terminates whatever is happening at the moment and usually "kills" all live microphones and stops all recorders. Some hand signals are used to give

FIGURE 2.9 When lit, the on-air or recording light indicates that a microphone is "live" in that audio studio.

directions to the talent regarding the microphone. To get the talent to **give mic level**, for example, hold one hand in front of you and open and close the thumb and fingers in a "chattering" motion to indicate that he or she should talk into the microphone so that levels can be checked.

Other hand signals are often used during a production to let the talent know how things are going or to convey some necessary information. Timing cues are given with the fingers with each finger indicating one minute. Using both index fingers to form a cross in front of you means there are 30 seconds left. Timing cues always indicate how much time remains in the program because there is nothing you can do about the time that has already gone by. When everything is going fine, the radio hand signal is

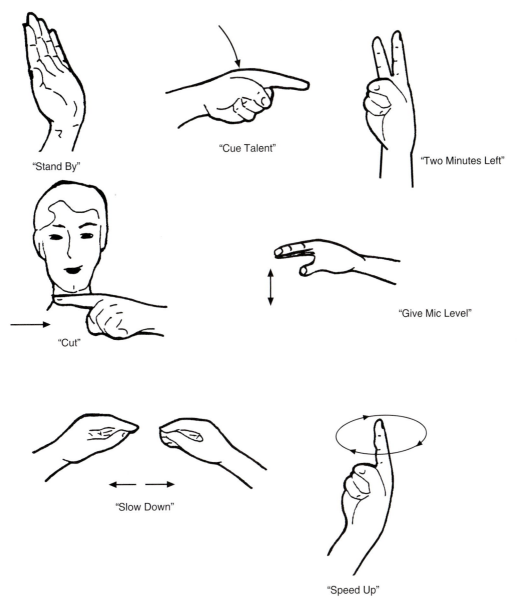

"Stand By"

"Cue Talent"

"Two Minutes Left"

"Cut"

"Give Mic Level"

"Slow Down"

"Speed Up"

FIGURE 2.10   Hand signals allow information to be conveyed in the audio studio when a "live" microphone prevents verbal communication.

the traditional "thumbs-up" given with clenched fist and extended thumb. There is no universal set of hand signals, so you may find that your facility uses some that are different, uses some not presented here, or doesn't use any at all. In any case, an understanding of hand signals should prove helpful in certain production situations.

2.11 NOISE AND DISTORTION

The next few chapters deal with the equipment that's housed in the audio production studio. Inherent in any of this electronic equipment is noise. The term **noise** refers to any unwanted sound element introduced in the production process that was not present in the original sound signal. For example, a microphone that employs an extremely

long cable might add noise to the audio signal. Recorders can introduce noise from mechanical gears or just through the electronic circuits used in amplifying or recording the signal. In all audio production, the noise level should be kept as low as possible. Most audio equipment is designed to produce a **signal-to-noise ratio (S/N)** of at least 60 to 1. S/N is an audio measurement, usually in decibels, that specifies the amount by which a signal at a standard test level exceeds the level of noise produced by an electronic component. The higher the signal-to-noise level, the better. For most analog equipment, an S/N of around 60 dB is considered good quality; modern digital equipment can show an S/N ratio of 98 dB. The S/N gives an indication of the equipment's ability to reproduce sound cleanly.

Distortion is an unwanted change in the audio signal due to inaccurate reproduction of the sound. One example

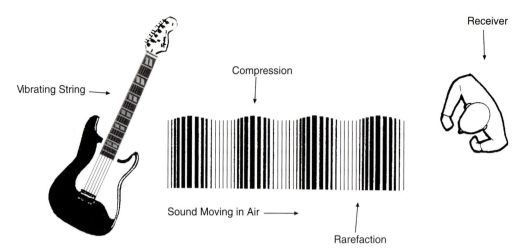

FIGURE 2.11   The production of sound requires vibrations, which are transmitted through a medium to a receiver.

is loudness distortion, which can occur when a signal is recorded at a level that is too loud for the equipment to handle. An overdriven or too loud signal sounds "muddy," and the reproduced signal does not have the same clarity or sharpness as the original. You should be aware of noise and distortion when working with audio equipment, especially analog equipment. Digital equipment frequently reduces the chance of introducing noise or distortion into your production work, but sometimes your work will be accomplished using a combination of analog and digital.

2.12 IS IT A SOUND SIGNAL OR AN AUDIO SIGNAL?

We've already mentioned how sound acts in the audio studio. It is worth your while to continue to consider sound, as this will help you understand many aspects of the production process discussed in the rest of the text. Much of what happens in the production studio has to do with manipulating sound, whether it involves a sound signal or an audio signal. When sound is naturally produced (for example, when talent speaks into a microphone), we think of that sound (his or her voice) as a **sound signal**.

In audio production, when that sound signal is then manipulated electronically (such as recorded into a digital recorder), is called an **audio signal**. Obviously, most audio production must start at some point with a sound signal, but during the actual production process, we are often recording and manipulating an audio signal. To further complicate things, these terms are sometimes interchanged when people talk about various production processes.

2.13 SOUND DEFINED

When something vibrates, sound is generated. For example, plucking a single guitar string causes a mechanical vibration to occur, which we can easily see by looking at the string.

Of course, we can also hear it. The vibrating string forces air molecules near it to come together, slightly raising the air pressure and pushing those molecules into motion, which in turn sets neighboring air molecules in motion, and on and on. Thus sound develops waves (like a stone dropped into water), which vibrate up and down and set the air molecules in a push (**compression**) and pull (**rarefaction**) motion, causing an area of higher pressure to move through the air. So in addition to the vibration noted previously, we need a medium for the sound to travel through. Of course, the medium we're usually concerned with is the atmosphere, or air. Sound can also travel through other materials, such as water or wood, but will often be distorted by the medium. Sound vibrations can't travel in a vacuum. Finally, for sound to exist technically, we need a receiver. Someone (a person) or something (a microphone) must receive it and perceive it as sound. The high-pressure area reaches receptors in our ear and we hear the vibrations as sound, or the pressure waves strike the diaphragm of a microphone, beginning the process of converting a sound signal into an audio signal.

Figure 2.11 shows a representation of sound being produced. We can't actually see sound waves, but they act very much like water waves as we've noted. The sine wave (shown in Figure 2.12C) is used to represent a sound waveform, because it can readily show the wave compression (the higher pressure portion of the wave above the center line) and the wave rarefaction (the lower pressure portion of the wave below the center line).

2.14 KEY CHARACTERISTICS OF SOUND WAVES

There are four key characteristics of sound that help determine why one sound is different from another: amplitude, frequency, timbre, and the sound envelope. A sound wave's **amplitude** relates to its strength or intensity, which we hear as **volume**, or loudness. The loudness of a sound can be thought of as the height of the sound wave. The louder

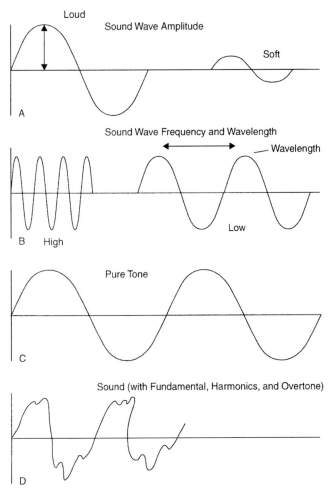

FIGURE 2.12 Characteristics of sound waves include volume, pitch, and tone, here visualized as sine waves.

the sound is, the higher the amplitude as shown in Figure 2.12A. As a sound gets louder, greater compression and rarefaction of air molecules takes place, and the crest of the wave will be higher while the trough of the wave will be deeper. A sound wave's actual amplitude is readily measured; however, loudness is a subjective concept. What is loud to one person isn't necessarily loud to another person. Sound amplitude is measured in **decibels** (abbreviated dB). The human ear is very sensitive and can hear a tremendous range of sound amplitudes, so the decibel scale is logarithmic. Near total silence is noted as 0 dB, a sound 10 times louder than this is 10 dB, a sound 100 times more powerful is 20 dB, and so on. Decibels represent the ratio of different audio levels and measure the relative intensity of sound. Sounds in the range of 0 Db (the threshold of hearing) to 120 dB (the threshold of pain) are detected by the human ear, but those sounds near and exceeding the high end can be painful and can damage your hearing. Any sound above 85 dB can cause hearing loss, but it depends on how close the listener is to the sound and how long he or she is exposed to it. The sound at many rock concerts has been measured around the 120 dB range, which explains why your ears often ring for a day or two after the show.

Frequency relates to the number of times per second that a sound wave vibrates (goes in an up-and-down cycle), which we hear as **pitch** (see Figure 2.12B). The faster something vibrates, or the more cycles it goes through per second, the higher the pitch of the sound. Like amplitude, frequency can be objectively measured, but like volume, pitch is subjective. In audio jargon, cycles per second are known as **hertz (Hz)**. A sound wave that vibrates at 2,000 cycles per second is said to have a frequency of 2,000 Hz. When the cycles per second gets higher—for example, 20,000 Hz—the term **kilohertz (kHz)** is often used. It denotes 1,000 cycles per second, so 20,000 Hz could also be called 20 kHz. (You'll learn more about frequency in the next section.)

A sound's **wavelength** is the distance between two compressions (**crests**) or two rarefactions (**troughs**). Sound wavelength can vary from around three-quarters of an inch for a treble sound near 16 kHz to around 36 feet for a bass sound near 30 Hz. There is an inverse relationship between wavelength and pitch, so higher-pitched sounds have a shorter wavelength.

A sound's **timbre** (which is pronounced "TAM-bur"), or **tone**, relates to the **waveform** of the sound. It's the characteristic of sound that distinguishes one voice from another, even though both may be saying the same thing at the same volume and pitch. A graphic representation of a pure tone is shown as the shape of a sine wave, as in Figure 2.12C. Each sound has one basic tone that is its **fundamental**; most sound, however, is a combination of many tones with different strengths at different frequencies, so the waveform is much more complex, as shown in Figure 2.12D. These other pitches are either exact frequency multiples of the fundamental (known as **harmonics**) or pitches that are not exact multiples of the fundamental (known as **overtones**). For example, striking an A note (above middle C) on a piano would produce a fundamental tone of 440 Hz. In other words, the piano string is vibrating 440 times per second. The harmonics of this note will occur at exact (or whole number) multiples of the fundamental tone, such as 880 Hz (twice the fundamental) or 2,200 Hz (five times the fundamental). The interaction of the fundamental, harmonics, and overtones creates the timbre of any particular sound.

When sound waves combine, they will be either **in phase** or **out of phase**. If the peaks and troughs of two waves line up, they will be in phase and combine into one wave with twice the amplitude of the original waves. If the peaks of one sound wave line up with the troughs of another, they will be 180 degrees out of phase and will essentially cancel each other out, producing no sound or greatly diminished sound. Most sound (such as voice or music) is made up of a combination of sound waves that are out of phase, but less than 180 degrees off, thus producing the complex waveform mentioned previously.

A sound's wave **envelope** relates to its **duration**, or the change in volume of a sound over a period of time, as shown in Figure 2.13. Normally, a sound's wave envelope

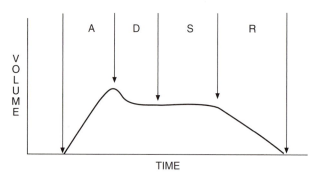

FIGURE 2.13 The sound wave envelope depicts the change in volume of a sound over a period of time.

develops through four specific stages: **attack**, the time it takes an initial sound to build to maximum volume; **decay**, the time it takes the sound to go from peak volume to a sustained level; **sustain**, the time the sound holds its sustain volume; and **release**, the time it takes a sound to diminish from sustain volume to silence. In essence, decay, sustain, and release refer to the time it takes a sound to die out. Some sounds, like a percussive drum beat, have a very fast attack; other sounds, like a piano chord, have a long decay-sustain-release. Audio equipment must be able to accurately reproduce any sound wave envelope.

2.15 FREQUENCY RESPONSE

In audio production, we often mention the frequency response of equipment or, for that matter, the frequency response range of human hearing. In very general terms, the human ear is able to hear frequencies within the range of 20 to 20,000 cycles per second. For most of us, it's not quite that low or that high. In any case, production equipment, such as an audio console or monitor speaker, should be able to reproduce an audio signal in that range, and most modern equipment is measured by how well it does so. For example, a monitor speaker may have a frequency response of 40 Hz to 18 kHz, meaning that the speaker can accurately reproduce all frequencies within that range. An inexpensive broadcast microphone may have a frequency response of only 80 Hz to 13 kHz. It would not be able to pick up any of the higher frequencies—those above 13,000 Hz. This may not be a problem if the microphone were used primarily to record speech because the human voice usually falls in a frequency range of 200 to 3,000 Hz. Obviously, if you wanted to record a musical group (which often produces sounds in the full range of frequencies), you would want to use a microphone with a wider frequency response.

A frequency response curve is often used to indicate the level of frequency response because some equipment may not pick up or reproduce certain frequencies as well as others. Broadcast equipment is designed to pick up all frequencies equally well, so its response curve is considered to be **flat**, although few components have a truly flat frequency response curve.

Although there are no standard figures, the audio frequency spectrum is often divided into three regions: bass, midrange, and treble. The low frequencies (bass) are those between 20 and 250 Hz and provide the power, or bottom, to sound. Too little bass gives a thin sound, and too much bass gives a boomy sound. The midrange frequencies fall between 250 and 4,500 Hz. These frequencies provide a lot of sound's substance and intelligibility. Too little midrange gives a lack of presence, but too much midrange gives a harsh sound. High frequencies (treble) are those from 4,500 Hz to 20,000 Hz. The treble frequencies provide the sound's brilliance and sharpness. Too little treble gives a dull sound, and too much treble gives excess sparkle as well as increasing the likelihood of hearing noise or hiss in the sound.

As frequencies change, we think in terms of the musical interval of the **octave**, or a change in pitch caused by doubling or halving the original frequency. For example, a sound going from bass to midrange to treble frequencies by octave intervals would go from 110 Hz to 220 Hz to 440 Hz to 880 Hz to 1,760 Hz to 3,520 Hz to 7,040 Hz and so on. As humans, we are subject to an awkwardly named **equal loudness principle**. That is, sounds that are equally loud will not be perceived as being equally loud if their pitch is different—we hear midrange frequencies better than either high or low frequencies. In audio production (and other forms of sound manipulation), we often compensate for this by equalization of the signal.

2.16 CONCLUSION

Unless you're building an audio production facility from the ground up, you will probably have little control over the construction of the studio; sound treatment is an important consideration, however, and methods of improving the sound environment can be put into practice in almost any situation. Although the audio studio may seem overwhelming at first, it is an environment you will become very comfortable in as you do production work. Completion of this chapter should have you in the audio production studio and ready to learn the procedures and techniques for operating all the equipment you see in front of you.

Self-Study

1. What does the radio expression "to work combo" mean?

   a) The announcer has an engineer to operate the studio equipment.
   b) The announcer operates the studio equipment and also announces.
   c) The announcer works at two different radio stations.
   d) The announcer is announcing in both the on-air and the production studio.

2. Which type of studio is least likely to contain an audio console?

   a) on-air studio
   b) production studio
   c) PDX studio
   d) performance studio

3. Which term describes sound produced in the audio studio that causes objects or surfaces within the studio to vibrate sympathetically?

   a) absorbed sound
   b) reflected sound
   c) reinforced sound
   d) diffused sound

4. In the production studio, sound that has bounced off one surface before reaching the microphone is called what?

   a) echo
   b) reverberation
   c) direct sound
   d) indirect sound

5. What does "reverb ring" in the production studio refer to?

   a) the circular route reflected sound takes before it reaches the microphone
   b) the time it takes reflected sound to go from full volume to silence
   c) just another common name for echo
   d) a sound that has bounced off two or more surfaces

6. What is the use of carpeting on the walls of some audio production facilities an example of?

   a) an inexpensive way of decorating the studio
   b) producing reverb in the studio
   c) producing a live sound in the studio
   d) soundproofing the studio

7. Studios with parallel walls produce less reflected sound than irregularly shaped studios.

   a) true
   b) false

8. Why do most production studios use a U-shaped layout?

   a) This design places equipment within easy reach of the operator.
   b) This design uses incandescent lights rather than fluorescent lights.

c) This design necessitates custom-built cabinets.

d) This design uses the least amount of wire to connect the equipment.

9. Static electricity is not a problem in the modern production studio, because state-of-the-art audio equipment is impervious to static.

a) true

b) false

10. Which hand signal almost always comes immediately after the standby hand signal?

a) 2 minutes to go

b) thumbs up

c) cue talent

d) give mic level

11. If you hold up the index, second, and third fingers of one hand in front of you, what are you telling the announcer?

a) There are 3 minutes left in the program.

b) There are 30 seconds left in the program.

c) He or she should move three steps closer to the microphone.

d) Three minutes have gone by since the beginning of the program.

12. What does one call the linking of a CD player to an audio console, the console to an equalizer, and the equalizer to an audio recorder?

a) audio road map

b) audio linking

c) audio processor

d) audio chain

13. What do we call the uneven sound that is produced when sound waves are reflected between parallel walls in such a manner that a wave reflected in one direction is combined with an identical wave going in the opposite direction?

a) a diffused wave

b) a standing wave

c) an absorbed wave

d) a sympathetic wave

14. When a "recording" light is on outside a production studio, it means a microphone is "live" in that studio.

a) true

b) false

15. If an audio studio has a live end/dead end design, the front of the studio is the "live end."

a) true

b) false

16. When sound produced in the production studio strikes a hard, flat surface, which of the following does not happen?

a) reflection

b) absorption

c) penetration

d) diffusion

17. A production studio wall that has an absorption coefficient of 0.50 will absorb half the sound striking it and reflect back half the sound.

    a) true
    b) false

18. Posters and other radio station paraphernalia should not be put up in a production studio as they will distract the announcer from doing good production work.

    a) true
    b) false

19. Which term describes what happens when the irregular surfaces of acoustic tiles break up sound reflections?

    a) absorption
    b) reflection
    c) penetration
    d) diffusion

20. What is an unwanted change in the audio signal due to inaccurate reproduction of the sound called?

    a) reverb
    b) noise
    c) distortion
    d) diffusion

21. Which statement about sound is not true?

    a) Sound is generated when something vibrates.
    b) Sound, to technically exist, must be heard.
    c) Sound vibrations develop waves by setting adjacent air molecules in motion.
    d) Sound vibrations travel faster in a vacuum than in air.

22. Which of the following is not part of a sound wave's envelope?

    a) attack
    b) decay
    c) sustain
    d) rarefaction

23. The number of times a sound wave vibrates (goes in an up-and-down cycle) per second determines which characteristic of the sound?

    a) frequency
    b) amplitude
    c) wavelength
    d) wave envelope

24. What is the standard unit of measure to gauge the relative intensity of sound?

    a) signal-to-noise ratio
    b) hertz
    c) absorption coefficient
    d) decibel

25. Sound (such as a talent's voice) that has been manipulated electronically (such as recorded on a digital recorder) is called a sound signal.

    a) true
    b) false

ANSWERS

If you answered A to any of the questions:

1a. No. This is not working combo. (Reread 2.3.)

2a. No. An on-air studio needs an audio console for sending the mixed signal out. (Reread 2.1 and 2.2.)

3a. No. If anything, absorbed sound would be diminished. (Reread 2.5.)

4a. Yes. Echo is sound that has reflected off a single surface.

5a. No. This answer nearly (but not exactly) describes reverb route. (Reread 2.5.)

6a. No. Painted walls would be less expensive, so this can't be correct. (Reread 2.6 and 2.8.)

7a. No. Just the opposite is true. (Reread 2.7.)

8a. Right. The operator can reach around the "horseshoe."

9a. No. Just the opposite is true. (Reread Production Tip 2 A.)

10a. No. The two-minute signal would not come until the end of a program. It would not be right after a standby signal. (Reread 2.10.)

11a. Yes. This is the correct hand signal.

12a. No. Although you could map out this audio signal route, this is not the best answer. (Reread 2.2.)

13a. No. Diffused waves would be sound reflections that have been broken up. (Reread 2.5 and 2.7.)

14a. Right. On-air and recording lights usually come on automatically when a microphone is on in that studio.

15a. No. This statement is not true because the front of the studio would be the "dead end" designed to absorb and diffuse sounds. (Reread 2.5.)

16a. No. Most of the sound that strikes a hard, flat surface will be reflected. (Reread 2.5.)

17a. Yes. This would be a true statement.

18a. Wrong. Posters and other studio decorations aren't likely to cause poor production work, and they do add atmosphere to the studio. (Reread 2.8.)

19a. No. Absorption would be the soaking up of sound reflections. (Reread 2.5 and 2.6.)

20a. No. Reverb is a form of reflected sound. (Reread 2.5 and 2.11.)

21a. No. This is a true statement. (Reread 2.13.)

22a. No. Attack is the time is takes an initial sound to build up to full volume. (Reread 2.14.)

23a. Yes. This is the correct answer.

24a. No. Although S/N is expressed in decibels, it measures the nominal output of audio equipment in relation to the equipment's noise level. (Reread 2.14.)

25a. No. This is not a true statement, because once natural sound has been manipulated electronically, it is correctly called an audio signal; however, be aware that sometimes these terms are interchanged. (Reread 2.12.)

If you answered B to any of the questions:

1b. Correct. The announcer is also the equipment operator when working combo.

2b. No. A production studio needs an audio console for mixing. (Reread 2.1 and 2.2.)

3b. No. Reflected sound is sound that has bounced off a surface. (Reread 2.5.)

4b. No. Reverb is sound that has reflected off two or more surfaces. (Reread 2.5.)

5b. Yes. This is what we call "reverb ring."

6b. Wrong. Carpeting absorbs sound and reduces reverb. (Reread 2.5 and 2.6.)

7b. Yes. This is the correct response.

8b. No. Lights have no relevance, so this can't be correct. (Reread 2.3 and 2.8.)

9b. Yes. Modern electronics, especially logic circuits, can be disrupted by static discharges.

10b. Wrong. You wouldn't know the production was going well if it hadn't started yet. (Reread 2.10.)

11b. No. Crossed index fingers indicate 30 seconds left. (Reread 2.10.)

12b. No. This is not correct. (Reread 2.2.)

13b. Correct. This is the right answer.

14b. No. This is exactly what it means. (Reread 2.9.)

15b. Yes. This is a false statement. The "live end" would be the back of the studio designed to add some reflected sound giving the studio sound a desirable sharpness.

16b. This isn't a bad choice, but some sound will be absorbed and dissipated even with hard surfaces. (Reread 2.5.)

17b. No. A coefficient value of 1.00 would mean total absorption and a coefficient value of 0.00 would mean no absorption. (Reread 2.6.)

18b. Yes. This is the correct answer.

19b. No. Reflection would be sound that has bounced off a surface. (Reread 2.5)

20b. No. You're close because noise is an unwanted element introduced into the audio signal that was not present in the original sound, but there's a better response. (Reread 2.11.)

21b. No. This is a true statement. (Reread 2.13.)

22b. No. Decay is the time it takes sound to go from peak volume to a sustain level. (Reread 2.14.)

23b. No. Amplitude relates to volume and the height of a sound wave. (Reread 2.14.)

24b. No. Hertz is another term for cycles per second and is a measure of frequency. (Reread 2.14.)

25b. Correct. This is a false statement because once natural sound has been manipulated electronically, it is correctly called an audio signal; however, be aware that sometimes the terms are interchanged.

If you answered C to any of the questions:

1c. No. This is not working combo. (Reread 2.3.)

2c. No. This is just another term for production studio. (Reread 2.1 and 2.2.)

3c. Right. This is the correct response.

4c. No. Direct sound doesn't bounce off any surface before reaching the microphone. (Reread 2.5.)

5c. No. Echo and reverb are both reflected sound but distinctly different. (Reread 2.5.)

6c. No. Just the opposite would happen. Soundproofing with carpeting would help produce a dead sound in the studio. (Reread 2.5 and 2.6.)

8c. No. In a cost-conscious facility, this could be a negative. (Reread 2.3 and 2.4.)

10c. Correct. "Standby" and "cue talent" hand signals are always given one after the other.

11c. No. There is another hand signal to move the announcer closer to the microphone, and exact steps are never indicated. (Reread 2.10.)

12c. No. You are way off base with this answer. An audio processor is used to alter the sound characteristics of an audio signal. (Reread 2.2.)

13c. No. Absorbed waves would be sound reflections that have been soaked up. (Reread 2.5 and 2.7.)

16c. No. Some sound will penetrate a hard surface and be transmitted to the adjoining space. (Reread 2.5.)

19c. No. Penetration would be sound that has been transmitted through a surface. (Reread 2.5.)

20c. Yes. You're correct.

21c. No. This is a true statement. (Reread 2.13.)

22c. No. Sustain is the time a sound holds its volume. (Reread 2.14.)

23c. No. Wavelength refers to the distance between two wave compressions or rarefactions. (Reread 2.14.)

24c. No. Absorption coefficient measures the degree to which materials can absorb sound. (Reread 2.14.)

If you answered D to any of the questions:

1d. No. This seems improbable and is not working combo. (Reread 2.3.)

2d. Correct. A performance studio usually only has microphones that are fed to an audio console in either a production studio or an on-air studio.

3d. No. (Reread 2.5.)

4d. You're partly right, but echo and reverb are both indirect sound, and one is a better response to this question. (Reread 2.5.)

5d. No. While this describes reverb, there is a better response. (Reread 2.5.)

6d. Correct. Carpeting walls helps to soundproof, as would use of acoustic tiles designed for the production studio.

8d.   While this may be true, it really is not the best reason. (Reread 2.3.)

10d. No. The "give mic level" signal, if used, would have been given before a "standby" signal. (Reread 2.10.)

11d. No. Time signals are usually given only to show how much time remains in a program. (Reread 2.10.)

12d. Correct. The term "audio chain" describes how broadcast equipment is connected together.

13d. No. Sympathetic waves would be sound reflections that have been reinforced. (Reread 2.5 and 2.7.)

16d. Correct. Sound is diffused when it strikes an irregular surface.

19d. Correct. This is diffusion.

20d. No. Diffusion is sound that has been broken up by an irregular surface. (Reread 2.5 and 2.11.)

21d. Correct. Sound vibrations can't travel in a vacuum.

22d. Correct. Rarefaction is not part of a sound's wave envelope.

23d. No. Wave envelope refers to a sound's duration. (Reread 2.14.)

24d. Right. The decibel is the standard unit or ratio used to measure a sound's volume.

Projects

PROJECT 1

Tour an audio facility and write a report describing it.

Purpose

To enable you to see a commercial production facility firsthand.

Notes

1. This project can be completed by touring a radio station, recording studio, or other audio production facility, but don't push a facility that seems reluctant to have you come. Although some smaller studios are happy to have you, others just aren't equipped to handle visitors.
2. Make sure that before you go you have some ideas about what you want to find out so that you can make the most of your tour.
3. Keep your appointment. Once you make it, don't change it.

How to Do the Project

1. Select a studio or station that you would like to tour. (If the instructor has arranged a tour for the whole class, skip to Step 4.)
2. Call and ask them if you could tour the facility so that you can write a report for an audio production class.
3. If they're agreeable, set a date; if they're not, try a different facility.
4. Think of some things you want to find out for your report. For example:
   a. How many production studios do they have?
   b. What types of equipment (CD player, audio recorder, and so on) do they have?
   c. What manufacturers (brand names) have they bought equipment from?
   d. How is the production studio soundproofed?
   e. How is the on-air studio different from the production studio(s)?
   f. Do they ever use hand signals during a production?
   g. Are their studios designed for stand-up operation?
   h. What is the physical layout of the studios and the station?
5. Go to the facility. Tour to the extent that they'll let you, and ask as many questions as you can.
6. Jot down notes so that you'll remember main points.
7. Write your report in an organized fashion, including a complete description of the production studio and the other points you consider most pertinent. It should be two or three typed pages. Write your name and "Audio Production Facility Tour" on a title page.
8. Give the report to your instructor to receive credit for this project.

PROJECT 2

Redesign your production studio.

Purpose

To suggest improvements to your production facility, utilizing some of the concepts mentioned in this chapter.

Notes

1. Although you may initially feel your production studio is perfect just the way it is, almost every studio can be reconfigured with improvements.

2. You won't be judged on artistic ability, but make your drawings as clear as possible.
3. You may find it useful to complete Project 1 before attempting this project.

How to Do the Project

1. Draw a rough sketch of your production studio, showing approximate dimensions, door and window location, equipment placement, and so forth.
2. Draw another sketch of the studio, suggesting changes or improvements to it. For example, if there currently is a CD player on the left side of the audio console and another on the right side, you may suggest moving them both to one side. If you notice a paneled or painted sheet rock wall in the studio, you may suggest putting acoustic tile on that area. You may want to employ an idea for your studio that you noticed when you did Project 1. Just be creative, and try to design the best possible production studio.
3. On a separate sheet of paper, provide a reason for each change you suggest.
4. Write your name and "Studio Design" on a title page, and put your two sketches and reasons together.
5. Turn in this packet to the instructor to receive credit for this project.

PROJECT 3

Draw an audio chain flowchart for your production studio.

Purpose

To help you understand that the audio chain maps the route an electronic audio signal takes as it goes from one place to another in the production studio.

Notes

1. It may be helpful to review Figure 2.2 before beginning this project.
2. Use simple shapes to represent equipment and arrowed lines to represent the sound signal.
3. You won't be judged on artistic ability, but make your drawings as clear as possible.

How to Do the Project

1. Pick a single sound source in your production studio, such as a CD player.
2. Draw a figure to represent the CD player toward the left side of a sheet of paper, and label it appropriately.
3. Determine where the sound goes as it leaves the output of the CD player. (Most likely, it goes to the audio console.)
4. Draw a figure to the right of the CD player to represent the audio console, and label it.
5. Draw an arrowed line going from the CD player to the audio console to represent the signal flow.
6. Now determine where the sound goes next. (It could go to a signal processor or maybe directly to an audio recorder.)
7. Continue in this manner until you've drawn all the possible signal paths that the CD player sound could take. (Don't forget to include the signal to the studio monitors.)
8. Pick another sound source, such as the studio microphone, and repeat the above steps. Do the same for all the other sound sources in your studio—audio recorders, and so forth.
9. Write your name and "Audio Chain" on your sketch, and turn it in to the instructor to receive credit for this project.

3

DIGITAL AUDIO PRODUCTION

3.1 INTRODUCTION

Digital technology has revolutionized how a production person can record, edit, and otherwise manipulate an audio sound signal. From creating a music bed to adding sound effects and editing out vocal mistakes, audio editing is a day-to-day part of audio production work—and it's one of the more important skills that you need to know as a production person.

This chapter introduces you to the world of digital audio production. First, some basic information on how analog sound is converted to digital audio is presented. Then the focus shifts to exploring some of the digital audio equipment and basic production techniques used in the modern audio studio. Finally, the chapter looks at digital audio editing and multitrack production work.

3.2 THE ANALOG ROOTS OF DIGITAL PRODUCTION

Before digital technology was developed, audio recording relied on an **analog** process. An analog signal is a continuously variable electrical signal whose shape is defined by the shape of the sound wave produced (see Figure 3.1A). In the analog recording process, a duplicate or electromagnetic representation of the sound wave of the original sound source can be stored on magnetic tape. For example, a microphone converts sound pressure changes to changes in voltage that are sent down the microphone cable and recorded onto audio tape as changes in magnetic strength.

Each time the analog signal is recorded or processed in some fashion, it is subject to degradation, because the signal changes shape slightly. Analog encoding is similar to creating a line graph to show a statistical analysis. All measurements are on a continuous line that curves up and down with no discrete points. The recording process is like trying to retrace a curve on a graph; the reproduction is always slightly different than the original. In addition to this generation loss, because analog recording relies on magnetic pulses stored on tape, any defect or decrease in the magnetic properties of the tape means a loss of signal quality.

3.3 THE DIGITAL PROCESS

In today's production studio, computers and other equipment use a digital recording process. By digital technology, we mean the process of converting original audio waveform information into an electrical signal composed of a series of on and off pulses. In other words, the digital process is a conversion into **binary** numbers. All computers handle information in this manner by associating a binary number with each letter of the alphabet and each number, and then manipulating this binary data. Digital encoding is accomplished in a discrete fashion, similar to looking at individual numbers in a statistical analysis and writing them down in a set order. The audio signal starts out as analog, but it can be converted to digital by going through four basic stages: filtering, sampling, quantizing, and coding.

First, the original analog sound signal is sent through a low-pass **filter** that strips off frequencies that are above the range of human hearing. Although originally inaudible, these frequencies can be shifted, or **aliased**, into an audible range during recording and playback, so this process is known as **anti-aliasing**.

The filtered analog signal is next divided many times a second in a process known as analog-to-digital conversion, or **sampling** (see Figure 3.1B). Each sample represents the amplitude of the audio signal at the moment the sample is taken. The more samples that are taken and converted to binary data, the more exact a reproduction of the original sound signal can be recorded. The process is much like that of film, in which 24 still photographs are taken per second. When these photographs are played back at

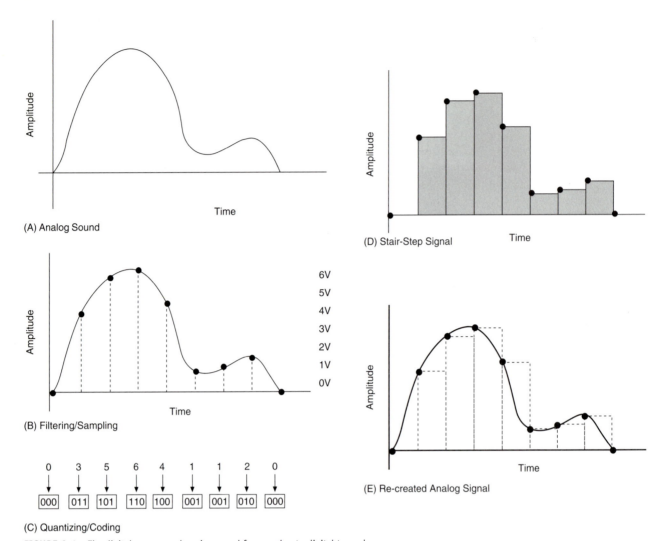

FIGURE 3.1   The digital process—changing sound from analog to digital to analog.

the same rate, they create the illusion of movement. When audio samples are played back, they create the illusion of a contiguous sound. To do so, however, many more than 24 samples must be taken per second. Most digital audio equipment utilizes **sampling rates** of 32, 44.1, and 48 thousand samples per second. The sampling rate must be at least twice the highest frequency in the audio signal to enable high-quality and accurate encoding and decoding. Because we can't hear sounds above 20 kHz, the sampling rate should be slightly greater than twice 20 kHz, which is one reason why the most common digital sampling rate is 44.1 kHz.

Quantizing and coding are the stages that assign a numerical value to each individual sample. The samples taken of the **amplitude** of the audio signal can occur at any point within the range of amplitudes, from absolutely silent to very loud. Between these two extremes—or indeed between any two points, as geometry tells us—there are an infinite number of other points. **Quantizing** breaks up these infinite points into a more manageable number, rounding samples up or down to the nearest

value. The term "bit depth" references the quantizing levels: the more levels, the more accurate information you would have about the signal. For example, a 1-bit system would signify just two quantizing levels—either no amplitude or maximum amplitude—which doesn't give much information about the sound. Each additional bit doubles the number of levels—2 bits give four levels, 3 bits give eight levels, and so on. The standard bit rate for most digital recording is 16 bits, with some CD and DVD recording now being done with 20-bit or 24-bit technology. Sixteen bits can represent 65,536 values. Higher bit depth equals lower noise and better fidelity of the digital recording.

Coding involves putting 0s and 1s in a precise order corresponding to the values measured during the quantizing process. This binary or digital "word" (see Figure 3.1C) represents each individual sample's quantized (rounded up or down) voltage level at that particular moment. The analog-to-digital (A/D) converter is the electronic circuit that accomplishes this task. Remember, it's the binary data that is actually recorded, not an analog representation of the signal. With digital technology, we can make numerous copies with no measurable loss of quality. Along with the improved **frequency response**, wide **dynamic range**, and drastically reduced **noise** and **distortion**, this ability to rerecord with no decrease in quality has contributed greatly to the acceptance of digital technology in audio production.

To transform the digital signal back to analog, the recorded numbers are sent to a digital-to-analog (D/A) converter where each sample is read and decoded. A signal of the corresponding analog amplitude is produced and "held" for the individual samples, producing a stair-step signal (see Figure 3.1D) that represents the analog signal. Finally, a filter employs an exact mathematical attribute for each sample to create a correct reproduction of the original analog signal, as shown in Figure 3.1E.

3.4 REASONS FOR EDITING

Why do you even need to edit audio in the first place? The answers are relatively obvious. For example, rarely will you produce the vocal track for a production exactly the way you want it on the first try. Although you could record the script over and over until you got it perfect, editing gives you the ability to eliminate mistakes without rerecording. Now you can just record a few takes and it's more likely you'll get part of it sounding great on one take, part of it sounding great on another, and so on. The best recording will probably be bits and pieces from various takes that you edit to take out fluffs and bad segments and keep only the exact words and phrases you want. Other production work may require you to edit out excessive pauses or "uhs" from a piece of news tape or language not allowed by the FCC from an artist interview.

In addition to eliminating mistakes, editing allows you to decrease the length of production work. Audio productions usually require exact times for commercials, news stories, and other programs, and editing can keep your work to the exact lengths required. You can either manually edit out excessive pauses in a vocal track or, in some instances, use audio editing software to automatically "time compress" a vocal segment to the exact length you need. Many half-hour interview programs are really edited down from an actual interview that went on much longer. Entire questions that didn't get a good response can be edited out, and long, rambling responses can be cut down to a more concise reply.

Audio editing also gives you the freedom to record out of sequence. For example, you might be putting together a production that uses the testimonials of several customers that you've recorded. It's probable that the one you want to use first in your commercial may not have been recorded first. Editing allows you to easily rearrange the order or, again, just use a portion of what you originally taped in the final production.

3.5 DESKTOP AUDIO PRODUCTION: THE DIGITAL AUDIO EDITOR

One of the simplest ways to get into digital production is to put together an inexpensive digital audio editor that utilizes a standard off-the-shelf computer system, plus some specialized equipment, to make up an audio editing system. Often referred to as "desktop audio," this type of production system has the potential of replacing almost an entire production studio. There are two main types of audio editors: 2-track and multitrack. If you're going to just edit phone calls, a simple 2-track system might be more than adequate. If you plan on doing complex commercial production, however, you will want a multitrack system. Many audio editing software programs incorporate both types of editors in a single program.

Almost any basic computer system today will be configured adequately to run audio editing software. In addition to the computer, the necessary specialized equipment includes a **DSP** (digital signal processing) **audio card**, normally a PCI-bus design, as shown in Figure 3.2. A standard computer audio card could be used, but professional audio hardware usually offers higher sampling rate capability, greater bit resolution, and broadcast-style connectors. The audio card functions as both the A/D and D/A converter, and the interface or I/O (input/output) device that moves the audio signal from its source to the editing system. In most production studios, an output from the audio console is fed into the audio card so that any equipment that runs through the audio board can be recorded into the desktop system.

The final component of a desktop audio system is a computer software program to perform the actual recording and editing of the audio. There are several software programs (see Figure 3.3) that can turn a PC into a powerful digital audio editor—*Digidesign Pro Tools*, *Sony Sound Forge 9*, *Steinberg Cubase Studio 4*, and *Adobe Audition 3*, to name a few. Most professional programs used in the audio studio fall within a range of $300 to $900—a relatively inexpensive investment. In addition, some bare-bones audio editing software can be found for less than $100. With a modest budget, anyone should be able to build a desktop system and begin doing digital audio production work.

PRODUCTION TIP 3A
Audacity

Audacity offers a free audio editor that you can download for Windows, Mac, and some other operating systems at http://audacity.sourceforge.net. Many of the key features found in professional programs and mentioned in this chapter are available in the Audacity program. You can record audio or digitize (analog sources) in 16-bit, 24-bit, or 32-bit resolution at a sampling rate of up to 97 kHz. Basic audio editing commands include cut,

FIGURE 3.2   A DSP audio card is an important component of any computer-based desktop audio editor. (Image courtesy of Digital Audio Labs.)

copy, paste, and delete with undo and redo functions. The program also facilitates audio effects like pitch change, noise reduction, equalization, echo, phasing, and more. Audacity can import and export several common sound file formats such as MP3, WAV, and AIFF. Audacity is released under the terms of a GNU General Public License. Users of this open source software can use the program, as well as study, copy, modify, and redistribute it under terms of the license.

3.6 DIGITAL AUDIO WORKSTATIONS AND OTHER DIGITAL EDITORS

The **DAW** or **digital audio workstation** is a hard disk–based system that incorporates proprietary computer technology but is quite similar to desktop audio systems. Because the workstation has been developed as a dedicated audio recorder and editor, it often has built-in specialized functions and features. The basic components of the DAW are packaged as a single unit similar to the one shown in Figure 3.4. A frame houses the computer chassis, power supply, and motherboard. An internal hard disk drive stores and manipulates the digital audio data.

A **user interface**, such as a keyboard, touch screen, or mouse, is necessary to actually operate the workstation. However, many workstations have tried to become more user-friendly by making the interface include typical audio production elements, such as **faders**, **cue wheels**, and **transport buttons**. Sometimes these interfaces are shown in graphics form on a computer screen, but other systems are part of a small audio mixer. A built-in audio card provides the connection between the workstation and the other audio equipment. Through the use of various ports, many workstations have the ability to network with other workstations or interface with printers, modems, and other components. So a DAW-based system can become part of an all-digital facility (see Figure 3.5) that can produce an audio spot, store it or several variations of it, play the production on air by sending the signal to a digitized transmitter, and even send logging and bookkeeping information about the airing to the appropriate personnel.

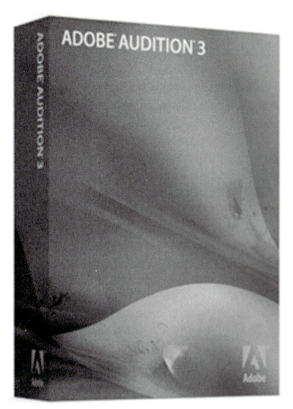

FIGURE 3.3 Audio editing software can transform an off-the-shelf computer into a desktop audio editor. (Adobe box shot reprinted with permission from Adobe Systems Incorporated.)

Another type of digital audio editor is the **personal audio editor**. One example is *360 Systems Short/cut*™. This editor is configured in a compact, portable case (as shown in Figure 3.6) and records audio directly to its internal hard drive.

Beneath a small 2-track waveform display are three distinct sections of controls. To the right are basic transport controls (like play and record), in the center are editing controls (like edit in and cut) and a large scrub wheel, and to the left are the system controls (like hot keys and menu directory) and a QWERTY keyboard for labeling functions. Editing is as easy as recording or loading in a file, moving to the edit-in point, and then moving to the edit-out point (see Figure 3.7). The marked section of audio will become highlighted and can then be removed, copied, or new material can be inserted. If you make a mistake, an undo function will allow you to correct it. This editor has a selectable 44.1 kHz or 48 kHz sample rate, and provides around 12 hours of recording time for stereo audio. This type of audio editor, which is less complex than some of the PC-based audio editors, is fairly commonplace in the digital production studio.

Other multitrack recorders and editors are designed to be rack-mounted in the studio or are part of a system that contains the recorder, audio mixer, and signal processing effects within an individual unit.

FIGURE 3.4 Some digital audio workstations resemble desktop audio editors, but employ specialized audio cards, customized boxes, and proprietary software. (Image courtesy of SADiE Inc.)

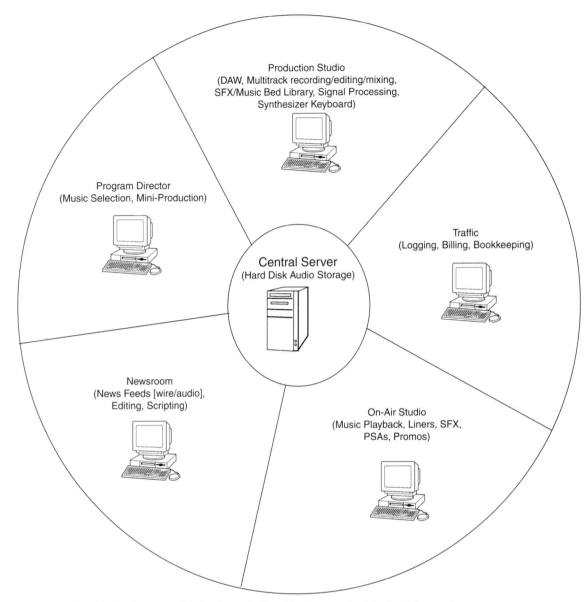

FIGURE 3.5 An all-digital facility integrates digital audio production with other aspects of the facility's operation.

FIGURE 3.6 This personal audio editor is a digital replacement for the two-track reel-to-reel recorder. (Image courtesy of 360 Systems. All rights reserved.)

FIGURE 3.7 360 Systems' waveform display showing EDIT IN and EDIT OUT marks set; the highlighted area will be cut out when the edit is completed. (Image courtesy of 360 Systems. All rights reserved.)

3.7 STRONG POINTS AND WEAK POINTS OF DIGITAL PRODUCTION

We know that digital equipment offers superior audio quality and that digital equipment doesn't suffer from various forms of audio distortion or build up any additional noise during recording or copying. But there are other advantages to digital recording that have helped endear the technology to the audio production person.

One operational advantage of the DAW is fast random access to all the material stored in the system. This ability to immediately cue up at any point leads to less time spent on basic production functions and potentially more time spent on the creative aspect of the production process.

If you record something, but then need to make it slightly shorter or longer, you can do so easily with digital equipment. For instance, if you record what is to be a 15-second commercial and it turns out to be 17 seconds long, you can remove short bits of silence throughout the commercial to get it to 15 seconds. In fact, many digital audio editing programs or workstations can do this time compression/expansion for you. You simply indicate how long you want something to be, and the program adjusts the material accordingly.

IDs and other types of label information can be encoded within the digital media. A table of contents can provide names, times, and other data through a front-panel window on the equipment or through the video monitor screen of a DAW.

As there are few internal operating parts, repair of digital equipment is often a simple substitution of one circuit board or component for another. On the other hand, when something goes wrong with a computer hard drive, for example, it's often not just the current project that is damaged or lost, but everything else contained on the hard drive can be corrupted as well. For this reason, the need for frequent backing up of hard drives cannot be overemphasized, especially if material contained on the drive is sensitive or difficult to re-create. Computer programs also have a tendency to crash at exactly the wrong moment, erasing hours of work in an instant if the audio files you are editing or recording haven't been backed up. Most computer audio-editing software has an option to perform periodic automatic backups of files currently being worked on, either at timed intervals or after a specified number of new edits. However, the automatic backup feature is not often turned on as a default after installation of the program, so it is worth looking in the index of the program's documentation for this feature so that you can enable it before you start working.

PRODUCTION TIP 3B
Maintaining Digital Equipment

There are few mechanical elements in digital equipment, but computer knowledge is becoming more and more important for what maintenance there is. To keep your studio computers running in their most efficient manner, you will need to reboot them every 7 to 10 days. Most computer programs, such as editing software, will cause the computer RAM to become fragmented as the program runs. You may not notice any problems with typical business programs (like word processing) on computers that run during the normal workday and then are shut down until the next day. However, studio computers are often running 24 hours a day, every day of the week. RAM can become so fragmented that the computer will lock up, and that's a condition that you don't want to happen for a production or on-air computer. Set up a regular maintenance reboot during some station quiet time and you'll have fewer computer problems.

In addition, memory management should become a regular part of your computer maintenance. As production work is accomplished, sound file fragments and completed productions may be left on the hard drive. But in a short period of time, hours of hard disc storage space will dwindle down to minutes unless old files are deleted from the system or archived onto a removable storage medium for later use.

There is also a potential noise problem with digital equipment—not audio noise, but noise from cooling fans in computers or disk drives. If this equipment has to be housed in a studio with live microphones, there could be a problem. Some production facilities solve this by putting computer CPUs in a separate equipment room, leaving only the keyboard/mouse and monitor in the actual studio. If computer equipment must be in the studio, try to place it as far from the microphone as possible, and build it into studio furniture to minimize any noise. Laptop computers may also be an option to consider, as their cooling components are usually much quieter.

3.8 AUDIO SYNCHRONIZATION

Digital audio signals are streams of digits broken up into digital words. If two digital signals are out of sync, then one may just be beginning a new digital word when the other is in the middle of a word. Switching from one to the other would result in an audible tick or pop. Synchronized audio signals start both new digital words at precisely the same time. Some digital production equipment is self-synchronizing, but digital audio consoles that accept many different types of digital inputs need to synchronize audio to a common clock.

Most digital audio workstations and many other pieces of digital broadcast equipment also have the ability to incorporate MIDI and SMPTE synchronization. **MIDI (musical instrument digital interface)** is an interface system that allows electronic equipment—mainly musical instruments like synthesizers, drum machines, and samplers—to "talk" to each other through an electronic language. **SMPTE (Society for Motion Picture and Television Engineers)**

time code is an electronic language developed for videotape editing that identifies each video frame with an individual address. The time code numbers consist of hour, minute, second, and frame. The frame digits correspond to the 30 video frames in each second. Both MIDI and SMPTE signals can be used to reference various individual pieces of equipment and accurately start, combine, or stop them.

Computers with faster CPU processing have helped, as has the development of audio drivers that bypass the Windows or Mac operating system, allowing audio signals to connect directly with the sound card. Still, latency can be an issue that the audio production person must be aware of and willing to work around if it becomes noticeable in his or her production work.

3.9 LATENCY ISSUES

Latency is the short amount of time required to convert analog audio into digital audio, or to add a digital effect to audio, or to move audio from one location to another. All digital equipment and computers dealing with audio will exhibit some latency. In most individual pieces of equipment, latency is usually not an audible issue, because it is often only a few milliseconds delay. However, latency can be cumulative as sound goes through several normal audio processes. For example, if you add EQ to an audio track, mix that track with several other audio tracks, and then monitor everything through an audio interface, your audio will have gone through several layers of software processing, each adding some latency effect.

In broadcast situations, latency issues also arise when a live broadcast is combined with audio from a satellite or telephone feed or similar link. The linking equipment often has enough latency to produce a noticeable time delay between the live broadcast and the other audio.

3.10 DIGITAL AUDIO EDITING

Editing normally begins after you've recorded audio into the system you're using. You can also import a previously recorded audio file, or directly "rip" audio from a CD into a file. Although there are many different systems available, to gain an understanding of digital audio editing, we'll look at one system—Adobe Audition. Adobe Audition has two main work areas. The "Edit View" screen (shown in Figure 3.8) puts the user in a single-waveform editor that is used to record, process, and edit mono and stereo audio segments. The "waveform display" shows the audio sound file and is utilized to edit or otherwise process the sound. The "transport" buttons control recording and playback functions of the audio. A "timeline display" shows timing information, and horizontal and vertical zooms allow you to scale the audio display to various sizes. Other options are available through either menu options or toolbar buttons.

To illustrate the basic audio edit, let's first record three words—*dog, cat, banana*—into our system. Basic editing

FIGURE 3.8 The main screen of an audio editing program shows various navigation and functional controls for manipulating the audio file. (Adobe screenshot reprinted with permission from Adobe Systems Incorporated.)

programs allow you to set the sampling rate and bit depth using the sound card and software. To begin recording, click on File from the top menu bar, select New, click the appropriate recording specifications (for example, sample rate = 44,100, channels = stereo, resolution = 16-bit), and then click on OK. We'll assume that you have a microphone plugged directly into your sound card or the output of your audio console feeds into the sound card. Click on the RECORD button (red circle) on the Transport controls and speak the three words into the microphone, pausing slightly between each word. You can check recording levels by watching the "Record Level Meters" at the bottom of the "Edit View" screen. Double-clicking activates the meters if they aren't already monitoring the audio amplitude. It's also probable that you can manipulate the source audio volume through an external control, such as an audio console or interface. Finally, click on the STOP button (gray square) on the Transport controls.

The audio you recorded will appear as a green waveform (see Figure 3.9) on the black background in the Waveform Display area of the screen. Silence (the pauses) will be shown as a flat green line. (These are the default screen colors, so you may see something different, depending on the settings for your system.) The audio can now be edited, processed, or stored on the editor's hard disk as a **sound file**. These large audio files consist of an information header (noting sample rate, bit depth, and so on) and the actual data (a long series of numbers—one for each sample). CD-quality audio at 44,100 samples per second times 16 bits of data adds up to around 10 MB for each minute of audio recorded. Even though some procedures and terminology will be different, many of the basic principles would apply to any equipment that's capable of digital audio editing.

Editing uses the mouse to define a **region** in a fashion similar to standard editing: that is, selecting a range (start point and end point) for each edit. In this case, the edit marks are made on the computer screen, which shows a "picture" of the audio (usually the actual **waveform**; see Figure 3.9) and can be easily moved, or **trimmed**, to the exact position desired.

If you wanted to edit out the word *cat*, you would click an edit point just to the left of the waveform for the word *cat* and then drag the mouse to the right, stopping just before the waveform for the word *banana*. Including the pause after the word maintains the natural pacing of the audio. Selecting edit points just before and immediately after the word *cat* would increase the pause between *dog* and *banana*. In a similar manner, selecting edit points just after the word *dog* and just before the word *banana* would eliminate any pause between those words, creating an unnatural flow to the words. The area you have selected will become highlighted in white (refer to Figure 3.9 again). You can hear the audio segment that you've highlighted by clicking on the PLAY button (single green forward triangle).

If you need to adjust either edit point, hold down the Shift key and click on the edit point. Move the edit point left or right as required. Most editor programs have a function to zoom in on the segment of audio you're working on to fine-tune any adjustments and get the mark exactly where you want it. To complete the edit, click on Edit on the top menu bar and select Cut or click on the appropriate toolbar icon. The selected audio will be cut to a clipboard and the remaining audio will automatically "heal" or be joined together, leaving the words *dog* and *banana*. It takes a lot longer to explain this process than it does to accomplish it—as you'll quickly learn!

Suppose you now want to paste the word *cat*, which we just edited out, in front of the word *dog*. Click a single edit point just to the left of the waveform of the word *dog*, then click on Edit on the top menu bar and select Paste. The audio from the clipboard will be edited back in at that point so the word order is now *cat*, *dog*, and *banana*. Should you decide you don't really want to do this, you can click on

FIGURE 3.9 A sound file is shown on the computer screen as the waveform of the audio. The vertical axis indicates amplitude and the horizontal axis indicates time. Editing is accomplished with a simple mouse-drag operation, with the area to be edited out highlighted. (Adobe screenshot reprinted with permission of Adobe Systems Incorporated.)

File and select Undo, which will cancel or undo your last action. Normally, Undo can be repeated to back out of several actions if necessary. One of the biggest advantages of digital audio editing is the **nondestructive** nature of the process. The original audio isn't actually altered; edit information (where to start and stop playing the audio) is simply recorded in an **edit decision list** that is held in the computer program. The same audio can be used in several places within a project.

To copy a word, you'd follow a similar process. Click an edit point just after the word *dog* and drag to the end of the word *banana*. The word *banana* and the pause before it should now be highlighted. Once again go to Edit and select Copy. Click an edit point right at the end of the word *banana* and go to Edit and select Paste. The word order should now be *cat, dog, banana, banana*.

In most cases and with most audio editing programs, you'll want to both export and save your project when you're done editing. You want to export your file when you are finished editing it and would like to write it to a CD or other medium to play later on the air. Most programs give you the option to export in various file formats, but the most popular are .wav (which gives you high quality, but uses lots of hard drive space) and .mp3 (which saves you space, but can sacrifice sound quality). How the audio will ultimately be used may well determine what sound format you want to employ if you have that option.

Saving the project creates a file that only your audio editing software can open. You would reopen this file either if you weren't finished with your project when you saved it last and wanted to work on it more, or if later you wanted to re-edit the material. Unlike the exported file, which exports a single mono or stereo file, the saved file keeps multiple tracks intact (if you used them in your project), making it possible to separate them again. This is especially helpful if, for example, you have created a project with dialogue or narration and an underlying music bed. Perhaps when you were creating it, you were using headphones and the mix between dialogue and music sounded balanced, so you exported it to play on the air. Later, however, when playing it on monitor speakers, you found that the music was too loud or not loud enough and distracted from the voice or didn't support it enough. If you had only exported the audio, but not saved the file, all you would have would be the file with the audio elements out of kilter, irretrievably mixed together. With the saved file, however, you have the music on one track and the voice on another. You can therefore turn up or down the voice or music to readjust the balance and then export the corrected audio again.

You'll find that regardless of what audio editor you're using, it's capable of a lot more than these few simple operations. The best way to learn what an editor can do is to try different things and, of course, reading the manual or help screens doesn't hurt either. You should also check the software manufacturer's web site, as many offer tutorials or hints on how to get the most out of their programs. Most digital audio editors also feature multitrack and signal processing capabilities, which we'll look at next as well as in other chapters.

3.11 MULTITRACK EDITING TECHNIQUES

Most editing programs allow the recording of several "tracks." Figure 3.10 shows the "Multitrack View" screen from Adobe Audition. In this view, the first few tracks of the system are shown with some of the controls associated with those tracks. **Multitrack recorders** give the production person a tremendous amount of creative flexibility. Each production element, such as a vocal track or music bed, can be recorded on a separate track. Once recorded, they can be individually manipulated (such as changing volume or adding some signal processing effect), but also played back simultaneously to hear the mix of the whole production.

Other software programs will have similar screens and functions. To start recording, click on the File menu and select New. This will pop up a window that allows you to create settings that control the recording process.

Like the editing portion of the program, pull-down menus provide access to all the multitrack functions, and toolbar icons also can be used to select the most commonly used functions. The audio data in each track is graphically displayed as a waveform block as shown in Figure 3.11. In the multitrack mode, audio can easily be mixed, moved, copied, or deleted, and information can be displayed on the screen in different sizes with a "zoom" control. Each track has various virtual faders and pan controls that allow for level setting and balance control during the mix of the production. To move a waveform block with Adobe Audition, right mouse click on it and continue to hold down the right mouse button. You can now drag and drop that audio from one track to another, from one part of a track to another part, or, with other simple mouse moves, mix, copy, divide, or delete the audio.

One of the most basic techniques used in multitrack work is **overdubbing**, or the process of adding new tracks to existing tracks. Refer to Figure 3.10 as you follow the steps of a basic overdub using the multitrack function of Adobe Audition. To begin recording click on File, select New Session, and choose the sample rate and bit resolution you want. Now click on the small red *R* button (to enable recording) for Track 1. Then when you click on the master Record button on the Transport Controls, you can record, for example, an announcer's voice onto this track. Click the Transport Stop button when you're done recording. To accomplish the overdub, click on the *R* button for Track 1 again, which will now make this track play back. Click on the *R* button for Track 2. This time, when you click on the master Record button, you will record another voice on Track 2. Click on the Stop button when you're done recording. Remember to click on the Track 2 *R* button when you've finished recording the vocal track to disable recording on this track.

FIGURE 3.10 Most digital audio editing programs incorporate a virtual multitrack recorder. (Adobe screenshot reprinted with permission from Adobe Systems Incorporated.)

FIGURE 3.11 Audio segments are shown as waveform blocks that can be manipulated with drag-and-drop mouse clicks. (Adobe screenshot reprinted with permission from Adobe Systems Incorporated.)

With a few other mouse clicks, you can adjust the volume levels between the two tracks. You could also import a musical .wav or .mp3 file into Track 3, providing a music bed for your production. With Adobe Audition, you can "rip" music into the system by clicking on File and then selecting the Extract Audio from CD option. There are a number of parameters you can choose, but the main options will be to select the track you want to import into the system or select the time to import just a portion of a track. Once you've set the various components and clicked on OK, the audio will be ripped into the system. The exact steps described are unique to this software, but most systems will employ a similar type of process.

Overdubbing allows you to build a production in layers, because you don't have to record everything at the same time. If you decided later to add a sound effect to the production, you could just record it on another track, move it

to the spot where you want it to occur, and set the proper volume. Playing back all the tracks at the same time would let you hear how all the elements fit together.

If you've recorded a vocal on one track, but a portion of the vocal contains a mistake, another multitrack technique known as the **punch in** allows you to record over just the part that contains the mistake, and leave the rest of the track undisturbed. To punch in using Adobe Audition, first highlight the section of audio you want to rerecord by clicking and dragging. Click Clip on the menu, select the Punch In option, and put the track into the record-enabled mode. Place the cursor a bit before the section where the punch in will occur. Click Record and you will hear the audio up to the point of the punch in where you begin your rerecording. You can record several different "takes," and the program will allow you to select the one you feel is best. It's important not to change volume levels or microphone position of the original setup so that the rerecording is consistent with the original recording.

Most multitrack recorders can be put in "record" mode by pressing a record button for the individual track you want to record on or putting that track into a "record ready" mode, then pressing a master record button on the multitrack. The technique is a punch in, because you play back the track to the point where you want to rerecord, punch in the record button, and record over the portion of the track that you wish to correct. You punch out of record mode at an appropriate point after you've fixed the mistake. Essentially you're doing an edit on the fly with a punch in; in fact, it's also known as an **insert edit**. You might need to practice a few times so you know exactly where you want to punch in and punch out. Try to choose logical spots, such as the end of a sentence or at a pause between words; otherwise, the punch in may be noticeable.

Bouncing or **ping-ponging** tracks is the process of combining two or more tracks on a multitrack recorder and rerecording and transferring them to another vacant track of the same recorder. If you were building a music bed, for example, record drums on Track 1 and a bass on Track 2. Then bounce those tracks to Track 3. Now you have Track 1 and Track 2 free, and you can record stereo strings on those two tracks, and, if you want, bounce all three tracks to Track 4. Bouncing is a technique to increase the number of tracks that you can utilize; however, bouncing tracks brings with it both advantages and disadvantages. For example, once several tracks are combined, they can't be uncombined, so you can't change the balance of the mixed tracks, and if you equalize or otherwise process the track, it affects all elements on the track.

On the other hand, you may need to bounce some tracks together to reduce the hard disk space and processing time needed to manipulate the audio. If you have a large number of tracks, making a "submix" of some of them will speed up CPU processing. Again, you can just highlight the tracks you want to combine and choose a "mix down" option for selected files. **Live bouncing** is a similar technique: at the same time that you're mixing several tracks onto a vacant track, you add a live track to the mix. Again, it's a technique to get a maximum number of sources onto a minimum number of tracks.

3.12 MULTITRACK VOICE EFFECTS

Multitrack techniques open the door to many special effects that can turn a basic production into a creative masterpiece. Voice doubling, chorusing, and stacking are three forms of overdubbing that can give your next production a unique sound. They are often used to add a "thickness" to the vocal by making it seem like several voices speaking at the same time. **Voice doubling** is exactly what the name implies. Record your voice on Track 1. Now, while monitoring Track 1, record your voice again on Track 2. Even

though you read the same script, it's impossible to record both tracks exactly alike. The effect, also known as "voice dubbing," will be closer to two people reading the same script at the same time.

Chorusing is taking voice doubling one step further. Record at least two additional tracks in sync with the original track, creating a "chorus" effect. The more additional tracks you record, the larger your chorus will sound. It's a way for one announcer to become a group of announcers. **Stacking** is a similar multitrack technique in which an announcer "sings harmony" to a previously recorded track. As it is actually a form of delay, chorus effects are often included on audio editing software. In this case, up to twelve voices can simulate various chorus effects, and even though only one voice recorded the script, the program will slightly change timing, intonation, and vibrato of the original audio to give each voice created a distinct sound.

One announcer can appear to be two *different* announcers trading lines using a technique referred to as **dovetailing**. On Track 1, the announcer records the *odd* lines of the script, while reading the even lines silently. This leaves space between the odd lines on Track 1. Now, record on Track 2 the *even* lines of the script while mentally reading the odd lines to keep the timing correct. When both tracks are played back, you get the effect of two announcers reading a dialogue script. Obviously, you must slightly change one of the voices so that it sounds like two different announcers, and you'll probably need to practice a few times or do some editing to get the timing correct. Remember, you usually "mentally" read lines slightly faster than you do when you actually speak them. It can take a little time to perfect this technique, but it can be well worth the effort.

Of course, the same effect can be produced in another fashion. Just record the lines for each announcer on the appropriate track of the multitrack, changing one voice slightly. Now cut, move, and paste the lines to create the dialogue. You can create the natural pacing of two announcers by slightly overlapping the end of one line with the beginning of the next line.

To produce a **slapback echo** with a multitrack recorder, record your voice on Track 1. Now, dub Track 1 to another track, but without synchronization. Play back both tracks, and you'll get a unique echo effect. As this is another form of delay, look for this special effect as a menu item on your editing software's special effects section.

3.13 TRACK SHEETS

As you can tell just by reading about the various techniques above, multitrack recording can become complicated. Good production practice dictates that you keep notes of what material is recorded on which track. Although there is no standard form, Figure 3.12 shows one possible **track sheet**, or format, for keeping notes regarding a multitrack production. The top of the page indicates the number of tracks the recorder has, the edge of the page indicates the various takes, and the boxes show what was put on each track during each take. As shown, during the first take, an announcer vocal was put on Track 1, a sound effect was put on Track 2, a music bed was put on Tracks 3 and 4, and Track 5 was left open. This doesn't mean that these elements were all recorded at the same time; most likely they were put down separately, but these were the first elements assigned to those tracks.

During the second take, the announcer vocal was not changed, but the sound effect on Track 2 and the music bed on Tracks 3 and 4 were all bounced to Track 5. On the third take, Tracks 1 and 5 did not change; however, a new music bed was put on Tracks 3 and 4, and the announcer vocal was rerecorded on Track 2. You could also put any signal processing settings, music bed cuts used, or special notes regarding the production on the track sheet.

With digital software, most programs allow you to name the tracks directly in the program, so that these track labels are saved along with the file and there is no need for a hard copy.

3.14 THE MIX DOWN

Regardless of how many tracks you work with in a multi-track production, you will probably ultimately mix the production down into a stereo mix with just a left and right channel. For many programs, including Adobe Audition, there is a menu item selection to "mix down" all files.

Certain tracks from the multitrack master may be panned to the right channel, some tracks may be panned to the left channel, and some tracks may be balanced to both left and right. This is where the production person needs a good monitoring system and some good judgment to create just the right mix.

	TRACK 1	TRACK 2	TRACK 3	TRACK 4	TRACK 5	TRA
TAKE 1	ANNOUNCER	SFX	MUSIC BED - LEFT	MUSIC BED - RIGHT	OPEN	
TAKE 2		OPEN	OPEN	OPEN	SFX + MUSIC BED - LEFT + MUSIC BED - RIGHT	
TAKE 3		ANNOUNCER RETAKE	NEW MUSIC BED - LEFT	NEW MUSIC BED - RIGHT		
TAKE 4						
TAK						

FIGURE 3.12 A track sheet shows what material is recorded on which track during a multitrack recording session.

Most likely you're working in stereo and hearing the final mix in stereo; however, you need to hear the same mix in mono, because sometimes a mix sounds great in stereo, but not in mono. Often by listening in cue (assuming that the cue signal is in mono), you can tell if a stereo mix is not going to be compatible with mono. It's possible that portions of the audio signal will be out of **phase** when the left and right channels are combined for the mono signal, causing a cancellation and diminishment of the sound at different spots. A fine-tuning of some track equalization, a slight volume change, or minor panning adjustment will usually correct the mono signal, but it's always important to make sure the stereo and mono signals are compatible.

3.15 MULTITRACK SPOT PRODUCTION

There is no "standard" way to record using multitrack techniques, but let's look at the production of a commercial spot that includes two announcer voices, a background music bed, and two sound effects. In most cases, the music bed would begin first at full volume for a few seconds, and then fade under the vocals and hold at a background level. The first announcer begins his or her voice-over on top of the music bed, probably trading lines with the other announcer until the end of the copy. Sound effects are added at the appropriate points, and the music bed is brought up to full volume at the end of the voice-over. The music bed ultimately ends cold or may fade out. Of course, all of this takes place in a 30- or 60-second time frame. Assuming a production studio setup with multitrack audio editing capability, here is what is happening during this "typical" production.

Each sound source (microphone, CD, etc.) should be assigned to a stereo track. Let's put one announcer on Track 1, the other announcer on Track 2, a sound effect on Track 3, a music bed on Track 4, and another sound effect on Track 5. The first track you record is extremely important because it's often the reference for all the other tracks. In audio production, the music bed or vocal track is often put down first. In this case, the music bed is a preproduced and timed music bed from a CD production library. We just have to dub it or rip it from the CD into our recorder, either by importing it or setting the multitrack recorder to record on Track 4 only (the music bed). In either case, you want to have the entire music bed at full volume in the recorder, even though you'll be fading it under the announcers. The various levels can be balanced during the final mix.

Next, put the recorder Track 4 into a "safe" and "sync" mode. This allows you to overdub on the other tracks at the same time that you monitor the music bed track. Set Tracks 1 and 2 into the record position. Since the announcers "trade" lines throughout the commercial, you should record them at the same time, which will provide a more natural feeling of interplay and continuity than if they were recorded separately. While monitoring Tracks 4, 1, and 2, record the vocals on Tracks 1 and 2. You should fade the music at the appropriate place, so the announcers get the proper feel of reading the spot, but remember the actual blend of all the elements will take place later. At this point, if the vocal tracks came out okay, the announcers could leave, and a production person would finish the spot. That makes sense to do if the announcers are high-priced talent, and that's why many multitrack productions are started by putting down the vocal tracks. Suppose one announcer misspoke the final line in the spot. Depending on the complexity of the spot, it would be possible to set up Tracks 4 and 1 to play, and have the announcer rerecord a portion of Track 2 to correct the mistake with a punch in.

By additional overdubbing, the various sound effects would be added by playing back the tracks that were previously recorded and recording only those tracks that were assigned to sound effects, doing one effect at a time. If you miscue a sound effect, you don't have to reset every element and start all over again. You would merely rerecord the track that had the mistake on it or click and drag the misplaced element to the desired location. Once you have all tracks recorded, you can begin to "mix down" the final spot. You'll probably play back all tracks several times now (through the mixer, monitoring the multitrack outputs) to adjust the levels. If you're using digital multitrack software, you can often adjust volume levels and pans so they will automate during playback and you don't have to manipulate a bunch of faders during the mix.

3.16 CONCLUSION

This chapter is a significant one in your development as a production person. Audio editing is a very important concept as more emphasis is being placed on sound bites and ear-catching productions. The modern production person must also be skilled in working in the multitrack environment to be successful. Although this chapter is only designed to give you some basic familiarity with the equipment and techniques, it should serve as a good starting point. Like most everything about audio production, the real learning comes when you go into the studio and try out different concepts. You'll only become really skilled in multitrack production work or audio editing if you spend time in the studio to understand the creative possibilities it offers. The type of equipment or particular software that is used is not nearly as important as *how* this equipment is used to convey information in a meaningful way.

Self-Study

1. In which area is digital technology superior to analog technology?

   a) signal-to-noise ratio
   b) frequency response
   c) dynamic range
   d) all of the above

2. Which of the following is a reason to edit audio?

   a) to eliminate mistakes
   b) to record out of sequence
   c) to cut to exact length
   d) all of the above

3. A standard off-the-shelf computer can be converted into a basic digital audio editor by adding appropriate software and what other component?

   a) an ESP audio card
   b) an ESPN audio card
   c) a DSP audio card
   d) an ASP audio card

4. An audio sound file that has been edited with a destructive system has been permanently altered so the original audio cannot be restored.

   a) true
   b) false

5. Musical instruments (such as synthesizers or samplers) can interface with digital audio equipment through an electronic communications language known as what?

   a) Short/cut
   b) Audacity
   c) MINI
   d) MIDI

6. Where would you place the edit marks to edit out the word *two* from the phrase *one . . . two . . . three*?

   a) just after letter *e* of *one* and just before letter *t* of *three*
   b) just before letter *t* of *two* and just before letter *t* of *three*
   c) just before letter *t* of *two* and just after letter *o* of *two*
   d) no correct way to mark this edit is shown here

7. Which stage of the digital recording process breaks down the analog signal into discrete values or levels?

   a) filtering
   b) sampling
   c) quantizing
   d) coding

8. Which term describes the process when two or more tracks of a multitrack recording are combined and rerecorded on another vacant track?

   a) overdubbing
   b) bouncing
   c) punching in
   d) combo-cording

9. In multitrack recording, what is the process of adding new tracks to existing tracks called?

   a) bouncing tracks
   b) overdubbing tracks
   c) punching in tracks
   d) ping-ponging tracks

10. Why can digital recordings be copied over and over with no measurable loss of sound quality?

   a) The sound signal is a continuously variable electrical signal, the shape of which is defined by the shape of the sound wave produced.
   b) The original sound source is sampled over 44,000 times per second.
   c) It is binary data that is recorded, and this can be accurately copied.
   d) The laser beam is focused directly on the data track.

11. One announcer can appear to be two different announcers reading a dialogue script using which multitrack recording technique?

   a) voice doubling
   b) chorusing
   c) dovetailing
   d) stacking

12. Most digital equipment promises a longer interval between breakdowns than comparable analog equipment; however, when there is a technical problem, repair time for the digital equipment will probably also be longer.

   a) true
   b) false

13. The main reason announcer voices are often recorded first on a multitrack recording is because vocal sources are usually assigned to Track 1 and Track 2.

   a) true
   b) false

14. Most audio editing software can save files in a number of different audio formats. Which are the two most common?

   a) .wav and .wma
   b) .mp3 and .aif
   c) .voc and .pcm
   d) .wav and .mp3

15. Which digital sampling rate is used most frequently?

   a) 32 kHz
   b) 44.1 kHz
   c) 48 kHz
   d) 88.2 kHz

16. A track sheet is a manufacturer specification sheet that lists the number of tracks that a multitrack recorder has.

   a) true
   b) false

17. Multitrack productions are usually mixed down to a 2-track stereo master. If the stereo master is slightly out of phase when combined into a mono signal, it can be corrected by all but which of these adjustments to one of the stereo tracks?

   a) change track equalization
   b) move track to a vacant track
   c) change track volume
   d) change track panning

18. During multitrack recording, which technique allows you to rerecord just a portion of a track to correct a mistake, while leaving the rest of the track undisturbed?

   a) punching in
   b) overdubbing
   c) voice doubling
   d) bouncing

19. What is another term for "bouncing tracks" on a multitrack recorder?

   a) chorusing
   b) overdubbing
   c) ping-ponging
   d) dovetailing

20. The "drag-and-drop" function of a multitrack audio editor would allow you to move audio segments from one part of a track to another, but not from one track to a completely different track.

   a) true
   b) false

ANSWERS

If you answered A to any of the questions:

1a. You're partially correct, but this is not the best response. (Reread 3.3 and 3.7.)
2a. Although this is one reason for editing audio, there is a better answer. (Reread 3.4.)
3a. No. You didn't "sense" the correct answer. (Reread 3.5.)
4a. You're not quite right with this answer. Although audio edited with a destructive system is ultimately physically changed, most editing systems provide an Undo function that can restore the original audio. (Reread 3.10.)
5a. No. 360 Systems' Short/cut™ is a personal audio editor, not a communications language. (Reread 3.8.)
6a. No. This would leave no space or pause between the words *one* and *three*. (Reread 3.10.)
7a. No. Filtering cuts off unwanted high frequencies before sampling begins. (Reread 3.3.)
8a. Wrong. Overdubbing is the normal technique for multitrack recording. (Reread 3.11.)
9a. No. This is another multitrack recording technique. (Reread 3.11.)
10a. No. This refers to an analog signal. (Reread 3.2 and 3.3.)
11a. Wrong. Though this is a "voice doubling" technique, it's another multitrack trick. (Reread 3.12.)

12a. No. Only half of this statement is true. Although digital equipment will probably break down less often than analog equipment, repair time for digital equipment also promises to be shorter in many cases. (Reread 3.7 and Production Tip 3B.)

13a. No. It really doesn't matter what sources are assigned to what tracks. (Reread 3.15.)

14a. No. Although audio editors might use both of these formats to save files, only one of them is very common. (Reread 3.10.)

15a. No. This is another sampling rate that some digital equipment is capable of utilizing. (Reread 3.3.)

16a. No. A track sheet is a way of keeping notes during a multitrack production. It usually lists track numbers and what is recorded on each track. (Reread 3.13.)

17a. Wrong. This will often correct the mono signal. (Reread 3.14.)

18a. Yes. The punch in is also known as an insert edit because you can just rerecord a portion of a track.

19a. No. This is a different multitrack technique. (Reread 3.11 and 3.12.)

20a. Wrong. You would be able to move the audio from track to track as well as anywhere on an individual track. (Reread 3.11.)

If you answered B to any of the questions:

1b. You're partially correct, but this is not the best response. (Reread 3.3 and 3.7.)

2b. Although this is one reason for editing audio, there is a better answer. (Reread 3.4.)

3b. No. You might have just taken a "sporting" guess to get this answer. (Reread 3.5.)

4b. Yes, because most destructive editing systems have an Undo function that enables edited audio to be restored.

5b. No. Audacity is an audio editing software program, not a communication language. (Reread 3.8 and Production Tip 3A.)

6b. Yes. This would edit out the word *two*, but it would maintain the natural pause between *one* and *three*.

7b. No. Sampling is when the signal is "sliced" into thousands of individual samples (voltages). (Reread 3.3.)

8b. Correct. Bouncing or ping-ponging tracks is the multitrack technique described here.

9b. Yes. This is a primary advantage of multitrack recording and one of the most basic techniques used in multitrack production.

10b. No. But you're heading in the right direction. Sampling rate is important for exact reproduction of the original sound, but it isn't really the reason why digital recordings can be copied over and over. (Reread 3.2 and 3.3.)

11b. Wrong. Although this is a technique for adding voices, it's another multitrack technique. (Reread 3.12.)

12b. Yes. Only part of this statement is true. Digital equipment repair time should be shorter than analog.

13b. Yes. It doesn't really matter what sources are assigned to what tracks, but announcers are often recorded first because it's easier to lay down other tracks to the vocals, and high-priced talent can be finished with their part of a production once their tracks are recorded, even if the entire spot isn't completed.

14b. No. Although audio editors might use both of these formats to save files, only one of them is very common. (Reread 3.10.)

15b. Correct. This is the most common digital sampling rate.

16b. Yes. This is a false statement. A track sheet is a way of keeping notes of what is recorded on each track of a multitrack production.

17b. Correct. Just moving a track's location won't help.

18b. No. This technique allows you to add additional tracks to a production. (Reread 3.11.)

19b. No. This is a different multitrack technique. (Reread 3.11 and 3.12.)

20b. Correct. This is false because you can move audio from track to track as well as anywhere on an individual track.

If you answered C to any of the questions:

1c. You're partially correct, but this is not the best response. (Reread 3.3 and 3.7.)

2c. Although this is one reason for editing audio, there is a better answer. (Reread 3.4.)

3c. Correct. A DSP audio card is a standard audio interface for the PC platform.

5c. No. You're probably confusing this with the minidisc. (Reread 3.8.)

6c. No. This would lengthen the pause between *one* and *three* and sound unnatural. (Reread 3.10.)

7c. Yes. This is correct.

8c. Wrong. Punching in is a technique that allows you to record a segment of a track without affecting the material before or after that segment. (Reread 3.11.)

9c. No. This is another multitrack recording technique. (Reread 3.11.)

10c. Correct. Binary data can be accurately recorded over and over, making digital copies sound exactly like the original.

11c. Correct. By reading even lines of a script on one track and then odd lines on another track, one announcer can sound like he or she is talking to another person with this technique.

14c. No. Although audio editors might use both of these formats to save files, neither of them is very common. (Reread 3.10.)

15c. No. This is another sampling rate that some digital equipment is capable of utilizing. (Reread 3.3.)

17c. Wrong. This will often correct the mono signal. (Reread 3.14.)

18c. No. This technique is a form of overdubbing that allows you to "voice double." (Reread 3.11.)

19c. Yes. This is another term for bouncing tracks.

If you answered D to any of the questions:

1d. Correct. Digital technology offers all these technical improvements over analog.

2d. Right. All of these are good reasons for editing audio.

3d. No. You got "bitten" on this answer. (Reread 3.5.)

5d. Yes. MIDI (musical instrument digital interface) is the correct response.

6d. No. One of the other answers is the correct way to mark this edit. (Reread 3.10.)

7d. No. Coding is when a series of binary digits are assigned to each individual sample. (Reread 3.3.)

8d. Wrong. There is no such thing. (Reread 3.11.)

9d. No. This is another multitrack recording technique. (Reread 3.11.)

10d. No. Although the use of a laser is an important part of CD technology, it is not the reason. (Reread 3.2 and 3.3.)

11d. Wrong. Although this is a technique for adding voices, it's another multitrack technique. (Reread 3.12.)

14d. Yes. These are the two most common formats that audio editors might use to save files.

15d. No. This is not a common sampling rate. (Reread 3.3.)

17d. Wrong. This will often correct the mono signal. (Reread 3.14.)

18d. No. This technique allows you to combine tracks and transfer them to a vacant track. (Reread 3.11.)

19d. No. This is a different multitrack technique. (Reread 3.11 and 3.12.)

Projects

PROJECT 1

Undertake digital audio editing.

Purpose

To gain practice editing a vocal audio tape using a digital editing system.

Notes

1. If you're not sure of what you're doing, ask the instructor for assistance.
2. Remember, you're to do several edits, not just one.
3. You'll be judged on how clean your edits are, so be sure you make your edit marks accurately.

How to Do the Project

1. Familiarize yourself with the operation of the digital editing system in your production studio. If you have questions, ask your instructor.
2. You may use the material on the CD-ROM enclosed with the text, or you may be allowed to record your own. If you can record your own, select some news copy or a weathercast from a news wire service, or write something similar and record it into your editing system. Label this sound file as required by your system.
3. Do your edits as follows:
   a. Press the "play" button, and listen to what is recorded.
   b. Select something you wish to edit. Write down on a piece of paper the part you plan to edit, with a few words before and after it. Put parentheses around what you plan to take out. For example: "Today's weather calls for (sunny skies and) a temperature of 70 degrees."
   c. Stop playback so that it's at the exact place you wish to edit—in our example, just in front of "sunny."
   d. Make your beginning edit mark.
   e. Continue playing the audio until you get to the end of your edit—in our example, just before "a."
   f. Make your end edit mark.
   g. Preview the edit. You can probably adjust either edit mark so that it is accurately positioned. If necessary, do so.
   h. Perform the actual edit, and listen to it. If you've made some type of error, "undo" the edit, and start again.
4. Repeat the above steps for another edit. Do a few more similar edits.
5. When you've done several edits, record them all.
6. Label your recording with your name and "Digital Audio Editing."
7. Turn in the recording to your instructor to receive credit for the project.

PROJECT 2

Using a digital audio editor, build a short music bed and record a "voice and music bed" spot.

Purpose

To continue to give you experience with digitally based recording and editing.

Notes

1. This project incorporates a single announcer voice and a music bed. There are many ways to accomplish it, so don't feel like you must follow the production directions exactly.

2. You will use music from the CD-ROM to build your music bed.
3. You'll be laying the same few seconds of music down several times, so select some music that will lend itself to this. Find a piece of music that won't sound like it has been cut off abruptly.
4. The project is written to make a music bed that is 60 seconds long.
5. You will also need to write a script that can be read in about 50 seconds. Write the copy about a desktop item, such as a pen, stapler, or paperclip holder.

How to Do the Project

1. Select music from the CD-ROM provided and record a sound file of about 20 seconds.
2. Activate your computer editing program.
3. Select a 10- to 15-second region of music from the sound file, and lay it down on one track made available through your computer editing program.
4. Lay the same material down again right next to the first region, and continue to do this until you have a 60-second segment.
5. Listen to the segment and improve upon it so that it could be used as a music bed under someone talking about a commercial product. You may want to change volume or edit to tighten it a bit. What you can do and exactly how you do it will depend on the computer program that you're using.
6. Now record the script. Rerecord or edit to correct vocal mistakes to get the timing correct, or just to make it sound the way you want.
7. Set playback levels for both the vocal track and the music bed. Both should start at full volume.
8. Record the spot. Start the music bed at full volume and then start the vocal track as you simultaneously fade the music slightly so that the vocal is dominant.
9. As the vocal ends, bring the music bed back to full volume and then fade it out at 60 seconds.
10. Make sure you have a good balance between the music bed and announcer voice. If you need to do it over, just cue up, make necessary adjustments, and try again.
11. Label the project with your name and "Voice and Edited Music Bed Spot."
12. Give the project to your instructor to receive credit for this project.

PROJECT 3

Write a report that compares various recording/editing software programs.

Purpose

To allow you to further investigate some of the computer software that is available for digital production systems.

Notes

1. Prepare a list of questions that you want answered before you begin your research.
2. This project requires obtaining material through the Internet from various manufacturers.
3. The manufacturers shown at the end of this project are not the only ones who produce audio editing software. You could also complete the project by looking at other programs.

How to Do the Project

1. Develop some questions that you want answered about audio editing software. For example:
   a. What are the computer system requirements for each software program?
   b. What exactly can each do in the area of radio production?
   c. How much do they cost?

d. Are there any problems associated with these programs?

e. What sample rate and bit depth does each program use?

2. Gather information by going to the web site of the manufacturers.

3. If your facility has this software or you know of a station in your area that does, try to talk with someone who uses it on a regular basis to further research the programs.

4. Organize your material into an informative report that compares the various software programs. It should be several pages long. Write your name and "Editing Software Programs Comparison" on a title page.

5. Turn in the report to your instructor for credit for this project.

Pro Tools
www.digidesign.com

Adobe Audition
www.adobe.com

SAW Studio
www.sawstudio.com

Sound Forge
www.mediasoftware.sonypictures.com

Sonar
www.cakewalk.com

Fast Edit
www.minnetonkaaudio.com

Cubase
www.steinberg.net

4

MICROPHONES

4.1 INTRODUCTION

In audio production, microphones are also used to record voice, music, or sound effects in both the studio and the field. The studio microphone (see Figure 4.1) takes on an important role, because it's the first element in the audio chain. It's the piece of equipment that changes the announcer's voice into an electrical signal that can then be mixed with other sound sources and sent to a recorder or broadcast over the air. Because the purpose of the microphone is to change sound energy into electrical energy, it's called a **transducer**, which is a device that converts one form of energy into another.

FIGURE 4.1 The studio microphone changes the announcer's voice into an electrical signal. (Image courtesy of Neumann/USA.)

Unlike much of the other studio equipment, microphones are generally analog-based, although some digital microphones are now on the market. Putting an analog-to-digital converter in an external microphone preamplifier or immediately after the microphone in the audio chain or within the microphone housing could quickly transform *any* microphone's electrical output to a digital signal. For example, Audio-Technica's AT2020 USB microphone, shown in Figure 4.2, has an analog-to-digital converter built into the microphone housing and a USB output for direct connection to a computer or digital recorder. Manufacturers including National Semiconductor and Akustia have developed integrated circuits that convert a microphone sound signal *directly* into a digital bit stream output signal, making for a truly digital microphone. Though such microphones are not yet in general use in the broadcast studio, it's highly likely that we'll continue to see more digital microphone developments in the future.

This chapter looks at different types of microphones and some of their key characteristics. Selecting the wrong microphone for a particular situation can result in a poor recording that can't be fixed with any postproduction processing. The astute audio production person takes advantage of a microphone's qualities to achieve the best possible sound quality for either live broadcast or digital recording.

4.2 CLASSIFYING MICROPHONES

There is no one correct microphone to use in audio production work, but specific types of microphones work better than others in certain situations. For example, a microphone that is perfect for voice-over work in the studio may not work well for recording a sound effect in the field. Microphones are usually described by two key specifications—their electrical operation and their **pickup pattern**. Categorized by their internal, sound-generating element, there are two types of microphones commonly

FIGURE 4.2 With a USB digital output, this microphone is ideal for computer-based recording. (Image courtesy of Audio-Technica U.S. Inc.)

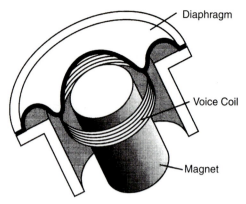

FIGURE 4.3 The internal components of a dynamic microphone include a diaphragm, magnet, and voice coil. (Image courtesy of Shure Incorporated.)

diaphragm caused by sound waves result in a disturbance of the magnetic field, and this induces a small electric current into the coil of wire, which is the audio output signal.

The dynamic microphone is a good general-purpose microphone commonly used in radio and audio production studios and has many advantages that make it popular. Because of its relatively simple construction, it is a modestly priced microphone that produces very low self-noise and has excellent **frequency response**, so that both highs and lows reproduce accurately. But the main reason it has seen such acceptance by broadcasters is its sturdy design. The dynamic microphone can withstand a moderate amount of abuse, which often occurs in the broadcast setting. Dynamic microphones can handle extremely high sound levels, making it almost impossible to overload them, and are not usually affected by extremes of either temperature or humidity. This style of microphone is also fairly insensitive to wind, and this feature, along with its ruggedness, makes it an excellent remote or field recording microphone.

The main disadvantage of the dynamic microphone is that it does not satisfactorily reproduce certain voices. With some announcers, the microphone exaggerates plosives (popping on *p*) and sibilance (hissing on *s*). Dynamic microphones also can lose some light, delicate sounds, because the mass of the diaphragm requires a fairly high sound level to move it. Even though the dynamic microphone is fairly rugged, all microphones are fragile to some extent and should be handled with care like any other piece of audio production equipment.

used in audio production work: the dynamic microphone and the condenser microphone. When considering their pickup patterns, there are also two main types: omnidirectional and cardioid. In both categories, as you will see, these are not the only types.

When selecting microphones, some radio stations use a standard microphone throughout the facility; however, the general audio production facility tends to take another approach, which is to have multiple microphones available. That makes sense, because it allows the facility the flexibility to handle a number of different recording situations.

4.3 DYNAMIC MICROPHONES

The **dynamic microphone** is sometimes known as the **moving-coil microphone** or occasionally the **pressure microphone**. This microphone's sound-generating element is constructed of a diaphragm, a magnet assembly, and a voice coil, as shown in Figure 4.3. The flexible diaphragm (usually made of thin plastic), which responds to the pressure of the sound, is positioned so that the attached small wire coil is within the field of a permanent magnet. Movements of the

4.4 CONDENSER MICROPHONES

The other common type of broadcast microphone is the **condenser microphone**. Less frequently known as a **capacitor microphone**, it uses an electronic component—the capacitor—to respond to the sound. The sound-generating element consists of a charged conductive diaphragm and an oppositely charged metallic backplate separated by an

Condenser Microphone

FIGURE 4.4 The internal components of a condenser microphone include two oppositely charged plates—a moveable diaphragm and a fixed backplate. (Image courtesy of Shure Incorporated.)

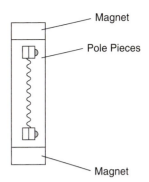

FIGURE 4.5 The internal components of the ribbon microphone center around a thin, corrugated metallic ribbon.

insulating material that creates an air space between them and forms a sound-sensitive capacitor (see Figure 4.4). The thin metal or metal-coated plastic diaphragm responds to sound waves, changing the distance between the diaphragm and the backplate; this alteration changes the capacitance (resistance to electrical voltage buildup) and generates a small electrical signal that is further amplified within the electronics of the microphone. This fluctuation of electrical current is the audio output signal.

The condenser microphone requires a power supply, such as a battery, to charge the backplate and diaphragm and related electronic components. To do this, condenser microphones utilize small internal power supplies or **phantom power** supplies. The latter usually comes from a recorder or an audio board through the microphone cable and back to the microphone. Because all condenser microphones are powered, the electronics of the microphone can produce a little noise, and there is a limit to the sound level signal that the microphone can handle. Still, the condenser microphone is an excellent microphone, because it's fairly rugged and produces excellent sound quality and wide frequency response. This microphone also has excellent transient response, but can be distorted at high recording volumes. Although the dynamic microphone is the most commonly used radio production microphone, the condenser microphone is also frequently found in the modern audio production facility. In addition, the built-in microphone on many portable audio recorders is often a condenser microphone that provides fairly good quality on both consumer and professional models.

Another form of condenser microphone is the **electret microphone**. Its capacitor is permanently charged during manufacture, but it still needs a power supply (albeit much less power) for its electronic circuit. The lower power requirement offers some flexibility in usage, but the electret microphone possesses less dynamic range than the regular condenser microphone, so you may not find an electret microphone in many radio production studios.

4.5 OTHER MICROPHONES

There are other types of microphones, but they are less likely to be encountered in the broadcast studio. For many years, the **ribbon microphone** was common in broadcasting and a few manufacturers still produce this style of microphone. Another form of a dynamic microphone, the ribbon microphone contains a sound-generating element that consists of a thin, corrugated metallic ribbon suspended in the field of a magnet. Sound waves vibrating the ribbon generate an electrical output signal (see Figure 4.5). The ribbon microphone has an excellent warm, smooth sound, but it is bulky and fragile and has been largely replaced by the condenser microphone, which has a similar high-quality sound.

A **regulated phase microphone** can be thought of as part dynamic and part ribbon microphone. A wire coil is attached to or impressed into the surface of a circular diaphragm. The diaphragm is suspended between two circular magnets that are designed to be acoustically transparent. In other words, the magnets don't impede the sound waves striking the diaphragm in any way. An electrical current is generated as sound waves vibrate the diaphragm. Because of its design, the regulated phase microphone exhibits some of the qualities of a ribbon microphone with some of the ruggedness of the dynamic microphone.

Most **tube microphones** are merely modern condenser microphones that incorporate a vacuum tube into the electronics of the microphone. Tube microphones provide superior dynamic range, outstanding clarity, and the "warmth" of classic analog sound that many find missing with solid-state and digital electronics. Although the microphones in this section are readily available, they're most often found in a high-end audio production facility.

4.6 SPECIAL-PURPOSE MICROPHONES

There are other microphone types that are not necessarily based on internal sound-generating elements. In fact, these microphones usually employ one of the basic designs mentioned in the previous sections; however, they are often

FIGURE 4.6 Lavaliere microphones are used more in television than radio because of their unobtrusive design. (Image courtesy of Audio-Technica U.S., Inc.)

FIGURE 4.7 Stereo microphones often employ multiple sound-generating elements as part of a single microphone. (Image courtesy of RODE Microphones.)

designed for a specific usage and are frequently considered to be another variety of microphone. For example, the **lavaliere microphone** (see Figure 4.6) mentioned previously is a tiny microphone that can be unobtrusively clipped to an announcer's lapel or tie. There are both dynamic and condenser models, and although the lavaliere microphone is occasionally used in a radio remote situation, its small size makes it more appropriate for television than radio.

A **stereo microphone** like the one shown in Figure 4.7 incorporates small, multiple sound-generating elements as part of a single microphone housing that can duplicate the various stereo microphone techniques. You'll learn more about these methods later in this chapter.

FM microphones—also known as **RF** (radio frequency), **wireless**, and **radio microphones**—are used mainly in production situations in which a microphone cable might hinder the recording or production. A wireless microphone is really a system—a microphone, a radio transmitter, and a radio receiver (see Figure 4.8). The audio signal generated (employing either a dynamic or condenser element) is sent out from the microphone by a low-power transmitter rather

FIGURE 4.8 Because of its wireless design, an FM microphone system can be used when a microphone cable would get in the way. (Image courtesy of Shure Incorporated. Used by permission.)

than a microphone cable. This transmitter is either in the microphone housing or contained in a small pack designed to be worn by the talent. The transmitted signal is picked up by a receiver located nearby and converted from a radio frequency signal back into an audio signal at that point. One problem associated with wireless microphones is interference. Because they broadcast on specific FCC-assigned frequencies that are not exclusive to FM microphones, they sometimes pick up interference from other radio frequency users.

The **pressure zone microphone** or **PZM** (also known as a **boundary**, **plate**, or **surface-mount microphone**), is a small microphone capsule mounted next to a sound-reflecting plate (or boundary), as shown in Figure 4.9. Designed to be used on a flat surface, such as a tabletop, the microphone picks up sound from all directions above the table surface and both direct sound and reflected sound reach the microphone at the same time, as the microphone is so close to the reflective surface. This design boosts the incoming sound signal, which improves the clarity of the sound.

Figure 4.10 shows that the **shotgun microphone** is appropriately named. A microphone capsule is at one end of a tube (or barrel) that is "aimed" like a gun toward the sound source. The design of the microphone rejects sound from the side and rear but picks up a very narrow angle of sound from the front of the microphone's barrel. The highly directional nature of the microphone makes it good at picking up sound from a considerable distance from the sound source; however, sound quality is somewhat lower than that achieved by microphones designed to pick up only nearby

sounds. There are other specialized microphones available, but in typical audio production work you aren't likely to run across them. In fact, many of the microphones mentioned in this section will only be useful on occasion, but an understanding of them may prove helpful from time to time.

4.7 MICROPHONE PICKUP PATTERNS

The other way of classifying microphones is by their **pickup patterns**. Microphones can be constructed so that they have different directional characteristics—in other words, how sensitive they are to sound from varying directions (Figure 4.11). Sound picked up at the front of the microphone, or at 0 degrees, is said to be **on-axis**. Sound picked up from the microphone's side is 90 degrees off-axis, and sound picked up from the rear of the microphone is 180 degrees off-axis. The microphone housing, through the use of small openings and ports, can be designed so that unwanted sound (often off-axis sound) is cancelled out or attenuated as it enters the microphone. The on-axis sound received directly from the front of the microphone fully impacts the microphone's diaphragm. An understanding of the microphone pickup patterns helps the user place the microphone relative to the sound source to maximize the pickup of desired sound and minimize the pickup of unwanted background noise.

The most common sound patterns are omnidirectional and cardioid, but there are other patterns. Although most microphones will have one fixed pickup pattern, **multidirectional microphones** have switchable internal elements that allow the microphone to employ more than one pickup pattern—usually cardioid and omnidirectional.

FIGURE 4.9 The PZM is designed to be used on a flat surface, such as a tabletop. (Image courtesy of Crown Audio, Inc.)

FIGURE 4.10 A shotgun microphone has a long tube or barrel that is "aimed" at the sound source. (Image courtesy of Sennheiser Electronic Corporation.)

FIGURE 4.11 On-axis sound, picked up directly from the front of the microphone, fully impacts the microphone's diaphragm.

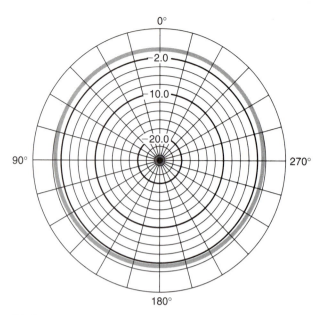

FIGURE 4.12 The omnidirectional pickup pattern shows that the microphone picks up sound equally well from all directions.

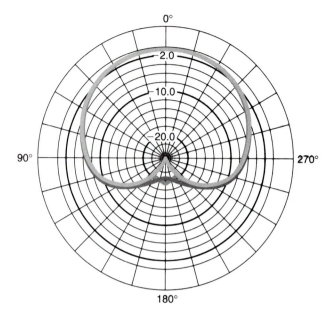

FIGURE 4.13 A cardioid pickup pattern shows that the microphone picks up sound mainly from the front and side, but not very well from the back.

4.8 THE OMNIDIRECTIONAL PICKUP PATTERN

The **omnidirectional** microphone is also known as a **non-directional** microphone. These two terms may seem to contradict each other—*omni* (all) and *non* (no). Both terms are correct, however. The microphone picks up sound in all directions, but that also means that it has no particular pickup pattern. Omnidirectional microphones pick up sound equally well in just about any direction. Think of an orange with a microphone right in the middle. No matter where the sound comes from around the orange, the microphone responds to it equally well. Figure 4.12 illustrates the pickup pattern for a typical omnidirectional microphone.

Omnidirectional microphones are used whenever it is desirable to pick up sound evenly from all sides of the microphone, including above and below it. Omnidirectional microphones are commonly used outside the studio when the ambience of the location needs to be picked up along with a person's voice. Of course, the fact that they pick up sound equally well from all directions can also be a disadvantage. You may pick up unwanted background noise (such as traffic noise) in addition to the voice when recording in a remote situation. Omnidirectional microphones used in a highly reflective room may also produce a "hollow" sound, because they tend to pick up more reverb than other types of microphones.

4.9 THE CARDIOID PICKUP PATTERN

The **cardioid** microphone picks up sound coming mainly from one direction—the front of the microphone. Its pattern is actually heart-shaped, hence the name cardioid (see

Figure 4.13). Another way to visualize this pickup pattern is to think of an upside-down apple, where the stem represents the microphone and the rest of the apple approximates the cardioid pickup pattern. Although the microphone picks up sound from the front and sides, the level of pickup from the sides is only about half that of the front. The microphone doesn't pick up sound well from the rear at all—less than one-tenth the sound it can pick up from the front.

Variations on the basic cardioid design include the **super-cardioid**, **hyper-cardioid**, and **ultra-cardioid** microphones. They continue to offer great rejection of the sound from the sides, but each microphone also picks up a narrower scope of on-axis sound. In other words, these microphones are even more directional in nature and are sometimes referred to as "unidirectional" because of this. All cardioid microphones are popular because they do reject unwanted sounds (excessive reverb, feedback, background noise), but the talent must be careful to stay "on mic" and not move too far off-axis, especially when using super-, hyper-, or ultra-cardioid microphones.

4.10 OTHER MICROPHONE PICKUP PATTERNS

As noted previously, while some consider all cardioid microphone pickup patterns to be **unidirectional**, many reserve that term for the "gun" microphones that employ the narrow cardioid patterns, such as the hyper-cardioid or ultra-cardioid, and therefore consider unidirectional to be another pickup pattern.

Another microphone pickup pattern is the **bidirectional** microphone, which picks up sound mainly from two directions: the front and the rear of the microphone, or

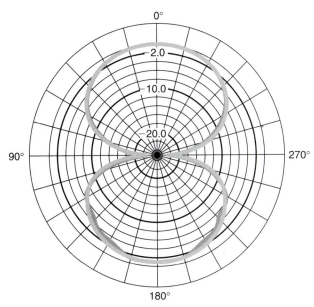

FIGURE 4.14 The bidirectional pickup pattern shows that the microphone picks up sound from the front and back of the microphone.

FIGURE 4.15 A three-dimensional view of the cardioid microphone pickup pattern. Image courtesy of Sennheiser Electronic Corporation.

on-axis and off-axis (see Figure 4.14). Its pickup pattern can be visualized as a figure eight, with the microphone located at the intersection of the two circles, or, to maintain the fruit analogy, think of two grapes sitting side by side. It was often used for radio dramas so that actors could face each other, but it is not a common pickup pattern for most of today's microphones. It is, however, a good microphone for the basic two-person interview.

A **hemispherical** pickup pattern is common to the PZM. This type of microphone picks up sound equally well within a 180-degree spherical angle or essentially a half-omnidirectional pattern.

4.11 POLAR RESPONSE PATTERNS

Microphone pickup patterns are sometimes referred to as **polar patterns**. The two are actually different. A pickup pattern refers to the three-dimensional area around the microphone in which it best "hears" or picks up the sound. The microphone's polar pattern is a two-dimensional drawing or representation of this. Compare the cardioid pickup pattern shown in Figure 4.15 with the cardioid polar response pattern shown in Figure 4.13. In practice, the terms are used somewhat interchangeably, and because it is difficult to show three dimensions on a printed page, the drawings that are used for polar response patterns are two-dimensional.

A polar pattern is drawn around a full circle, or 360 degrees. As noted earlier, the line from 0 to 180 degrees represents the microphone's axis, and sound entering the microphone from the front (0 degrees) is on-axis. The concentric circles show decreasing dB levels and allow us to see how the sound will be attenuated as it is picked up off-axis. For example, Figure 4.13 shows that sound picked up directly in front of the microphone will experience no

attenuation. On the other hand, sound picked up from either side (90 degrees off-axis) will be attenuated about 5 dB, and sound coming directly from the rear of the microphone (180 degrees) will be attenuated almost 20 dB.

4.12 IMPEDANCE OF MICROPHONES

Another factor sometimes used to categorize microphones is **impedance**, a characteristic similar to resistance and common to audio equipment. Impedance is expressed in ohms, and microphones can be either high-impedance (10,000 ohms or higher) or low-impedance (600 ohms or less). Some microphones may fall between the 600–10,000 ohm range and are medium impedance mics. Most professional microphones are low-impedance, as they provide the best frequency response, and most pro audio equipment is designed to accept this type of microphone. High-impedance microphones are also quite limited in the length of microphone cable that can be used with them before hum and severe signal loss occurs. High-impedance microphones should not be plugged into audio recorders or other equipment designed for low-impedance; similarly, low-impedance microphones should not be used with high-impedance equipment, although the negative effects aren't as noticeable with this combination. If impedance is mismatched, sound will be distorted. There are impedance converters that can convert one type of impedance to the other and some microphones can switch from one impedance level to another.

4.13 SENSITIVITY OF MICROPHONES

Sensitivity refers to a microphone's efficiency or ability to create an output level. For the same sound source (say, one particular announcer's voice), a highly sensitive microphone produces a better output signal than a less sensitive microphone. To compensate for this, the gain control (volume) must be increased for the less-sensitive microphone; this increased gain produces more noise. Although different sensitivity-rating systems can be employed, condenser microphones generally have high-sensitivity specifications, and dynamic microphones have medium sensitivity. Obviously, if you're trying to pick up a loud or close-up sound, a microphone with a lower sensitivity rating would be desirable.

4.14 PROXIMITY EFFECT AND BASS ROLL-OFF

Using a microphone sometimes produces a sound phenomenon known as the **proximity effect**. This is an exaggerated bass boost that begins as the sound source gets about 2 feet from the microphone. The effect should be most noticeable as the announcer gets about 2 or 3 inches from the microphone and is especially noticeable with microphones that have a cardioid pickup pattern. Although it could help deepen or add fullness to a normally high voice, the proximity effect is usually compensated for by a **bass roll-off switch** on the microphone. This switch, when turned on, will electronically "roll off," or turn down, the bass frequencies that would be boosted by the proximity effect, thus leaving the desired flat response.

4.15 MICROPHONE FEEDBACK

Feedback is a "whine" or "howl" generated when a sound picked up by a microphone is amplified, produced through a speaker, picked up again, amplified again, and so on, creating a loop. Generally, reducing the volume or turning off the microphone ends the feedback. Feedback is a common microphone problem in public address situations but is usually not a problem in media production, because the speaker is muted when the microphone is switched on. Occasionally, announcers can produce feedback in the production studio by operating their headphones at an excessive volume or accidentally picking up a stray speaker signal from an outside source, such as another studio speaker.

4.16 MULTIPLE-MICROPHONE INTERFERENCE

Sometimes, when two or more microphones receiving the same sound signal are fed into the same mixer, the combined signal becomes electronically **out of phase**. What happens is that the sound reaches each microphone at a slightly different time so that while the sound wave amplitude is up on one microphone, it's down on the other. Under these circumstances, the resulting sound will have frequency peaks and cancellations causing very poor sound quality. This situation is known as **multiple-microphone interference** and can be avoided by remembering a 3-to-1 ratio. That is, if the microphones are about 1 foot from the announcer (sound source), they should be at least 3 feet apart from each other. In this way the signals won't overlap (see Figure 4.16A).

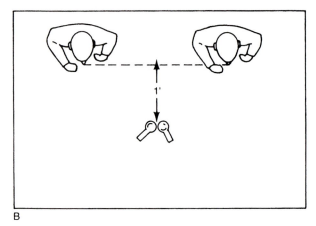

FIGURE 4.16 Avoid multiple-microphone interference by keeping the distance between the two microphones three times the microphone-to-source distance (A) or by keeping the microphones head-to-head (B).

Another solution to this problem is to place microphones that must be close together head-to-head, so they will receive the signal at the same time (see Figure 4.16B). Although multiple-microphone interference isn't usually a problem in the studio, it can occur in some remote situations.

4.17 STEREO

We hear sound in stereo because most sounds arrive at one ear before the other. In other words, the right ear hears a slightly different sound perspective from the left ear. This occurrence allows us to locate sound by turning our head until the sound is "centered." When stereo sound is compared with monophonic sound, it's soon apparent that stereo adds both "depth" and "imaging" to the sound.

Imaging is the apparent placement of the sound between the left and right planes and, as noted, provides location of the sound in space. **Depth** is the apparent placement of the sound between the front plane and the back plane and often provides the ambience of the space where the sound is produced. Good stereo sound allows us to record and reproduce sound as it is in real life.

FIGURE 4.17   The most common techniques to microphone sound for stereo.

4.18 STEREO MIKING TECHNIQUES

Much audio production work is done with a mono microphone. Even in stereo studios, often the same mono microphone signal is simply sent to the left and right channels. However, there may be times when you will want to employ true stereo microphone techniques. There are a number of different techniques for stereo miking, but the three most common techniques are A-B, X-Y, and M-S miking (see Figure 4.17).

As the ultimate goal of stereo recording is to have separate sound signals come from the left and right speakers, one common way to accomplish this is through **A-B miking**, which splits a pair of omnidirectional or cardioid microphones to the left and right of center about 3 to 10 feet apart. A good rule to follow is to separate the microphones by about half the width of the sound source. For example, if you were recording a band on a 10-foot-wide stage, you'd space your microphones about 5 feet apart. This A-B technique (also known as **spaced pair** or **split pair**) uses one microphone to feed the left channel of the stereo signal and another one to feed the right channel. As long as phase problems are watched and the sound source is kept a relatively equal distance from the microphones, a true stereo signal will be obtained. However, when using this technique, the sound is often "spacious," with a great deal of separation, especially as you place the microphones farther and farther apart. Room ambience may be overbearing, with individual sounds seeming to "wander" in the stereo image.

The **X-Y miking** (also called **cross-pair**) technique requires placing two cardioid microphones facing left and right like crossed swords forming an X- and Y-axis, as shown in Figures 4.7 and 4.17. The angle formed between the heads of the microphones is usually 90 degrees, but can vary from 60 to around 135 degrees, with the right microphone facing the left side of the sound source and the left microphone facing the right side. This angle has an impact on the stereo effect and requires some experimenting to get it right. If the microphones become too parallel, the stereo effect is minimal; if the angle is too wide, there will seem to

be a "hole" in the stereo image. If the heads of the microphones are close together, this X-Y miking allows the sound signal to reach both microphones at the same time and there will be no phase problems. Although this approach solves some of the split-pair arrangement problems, it can cause a loss of "focus" on the image, because the microphones are off-axis to the center of the stereo image.

M-S miking, or **mid-side miking**, offers superior imaging by using microphones arranged in an upside-down "T" pattern. The mid microphone (often a cardioid or supercardioid, but sometimes an omnidirectional) is aimed at the sound source, and the side microphone (usually a bidirectional) is placed parallel to the sound source and at a 90-degree angle to the mid microphone to pick up the sound to the left and right. Both microphones must be fed into a mixer designed to matrix, or form the incoming signals into a stereo signal. Mid-side miking generally provides a very accurate stereo recording of the localization of the actual sound sources.

Variations of these techniques, using different types of microphones and microphone placements, are also employed to achieve stereo miking. If you intend to do a great deal of stereo recording, you may employ a number of other techniques, such as the Decca Tree, ORTF, or NOS technique, and Blumlein or stereosonic miking. Furthermore, stereo microphones can duplicate the X-Y or M-S techniques using a single microphone with specially designed internal sound-generating structures (review Figure 4.7).

4.19 SURROUND SOUND

Surround sound is more difficult to record than stereo sound, so it is often put together in a postproduction environment. The difficulty occurs because of the number of channels involved. Surround sound, in its most common form, provides a 5.1-channel sound, that is, six separate audio channels. To accomplish this, a center channel is added to the stereo left and right channels (to the front of the listener), and left and right surround channels are added (to the rear of the listener). These are all full-frequency response main channels. The sixth channel, designated as ".1", is a limited-response channel for bass frequencies only, often reproduced by a powered subwoofer. Surround sound that is designated at 7.1 would add a left and right side channel to the 5.1 configuration and 6.1 would add just a "top" channel.

It is possible to record audio to accommodate all these channels. One way involves placing cardioid and/or supercardioid microphones in a circle, each pointing at a different place on the circumference of the circle to approximate the various channels. A variation of the stereo spaced pair technique can also be used with multiple omnidirectional or cardioid microphones. Arrange three front microphones (left, center, right) about a foot apart and two rear microphones (left, right) about 2 feet behind the front microphones and about 2 feet apart from each other. Of course, if you're using cardioid microphones, the rear mics should be rear facing. Generally, the .1 or bass channel is just a low-pass signal from one of the microphones or a combination of the bass signals from all the mics. Another method is to use a surround sound microphone (see Figure 4.18), such as the Holophone. Its elliptical shape emulates the characteristics of the human head. Sound waves bend around the microphone as they do around the head, providing sound spatiality and directionality. This microphone captures the sound with miniature mic elements positioned around and flush with the oval surface of the microphone.

As with stereo recording, however, it is often easier to send a mono signal to all the channels than to try to record all of them. The problem with making realistic surround sound is that there are so many channels, front and rear, that the mono signal often needs to be altered so that it conveys the characteristics people expect as they hear sound coming from different directions. This is best undertaken in postproduction, where the sounds can be manipulated in a more leisurely, technical fashion.

Surround sound isn't currently used much for radio; it is fairly standard for motion pictures, in which the dialogue is mostly handled by the left-center-right speakers, ambient sounds and some special effects are handled by the rear surround speakers, and big explosive sounds are handled by the subwoofer. Surround sound helps convey "movement" of sound as effects and other sounds can swirl around the listener.

4.20 MICROPHONE ACCESSORIES

In addition to the basic microphone, a production person will find one or more of the following accessories necessary for proper audio production work: windscreens, shock mounts, and stands or booms. The most common **windscreens** are ball-shaped foam accessories that can be placed over the head or front of the microphone (as shown in Figure 4.19) to help reduce the chance of a plosive sound. Not only do they prevent popping, but they also help keep dust out of the internal elements of the microphone and can provide some cushion if the microphone is accidentally dropped. Windscreens can also be built into the grill of the microphone.

Another design consists of a porous, film-like material that is suspended within a circular frame. This **pop filter**

FIGURE 4.18 A microphone designed specifically for surround sound recording. (Image courtesy of Holophone, a Division of Rising Sun Productions Limited.)

FIGURE 4.19 Microphone windscreens help reduce plosive sounds. (Image courtesy of Shure Incorporated.)

or **blast filter** apparatus is then attached to the microphone stand and positioned in front of the microphone rather than placed on the microphone itself, as shown in Figure 4.20. Announcing words that emphasize the *p*, *b*, or *t* sounds naturally produce a sharp puff of air and can produce a pop or thump when hitting the microphone (especially when a dynamic microphone is closely worked). The windscreen or pop filter eliminates or reduces this problem. Of course, in field recording, it also reduces the effects of wind noise.

Another microphone accessory, a **shock mount**, is often employed to isolate the microphone from any mechanical vibrations (or shocks) that may be transmitted through its stand. The microphone is physically suspended (usually by an arrangement of elastic bands) and isolated from the stand or boom to which it is attached (see Figure 4.21). If the microphone stand is accidentally bumped, the sound of this thud will not be passed on and amplified by the microphone.

Various microphone stands or **booms** are used to position the microphone for different recording situations. Some microphone stands consist of two chrome-plated pipes, one of which fits inside the other. A rotating clutch at one end of the larger diameter pipe allows the smaller pipe to be adjusted to any height desired. At the other end of the larger pipe is a heavy metal base (usually circular) that supports the pipes in a vertical position. Other microphone stands utilize a single pipe that's at a fixed height. In either case, the microphone is attached to the top of the pipe by a standard thread and microphone-stand adapter (see Figure 4.22A). Floor stands adjust for the announcer in a standing position, and desk stands are used for the seated announcer. A **boom stand** is a long horizontal pipe that attaches to a large floor stand (see Figure 4.22B). One end of the boom is fitted with the standard thread (for the microphone), and the other end is weighted to balance the microphone. The horizontal pipe allows the boom stand to be away from the announcer and positions the microphone in a workable relationship to him or her. The boom stand is frequently found in the TV studio when the microphone must be out of the picture. A **boom arm** (see Figure 4.22C) is a microphone stand especially designed for use in the radio studio. It consists of metal rods and springs designed somewhat like a human arm; the microphone attaches to one end, and the other end goes into a mounting base. The whole unit can then be attached to the countertop or other production studio furniture so that the microphone can be placed in close proximity to the audio console.

4.21 MICROPHONE USAGE

An understanding of the microphone types, pickup patterns, and other microphone characteristics is useful only if you can apply this knowledge to everyday audio production use.

FIGURE 4.20 A pop filter is a porous, film-like material suspended within a circular frame that is positioned in front of the microphone. (Image courtesy of Shure Incorporated. Used by permission.)

FIGURE 4.21 The microphone shock mount isolates the microphone from the microphone stand. (Image courtesy of Neumann USA.)

FIGURE 4.22 Microphone stands: (A) desk stands; (B) boom stand; (C) boom arm. (Images courtesy of Atlas Sound.)

It seems reasonable to assume that the microphone in a studio will be a dynamic microphone, because that's the one most commonly used in broadcasting, but it could also be a condenser microphone. Perhaps the more important consideration is its pickup pattern. In the studio, we mainly want to pick up voices and some studio ambience. A cardioid pickup pattern, with its pickup of front and side sounds, works best to accomplish this but not pick up unwanted sounds from the rear.

Studio interviews may require you to mic a group of people seated around a table. You could use a single omnidirectional microphone in the center of the table, or you could use a separate cardioid microphone for each individual at the table. Another option is to use the PZM.

There are many other situations that will require proper microphone selection and proper placement of those microphones. In other chapters, you will be exposed to some additional microphone usage techniques.

PRODUCTION TIP 4A
Microphone-to-Mouth Relationship

You see it on MTV or at a live concert: your favorite singers practically "eating" the microphone as they perform their latest hits. Don't emulate this! "Swallowing" the microphone is not good microphone technique. When using a microphone in the standard studio setup, keep in mind two basic rules concerning

distance from the microphone and position of the microphone. First, your mouth should be about 6 inches away from the microphone. That's about the length of a dollar bill—a good way to remember mic-to-mouth distance. This is a good starting point for using a microphone. You may find that you need to be closer or farther away because of the strength of your voice or the vocal effect that you're trying to achieve. Second, position the microphone so that you are not talking directly into it. Position the microphone level with your nose and tilted down toward your mouth, and talk beneath the front of the microphone, or place the microphone below your mouth with the front of it tilted up toward your mouth, allowing you to talk across the top of it.

PRODUCTION TIP 4B
Setting Microphone Levels

Beginning announcers often misuse a microphone by blowing into it to see whether it's live or to set a level. This is the worst way to test a microphone and can result in serious damage to the microphone. In fact, the higher the quality of the microphone, the more likely that it will be damaged in this manner. The best way to set a microphone level is to read several sentences of your script or ad lib some material into the microphone. If you just count (such as saying, "Testing . . . 1 . . . 2 . . . 3 . . .") or simply say "check" over and over, you're really not getting enough constant sound to set an accurate level. Also, most people don't count or say a single word in quite the same tone and volume as when they speak several sentences.

4.22 CONCLUSION

We said earlier that there is no one correct microphone to use in audio production. When using microphones, don't be afraid to experiment in each particular situation. The bottom line in any production should be how it sounds. It's good to be flexible in audio production work, because sometimes you won't have a wide variety of microphones available. But if you do have a full complement of microphones in your audio production facility, don't be afraid to try different ones. If you use what you've learned in this chapter, you should be able to obtain clear, appropriate sound under a variety of circumstances.

Self-Study

1. What is another name for the dynamic microphone?

   a) condenser
   b) pressure
   c) capacitor
   d) PZM

2. The dynamic microphone's sound-generating element is constructed of a diaphragm, a permanent magnet, and a voice coil. Into which of these is a small electrical current induced during use?

   a) diaphragm
   b) magnet
   c) coil
   d) none of the above

3. In what way does the condenser microphone differ from the dynamic microphone?

   a) The condenser microphone needs a power supply, and the dynamic microphone doesn't.
   b) The dynamic microphone has a diaphragm, and the condenser microphone doesn't.
   c) The dynamic microphone has better sound quality than the condenser microphone.
   d) The condenser microphone is bidirectional, and the dynamic microphone is omnidirectional.

4. True 5.1 surround sound is accomplished by adding what to the basic stereo setup of left and right front channels?

   a) a single rear or surround channel
   b) both left and right rear or surround channels
   c) both left and right rear or surround channels plus a center front channel
   d) both left and right rear or surround channels plus a center front channel plus a bass channel

5. Which microphone pickup pattern picks up sound on all sides?

   a) hyper-cardioid
   b) cardioid
   c) omnidirectional
   d) bidirectional

6. Which microphone would probably be most appropriate for conducting an interview on the sidelines at a football game?

   a) unidirectional
   b) omnidirectional
   c) bidirectional
   d) hyper-cardioid

7. Which microphone would probably be most appropriate for picking up a sportscaster announcing at a baseball game?

   a) cardioid
   b) nondirectional

c) bidirectional

d) omnidirectional

8. Which characteristic is true of most broadcast-quality microphones?

   a) low cost
   b) high impedance
   c) low sensitivity
   d) low impedance

9. Which of the following is most likely to exaggerate the bass sounds of a person's voice?

   a) feedback
   b) proximity effect
   c) multiple-microphone interference
   d) bass roll-off

10. What is the purpose of a shock mount?

    a) to reduce plosive sounds
    b) to keep the announcer's head at least 12 inches away from the microphone
    c) to isolate the microphone from mechanical vibrations
    d) to prevent static electricity discharges

11. Which type of microphone stand can be farthest away from a person and still allow the person to be close to the microphone?

    a) boom stand
    b) floor stand
    c) desk stand
    d) shock mount

12. Which stereo miking technique uses two microphones crossed (like swords) at a 90-degree angle to each other?

    a) split-pair miking
    b) mid-side miking
    c) M-S miking
    d) X-Y miking

13. Which type of microphone uses small, multiple sound-generating elements within a single microphone housing?

    a) ribbon mic
    b) wireless mic
    c) stereo mic
    d) boundary mic

14. A microphone's pickup pattern is exactly the same thing as a microphone's polar response pattern.

    a) true
    b) false

15. Which microphone has a permanently charged capacitor as part of its sound-generating element?

    a) condenser mic
    b) regulated phase mic
    c) electret mic
    d) ribbon mic

16. Which microphone would be best at picking up sound when the sound source is a considerable distance from the microphone?

    a) lavaliere microphone
    b) PZM
    c) RF microphone
    d) shotgun microphone

17. Sound picked up from the rear of a microphone is 90 degrees off-axis.

    a) true
    b) false

18. Which microphone pickup pattern describes a microphone with the narrowest scope of on-axis sound pickup?

    a) cardioid
    b) ultra-cardioid
    c) hyper-cardioid
    d) super-cardioid

19. Microphone impedance refers to a microphone's ability to create an output signal.

    a) true
    b) false

20. Which term describes a "screech" that occurs when sound is picked up by a microphone, amplified, fed back through a speaker, and picked up again, over and over?

    a) proximity effect
    b) multiple-microphone interference
    c) feedback
    d) bass roll-off

21. Which of the following is *not* a way that microphones are commonly classified?

    a) a microphone's sound-generating element
    b) a microphone's size
    c) a microphone's pickup pattern
    d) a microphone's impedance

22. Which stereo miking technique splits a pair of omnidirectional or cardioid microphones to the left and right of center about three to ten feet apart?

    a) ORTF miking
    b) M-S miking
    c) X-Y miking
    d) A-B miking

23. Which microphone has a wire spiral embedded in a circular diaphragm as part of its sound-generating element?

    a) dynamic microphone
    b) electret microphone
    c) moving coil microphone
    d) regulated phase microphone

24. Multiple-microphone interference can be avoided if the microphones employed are at least three times as far from each other as they are from the sound source.

    a) true
    b) false

25. Which of the following is *not* another term for a wireless microphone?

    a) FM microphone
    b) RF microphone
    c) radio microphone
    d) PZM

ANSWERS

If you answered A to any of the questions:

1a. No. This is a different type of microphone. (Reread 4.3 and 4.4.)

2a. Wrong. The diaphragm feels the pressure. (Reread 4.3.)

3a. Right. The condenser microphone power supply is needed to charge the backplate and diaphragm.

4a. No. This would not provide surround sound. (Reread 4.19.)

5a. No. Hyper-cardioid microphones pick up sound mainly from the front. (Reread 4.7 to 4.10.)

6a. Wrong. Although a cardioid microphone can be used in the field, it picks up sound from mainly one direction, so it might not pick up enough of the crowd ambience. (Reread 4.7 to 4.10.)

7a. Yes. It would pick up the sportscaster without much of the background noise.

8a. No. Most broadcast studio microphones cost $300 to $500. Although remote microphones may be less, they are usually not inexpensive. (Reread 4.12.)

9a. No. Feedback is a howling noise caused by having open microphones near speakers. (Reread 4.14 to 4.16.)

10a. No. A pop filter or windscreen is used to reduce plosive sounds. (Reread 4.20.)

11a. Right. This is the best selection.

12a. No. This is a different stereo miking technique. (Reread 4.18.)

13a. No. As the name implies, a ribbon microphone employs a thin metallic ribbon as part of a single sound-generating element. (Reread 4.5 and 4.6.)

14a. Wrong. A pickup pattern is the three-dimensional shape of the area around the microphone in which it hears the sound best; a polar response pattern is the two-dimensional representation of this. (Reread 4.7 and 4.11.)

15a. You're close to the correct response, but normal condenser microphones require a power supply to charge the capacitor. (Reread 4.4.)

16a. Wrong. Lavaliere microphones are designed to be attached to the announcer's clothing. (Reread 4.6.)

17a. No. Sound that is 90 degrees off-axis would be coming from the side of a microphone. (Reread 4.7.)

18a. All cardioid microphones pick up sound mainly from the front, but this is not the correct answer. (Reread 4.9.)

19a. No. Impedance is an electrical characteristic similar to resistance. (Reread 4.12 and 4.13.)

20a. No. Proximity effect is a characteristic of microphones that accents the bass response. (Reread 4.14 to 4.16.)

21a. No. Microphones are categorized by their sound-generating elements. (Reread 4.2.)

22a. No. With this technique the microphones are crossed to form a 110-degree angle. (Reread 4.18.)

23a. Wrong. Dynamic microphones do have a wire coil as part of their sound-generating element, but it's not configured like this. (Reread 4.3 and 4.5.)

24a. Yes. This is a true statement.

25a. No. FM microphone is another term for a wireless microphone. (Reread 4.6.)

If you answered B to any of the questions:

1b. Correct. The dynamic microphone is also called a pressure or moving-coil microphone.

2b. Wrong. The magnet sets up the field. (Reread 4.3.)

3b. No. Both microphones have a diaphragm. (Reread 4.3 and 4.4.)

4b. No. This would not provide surround sound. (Reread 4.19.)

5b. Wrong. The cardioid picks up sound on all but one side—usually the one right behind the microphone. (Reread 4.7 to 4.10.)

6b. Correct. An omnidirectional microphone would pick up from all sides, thus easily miking both the interview and some crowd noise.

7b. No. The crowd noise would tend to drown out the announcer. (Reread 4.7 to 4.10 and 4.21.)

8b. No. Consumer-quality microphones are usually high-impedance, but not of broadcast quality. (Reread 4.12.)

9b. Right. When an announcer gets too close to the microphone, the bass may be exaggerated.

10b. No. For one thing, the announcer's head should be about 6 inches away, not 12 inches away. (Reread 4.20 and Production Tip 4A.)

11b. No. A person must stand right beside a floor stand. (Reread 4.20.)

12b. No. This is a different stereo miking technique. (Reread 4.18.)

13b. No. Wireless microphones employ a transmitter (often part of the microphone) and a receiver, but this is not a description of this system. (Reread 4.6.)

14b. Right. This is the correct response.

15b. No. The regulated phase microphone doesn't require phantom power or have a capacitor as part of its sound-generating element. (Reread 4.4 and 4.5.)

16b. Wrong. PZMs are designed to be placed on a flat surface, such as a tabletop. (Reread 4.6.)

17b. Yes. This statement is false. Sound that is picked up from the rear of a microphone is 180 degrees off-axis.

18b. Yes. This is the correct response.

19b. Correct. Microphone sensitivity refers to a microphone's ability to create an output level.

20b. No. This is not correct. Multiple-microphone interference is a phase problem that creates peaks and cancellations in the sound. (Reread 4.15 and 4.16.)

21b. Correct. Although microphones come in a wide variety of sizes, they are not usually categorized by size.

22b. Wrong. This technique requires the microphones to be close together. (Reread 4.18.)

23b. No. The electret microphone is a type of condenser microphone that uses a capacitor as its sound-generating element. (Reread 4.4 and 4.5.)

24b. No. The statement is true. (Reread 4.16.)

25b. No. RF microphone is another term for a wireless microphone. (Reread 4.6.)

If you answered C to any of the questions:

1c. No. This is another name for the condenser microphone. (Reread 4.3 and 4.4.)

2c. Correct. The current is in the coil.

3c. No. The condenser microphone usually has slightly better sound quality than the dynamic microphone. (Reread 4.3 and 4.4.)

4c. No. This wouldn't provide true surround sound although you're getting close. (Reread 4.19.)

5c. Yes. An omnidirectional microphone picks up on all sides.

6c. No. Although this microphone could pick up the interview nicely, it wouldn't get much crowd noise. (Reread 4.7 to 4.10 and 4.21.)

7c. No. A bidirectional microphone picks up on two sides, and the sportscaster would be on only one side. (Reread 4.7 to 4.10 and 4.21.)

8c. No. Condenser microphones have a high sensitivity, and dynamic microphones have medium sensitivity. Neither has low sensitivity. (Reread 4.12 and 4.13.)

9c. No. This will create a distorted signal. (Reread 4.14 and 4.16.)

10c. Yes. This is a special type of microphone holder that suspends the microphone.

11c. No. A desk stand has to be right in front of the person. (Reread 4.20.)

12c. No. This is a different stereo miking technique. (Reread 4.18.)

13c. Yes. This is the correct answer.

15c. Yes. A type of condenser microphone, the electret microphone, has a capacitor that is charged during manufacture.

16c. No. RF microphones are wireless, but they don't have exceptional distance pickup characteristics. (Reread 4.6.)

18c. Although the hyper-cardioid microphone does have a narrow, unidirectional pickup pattern, this is not the best response. (Reread 4.9.)

20c. Correct. That screeching, howling sound is feedback.

21c. No. Microphone pickup patterns are used to categorize microphones. (Reread 4.2 and 4.7.)

22c. Wrong. This miking technique requires crossed microphones at an angle that can vary from 90 to 140 degrees. (Reread 4.18.)

23c. No. The moving coil microphone is just another name for the dynamic microphone. (Check the response to 23a; reread 4.3 and 4.5.)

25c. No. Radio microphone is another term for a wireless microphone. (Reread 4.6.)

If you answered D to any of the questions:

1d. No. A PZM does not indicate a type of construction. (Reread 4.3 and 4.6.)

2d. Wrong. (Reread 4.3.)

3d. No. Both dynamic and condenser microphones can have omnidirectional or bidirectional pickup patterns. (Reread 4.3, 4.4, 4.8, and 4.10.)

4d. Yes. These components when added to the stereo left and right front channels make up 5.1 surround sound.

5d. No. A bidirectional microphone picks up sound from the front and back of the microphone. (Reread 4.7 to 4.10.)

6d. No. This type of cardioid microphone has a very narrow pickup pattern. It isn't a good interview mic and wouldn't really give you full background crowd noise, although it might be useful for picking up one specific section of the crowd. (Reread 4.7 to 4.10 and 4.21.)

7d. No. This is another term for nondirectional. (Reread 4.7 to 4.10 and 4.21.)

8d. Right. Most broadcast equipment is low-impedance.

9d. Wrong. Bass roll-off is an electronic "turn down" of bass frequencies. (Reread 4.14.)

10d. No. This is not the correct answer. (Reread 4.20.)

11d. No. Although this is often used in conjunction with a microphone stand, it won't determine the distance between announcer and microphone stand. (Reread 4.20.)

12d. Correct. This is a description of X-Y stereo miking technique.

13d. No. Boundary microphones employ a single sound-generating element in conjunction with a sound-reflecting plate. (Reread 4.6.)

15d. No. The ribbon microphone doesn't require a power supply or have a capacitor as part of its sound-generating element. (Reread 4.4 and 4.5.)

16d. Right. Shotgun microphones are designed with a narrow tube that can be aimed at, and will pick up sound from, a point some distance away.

18d. Although the super-cardioid microphone does have a narrow, unidirectional pickup pattern, this is not the correct response. (Reread 4.9.)

20d. No. Bass roll-off is a switch on some microphones that electronically turns down the lower frequencies. (Reread 4.14 and 4.15.)

21d. No. Microphone impedance is used to categorize microphones. (Reread 4.2 and 4.12.)

22d. Correct. This describes the A-B miking or spaced pair technique.

23d. Yes. This is the correct response.

25d. Yes. The PZM is a type of boundary microphone that is designed to be placed on a flat surface, such as a tabletop.

Projects

PROJECT 1

Position microphones in various ways to create different effects.

Purpose

To enable you to experience proximity effect, feedback, multiple-microphone interference, and the differences in sound quality that occur when a microphone is placed at different distances and angles from an announcer.

Notes

1. You may need some help from your instructor or the engineer in setting up the equipment.
2. For the proximity effect, try to find a microphone that doesn't have a bass roll-off switch, or make sure it's switched off if it does.
3. Don't allow feedback to occur for too long. It can be damaging to all the electronic equipment— and your ears. You may have to plug the microphone into something other than the audio board if the board automatically shuts off the speakers when the microphone is turned on.
4. For multiple-microphone interference, make sure that the microphones are closer than 3 feet apart. Omnidirectional microphones will demonstrate the effect the best.
5. Use a cardioid microphone for the distance and angle experiments, because it will demonstrate the points better.

How to Do the Project

1. Set up an audio board so that two microphones are fed into it and so that the sound of those two microphones can be recorded on an audio recorder.
2. Put the recorder in record mode and activate one of the microphones. Start talking about 2 feet away from the microphone, and keep talking as you move closer until you are about 2 inches from it. As you talk, say how close you are to the microphone, and mention that you're experimenting with the proximity effect. Stop or pause the recorder.
3. Position a microphone so that it's close to an activated speaker. Turn on the audio recorder and talk into the microphone. Record a short amount of the feedback and turn off or pause the recorder.
4. Position two microphones in front of you that are less than 3 feet apart. Put the audio recorder in record mode and talk into the microphones, saying that you're testing for multiple-microphone interference. Turn off or pause the recorder.
5. Position one microphone in front of you. Put the audio recorder in record mode. Position yourself 12 inches from the microphone and talk into it. Then position yourself 6 inches from the microphone and talk directly into it. Then talk across the top of the microphone. Move 6 inches to the side of the microphone, and talk into it with your mouth positioned to speak across the top of it. Get behind the microphone, either by moving behind it or by turning it around, and talk from about 6 inches away. Describe each action as you do it.
6. Listen to the recording to hear the various effects and to see that you have, indeed, recorded all the assignments. If some of them didn't turn out as well as you would have liked, redo them.
7. Write a brief observation of each effect explaining what you hear on your recording.
8. Turn in your recording and your observations to your instructor to receive credit for the project. Make sure you put your name on it and label it "Microphone Placement."

PROJECT 2

With several other students, make a recording using stereo miking techniques.

Purpose

To give you experience using standard microphones to employ various stereo miking techniques.

Notes

1. Which technique you employ will depend on the microphones that are available at your facility.
2. Because this project requires several people, your instructor may assign it as a group project.
3. The "How To" section that follows uses X-Y techniques for illustration purposes; you can adjust it for any of the other techniques.

How to Do the Project

1. At one end of your studio (or room) arrange at least three students in a left–center–right configuration. This could also be three groups of students or even a small musical group, as long as they're arranged so that specific sections can be identified as left, center, or right.
2. Set up two cardioid microphones to record onto an audio recorder.
3. Arrange the microphones in an X-Y position as described in the text, in line with the "center" of the students or group.
4. Begin recording and have the students or group do the following:
   a. have the left say something
   b. have the right say something
   c. have the center say something
   d. have all three sections say something different, but at the same time
   e. have just the center say something
   f. have the left and right say something
   g. have all three sections say something
5. As you are recording the variations in Step 4, make sure to identify each segment by having one student say something like, "This is just the 'left' group," before the group says anything.
6. Play back your recording. Are you able to "hear" the stereo image correctly? Does the left group "appear" to be located left? Make some observations about the recording results and write them down.
7. Repeat the same recording, but use a single microphone; that is, record in mono.
8. Listen to the second recording. What differences do you hear between the two recordings? Write down your observations again.
9. Turn in your recording and the observation sheet labeled with your name and "Stereo Miking" to your instructor to receive credit for this project.

PROJECT 3

Compare sound from different types of microphones.

Purpose

To learn the differences between dynamic and condenser microphones and between cardioid and omnidirectional pickup patterns.

Notes

1. You may need help from your instructor or engineer in setting up the equipment.
2. Don't be concerned if you can't discern differences between the dynamic and condenser microphones. The pop and hiss effect doesn't occur for all voices.

3. If your facility has microphones with other sound-generating elements (such as ribbon or regulated phase) or other pickup patterns (such as bidirectional or ultra-cardioid), add those to the exercise.

How to Do the Project

1. Select a dynamic and a condenser microphone from those at your facility.
2. Attach the microphones to an audio recorder. You can put both microphones through an audio console and use them one at a time, or you can attach each microphone to the recorder in its turn.
3. While you're recording, say the following into the dynamic microphone: "Peter Piper picked a peck of pickled peppers," and "She sells seashells by the seashore." Turn off or pause the recorder.
4. Repeat Step 3, but use the condenser microphone.
5. Select a microphone with a cardioid pickup pattern and another microphone with an omni-directional pickup pattern from those at your facility.
6. Attach the microphones to an audio recorder as in Step 2.
7. Position the cardioid microphone on a stand and, while recording, walk all the way around the microphone, saying where you are as you move: for example, "Now I'm right in front of the microphone; now I'm 90 degrees to the right of the front of the microphone." Turn off or pause the recorder.
8. Repeat Step 7, using the omnidirectional microphone.
9. Listen to the recording, and write down any observations you have about the differences among the various microphones.
10. Turn in the paper and your recording to your instructor to receive credit for the project. Be sure to include your name on both and call the assignment "Microphone Comparisons."

5

THE AUDIO CONSOLE

5.1 INTRODUCTION

In the modern audio studio, the spotlight is often on computer editing rather than the **control board**; however, the **audio console** is still a primary piece of equipment in most production facilities. It can sometimes be more difficult to understand than other equipment, but it is important that you are familiar with its operation, because most other pieces of equipment operate in conjunction with the audio console. Therefore, unless you can operate the audio console, you can't really utilize other studio equipment, such as a compact disc player or audio recorder. Audio consoles can range from a simple field mixer (see Figure 5.1) to a typical on-air radio console (see Figure 5.2) or a complex control board used for music recording (see Figure 5.3). Regardless of their complexity, all control boards have basic similarities. Even though you may run across many different audio consoles in your production work, a thorough knowledge of any one should enable you to use any control board after a brief orientation.

Most boards include some method for input selection (such as source selectors), and volume control (such as faders), as well as some method for output selection (such as program/audition switches). They should also have some method of indicating to the operator the strength of the signal (through VU meters), and a way of allowing the operator to hear the mix of sources (through monitor/cue speakers or headphones). Boards also have amplifiers at various stages so that the signal is loud enough when it eventually goes to the transmitter or an audio recorder. These amplifiers are buried inside the board and are not something the board operator can usually control. In addition, audio consoles can have many other special features to help the board operator work more efficiently and

FIGURE 5.1 Even a small audio mixer often provides several inputs, equalization, and other audio processing effects. (Image courtesy of Behringer North America, Inc.)

FIGURE 5.2 Some digital audio consoles feature a self-contained, modular architecture, much like older analog boards. (Image courtesy of Radio Systems.)

FIGURE 5.3 Audio boards found in recording studios and some production facilities are often more complex and have more features than basic audio consoles. (Image courtesy of AMS Neve.)

creatively. The board may look intimidating because of all the buttons, knobs, and levers, but most of these are repeats, as the board has many different inputs and outputs. These will be explained in detail as we begin to explore the operation of the audio console.

5.2 THE DIGITAL AUDIO CONSOLE

The majority of audio consoles that you'll find in various production facilities will be digital, like the one shown in Figure 5.2. Although the first generation of digital boards were quite expensive, most current digital audio consoles are just slightly more expensive than their analog counterparts and often include additional features that justify any small extra expense. Most digital boards also have the capability to handle both analog and digital inputs with modular designs that include plug-in channels that can be easily updated from an analog to a digital format as the studio adds additional digital equipment.

There are several options for digital audio console design. Some boards emulate traditional audio consoles and are self-contained units, as shown in Figure 5.2. The various audio sources are fed directly into the stand-alone console, which follows the most common wiring practice and allows console replacement to be a simple matter of "pick up the old, drop down the new." Other digital consoles are designed so that the "board" is merely an interface or control surface for an audio "engine" that can be installed in a rack in the studio or in an equipment room down the hall (see Figure 5.4). In this instance, the audio

FIGURE 5.4 Many digital audio consoles are merely control surfaces that work in conjunction with a separate audio router that allows the electronics to be centralized in a rack or equipment room. (Image courtesy of Wheatstone Corporation.)

console works like the keyboard for your computer. The audio engine is essentially a router that accepts both analog and digital inputs with a capacity that usually exceeds even the largest analog board. Generally, analog inputs are converted to digital signals, and digital signals with different sample rates are synchronized at the audio engine.

Another feature of many digital audio consoles is the inclusion of a touch screen interface (review Figure 5.4) or similar type of LCD (liquid crystal display) window. Because digital boards can be so readily customized to individual users, assigning different sources to different channels, a visual display helps with programming the board setup and operating the console.

5.3 AUDIO CONSOLE FUNCTIONS

Any control board has three primary functions: mix, amplify, and route audio. First, the audio console enables the operator to select any one or a combination of various inputs. In other words, it must first be determined where the signal is coming from: a microphone, a CD player, or an audio recorder, for example. Audio consoles are sometimes referred to as "mixing boards," because of their ability to select and have several inputs operational at the same time. Much of the production work you do will be a mix of voice, music, and sound effects through the audio console.

The second function of the control board is to **amplify** the incoming audio signal to an appropriate level. Although all sound sources are amplified to a degree, some sound sources (such as microphones) produce such a small electrical current that they must be further amplified to be used. What is also meant by "amplify" is that the volume of an audio signal going through the console can be raised or lowered. You'll learn more about this level adjustment later in this chapter. The third function of the audio console is to enable the operator to route these inputs to a number of outputs, such as monitor speakers, the transmitter, or an audio recorder. This function allows the operator to determine where the signal is going and to provide a means for listening to the signal.

5.4 COMPUTERS AND AUDIO CONSOLES

Rather than having a physical audio board containing individual input and output modules with multiple controls, in some instances, the operator may simply manipulate a "virtual console" on a computer screen, as shown in Figure 5.5. This is common practice on digital audio workstations that include mixing functions and other audio software programs. Such virtual boards are often part of a digital audio storage and studio system, such as Broadcast Electronics' AudioVAULT, which is a complete suite of software modules. The primary sections include a control screen for live or automated announcer operation and a waveform editor, and additional sections incorporate traffic and music scheduling, among other things. Google, ENCO, and other companies also offer computerized radio automation systems.

5.5 BASIC AUDIO CONSOLE COMPONENTS

All control boards, whether digital or analog, operate in basically the same way. For the purpose of simplicity, let's consider a small audio console with just two channels. Figure 5.6 shows such a board. Each channel (M-1 and L-1) has two inputs (labeled A and B), so that, for example, a microphone could be assigned to channel M-1 (position A), and channel L-1 could have a CD player assigned to

FIGURE 5.5 "Virtual" audio console controls emulate the functions of the traditional audio board. (Image courtesy of Arrakis Systems, Inc.)

input A and an audio recorder assigned to input B. In general terms, a channel refers to the path an audio signal follows. On an audio console, a **channel** refers to a group of switches, faders, and knobs that are usually associated with one or two sound sources (glance ahead to Figure 5.9). On the board in Figure 5.6, note the individual input selectors, output selectors, volume controls, and on/off switches associated with each individual channel. The cue, headphone, and studio monitor gain controls are associated with both channels, as are the VU meters.

5.6 INPUT SELECTORS

The **input selectors** on this particular audio console are pushbuttons that can be put in either an A or B position. This feature allows two different sound sources to be associated with each channel. Although channel M-1 and channel L-1 look identical, there is a major difference between them. Channel M-1 has been designed to accept only microphone-level inputs. Microphones generally do not have amplifiers built into them, whereas CD players and audio recorders have already put their signals through a small amount of amplification. When a signal from a sound source comes into channel M-1, it is sent through a preamplification stage that is not present for signals coming into channel L-1. In other words, a microphone-level input allows a signal to catch up to a stronger signal coming into the line position in terms of amplification. Then both signals often go through additional amplification.

The way the input selector switches in Figure 5.6 are arranged, a microphone comes into the M-1 channel (A input), a CD player comes into the L-1 channel (A input), and an audio recorder comes into the L-1 channel (B input). Nothing is assigned to the B input of channel M-1. Wiring the equipment to the board involves running a cable

FIGURE 5.6　A simple two-channel audio console.

from the microphone, CD player, and audio recorder to the back (or bottom) of the audio console. Such wiring is usually done in a semipermanent way by the engineer.

Not all audio boards have input selector switches. Some radio production boards have only one input per channel that must be at the **microphone level**, or other inputs that can only accommodate equipment that has been preamplified and is ready for a **line level**. On boards of this type, usually only microphones can be patched into the first two inputs, and only CD players, audio recorders, and other line-level equipment can be patched into the remaining inputs.

On the other hand, some boards have input selector switches that have three or more positions for one input. For these boards, it's possible to patch a CD player at position A, another CD player at position B, and an audio recorder at position C all into the same input. The use that the facility is going to make of the various pieces of equipment has to be carefully studied, because of course no two pieces of equipment could be used at the same time on a single channel. Regardless of the configuration of an audio

board, the first two channels (from the left) are often utilized as microphone-level channels. Channel 1 is normally the main studio microphone, and channel 2 is often an auxiliary microphone.

Digital audio consoles are changing the concept of input selection somewhat. Most digital boards allow the user to assign *any* audio source to *any* channel using a type of audio router, as shown in Figure 5.7. In other words, the console configuration can be personalized for each individual user, so that channel 3 can be associated with a CD player for one person, a DAT recorder for another person, and a microphone for the next person. Once the source is selected for any of the console's channels, the source name is usually displayed on an alpha display for that channel module.

5.7 INPUT VOLUME CONTROL

The input **volume controls** shown in Figure 5.6 are called **sliders**, or **faders**. They are merely **variable resistors**.

FIGURE 5.7 On most digital consoles, any available audio source can be assigned to any one of the console's input channels. (Image courtesy of Wheatstone Corporation.)

Although they are called volume controls, or **gain controls**, they don't really vary the amount of amplification of the signal. The amplifier is always on at a constant volume. Raising the fader (moving it from a south to a north position) decreases the amount of resistance to this signal. When the fader is raised and the resistance is low, a great deal of the signal gets through. The dynamic is like that of a water faucet. The water volume reaching the faucet is always the same, even when the faucet is closed. When you open the faucet (decrease the resistance), you allow the water to flow, and you can vary that flow from a trickle to a steady stream.

Some older boards have rotary knobs called **potentiometers**, or **pots**, instead of faders, although these are getting harder and harder to find. Pots provide the same function as faders. As the knob is turned clockwise, the resistance is decreased and the volume is increased. Most production people consider the fader to be easier to work with. For one thing, the fader gives a quick visual indication of which channels are on and at what level which is much harder to see with a rotary knob.

The numbers on both rotary knobs and faders may be in reverse order on some audio consoles to show their relationship to resistance. For example, if a knob is turned completely counterclockwise, or off, it may read 40; at a 12 o'clock position, it may read 25; and completely clockwise, it may read 0. These figures represent decreasing amounts of resistance and thus higher volume as the knob is turned clockwise. Modern boards with fader volume controls often use a range of numbers from −55 to 0 to +10 or +15. Although the same relationship to resistance is true (the more the fader is raised, the less resistance), these numbers actually relate to decibels and the VU meter. If the board has been set up properly, the 0 setting on the fader will produce a 0 reading on the VU meter. Some boards avoid using any numbers at all and merely use equally spaced indicator lines to provide some kind of reference for various knob and fader settings.

Of course, most boards have more than the two channels of our example board. In most production studios, boards have 10 to 20 channels, but there are smaller and larger boards. Each channel has its own gain control and with two inputs per channel, more than 30 individual pieces of audio equipment can be manipulated through the console.

In professional audio production facilities, consoles with more than 20 channels are not uncommon. With the digital board's ability to assign various sources to channels, the trend is for smaller boards, as you usually work with only two to four channels active at any one time.

In addition to the gain controls just mentioned, some boards have a **gain trim**, or **trim control**, that fine-tunes the volume of each input. For example, if the sound signal coming from a CD player has the left channel louder (stronger) than the right channel, a stereo trim control can decrease the left level or increase the right level until the sound signal is equal for both channels. Each input channel on an audio console usually has a gain trim feature, and often there is a similar trim adjustment for the program and audition output of the audio board. Although these trim controls may be on the face of the audio board, they are more often an internal adjustment that is taken care of by the engineer when the control board is initially set up.

5.8 MONITORING: SPEAKERS AND HEADPHONES

Once the signal is through the input gain controls, it's amplified in a program amplifier and then sent several places (see Figure 5.8). One of these is a **monitor amplifier**. This amplifies the signal so that it can be sent into a **monitor speaker** to enable the operator to hear the signal that is going out. Boards usually contain a simple potentiometer to control the gain of the monitor speaker. For instance, our example board has a pot labeled STUDIO, which controls the volume of the monitor speakers. This control in no way affects the volume of the sound being sent out to an audio recorder (or transmitter, for example). It controls only the volume for the person listening in the control room. A common mistake of beginning broadcasters is to run the studio monitors quite loud and think all is well, while in reality they have the signal going through the audio board (and therefore to a recorder or on the air) at a very low level. It's important for the operator to be aware of the level of sound going out the line.

Most audio consoles also have a provision for listening to the output of the board through **headphones**. Because live microphones are often used in production work, the monitor

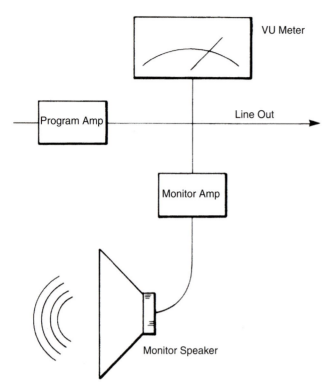

FIGURE 5.8 A block diagram of the monitor amplifier section of an audio console.

FIGURE 5.9 Whether digital or analog, a single channel of an audio console consists of a group of switches, pushbuttons, and a fade that can be used to manipulate a sound source that is assigned to that channel. (Image courtesy of Wheatstone Corporation.)

speakers are muted when the microphone is on so that **feedback** doesn't occur. To be able to hear an additional sound source, such as a CD, headphones are necessary. Audio consoles often allow you to monitor any of the outputs with headphones by selecting an appropriate switch. There is usually a volume control to adjust the signal level going to the headphones. On our example board, this control is labeled HDPN.

5.9 CUE

Another function found on most audio boards is called **cue**, which allows you to preview an input sound source. Both rotary pots and fader controls go into a cue position, which is below the off position for that control. If you turn the rotary pot all the way counterclockwise to off, it will reach a detent, or stop. If you keep turning the knob (with a little extra pressure), it will click into the cue position. Faders are brought down, or south, until they click into cue (see Figure 5.6 again). Some faders can be put into cue with a separate push button (see Figure 5.9) that, when depressed, puts that channel into cue regardless of where the fader control is set. Cue position is usually marked on the face of the audio console.

In the cue position, the audio signal is routed to a cue amplifier and then to a small speaker built into the control board. As the quality of this small internal speaker is usually marginal at best, the cue signal is often sent to a small,

but better quality, external speaker located near the audio console. Some audio consoles send the cue signal to the main studio monitor speakers. The program signal is automatically turned down, or dimmed, when a channel is put into cue and the cue signal is heard on top of the program signal. On our example audio console, the cue volume level is controlled with the pot labeled CUE.

As the name implies, this position is designed to allow the operator to cue up a sound source. For example, an audio recording can be cued to the exact beginning so that the sound will start immediately when the recorder is turned on. If an input is in cue, the signal doesn't go to any other output such as the transmitter or an audio recorder. Its only purpose is to allow off-air cueing. Many beginning announcers and production people forget to move the volume control out of the cue position after cueing up the sound source. If the control is left in the cue position, the signal won't go out on the air or be routed to an audio recorder. It will play only through the cue speaker.

FIGURE 5.10 The standard VU meter incorporates both a percent and decibel scale.

FIGURE 5.11 VU meters with fluorescent or liquid crystal displays can indicate volume changes more quickly and accurately than electromechanical meters. (Image courtesy of Dorrough Electronics.)

5.10 VU METERS

Another place the signal is sent after program amplification is the volume unit indicator, or **VU meter** (see Figure 5.10). This is a metering device that enables the operator to determine what level of sound is going out the line.

One common type of VU meter has a moving needle on a graduated scale. Usually the top position of the scale is calibrated in **decibels (dB)**, and the lower portion of the scale is calibrated in percentages. In audio engineering, a reading of 0 dB is 100 percent volume, or the loudest you want the signal to go. The VU meter is important for consistent audio production work. As noted in Chapter 2, "The Studio Environment," how loud something sounds is very subjective. What is loud to one announcer may not be deemed loud by another, especially if they each set the monitor speaker volume differently. The VU meter gives an electronic reading of volume that is not subjective.

The accuracy of VU meters is sometimes questioned in two areas. First, VU meters have trouble indicating transients—sudden, sharp, short increases in volume of the sound signal. Most VU meters are designed to indicate an average volume level and ignore these occasional sound bursts. Second, VU meters tend to overreact to the bass portion of the sound. In other words, if a sound signal is heavy in the bass frequencies, it will probably show a higher VU reading than it would if the total sound signal were being accurately read. In spite of these concerns, the VU meter remains the best indicator of volume levels in broadcast production.

Generally, an operator should control the signal so that it stays approximately between 80 percent and 100 percent. When the needle swings above 100 percent, we say the signal is **peaking in the red** because that portion of the VU meter scale is usually indicated with a red line. This is a warning to the operator to lower the gain with the fader or pot because the sound is **overmodulated**. Digital equipment is very unforgiving in regard to recording "in the red." Most digital equipment will not tolerate recording at any level above 100 percent and will distort or add "pops" to any recorded signal that exceeds it. Analog equipment

is more forgiving in that it simply distorts sound, but good production practice dictates recording everything below 100 percent.

Often there is a metal peg at the far end of the VU meter to prevent the needle from going off the dial. Allowing the gain to become so high that the needle reaches the upper peg is called **pegging the meter**, or **pinning the needle**, and should be avoided to prevent damage to the meter as well as distortion of the signal.

When the signal falls below 20 percent consistently, we say the signal is **undermodulated** or **in the mud**, and the operator should increase the volume. If it's necessary to adjust the level during the program, we say that the operator is **riding the gain** or **riding levels**. "Gain" is an audio engineer's term for loudness or volume. This is why a radio operator was first called a disc jockey. He would play record "discs" and "ride" the gain.

Our example audio board (Figure 5.6) has a set of VU meters that indicates the left and right volume of the program sound going out and another set of meters that shows the audition output. Most boards have multiple VU meters. For example, they might have separate meters for each individual channel. Boards that have multiple outputs also have multiple meters. For example, a board that is stereo, like our example board, will have one meter for the right channel and one for the left.

On some boards, the VU meter isn't an electromagnetic meter at all, but is rather a succession of digital lights (LEDs, or light-emitting diodes) that indicate how high the volume is. Other electronic meters (see Figure 5.11) replace the LEDs with liquid crystal or fluorescent displays, and the advantage of these over mechanical meters is that they can indicate volume changes more quickly and accurately.

5.11 OUTPUT SELECTORS

The most common arrangement for the **output selectors** on an audio board is a bank of three buttons for **program**,

audition, and **auxiliary** outputs. The example board in Figure 5.6 has this type of configuration except the auxiliary output is labeled UTL for **utility**. When no button is pushed in, the output is stopped at this point. When the program button (PGM) is pushed, the signal normally goes to the transmitter if the board is in an on-air studio, or to an audio recorder if the console is in a production room. The program position would be the normal operating position when using an audio console.

If the audition button (AUD) is depressed, the signal is sent to an audition amplifier and can then be sent to the monitor speakers, an audio recorder, another studio, and so on. The audition signal will *not* normally be sent to the transmitter. The purpose of the audition switch is to allow off-air recording and previewing of the sound quality and volume levels of a particular signal. For example, you could be playing a CD on one CD player through channel 3 of the audio console (in the program position) and at the same time be previewing another CD on a different CD player through channel 4 in the audition position. Each channel of the audio console can be used either in the program or audition position.

The auxiliary (AUX) or utility (UTL) position is just like either the program or audition position and is another output for the audio board (see Figure 5.6). For instance, some studios are set up so that the auxiliary position of one control board feeds another studio and becomes an input on the audio console in the other studio. Unlike most input selectors, which allow only one input to be selected at a time, output selectors usually allow more than one output to be active. If all output buttons were depressed, you could send the same audio signal to three different locations at the same time.

The configuration of output selector buttons varies from board to board. If there are a large number of outputs— six, for example—then there may be six output buttons for each input. The input signal will be sent to whichever buttons are depressed, or selected. Sometimes there are no output selectors; every input either goes out or it doesn't, depending on the master volume control. Other boards have buttons labeled SEND that determine where the signal goes. Some boards just use a single toggle switch in place of push buttons. The functions are exactly the same, depending on which way the toggle is switched; if the toggle is in the middle, or neutral position, the signal stops at that point (just like having no button pushed in a three-button bank).

Audio boards are often referred to by their number of inputs and outputs, so a 16-in/4-out board has 16 inputs and 4 outputs.

5.12 OUTPUT VOLUME CONTROL

There is no output volume control on our example board in Figure 5.6 that can be adjusted by the operator. Some audio consoles include a **master fader** that controls the volume of the signal leaving the board. Even if an input sound source is selected, program output is selected, and fader volume is up, if the master fader is all the way down, no signal will go from the console. Many boards have more than one output gain control. Again, a stereo board requires two masters: one for the right channel and one for the left. If there are multiple volume controls, then there's usually a master gain control that overrides all the other output volume controls. In other words, if the master is down, the signal won't go anywhere, even though one or more of the output volume controls are up.

5.13 REMOTE STARTS, CLOCKS, AND TIMERS

Other bells and whistles that frequently appear on audio boards include **remote start switches** (see Figures 5.6 and 5.9). These are usually located below each individual channel fader, and if the equipment wired into that channel (such as a CD player or audio recorder) has the right interface, it can be turned on, or started, by depressing the remote start. This makes it easier for the operator to start another sound source while talking into the microphone without having to reach off to the side and possibly be pulled off microphone. For most consoles, these switches also turn that channel on and off. In other words, even if you have the fader for that channel turned up, no sound signal will go through the channel until it has been turned on. However, some consoles are set up so that they will automatically turn the channel on when the fader is moved upward.

Many control boards include built-in clocks and timers. Digital clocks conveniently show the announcer the current time (hours, minutes, and seconds), and timers (see Figure 5.6) can be reset at the start of a CD to count up the elapsed time or count down the remaining time. Many timers will begin automatically when an "on" or remote start button is pressed.

5.14 EQUALIZERS AND PAN POTS

Many sound boards include simple **equalizers** (EQ). These increase or attenuate certain frequencies, thus altering the sound of the voice or music by changing the tonal quality of the sound. In some instances, they help eliminate unwanted sound. For example, an audio recording might include an electronic hum that could be lessened by filtering out frequencies around 60 Hz. Equalizers can also be used for special effects, such as making a voice sound like it is coming over a telephone. It's important to note that when you equalize a sound, you can affect both the unwanted and wanted sound; equalization is often a compromise between eliminating a problem and keeping a high-quality, usable audio signal.

Usually the equalizers are placed somewhere above each input volume control. In Figure 5.9, the input signal of the analog channel is split into three frequency ranges: high, midrange, and low. Turning the control clockwise increases the volume of that range of frequencies; counterclockwise rotation of the control will decrease its level. The "EQ in" button on this channel is actually a bypass switch that allows the operator to hear and compare the signal with and without equalization. Equalizers and other similar equipment will be discussed in further detail in Chapter 8, "Signal Processing Equipment."

Audio console channel inputs that are **monaural** (such as a microphone channel) often have a **pan pot**, or **pan knob**. By turning (panning) this knob to the left or right, you can control how much of the sound from that input goes to the right channel and how much goes to the left channel output. In other words, if the pan pot of a microphone channel is turned toward the L position, the vocal would sound stronger, or louder, from the left speaker. Normally, the pan pot would be in the center position and the input sound would be directed equally to the left and right outputs of that channel. **Stereo** input channels may have a **balance control**, which serves a similar purpose.

5.15 OTHER FEATURES

Some boards have a built-in **tone generator**. This reference tone is usually placed on an audio recording before the actual program material. The tone generator sends out a tone through the board that can be set at 100 percent, using the board VU meter. The VU meter on the source to which the signal is being sent (such as an audio recorder) is simultaneously set at 100 percent. After the two are set, any other volume sent through the board will be the exact same volume when it reaches the recorder. A tone generator allows for this recording consistency; otherwise, sounds that register at 100 percent coming through the board might peak in the red and be distorted on the audio recorder. The tone on the recording is also used during playback. The audio engineer or board operator listens to the tone and sets the recorder VU meter to 100 percent. That way the recording will play back exactly as it was recorded.

Some audio consoles have a **solo switch** above each input. When this switch is on, only the sound of that particular input will be heard over the monitor. Other boards have a **mute switch** for each channel, which prevents the signal from going through that channel when it's depressed. A mute switch acts just like an on/off switch.

A few boards have a **talk-back switch**, which is a simple intercom system consisting of a built-in microphone and a push-button control that turns the microphone on or off. The normal position of this switch is "off" so that the button must be pushed in to activate the microphone. The signal from the talk-back microphone is sent to a speaker in another studio—for example, a performance studio—which would allow the operator at the audio console to communicate with the announcer in a studio at a separate location.

PRODUCTION TIP 5A
Manipulating Faders

The type of transition that you are planning to have can affect how you are operating the faders of your board. If you know you will be doing a segue (explained shortly), you can set the faders for the new sound you will be bringing in ahead of time by using the cue function. Then, when it's time to take out one sound and bring in the other, you can simply hit the appropriate off and on buttons below the faders. That way you don't need to be concerned about getting the fader to the right position in order to have the new sound at the right level.

Working with the on/off buttons instead of the faders is also a good idea if you are doing a program where people are speaking. You can set the faders for each person's speaking level ahead of time and then, when the program begins, you can just push the "on" buttons and all the levels will be correct. This mode of operation is also advantageous if you are both talking and playing music. Set your microphone level ahead of time and then each time you will be talking, you can simply push the "on" button and not have to look down to make sure you have set the fader in the right position.

Of course, if you need to do a fade-in, fade-out, or cross-fade, this method won't work. For these transitions, you will want to have the "on" buttons already pushed and then bring the faders up or down to execute the fade.

5.16 SOUND TRANSITIONS AND ENDINGS

As mentioned earlier in this chapter, one of the functions of the audio console is to mix two or more sound sources together. Often this mix is really a sound transition, or the merging of one sound into another. In audio production, one basic transition is the **fade** (gradually increasing or decreasing volume), in which you mix one sound with silence. For example, to **fade-in** a CD means to slowly increase the volume from silence to the desired level (see Figure 5.12A). A **fade-out** accomplishes just the opposite, as the CD goes from full volume to silence (see Figure 5.12B). Most compact discs are recorded so that they fade out at the end naturally, but in production work it's sometimes necessary to end a song early, and the production person can do so with a manual fade-out.

The other common transitions are the cross-fade and segue. As the name implies, a **cross-fade** occurs when one sound is faded down as another sound is faded up (see Figure 5.12C). There is a point as the two sounds cross

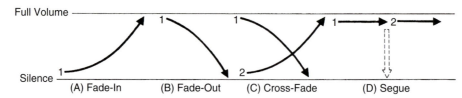

FIGURE 5.12   Sound transitions are used frequently in audio production work.

when both sounds are heard. Because of this, care should be taken in choosing music to cross-fade. Some combinations of songs can sound extremely awkward. The speed of a cross-fade is determined by the board operator and depends on the type of effect desired; however, most cross-fades are at a medium speed to give a natural, brief blending of the two sounds. A **segue** is quite different; it is the transition from one sound to the next with no overlap or gap (see Figure 5.12D). A segue can best be accomplished when the first song ends cold. Music with a **cold ending** doesn't fade out, but rather it has a natural, full-volume end. Unlike fades of any kind, segues are accomplished with both sounds at full volume. Most disc jockey work is a mixture of cross-fades and segues, but all the sound transitions are used frequently in audio production work.

In addition to the fade-outs and cold endings, one other music ending that should be noted is the **sustain ending**.

Songs with a sustain ending will hold the final chord or notes for a short period of time and then very gradually fade out. This is distinctly different from either a normal fade-out or a cold ending.

5.17 CONCLUSION

If you have followed the descriptions and explanations offered in this chapter, the audio console should be a less frightening assemblage of switches, knobs, and meters than it was when you began. You should begin to feel comfortable working with the controls of the board in your own studio. You should also be aware that most modern audio consoles will be a digital board or it may be a virtual audio console that you maneuver with a few mouse clicks or a touch screen.

Self-Study

1. It's possible to have music from an audio recorder go into a control board and then come out and be recorded on another recorder.

   a) true
   b) false

2. In Figure 5.9, according to the pan pot position on the analog channel, what is the relationship between the sound signal going to the left channel and the signal going to the right channel?

   a) Left channel volume would be less than right channel volume of the same signal.
   b) Left would be the same as right (similar change).
   c) Left would be greater than right (similar change).
   d) There would be no signal going to the right channel.

3. If the digital fader in Figure 5.9 was at 3 and you moved it to 7, what would you have accomplished?

   a) amplified the signal
   b) put the channel in cue
   c) decreased the resistance
   d) decreased the volume

4. In Figure 5.6, sound on channel L-1 would not get to program out to be broadcast or recorded unless what happened?

   a) The fader is at 0.
   b) The PGM output selector switch is on.
   c) The HDPN volume control is at 3.
   d) The A input selector switch is set to CD.

5. Audible sound comes from what in Figure 5.8?

   a) the VU meter
   b) the monitor amplifier
   c) the program amplifier
   d) the monitor speaker

6. In Figure 5.10, a reading of 50 percent on the scale is roughly equivalent to which reading on the dB scale?

   a) −6 dB
   b) −4 dB
   c) 50 dB
   d) −10 dB

7. Which expression describes a 20 percent reading on the VU meter in Figure 5.10?

   a) peaking in the red
   b) turning up the pot
   c) being in the mud
   d) riding the gain

8. Which expression describes a 3-dB reading on the VU meter in Figure 5.10?

    a) riding the gain
    b) broadcasting in stereo
    c) peaking in the red
    d) pegging the meter

9. A line-level channel of an audio console would have what type of equipment assigned to it?

    a) CD player and audio recorder
    b) microphone and CD player
    c) microphone and audio recorder
    d) only microphones

10. Which choice most accurately describes the monitor/speaker?

    a) an input
    b) a mix
    c) an output
    d) an equalizer

11. Look at Figure 5.6. What happens if the PGM/AUD/UTL output selector switch of channel M-1 is in the audition position?

    a) Sound will not reach the input A switch.
    b) Sound can be going to an audio recorder.
    c) Sound can be going to the transmitter.
    d) Sound will go to the cue speaker.

12. Which statement about the master volume control on an audio board is true?

    a) must be up for sound to leave the board
    b) is required only if the board is stereo
    c) controls only the volume of the line inputs
    d) controls only the volume of the microphone inputs

13. Which control found on an audio console might be used to help eliminate electronic hum on an audio recording?

    a) the pan knob
    b) the gain trim
    c) the solo button
    d) the equalizer

14. Which statement about the cue position on a fader is true?

    a) allows sound to go to the transmitter
    b) sometimes substitutes for the trim control
    c) sends sound to a small speaker in the audio board
    d) allows sound to fade from the left to right channel

15. Which of the following can help assure that the level that's being recorded on an audio recorder is the same as that coming from the audio board?

    a) tone generator
    b) remote switch
    c) digital timer
    d) pan pot

16. Which of the following statements about digital audio consoles is *not* true?

    a) Digital consoles are more expensive than analog consoles.
    b) Digital consoles include some type of display screen.
    c) Digital consoles do not accept analog inputs.
    d) Digital consoles offer several design architectures.

17. Which sound transition occurs when one CD is faded down at the same time as another CD is faded up?

    a) fade-in
    b) fade-out
    c) segue
    d) cross-fade

18. On an audio console, which term refers to a group of switches, faders, and knobs that are usually associated with one sound source, such as a CD player?

    a) input selector
    b) remote start switch
    c) channel
    d) output selector

19. A segue is the basic sound transition in which one sound is mixed with silence.

    a) true
    b) false

20. Most audio consoles used in radio broadcasting are identical to the consoles used in music recording.

    a) true
    b) false

21. Which feature of an audio console would allow the operator to alter the tonal quality of a sound going through the board?

    a) mute switch
    b) gain trim control
    c) equalizer control
    d) talk-back switch

22. How can a channel of the digital audio console shown in Figure 5.9 be put into cue?

    a) by moving the fader up to 0
    b) by moving the fader down to 7
    c) by depressing the START button
    d) by depressing the CUE button

23. Which feature of an audio console is a simple intercom system?

    a) talk-back switch
    b) tone generator
    c) pan knob
    d) output selector

24. On an audio console, a pan pot and a balance control both serve a similar function.

    a) true
    b) false

25. If you were attempting to segue from one song to another, how should the first song end?

   a) fade-out
   b) cold ending
   c) fade-in
   d) sustain ending

ANSWERS

If you answered A to any of the questions:

1a. Right. A tape recorder can be both input and output and an audio console can link two recorders.
2a. No. Check the setting of the pan pot. (Reread 5.14.)
3a. No. The fader never actually amplifies the signal. This is done with preamp or amplifier circuits. (Reread 5.7.)
4a. No. When a fader or pot is at 0, it is usually on. (Reread 5.7 and 5.11.)
5a. No. This indicates level, but you hear nothing from it. (Reread 5.8 and 5.10.)
6a. Right. You read the scale correctly.
7a. No. The needle would be at the other end of the scale for this. (Reread 5.10.)
8a. No. "Riding the gain" means to keep the volume at proper levels, and this is not being done. (Reread 5.10.)
9a. Correct. Both a CD player and an audio recorder are line-level inputs.
10a. No. You're at the wrong end. (Reread 5.3, 5.5, and 5.8.)
11a. No. The input selector switch is before the output selector switch and really has nothing to do with it. (Reread 5.6 and 5.11.)
12a. Right. The purpose of the master volume is to allow all appropriate sounds to leave the audio console.
13a. No. This controls how much sound is going to the left and right channels. (Reread 5.14.)
14a. No. When a channel is in cue, sound will not go to the transmitter. (Reread 5.9.)
15a. Right. If the board VU meter and the tape recorder VU meter are both set at 100 percent tone, the levels should be the same.
16a. No. Although the difference between the price of an analog board and a digital console is becoming less and less, many digital boards are slightly more expensive than their analog counterparts. (Reread 5.2.)
17a. No. This is a different sound transition. (Reread 5.16.)
18a. No. This is one of the switches involved, but this is not the correct term. (Reread 5.5 and 5.6.)
19a. No. You've confused this with the fade. (Reread 5.16.)
20a. No. Although there are similarities between all audio consoles, those most often found in radio are more basic than those used in the music recording studio. (Reread 5.1.)
21a. No. This control turns off a console channel. (Reread 5.14 and 5.15.)
22a. No. This will turn the volume of the channel up. (Reread 5.7 and 5.9.)
23a. Correct. The talk-back feature allows a board operator to talk with an announcer in another studio via a simple intercom system.
24a. Yes. Both can be used to adjust how much of the audio signal goes to either the left or right channel output.
25a. No. A segue should happen with both songs at full volume with no overlap or silence between songs; if the first song fades out, this won't happen. (Reread 5.16.)

If you answered B to any of the questions:

1b. Wrong. A tape recorder can be fed into an audio console and another tape recorder can be placed at the output. (Reread 5.3 and 5.5.)
2b. No. Check the setting of the pan pot. (Reread 5.14.)

3b.   No. Cue would be even below the "infinity" mark. (Reread 5.7 and 5.9.)

4b.   Right. When the PGM output selector switch is in the "on" position, normally sound would be sent to the transmitter or an audio recorder.

5b.   No. This amplifies so that the sound can come out, but you don't hear the sound from it. (Reread 5.8.)

6b.   No. You went in the wrong direction. (Reread 5.10.)

7b.   No. If anything, the pot is being turned down. (Reread 5.10.)

8b.   No. This is not correct. (Reread 5.10.)

9b.   No. A microphone should come into a microphone input, because it needs to be amplified to reach the line level of amplification. A CD player would be plugged into the line position. (Reread 5.3 and 5.6.)

10b.   No. This is incorrect. (Reread 5.3, 5.5, and 5.8.)

11b.   Yes. The purpose of the audition position is to send the sound somewhere other than the transmitter. Sound would not necessarily have to go to an audio recorder, though it could.

12b.   No. A master volume control functions the same for both mono and stereo. Stereo boards, however, usually have two master volume controls, one for each channel. (Reread 5.12.)

13b.   Wrong. This allows fine-tuning of input or output levels on an audio board. (Reread 5.7 and 5.14.)

14b.   No. The two have nothing to do with each other. (Reread 5.7 and 5.9.)

15b.   No. This will turn on the recorder remotely but will do nothing about levels. (Reread 5.13 and 5.15.)

16b.   No. Whether it's a simple alpha display on the channel module or a full LCD screen, because they can be readily reconfigured, all digital boards have some type of display screen. (Reread 5.2.)

17b.   No. This is a different sound transition. (Reread 5.16.)

18b.   No. This is one of the switches involved, but this is not the correct term. (Reread 5.5 and 5.13.)

19b.   Correct. The basic sound transition that mixes one sound with silence is the fade, not the segue.

20b.   Yes. This is false, because radio consoles are usually not as complex as the boards used in music recording.

21b.   Wrong. This control varies the input level of a sound source of a console channel. (Reread 5.7 and 5.14.)

22b.   No. Although some consoles are put into cue by moving the fader down, it would have to go all the way down and usually "click" into a cue position. (Reread 5.7 and 5.9.)

23b.   Wrong. The tone generator provides a reference level for setting correct recording levels. (Reread 5.15.)

24b.   No. This is not false because both controls can be used to adjust the amount of audio signal that is sent to the left or right output. (Reread 5.14.)

25b.   Yes. The first song should have a cold ending if you're going to segue into the next song.

If you answered C to any of the questions:

2c.   Right. The pan pot is set so that more of the sound from the input goes to the left channel.

3c.   No. Changing the level from 3 to 7 would increase resistance. (Reread 5.7.)

4c.   Wrong. The HDPN volume control only controls the volume of the headphone's audio. (Reread 5.8 and 5.11.)

5c.   No. This amplifies sound, but you don't hear sound from it. (Reread 5.8.)

6c.   There is no such reading on a VU meter. (Reread 5.10 and review Figure 5.10.)

7c.   Right. "In the mud" is the term for an extremely low reading.

8c.   No. It is worse than that because the needle is all the way to the end of the scale. (Reread 5.10.)

9c. No. A microphone should come into a microphone input because it needs to be amplified to reach a usable level. An audio recorder would be plugged into the line position. (Reread 5.3 and 5.6.)

10c. Right. Sound comes out to the monitor/speaker.

11c. No. The audition position is not normally used to send the sound to the transmitter. (Reread 5.11.)

12c. No. It controls all the sound that is set to leave the board. Line and microphone positions have no bearing on it. (Reread 5.6 and 5.12.)

13c. No. This allows you to hear one input channel by itself. (Reread 5.14 and 5.15.)

14c. Right. Cueing is just for the person operating the board.

15c. No. This is simply a type of clock. It has nothing to do with levels. (Reread 5.13 and 5.15.)

16c. Yes. Digital boards have modules that accept analog signals and convert them to digital.

17c. No. This is a different sound transition. (Reread 5.16.)

18c. Yes. This is the correct term.

21c. Right. EQ controls increase or decrease certain frequencies of the sound, thus changing the tone.

22c. No. If the fader was up, this would let us hear audio, but not in cue. (Reread 5.9 and 5.13.)

23c. Wrong. Pan pots control the amount of sound that goes to the left or right output of a channel. (Reread 5.14 and 5.15.)

25c. No. You're confused here; a fade-in isn't a way a song ends. (Reread 5.16.)

If you answered D to any of the questions:

2d. No. That would not be correct. (Reread 5.14.)

3d. Right. This is an increase in resistance to the signal; not as much of the signal gets through, and it's at a lower volume.

4d. Wrong. It wouldn't matter if you assigned the A input to a CD, audio recorder, or some other piece of equipment. (Reread 5.6 and 5.11.)

5d. Right. You hear sound from the monitor speaker.

6d. You might be thinking of half of the dB scale, but that isn't correct. (Reread 5.10.)

7d. No. If anything, the operator is not properly riding the gain. (Reread 5.10.)

8d. Right. "Pegging" the meter is correct. We could also have used the term "pinning the needle."

9d. Wrong. Microphone signals must be amplified to reach line level and should only come into a microphone input. (Reread 5.3 and 5.6.)

10d. No. An equalizer affects frequencies. (Reread 5.3, 5.5, 5.8, and 5.14.)

11d. Wrong. The cue speaker will be activated when a channel is put into cue, regardless of where the PGM/AUD/UTL switch is. (Reread 5.9 and 5.11.)

12d. No. It controls all the sound that is set to leave the board. Microphone and line positions have no bearing on it. (Reread 5.6 and 5.12.)

13d. Right. This can help eliminate high frequencies where scratches reside.

14d. No. You're confusing this with a pan pot. (Reread 5.9 and 5.14.)

15d. No. This allows sound to fade from the left to right channel. (Reread 5.14 and 5.15.)

16d. Wrong. Digital boards have more than one design approach, for example, the mainframe and control-surface system. (Reread 5.2.)

17d. Yes. This is the correct response.

18d. No. This is one of the switches involved, but this is not the correct term. (Reread 5.5 and 5.11.)

21d. Wrong. This control is a form of studio intercom. (Reread 5.14 and 5.15.)

22d. Yes. On this console, any channel can be put into cue merely by pressing the cue button associated with that channel, regardless of where other switches or buttons are set.

23d. Wrong. Output selectors determine where sound goes when it leaves the audio console. (Reread 5.11 and 5.15.)

25d. No. A segue should have no overlap or silence between songs; if the first song has a sustain ending, this won't happen. (Reread 5.16.)

Projects

PROJECT 1

Learn to operate an audio console.

Purpose

To make you proficient operating some functions of the audio console, and to practice basic sound transitions.

Notes

1. Audio boards are generally one of the more complicated pieces of audio equipment. It may take you a while to master a board, but don't despair. Take it slowly, and don't be afraid to ask for help.
2. Audio boards all have the same general purpose. Sounds come into the board, are mixed together, and are sent out to somewhere else.
3. The actual exercise should be done rapidly. You won't be judged on aesthetics. In other words, when you're fading from one source to another, do it quickly. Don't wait for the proper musical beat, phrase, or pause.

How to Do the Project

1. Familiarize yourself with the operation of the audio console in your production studio. Learn the inputs, the outputs, the method for changing volume, and other special features of the board.
2. As soon as you feel you understand the board, do the following exercise while recording it on an audio recorder. Practice as much as you like first.
   a. Cue up a CD, play part of it, and fade it out.
   b. Using the studio microphone, announce your name and the current time.
   c. Begin a second CD.
   d. Cross-fade to another CD, and then fade it out.
   e. Bring in an auxiliary microphone, and ad-lib with another announcer.
   f. Fade-in a CD, segue to another CD, and fade it out.
   g. Announce something clever on the studio microphone.
3. Listen to your recording to make sure it recorded properly.
4. Label your recording "Audio Console Operation" and include your name. Hand the assignment in to your instructor to receive credit for the project.

PROJECT 2

Diagram and label an audio board.

Purpose

To familiarize you with the positioning of the various switches and controls so that you can access them quickly.

Notes

1. Some boards are very complicated and have more functions than are discussed in this chapter. Usually, this is because they're intended to be used for sound recording of music. If you have such a board, you need to label only the parts that you will be using frequently.

2. If you can't find controls for all of the functions given in this chapter, ask for help. Because there are so many different brands and types of boards, sometimes functions are combined or located in places where you cannot identify them easily.
3. You don't need to label each switch and knob. If your board has ten inputs, it will obviously have ten channel-volume controls. You can circle them all and label them together, or make one label that says "Input Volume Controls" and draw arrows to all ten.
4. You will be judged on the completeness and accuracy of your drawing. You won't be graded on artistic ability, but be as clear as possible.

How to Do the Project

1. Sketch the audio console in your production studio.
2. Label all the basic parts: input selectors, channel gain controls, VU meters, output selectors, and master gain controls (if your board has them).
3. Also label any other parts of the board that you will be using frequently, such as equalizers, cue positions, and headphone connections.
4. Label your sketch with your name and the title, "Audio Console Diagram." Give your completed drawing to the instructor for credit for this project.

PROJECT 3

Record a two-voice commercial.

Purpose

To develop your skill in creating a spot while working with another announcer.

Notes

1. This project assumes that you have enough familiarity with your studio equipment to accomplish basic recording and production techniques.
2. The production incorporates two announcer voices and a music bed.
3. You will need to write a dialogue script that can be read in about 23 seconds. You might write copy about a restaurant you eat at frequently or some cosmetic or health product you are familiar with.
4. There are many ways to accomplish this project, so don't feel you must follow the production directions exactly.

How to Do the Project

1. Record the script (voices only) onto an audio recorder. Make sure both voices are close to the same volume level. Rerecord to correct mistakes or just to get it to sound the way you want.
2. Select a music bed that is appropriate for the style of the spot. You might find something on the CD-ROM that accompanies this text.
3. You can play back the music bed directly from a CD, or you may have to record it on another recorder.
4. Set correct playback levels for both the vocal track and the music bed. Both will start at full volume. Then cue both to the beginning sound.
5. Record your completed spot onto a CD-R, so set your recorder to record mode. (Your instructor may advise you to record on different media.)
6. Begin recording. Start the music bed at full volume. Start the vocal track and simultaneously fade the music bed slightly so the vocal track is dominant.

7. As the vocal ends, bring the music bed back to full volume and then quickly fade it out as you approach 30 seconds.

8. It may take you several attempts to get the spot to come out correctly. If you need to do it over, just cue everything and try again.

9. Listen to the finished commercial. Make sure that you've gotten a good balance between the music and the voice and all recording levels are proper.

10. Label the assignment with your name(s) and "Two-Voice Radio Spot." Turn it in to your instructor to receive credit for this project.

6

DIGITAL AUDIO PLAYERS/ RECORDERS

6.1 INTRODUCTION

Digital technology has essentially replaced conventional technology in various applications around the audio production studio. For example, the compact disc player has replaced the turntable as a necessary piece of production equipment. In fact, even CD players have become a less important production tool as audio files are merely moved around on computer platforms for various production processes. Other analog equipment, such as reel-to-reel or cassette tape recorders are also rarely found in today's production facilities. This chapter looks at some of the digital equipment that offers a number of available formats to work with in the audio production environment. Although it is not intended to be a comprehensive survey, most of the equipment mentioned still plays a role in digital playback and recording in many audio production studios.

6.2 THE CD PLAYER

The **compact disc player** was the first piece of digital equipment to be embraced in audio production and broadcast work, and is still one of the key sources for playing back pre-recorded material. Because CDs are often aired one right after the other, there are usually at least two CD players in each production room or on-air studio. This way, one can be cued while the other is playing on the air or recording.

CD players offer superior sound quality—greater **frequency response**, better **signal-to-noise ratio**, improved **dynamic range**, and almost no **distortion**—when compared to an analog component. In addition, there is no physical contact between the player and the actual CD so little wear takes place.

The CD format also offers the convenience of random access to the material stored on the disc. CD players can instantly move from one track to another track anywhere on the disc in a second or two. Another plus of the CD player, from a production viewpoint, is its ability to "cue to music." CD players allow the announcer to find the exact beginning of the music and start the CD instantly at that point. CD timing information (elapsed/remaining time and track length) is helpful for production work, and the ability to select and play segments of music or to automatically fade in at any point in the music can be a creative production tool.

The CD player shown in Figure 6.1 is typical of a unit designed specifically for broadcast use. Some facilities just use consumer CD players, but these often require special interfaces to be compatible with other audio equipment and are not really designed for day-in and day-out use.

One of the main operational features of many broadcast-quality units is a **cue wheel** that allows the operator to "rock" or "scrub" the CD back and forth. In this manner, the exact start point of the music can be found, and then the player can be paused at that spot, ready for play. Most

FIGURE 6.1 The professional-quality CD player is built for rack-mounting, heavy-duty use, and may have features not available on consumer units. (Image courtesy of Denon Professional.)

CD players will also automatically cue to the start of the music when you cue up to any specific track on the CD or cue to an index point within an individual track. Other normal CD controls include a play button to start the CD, several controls to select or program specific tracks on the CD, and an open/close control to load the CD into the machine. Regardless of the exact design, the CD ends up in a **tray** or **well**, where it spins so the laser can read it.

The internal structure of the CD player centers around three major components: a drive motor, a **laser** and lens system, and a tracking mechanism. The drive motor spins the disc at a variable rate between 200 and 500 RPM (revolutions per minute). To keep the data on the disc read by the laser at a constant rate, the drive motor slows down as the laser moves to the outside of the disc. In the laser and lens system, a **laser diode** generates a laser light beam, and a **prism system** directs it toward the disc surface. Different types of lenses focus the laser beam exactly on the pits of data encoded on the disc. Reflected light is directed back through the lens and prism to another wedge lens and a **photodiode**, which provides the data signal that will be converted to an audio signal. The tracking mechanism moves the laser assembly so that it follows the spiral track of data on the disc.

A different design approach to CD players has been to build them so that the CD must be put into a plastic housing before it can be played in the unit (see Figure 6.2). The plastic cartridge increases the cost of this system, but it also affords the CD extra protection from dirt and damage.

Another type of player is the **multiplay** CD player. With the ability to hold up to 300 CDs and with interfacing capability, this type of unit has been used as a music source in some automation systems. Not only does the operator have random access to thousands of individual songs, but also all the CDs can be secured under lock and key. However, since the advent of digital hard disk storage systems, this type of CD player has seen little use in the broadcast studio.

Regardless of the type of CD player utilized, some compact discs seem to display an overly bright, metallic, or even harsh sound—a distinctive "digital sound." The "problem" actually has nothing to do with the CD player or even the CD process. It occurs with some CDs because the original recording was intended for vinyl playback. Engineers often added equalization to compensate for sonic limitations of vinyl recording. Many early CDs were mastered with this same equalization applied rather than removed for transfer to the CD medium, thus the bright or shiny sound. Material that has been recorded essentially for CD use does not display this problem, nor should older material that has been carefully prepared or remastered for transfer to CD.

6.3 COMPACT DISCS AND CARE OF CDS

The **compact disc (CD)** is a small plastic disc, 12 centimeters (about 4.7 inches) in diameter. On one side of the disc,

the music is stored as a single spiral of microscopic pits and lands (or flat areas) that contain the encoded information about the sound. In addition to music information, data encoded on the disc tells the CD player where each track begins and ends, how many tracks are on the disc, and other timing and indexing information.

A CD stores music as 16-bit digital words, going from the center hole to the outside rim of the disc. With the standard digital sampling rate, 44,100 of these digital "words" are required for each channel every second! In fact, around 650 MB (megabytes) of data is stored on a standard 74-minute CD. A thin aluminum reflective coating (some CDs use a gold-coated reflective surface) makes it possible for the laser light to read the encoded data, and a layer of clear polycarbonate plastic protects the encoded information. The reverse side of the CD is made up of the label and a protective lacquer coating (see Figure 6.3).

CDs were originally designed to hold 60 minutes of recorded material; however, about 74 minutes of music has become the standard CD length, with 80-minute lengths also being used. CD singles (3-inch CDs) were developed that are capable of holding about 20 minutes of music, but these never really caught on and are not frequently seen today.

FIGURE 6.2 A compact disc must be put into a plastic housing before it can be played in a cart-style CD player. (Image courtesy of Denon Professional.)

PRODUCTION TIP 6A
CD Information and Codes

The number of tracks and timing information about songs have always appeared on the display of CD players, but why not other information, such as song titles? Although it has been technically possible to provide such information, such provisions were not put into the original CD "standards." If the codevelopers of the compact disc, Sony and Philips, revise the CD standard so that information about the artists, albums, and songs can be included with the music, then a text-capable audio CD player will be required. Computer CD-ROMs are text-capable players, and some music CDs do contain additional information that can be accessed with a PC or with CD players manufactured to read it.

The Society of Professional Audio Recording Services (SPARS) developed a code for CD packaging to show just how "digital" the CD was. The code told whether the recording was from a digital or analog master and whether it was mixed and mastered in analog or digital. For example, an AAD disc was recorded and mixed in analog but mastered in digital. Many AAD- or ADD-coded CDs didn't appeal to digital purists looking for that completely digital CD, labeled DDD, so the code was dropped for a few years. However, in 1995, SPARS recommended the code's return, and many of today's CDs again show this code, although it is not required on CD packaging.

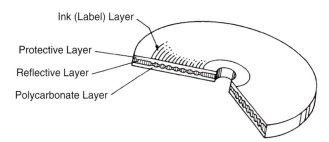

FIGURE 6.3 A compact disc is made up of several layers, as this cutaway view shows.

The compact disc is not as indestructible as it was originally promoted to be. Practical use has shown that CDs do require some care. When removing a CD from its **jewel box** case, put your thumb on the center spindle of the jewel box and your index or middle finger on the rim of the disc. Press down with your thumb and gently pull up on the disc until it is free of the case. When handling a disc, continue to hold only the outer edges or the edges of the hole, and avoid bending the CD in any manner. Never touch the surface of the disc.

Some CD players will not track properly with dust or fingerprints on the CD surface, and serious scratches can also render the CD unplayable. CDs can be cleaned by gently wiping the aluminum side (the side without the label) with a lint-free cotton cloth from the center hole of the CD directly toward the CD rim. Do *not* use a circular cleaning motion because this could cause a scratch that follows the spiral data on the disc, causing the disc to track improperly. Use a special CD-cleaning solution, isopropyl alcohol, or methanol to remove dirt or other material from the disc.

Flexing a disc or touching it with oily fingers can damage the CD's protective coating and ultimately allow oxidation of the aluminum layer, which can ruin the CD. If your CD player has a tray that opens and closes, be sure to stop the CD *before* you open the tray. Hitting the open (eject) button while the CD is still playing can cause damage to the CD as it continues to rotate while the tray is opening.

If you must mark the disc, do not use pen, pencil, fine-tip markers, or adhesive labels; rather, use a non-solvent-based felt-tip permanent marker on the label side of the disc. To get the maximum life span out of a compact disc, it should be stored in its plastic jewel box in an upright position, like a book.

6.4 THE CD RECORDER

CD recorders (see Figure 6.4) are found in most audio production studios. Although the first CD players were merely "turntables" for prerecorded CDs, shortly after their development, manufacturers produced a recordable CD. Broadcast

FIGURE 6.4 Most CD recorders found in the audio production studio can record in both the CD-R and CD-RW format. (Image courtesy of Tascam®.)

companies like Tascam, Marantz, Denon, and HHB all offer CD recorders that work in the CD-R and/or CD-RW format.

CD-R (CD-recordable) is a WORM (write once, read many) design. The CD consists of a photosensitive dye layer and a reflective layer, encased in the normal protective polycarbonate. When heated by high-power laser pulses, the dye melts or "burns." This creates bumps (and pits) that have a different reflective nature, similar to those of a regular CD. The data is read off the disc by a lower powered laser. The recording laser follows a preformed spiral track so the data can be played back on any standard CD player. Actually, the CD-R recorder allows you to record during several different sessions or until the disc is full (99 separate tracks, up to 80 minutes total); however, you may not be able to play the disc on a regular CD player until you "finalize" the disc and permanently write the table of contents of the disc. A partially recorded CD-R *will* play on the CD-R recorder at any time. The biggest drawback to the WORM design is the inability to record over old material; if you make a mistake in the recording process, you have ruined that disc or at least a section of it, and once you finalize the disc, you cannot add any new material to it.

The **CD-RW** (CD-rewritable) disc is used in a similar fashion; however, the last track recorded can be erased (before the disc has been finalized), and the space on the disc can be reused for recording other material. CD-RW discs that have been finalized can also be totally erased and rerecorded. The CD-RW format uses a phase-change technology; the material in the recordable CD surface goes from crystalline to amorphous when heated during the recording process, which changes its reflectivity. During playback, the laser light is reflected differently from opposite-phase areas, allowing the player to distinguish binary zeros and ones and thus reproduce a digital signal. An audio CD recorded in the CD-RW format may not play back correctly on all CD players, although it will play on its own recorder, which will also play standard CDs.

Another development in the CD recording area is a small, digital workstation component (see Figure 6.5) that combines a CD recorder with a small mixing console to provide recording, editing, and mixing features. The mixer section can handle up to eight tracks of simultaneous recording with built-in EQ and effects, such as reverb or delay. The recorder section uses 16-bit or 24-bit recording at a 44.1-kHz sampling rate. Other features include an internal hard drive (usually at least 40 GB), up to 24 playback tracks, and stereo mastering to the built-in CD-RW drive. Similar digital workstations use a MiniDisc or compact flash as the recording medium.

Even though there is intense competition with other digital recording media (such as the MiniDisc or hard disk recorder), the CD recorder has found a place in the digital production studio. Some stations record jingles, commercials, custom sound effects, and other production elements on CD. Other stations might prerecord a block of programming onto CD for later playback, perhaps through an

FIGURE 6.5 This multitrack recorder can function as a portable mini-studio and record on compact disc. (Image courtesy of Roland Corporation.)

automation system. In addition, most sound effect and production music libraries that used to be available on vinyl records are now produced on compact disc.

6.5 SACD (SUPER AUDIO CD)

Although the CD format still appears to have a long life ahead of it, there are "new and improved" audio formats that offer some competition to the venerable compact disc. The two most similar to CD, but offering higher quality, are DVD-Audio and SACD. Developed by the originators of the compact disc, Sony and Philips, **SACD** employs a new digital process rather than standard digital technology. Direct Stream Digital uses a simplified 1-bit, 2.82-mHZ digital method that touts increased resolution and clarity while providing a warmer, more natural sound. An SACD can hold more information, so multiple mix capabilities are usually provided—often a stereo mix and a 5.1 surround sound mix. (Review the section on surround sound in Chapter 4, "Microphones.") Most, but not all, SACDs are backward-compatible, because they offer a hybrid disc (see Figure 6.6) with a standard CD layer and the SACD layer. The bottom layer contains data for both a stereo mix and 5.1 channel mix of the audio, along with video or graphic information, if employed. The separate top layer contains standard CD data. Standard CD players would read this information and reproduce CD-quality sound. Players with SACD capability would read the high-density layer and reproduce the higher quality audio. At the moment, there are only a limited number of titles available in the SACD format and there are no recorders for this format. The main competitor for the SACD is DVD-Audio, as noted in the next section.

CD Layer

High Density Layer
Extra Data

Six-Channel Mix
Two-Channel Stereo

FIGURE 6.6 The high-density layer of a hybrid SACD can contain stereo and multichannel mixes, along with video and graphic information.

FIGURE 6.7 The MiniDisc recorder in a rack mounted configuration (and combined with a CD player) can be found in many audio production facilities. (Image courtesy of Tascam®.)

6.6 DVD-AUDIO

The next generation of audio disc may well be the **digital versatile disc (DVD)** or a variation of it. Originally called a digital *video* disc, the DVD was designed to hold a feature-length movie on a compact disc–sized medium. Primarily a video format, it also has applications for computer data and music. Physically, the DVD is the same size as a CD; however, it can have two data layers that can both be read from one side of the disc by refocusing the laser in the DVD player. The data information is spaced much closer together than on a CD, so by using a data compression scheme (around 2 to 1) and a two-sided, dual-layer disc, the DVD could hold up to 17 gigabytes of data, or the content of about 25 current CDs! Even a standard, single-sided DVD-Audio disc holds more data than the CD—about 4.7 gigabytes.

In addition to greater storage capacity, the DVD-Audio specifications offer a wide variety of possible formats of equal or better quality than the CD. An audio-only DVD can have sampling rates of 44.1, 48, 88.2, 96, 176.4, and 192 kHz, plus 16-, 20-, and 24-bit quantizing compared to the CD's 44.1 kHz/16-bit standard. Most broadcasters prefer a DVD-Audio standard of 96 kHz/24-bit, and this has become the most popular format. Like SACD, DVD-Audio also offers the advantage of multichannel sound—from a simple mono mix up to a maximum of six channels (5.1 surround sound).

In addition to musical content, DVD-Audio discs can also record text, still images, and short video clips.

Although there are DVD recorders, they are primarily for recording video or for data storage on personal computers. DVD-RW discs and drives also exist, with the same advantages as the CD-RW. Veteran users of CD-RW and DVD-RW discs, however, will point out that the medium is not as stable as the CD-R or DVD-R medium, so they are hesitant to put any vital or one-of-a-kind data on an RW disc.

Though prerecorded SACDs and DVD-Audio discs are available, neither format has really been embraced by consumers or audio professionals. Competing audio formats and even newer technologies seem to have bypassed both SACD and DVD-Audio before they have had time to become mainstream formats.

6.7 THE MD RECORDER/PLAYER

MiniDisc (MD) recorders and players of different styles and applications have seen moderate success in the audio production studio. Originally developed by Sony as a digital replacement for the cassette, the MiniDisc can be a handheld, tabletop, or rack-mounted (see Figure 6.7) system. Employing a small disc, the MD can still hold up to 80 minutes of music because of a data compression

FIGURE 6.8 A portable MD allows recording and editing in the field, as well as all the other features of the MiniDisc format. (Image courtesy of **HHB** and Sennheiser Electronic Corporation.)

scheme. The MiniDisc is *not* actually CD quality, but is still an extremely high-quality audio medium. The MD also features a "shock absorber" system that uses a memory buffer to store music that can continue to play for a few seconds if the player mistracks, until the pickup can return to its correct position.

The portable MD recorder, an example of which is shown in Figure 6.8, is a serious competitor for other recorders when it comes to news gathering or any production situation that requires recording in the field. The stand-alone unit offers recording, playback, and editing tracks on the move.

6.8 THE MINIDISC

The MiniDisc is permanently sealed in a plastic cartridge (see Figure 6.9), so it can be handled without worrying about dust, dirt, or fingerprints getting on the disc. The MD comes in both a prerecorded and recordable format. The actual disc is much smaller than a compact disc—about 2.5 inches in diameter—but otherwise shares many of the CD characteristics, including its digital data in a spiral of microscopic pits. The MiniDisc, like a computer disk, has a sliding protective shutter that automatically opens when the disc is put into a recorder/player.

Recordable MDs employ a **magneto-optical design**. A magnetically active layer of the disc is heated (by a laser) to the point where its magnetic orientation can be changed by a magnetic recording head. As the heated spot moves out of the laser beam, it rapidly cools, "freezing" its magnetic polarity according to the data applied to the recording head corresponding to a digital zero or one. During playback, the laser senses variations in reflected light in relation to the magnetic orientation. New material is recorded directly over the old with the MiniDisc format.

FIGURE 6.9 The MiniDisc is housed in a plastic case to keep it free from scratches, dust, and fingerprints.

6.9 DATA COMPRESSION

In order for the MiniDisc to record the large amount of necessary digital data and still employ its small disk-recording medium, the MD recording process uses a data **compression** system developed by Sony known as **ATRAC (Adaptive Transform Acoustic Coding)** to provide digital-quality sound. Like any other data compression scheme, data compression occurs because only audible sounds are encoded. In other words, sound below the threshold of hearing or too soft to hear, and sounds masked by louder sounds heard at the same time, are excluded, according to a "perceptual coding" model. In addition, those sounds that are encoded use only the number of data bits necessary for near-CD-quality sound. This allows the MiniDisc recording to cut down the amount of data that must be recorded by about one-fifth, with no apparent sound-quality change or loss.

There is no standard method of data compression, and other digital equipment uses other types of audio data reduction schemes. There has been some concern about the audible effects on sound that has been compressed more than once. For example, a MiniDisc could be played through a signal processor that also uses data compression. Some tests have shown a degradation of the audio signal with some combinations of data compression; however, this doesn't appear to be a major problem.

Data compression can also be used with any of the digital media mentioned previously, thus making their audio capacities even greater. A CD-R or CD-RW can hold a maximum of 80 minutes of uncompressed audio, but were those audio tracks to be compressed into, for example, the very popular MP3 format, 10 to 12 times that amount of audio could be stored on the same disc, or around 800 minutes. A standard DVD, with 4.6 GB of space, could store nearly 4,000 minutes of compressed, CD-quality audio. Looking at these numbers, storage space is obviously not a problem anymore. Ease of organization and utilization then becomes the issue. Here many compressed formats, such as MP3, also provide great flexibility, as the files can contain text and other data that can help to categorize and identify the files. Much of this additional data is user-definable. If you think a song fits better in the Bluegrass genre than the Country genre, switching this is a snap and will be reflected in all future searches of the content.

In addition to being playable in computers, MP3 and other popular audio compression formats are increasingly playable in CD and DVD players, as well as MiniDisc players and, of course, stand-alone MP3 players.

6.10 COMPACT FLASH AND OTHER DIGITAL RECORDERS

The digital recorders that are enjoying the most prominent place in audio production work are **solid-state recorders** that record on a removable media card, such as a **Compact Flash (CF)** or **Secure Digital (SD)** card. Portable, rackmount, and mixer/recorder workstation units have all found their way into audio production work. The portable recorder shown in Figure 6.10 is one of many popular handheld recorders. The front panel of the unit shows an LCD screen and typical recorder controls. Most recorders allow both wav and MP3 recording with built-in or external microphones. One-button recording is often featured, and additional controls are used to set various digital parameters, such as sample rate, data compression, or other effects.

Once recording is complete, basic nondestructive editing can be accomplished by manipulating a waveform display on the LCD screen, or the audio files can be fed to a laptop or desktop PC for editing or archiving. Perhaps the biggest plus for the Compact Flash recorder is that the recording system does not rely on moving parts and, once recorded, files can be directly downloaded into an editing system via USB cable rather than having to wait on "real-time" transfers.

As noted earlier, some other production recorders are designed to be rack mounted in the studio. In addition to providing multiformat recording capability and normal transport controls, these recorders often feature an LCD screen for file manipulation or basic editing, and analog, digital, and

FIGURE 6.10 Many solid-state digital audio recorders fit easily into the palm of your hand and have become popular for news gathering and other field recording uses. (Image courtesy of M-Audio.)

FIGURE 6.11 The HHB FlashMic is a professional digital recording microphone with a flash recorder built right into the base of the microphone. (Image courtesy of HHB and Sennheiser Electronic Corporation.)

FIGURE 6.12 The DAT tape cassette is similar in design to a VCR tape. (Image courtesy of TDK Electronics Corporation.)

medium, these machines have used internal Zip drives or removable IDE (Integrated Drive Electronics) computer drives. Most **digital cart recorders** offer selectable sampling rates, the usual operational controls, and can easily add an electronic "label" (through the use of a keyboard), which can show the cart name and timing information on an LCD screen. Two such recorders that still have a presence in the audio studio are 360 Systems DigiCart/E Hard Disk Recorder and the Alesis ADAT 24-Track Recorder. Both units are actually hard disk recorders, but both use removable disks to move audio from one location to another or to archive projects.

6.11 TAPE-BASED DIGITAL RECORDERS

Although tape-based formats have essentially been made obsolete by the type of recorders mentioned above and many models are no longer in production, some of these recorders can be found in recording studios and other audio production facilities. One is **DASH**, which stands for **digital audio stationary head**, a reel-to-reel standard for digital recorders, like the Sony PCM-3202 or Mitsubishi X-86. Because of their high costs, multitrack reel recorders like these were used mainly in recording studios.

Another tape-based digital format that did find some broadcast application was DAT; however, it was never widely used. The **DAT** (**digital audio tape**) recorder, also known as **R-DAT** (**rotary head digital audio tape**), used technology based on the VCR, traditional cassette recorder, and CD player. The DAT system recorded with rotating heads, putting digital data on $\frac{1}{8}$-inch tape in a series of diagonal tracks similar to VCR recording. DAT recording was 16-bit at sampling rates of 32, 44.1, or 48 kHz.

The actual DAT cassette tape was designed similarly to a VCR tape and consisted of two small tape reels encased in a plastic housing about the size of a pack of playing cards (see Figure 6.12). DAT, like CD, had several controls for

USB ports. A 1-GB card can hold over 1 hour of uncompressed stereo audio or up to 36 hours of MP3 mono audio.

Another type of portable recorder is HHB's FlashMic portable internal flash recording microphone. Shown in Figure 6.11, this digital recording microphone has a flash recorder with 1 GB of recording memory built right into the base of the microphone. A single button initiates recording with a high-quality Sennheiser omnidirectional or cardioid mic capsule or external line input. As the unit is entirely solid state, there is no internal noise generated that often plagues built-in microphones on portable units. The recorder also has a USB interface to export audio files for editing or adding effects to the recording. The immediate advantage of this type of recorder is its efficient design as one single unit and its rugged design making it a durable, portable recording device for anyone recording in the field.

Over the years, broadcast audio manufacturers have developed numerous other digital recorders. Instead of an analog audio cart, MD, CD, or DVD as the recording or storage selecting specific songs on the tape. An **AMS (Automatic Music Sensor)** button allowed the operator to skip forward or backward to the start of the next or previous recorded track.

Although DAT recorders had the same superior sound quality associated with all digital equipment—exceptional frequency response and signal-to-noise ratio; wide dynamic range; and virtually no wow, flutter, hiss, hum, or distortion—being tape-based became a disadvantage because audio tape was subject to breaking, deterioration, and manufacturing defects.

6.12 CONCLUSION

With the advent of digital audio equipment and the advantages in quality and convenience it offers, the use of older analog equipment continues to diminish and in many instances has been discontinued. Being comfortable working with various kinds of digital equipment, especially the recorders and players noted in this chapter, will be a necessary skill for most audio production people. It's also probable that new types of digital-based equipment will continue to be developed, and equipment not yet thought of will find a home in future audio production facilities.

Self-Study

1. What does the MiniDisc recorder use as its recording and storage medium?

   a) standard audio cassette
   b) 2.5-inch computer-type disk
   c) 3.5-inch computer-type disk
   d) DAT cassette

2. What is one reason for using a professional-quality CD player rather than a consumer model in the audio production studio?

   a) Professional-quality players use a higher powered laser than a consumer model.
   b) Professional-quality players offer a better signal-to-noise ratio and less distortion than consumer models.
   c) Professional-quality players offer a greater frequency response and better dynamic range than consumer models.
   d) Professional-quality players are built for heavy-duty, continuous operation, and consumer models are not.

3. The lacquer coating on a compact disc makes it virtually indestructible in normal use.

   a) true
   b) false

4. What is ATRAC (Adaptive Transform Acoustic Coding) used for?

   a) auto-reverse on a DAT recorder
   b) synchronization of CD-R and CD-RW discs
   c) data compression
   d) recording audio on a DVD

5. Which format allows a CD recorder to record a blank CD only once?

   a) CD-RW
   b) DASH
   c) WORM
   d) DVD

6. Compact discs are best cleaned with a cloth wiped in a circular motion over the playing surface of the disc.

   a) true
   b) false

7. Most digital recorders allow the user to add to the recording an electronic label that can show track name, timing, and other information on an LCD screen.

   a) true
   b) false

8. The DVD-Audio disc can utilize music encoded at each of the sampling rates and bit lengths shown. Which one is also shared with the CD?

   a) 44.1 kHz/16-bit
   b) 48 kHz/24-bit

c) 96 kHz/24-bit

d) 192 kHz/16-bit

9. Once a CD-RW disc has been "finalized," it cannot be erased and rerecorded.

   a) true

   b) false

10. The MD is one type of digital player featuring a memory buffer that helps prevent mistracking if the player is bumped during playback.

    a) true

    b) false

11. Which of the following is *not* an advantage of the CD player?

    a) random access to material on the CD

    b) lack of physical contact between player and CD

    c) large signal-to-noise ratio

    d) ability to hold more information than a DVD

12. You know that a compact disc should be marked only on the label side, but which type of writing instrument should you use to mark a CD?

    a) ball-point pen

    b) No. 2 lead pencil

    c) felt-tip permanent marker

    d) none of the above; use an adhesive label

13. Which of the following is *not* one of the main internal components of the compact disc player?

    a) drive motor

    b) laser and lens system

    c) compact flash card

    d) tracking mechanism

14. The DVD Direct Stream Digital recording process promises increased resolution and a more natural sound than other digital recording methods.

    a) true

    b) false

15. Digital recorders that employ a Compact Flash card have the ability to dub recordings using USB direct downloading rather than having to wait for real-time dubs.

    a) true

    b) false

ANSWERS

If you answered A to any of the questions:

1a. Wrong. The audio cassette is the recording and storage medium for the analog cassette recorder that the MiniDisc was designed to replace. (Reread 6.7 and 6.8.)

2a. No. Both professional and consumer-model CD players use a similar laser system. (Reread 6.2.)

3a. No. Although the lacquer coating helps protect the CD, it is far from indestructible—fingerprints, dust, and scratches can damage CDs. (Reread 6.3.)

4a. No. This is not a feature found on DAT recorders. (Reread 6.9 and 6.11.)

5a. No. This is a recordable/erasable format. (Reread 6.2.)

6a. Wrong. CDs should be wiped only in a straight line from the center hole toward the outer rim. (Reread 6.3.)

7a. Correct. This is a feature of most digital recorders.

8a. Yes. This is the standard CD recording format that can also be used by DVD-Audio.

9a. Wrong. CD-RW discs can be completely erased and rerecorded even after they have been finalized. (Reread 6.3.)

10a. Yes. This is true of the MiniDisc as well as many other digital players.

11a. No. Being able to instantly move from one track to another on the CD is a big advantage. (Reread 6.1.)

12a. No. You should not use a ball-point pen to label a CD. (Reread 6.3.)

13a. Wrong. The internal structure of a CD player centers around a drive motor. (Reread 6.2.)

14a. No. This is a false statement because Direct Stream Digital is associated with SACD, not DVD. (Reread 6.5 and 6.6.)

15a. Correct. This feature is one of the main advantages of the Compact Flash recorder.

If you answered B to any of the questions:

1b. Yes. MiniDisc recorders utilize a small CD-type disc encased in a plastic housing similar to a computer disk.

2b. Wrong. All CD players have similar S/N and distortion characteristics. (Reread 6.2.)

3b. Yes. CDs require careful handling even though the lacquer coating helps prevent problems.

4b. No. This answer doesn't really make any sense. (Reread 6.4 and 6.9.)

5b. No. DASH is a digital reel-to-reel system. (Reread 6.4 and 6.11.)

6b. Correct. Although a circular cleaning motion works for vinyl, it can damage a CD.

7b. Wrong. Most digital recorders do offer this operational feature. (Reread 6.10.)

8b. No. This is a DVD-audio format, but it is not used by CDs. (Reread 6.6.)

9b. Correct. CD-RW discs can be erased even after they have been finalized.

10b. No. This is a true statement. The MD (and other digital players) offers this feature. (Reread 6.7.)

11b. No. Because the CD is read by laser, there is no wear on the CD and this is a big advantage. (Reread 6.2.)

12b. No. You should not use a pencil to label a CD. (Reread 6.3.)

13b. Wrong. The internal structure of a CD player centers around a laser and lens system. (Reread 6.2.)

14b. Yes. Direct Stream Digital is associated with SACD, not DVD, making this a false statement.

15b. Wrong. This is a true statement and this feature is one of the main advantages of the Compact Flash recorder. (Reread 6.10.)

If you answered C to any of the questions:

1c. No. The regular computer disk has been used in another type of digital "cart" recorder, but not the MiniDisc. (Reread 6.7, 6.8, and 6.10.)

2c. No. All CD players have similar frequency response and dynamic range characteristics. (Reread 6.2.)

4c. Correct. This is Sony's data reduction scheme, which allows a long recording time on a small recording medium.

5c. Yes. This is the "write-once, read-many" format used by CD-R machines.

8c. No. This is a DVD-Audio format, but it is not used by CD. (Reread 6.6.)

11c. No. The larger the S/N ratio the better, so this is an advantage. (Reread 6.2.)

12c. Yes. If you must label a CD, use a soft, felt-tip permanent marker.

13c. Correct. The compact flash card is a removable recording medium for other digital recorders.

If you answered D to any of the questions:

1d. No. DAT tapes are used only in DAT recorders and players. (Reread 6.7, 6.8, and 6.11.)

2d. Yes. Most consumer-model CD players can't stand up long under the constant use of a broadcast facility.

4d. Wrong. Although there are different data compression schemes for recording onto digital media, ATRAC is associated with the MiniDisc. (Reread Sections 6.6 and 6.9.)

5d. No. DVD is a different type of format. (Reread 6.4 and 6.6.)

8d. No. This is a DVD-Audio format, but it is not used for CDs. (Reread 6.6.)

11d. Correct. A DVD can hold more information than a CD.

12d. No. You should not use adhesive labels to mark a CD. (Reread 6.3.)

13d. Wrong. The internal structure of a CD player centers around a tracking mechanism. (Reread 6.2.)

Projects

PROJECT 1

Record a public service announcement that uses a sound effect.

Purpose

To develop your skill in creating a radio spot that incorporates a sound effect to provide a transition.

Notes

1. This project assumes that you have enough familiarity with your studio equipment to accomplish basic recording and production techniques.
2. The production incorporates a single announcer voice, two distinct music beds, and a sound effect to provide a transition between the music beds.
3. You will need to write a simple script that can be read in about 20 seconds. Write the copy about an environmental concern, such as water pollution, littering, or forest fire prevention. The spot should follow a "problem–solution" format.
4. There are many ways to accomplish this project, so don't feel like you must follow the production directions exactly.

How to Do the Project

1. Select music beds that are appropriate for the style of the spot. You should use a more somber-sounding bed for the "problem" and a more upbeat sound for the "solution." The CD-ROM that came with this text contains a variety of musical styles that may provide what you need, or you can find your own music on another CD.
2. You can play back the music beds directly from the CD.
3. Record the music bed and script (voice) onto a recorder. First record the "problem" part of the spot, using a serious tone of voice and mixing the appropriate music bed with it. Then record the "solution" with a lighter vocal delivery, slightly faster pace, and more up-tempo music.
4. Begin recording the music bed at full volume. Start the vocal track and simultaneously fade the music bed slightly so that the vocal track is dominant while you record the rest of the script.
5. Now, find an appropriate sound effect. It will be used to separate the two music beds and provide a transition between the "problem" and "solution" parts of the spot. (There are several on the CD-ROM.)
6. Record the sound effect onto another recorder.
7. Set correct playback levels for the vocal/music bed tracks and the sound effect. Then cue both to the beginning sound.
8. It may take you several attempts to get the spot to come out correctly. If you need to do it over, just cue everything and try again.
9. On the finished commercial, write your name and "Sound Effect Radio Spot," and turn it in to your instructor to receive credit for this project.

PROJECT 2

Prepare a report on a digital player/recorder that is not discussed in this chapter.

Purpose

To keep you up to date on what is happening in this field.

Notes

1. Technological developments in this field are changing rapidly. Undoubtedly there will be new products available by the time you read this text that were not available when it was written. It behooves anyone in the audio production field to keep up to date. However, audio equipment also comes and goes, so don't be surprised if the player/recorder that you write about today is no longer available a year from now.
2. You can select equipment that does more than play and/or record. For example, some of the current recorders also allow for editing or mixing.
3. The Internet is an excellent place to find this information. The major manufacturers place a great deal of material about their products on their web sites. Companies that are particularly active in this field include 360 Systems, Sony, Marantz, Roland, and Tascam.

How to Do the Project

1. Find a piece of equipment that qualifies as a digital player/recorder. As suggested, you can do this on the Internet or you can write to companies for their catalogues.
2. Research the characteristics of the piece of equipment. If you know a facility that has this equipment, talk with the engineer or an operator who uses it. You could also call a distributor who sells the equipment for additional information.
3. Organize your report, taking into consideration some of the following points:
   a. What is the primary purpose of the piece of equipment?
   b. How does it operate—with regular transport controls (play, record, stop, and so on), attached to a computer, with the use of a rotary dial?
   c. Is it designed to replace an older piece of equipment, or is it designed for a new application?
   d. What compression format does it use, if any?
   e. What type of recording medium does it use—tape, computer disk, flash card, specially designed material?
   f. When was it introduced to the market?
   g. What does it cost?
   h. Are there optional features of this equipment?
   i. What is your assessment of whether this will be a successful product?
4. Write your report; remember to include your name and "Digital Player/Recorder" as a title on it.
5. Turn in the report to your instructor to receive credit for this project.

PROJECT 3

Play and record several compact disc selections.

Purpose

To familiarize yourself with the operation of CD players.

Notes

1. For this exercise you will need to work with a microphone, audio board, and audio recorder, as well as a CD player.
2. Different brands of CD players have slightly different features, so you will need to learn the particular characteristics of your player.
3. You can play several selections from one CD or use several CDs. If you have only one CD player, you would be advised to use three cuts from one CD, as you will probably not have time to change discs. If you have two CD players, you would be better off playing selections from at least two CDs.

How to Do the Project

1. Make sure that your CD player is connected so that it can be faded out and will record onto an audio recorder.
2. Make sure that a microphone is available so that you can announce the title of the selections you choose.
3. Examine the CD player and practice with it so that you can cue, play, and pause it with ease.
4. When you feel familiar with the player and have decided on three selections to play, start the recorder.
5. Complete the project by doing the following:
   a. Announce the name of the first musical selection, bring it in, and then fade it out after about 30 seconds.
   b. Announce the name of the second selection, bring it in, and fade it out after about 30 seconds. (If you have two CD players, you can cue the second one while the first is playing. If not, you'll need to cue a second selection while you are introducing it. This is not particularly difficult, because most CD players enable you to cue easily.)
   c. In the same manner, announce the name of the third selection, bring it in, and then fade it out.
6. Label the assignment with your name and "CD Recording."
7. Turn in the assignment to your instructor to receive credit for the project.

MONITOR SPEAKERS AND STUDIO ACCESSORIES

7.1 INTRODUCTION

This chapter looks at some audio studio items that are often treated as passive devices that simply exist in the studio, but they are actually quite significant. **Monitor speakers** (see Figure 7.1) are used to listen to sound in the studio. The speakers convert the audio signal, stored on recording media like CDs or digital recorders, back into sound we can actually hear. The sound that comes from them is the final product, so they are important in determining the quality of that product. What you hear on the monitor speakers is an accurate gauge of what you recorded and what the listener will hear.

The various pieces of equipment used in the audio production studio, including monitor speakers, are all interconnected. This chapter also looks at the **cables** and **connectors** used for this interconnection, as well as some of the accessories that make work in the production studio easier. Some accessories, such as windscreens and pop filters, have been previously mentioned.

FIGURE 7.1 Studio monitor speakers help you judge the sound quality of your audio production. (Image courtesy of Behringer North America, Inc.)

7.2 TYPES OF SPEAKERS

You may want to review the sections on sound in Chapter 2, "The Studio Environment," as it will help you understand how speakers work. **Speakers** are transducers. They work in a manner opposite to that of microphones. Instead of converting sound waves into electrical energy, speakers produce sound from an electrical signal by converting the signal into mechanical energy that produces sound waves or audible sound.

The most common type of monitor speaker is a **dynamic speaker**. Also known as a **moving coil** or an **electromagnetic speaker**, its transducing element, called a driver, produces sound by moving a flexible cone or diaphragm in and out very rapidly. The paper diaphragm, which also may be plastic or metal, is suspended in a metal frame. Attached at the narrow end of the cone is a voice coil (a cylinder wound with a coil of wire), which is located between powerful circular magnets (see Figure 7.2). When an electrical current is generated in the voice coil, it creates another magnetic force that moves the coil (and cone) back and forth, according to the electrical signal entering the coil. The cone vibration causes the surrounding air to move in a like manner, which our ears pick up as sound. Instead of a cone, some speakers use a dome, which is just another type of diaphragm that bulges out rather than tapers in. Other speaker drivers, such as **electrostatic** or **planar-magnetic**, are usually considered fairly exotic, and you aren't likely to run across them in the typical production studio.

As the modern audio production facility is typically an all-digital environment, several manufacturers now offer digital monitor speakers (see Figure 7.3). The speakers have digital inputs, in addition to analog inputs, which can identify up to a 24-bit digital signal with a sampling rate as high as 192 kHz. When a digital signal is detected, the speaker's internal D/A converter becomes activated. Does the digital speaker sound better? There really is no monumental sound difference between an analog and a digital

FIGURE 7.2   The most common type of speaker driver is the dynamic cone driver.

FIGURE 7.3   Digital monitor speakers feature an input that allows for direct digital hookup from an audio console or workstation. (Image courtesy of Genelec, Inc.)

input; however, the convenience of attaching directly to the digital output of an audio console or digital audio workstation is a plus for the digital monitor speaker. In addition, digital monitor speakers help eliminate line loss and possible hum sometimes associated with analog speakers.

7.3 BASIC SPEAKER SYSTEM COMPONENTS

The basic components of the typical speaker system (see Figures 7.1 and 7.4) are the woofer, tweeter, crossover, and speaker enclosure. **Woofer** and **tweeter** are names given to drivers or individual speakers used in a speaker system. Because no one speaker design can reproduce the entire frequency range adequately, different speakers were developed to handle different portions of it. A woofer is designed to move the large volume of air necessary to reproduce lower frequencies. The cone should be large in size (usually anywhere from 8 to 12 inches) or be able to make large movements, and often a woofer utilizes a combination of both. However, this bulk prevents the speaker from

FIGURE 7.4   The basic two-way speaker system consists of a tweeter, a woofer, and a crossover housed within an enclosure.

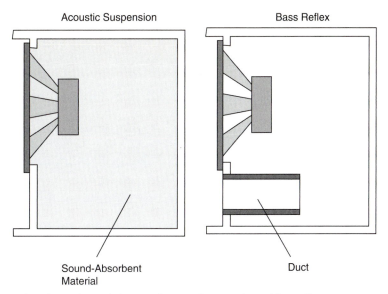

FIGURE 7.5 The most widely used speaker enclosure designs are the acoustic suspension and bass reflex systems.

adequately reproducing the higher frequencies that require rapid cone movement. The tweeter uses a lighter and smaller design; often a convex dome (1 inch or less in diameter) replaces the cone. There are also midrange speakers with cones from 3 to 5 inches in diameter that are designed to reproduce higher-bass and lower-treble frequencies.

An individual speaker is really a speaker system, in that most modern speakers use at least a woofer and a tweeter driver. To divide the audio signal and send the proper frequencies to the proper driver, another element of the speaker is used: the **crossover**. A crossover is a network of filters (mainly capacitors and inductors) between the input to the speaker and the individual speaker drivers. In the two-way system, an inductor would pass all audio *below* a certain frequency, sending it to the woofer. A capacitor would pass all audio *above* a certain frequency, sending it to the tweeter. Although there is no universal design for the crossover, most dividing points between the bass and treble frequencies are between 500 and 1,500 hertz. A speaker that has just a woofer, a tweeter, and a crossover is a **two-way speaker system**, like the one shown in Figure 7.4. A speaker that employs another driver (such as a midrange) is a **three-way system**.

7.4 SPEAKER SYSTEM ENCLOSURE DESIGNS

The speaker drivers and crossover are encased in a box (enclosure) that also plays a role in how the speaker sounds. Although there are different speaker system designs, each is intended to handle the rearward sound wave. Every speaker produces sound both behind and in front: the back sound wave is exactly opposite to the one that goes into the forward listening space. If the two sound waves are allowed to combine naturally, they would be acoustically out of phase (see Section 7.7) and cancel each other out, producing no sound or greatly diminished sound in a good portion of the frequency range, especially the bass part of the range.

The two most widely used speaker enclosure designs are the acoustic suspension and bass reflex systems shown in Figure 7.5. The **acoustic suspension** (or **sealed-box**) design puts the speaker drivers (and crossover) in a tightly sealed enclosure that produces an accurate, natural sound with a strong, tight bass. By containing and absorbing the back wave in the enclosure, the acoustic suspension design prevents the rear sound from radiating and disrupting the main sound of the speaker. Because half the sound energy is trapped and absorbed in the box, acoustic suspension speakers are less efficient than other designs and require a more powerful amplifier to drive them. The acoustic suspension design also demands a rather large, sturdily built physical enclosure to ensure accurate reproduction of the lowest bass notes.

On the other hand, the **bass reflex** (or **vented-box**) design is quite efficient and produces a strong bass sound with less power required. The bass reflex speaker enclosure is designed with a vent, duct, or port—an opening that is tuned to allow some of the rear sound (mainly the lower frequencies) to combine in phase and reinforce the main sound from the speaker. Some bass reflex design speakers have been criticized for not having tonal accuracy that is quite as good as the acoustic suspension design and for even adding a "boomy" quality to the sound. These problems, however, are often the fault of a particular speaker's tuning and construction and not caused by the bass reflex design. There are many different vented-box designs, and most modern bass reflex speakers produce a clean, wide-ranging bass.

7.5 SPEAKER SOUND QUALITIES

There's a wide variety of speaker systems to choose from, and, as with some other audio equipment, the differences between various models may be minimal. One of the important qualities that a good monitor speaker must have is excellent frequency response. As we've already noted, we are able to hear sounds or frequencies in the range of 20 hertz to 20 kilohertz, although most of us don't hear quite that low or that high. Top-line broadcast monitors often provide a frequency response range from 35 to 45 hertz at the low end, to 18 to 20 kilohertz at the high end. Increased use of digital equipment has made it necessary to have speakers that produce as much of this range as possible.

Another important quality for the broadcast monitor speaker is its ability to produce a **flat frequency response**. The speaker should be able to reproduce low, midrange, and high frequencies equally well to produce a natural sound. The speaker itself shouldn't add anything to the audio signal, such as a boosting of the highs. Perhaps what is most important is merely how a speaker sounds. Among the combinations of driver types, speaker enclosure design, and crossover frequencies, there is no one speaker configuration that produces the "best sound." It is agreed, however, that a good speaker sound doesn't depend only on the speaker itself. How a speaker sounds is also dependent on the program (what is being played through it), the dimensions and acoustic properties of the room in which the speakers are heard, the location of the speakers (in relation to the listener), and the listener.

7.6 SPEAKER PLACEMENT

In the audio studio, there may not be many options as to where the monitor speakers are located. Usually they are positioned one on each side of the audio console, but exactly how they are positioned after that is open to various schools of thought. If nothing else, you should try to achieve an acoustically symmetrical layout. Don't put one speaker in the corner next to a glass window and the other speaker in the middle of a wall that's covered with acoustic tiles. That would be a mismatched acoustic environment for the two speakers, rather than a similar one. One thought is to mount the speakers in the wall. As long as the speakers are isolated from the wall structure—using rubber shock mounts, for example—this flush mount creates an infinite baffle that prevents back wave problems.

Large speakers can be built into the wall, providing a loud, clear sound with plenty of "heavy" bass; unfortunately, this type of installation is often not practical for a particular studio. Some production people feel the ideal sound is obtained when speakers are even with or a bit above ear level. This installation is called **near-field** or **close proximity monitoring** and can be accomplished by putting small speakers, such as those shown in Figure 7.3, on the audio console "bridge" or on short stands to the left and right of the console, about 3 feet apart. Keeping the speakers a couple of feet from the back wall will prevent any excessive bass boost. As the speakers are so close to the listener, you hear mostly direct sound and don't need to worry much about the effect from room acoustics. "Toeing in" the speakers (angling them toward the listener) or pointing them straight away from the

wall will control the treble, with speakers pointing toward you providing the greatest high-frequency response. Very clear detail and excellent stereo imaging are characteristics usually associated with near-field monitoring setups.

Another concern with monitor speaker placement, especially true of studios that employ near-field monitoring, has to do with the increased use of computer equipment in the broadcast studio. Unless the monitor speakers are magnetically shielded, they must be positioned far enough away from the screen of the computer equipment so that they don't distort the picture. Perhaps the most practical monitor installation in many production studios is when the speakers are hung from the ceiling or attached to the wall behind the audio console. For the best sound dispersion, the speakers should be hung toward the upper corners of the production room. Keeping them close to the wall prevents a great deal of reflected sound and should produce full bass at a higher sound level than other possible positions.

When speakers are placed closer to a wall, there is more bass sound produced, because the usual omnidirectional sound field is cut down, and the sound is concentrated into a smaller dispersion area. Putting speakers totally into the corners of a room (such as the upper corners) may result in too much bass boost, but this is not an uncommon location. Hung speakers also keep counter space available for other production room equipment, and this is an important consideration in many settings.

Regardless of where the speakers are ultimately placed, the location of the operator in relation to the speakers also plays a role in how they sound, especially with stereo programming. Ideally, the operator is located directly between the two speakers and far enough back from them so that an equilateral triangle is formed if a line were drawn from speaker to speaker and from operator to speaker (see Figure 7.6). If the layout of the production room positions the operator closer to one speaker than the other, the source of all the sound appears to shift toward that one speaker. As a

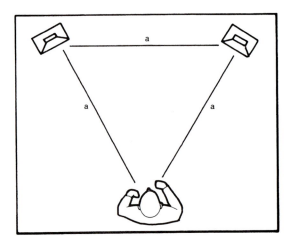

FIGURE 7.6 The most basic rule of speaker placement dictates that the distance between the speakers equals the distance from speaker to listener.

production person, you may not have any control over the speaker placement, but it's important that you realize the effects of speaker placement on the sound you hear.

7.7 PHASE AND CHANNEL ORIENTATION

The concept of **phase** was previously mentioned in Chapter 4, "Microphones." Wiring monitor speakers incorrectly can also cause phase problems. Each speaker is fed its sound signal from the audio console monitor amp (or sometimes an external amp) by a positive and negative wire. If the wires are reversed on one of the speakers (i.e., the positive wire is connected to the negative terminal), the two speakers will be out of phase. As the driver moves the cone of one speaker in and out, the driver on the other speaker is moving out and in, so that the two speaker sounds are fighting each other and tend to cancel out individual sounds, diminishing the overall sound quality. This would be especially noticeable if the speakers were reproducing a mono signal.

Another concern about speaker wiring is channel orientation. Most studio monitors are wired so that moving a balance control from left to right will shift the sound image from left to right *as you face the speakers*. In other words, while looking at the speakers, the left speaker is in line with your left hand. This setup is important for true stereo sound reproduction. For example, if you were listening to a classical music piece and the channel orientation were reversed, the violins would sound as if they were to the right of the sound stage, which would be contrary to normal symphony orchestra arrangement. However, as most speakers are wired by an engineer, phase and channel orientation should not be a problem in most audio studios.

7.8 MONITOR AMPLIFIERS

As you've previously learned, most audio consoles have an internal monitor amp that provides the signal to drive the monitor speakers. Although this is adequate for many studio applications, some production rooms (and control rooms) are set up with external monitor amplifiers. These are merely more powerful **amplifiers** that provide higher volume levels and clearer reproduction of the sound signal. Remember, the volume of the monitor speakers is only for the pleasure of the operator and has no relationship to the volume of the signal being broadcast or recorded.

7.9 SPEAKER SENSITIVITY

A speaker's **sensitivity** is the amount of sound (output level) that a speaker can produce from a given input level, much like the sensitivity of a microphone studied in Chapter 4. It

is measured in decibels of sound-pressure level (SPL), and a good-quality broadcast monitor will usually have a sensitivity of more than 90 db SPL measured at one meter with 1 watt of input level. There are speakers that range from low sensitivity to high sensitivity, but, in reality, this characteristic of a speaker has little bearing on its quality. What it does mean is that a low-sensitivity speaker will need more power to drive it to any given volume level than a high-sensitivity speaker.

Speaker size, sensitivity, and bass response are also related. To increase a speaker's low-frequency response, its enclosure can be made larger, or its sensitivity can be decreased. For many audio studio situations, a smaller speaker size offers a lot more flexibility in placement of the speaker and thus is preferred, even if it means a low-sensitivity speaker that might require a more powerful monitor amplifier.

7.10 HEADPHONES

Headphones are another type of monitor—they are tiny speakers encased in a headset. Headphones are necessary in audio production, because the studio monitor speakers are muted when the microphone is on, and the operator must be able to hear sound sources that are also on. For example, if a radio announcer was talking over the introduction of a song or a voice-over announcer was reading a commercial over the background of a music bed, headphones would allow him or her to hear both the other sound and the microphone sound so that you can balance the two or hit appropriate cues. Headphones are also portable, so sounds can be monitored when an actual monitor speaker might not be available.

Like regular monitor speakers, headphones come in a variety of designs and styles. The two main types of headphones found in the production studio are closed-cushion headphones and open-air or hear-through cushion headphones. **Closed-cushion headphones**, also known as **circumaural**, have a ring-shaped muff that rests on the head around the ear and not actually on the ear. The enclosure around the muff is solid or closed, as shown in Figure 7.7. These headphones are probably the most common, as they usually provide a full bass sound and attenuate outside noise better than other styles. Closed-cushion headphones are also less likely to leak sound into the studio; however, they're often heavier and more cumbersome than other styles.

Hear-through cushion headphones, also known as **supra-aural** or **open-air**, have a porous muff, instead of an ear cushion, that rests directly on the ear (see Figure 7.8). The enclosure around the muff typically has holes or other types of openings to give it the open-air design. Often made of very lightweight material, this design can be very comfortable for the wearer. However, open-air headphones are subject to possible feedback, because the audio signal can leak out if driven at high volume levels, so some audio production people avoid them.

FIGURE 7.7 Closed-cushion or circumaural headphones have a ring-shaped muff that rests on the head around the ear. (Image courtesy of Audio-Technica U.S., Inc.)

FIGURE 7.8 Hear-through or supra-aural headphones have a porous muff that rests directly on the ear. (Image courtesy of AKG Acoustics.)

FIGURE 7.9 A patch panel simplifies rewiring individual audio components into an audio console or studio. (Image courtesy of Gentner Broadcast Systems.)

Other headphone types include the tiny **earbud**, which is designed to fit in the ear; **electrostatic headphones**, which are extremely high-quality and require external amplification and special couplers to hook up; and **wireless headphones**, which operate similarly to wireless microphones by transmitting an RF or infrared (IR) audio signal from the source to the headphones.

Unlike consumer headphones, many professional-quality headphones are purchased "barefoot"; that is, they have no end connector on them. Although most audio equipment that allows headphone use requires a standard 1/4-inch phone connector, there are other situations as well, and the barefoot headphone allows the engineer to wire them as necessary.

Which headphone style is most appropriate is often determined by the personal taste of the user; however, professional-quality headphones should always feature large drivers and full (but comfortable) ear cushions and headband. One note of caution for all headphone users: *Listening at extremely high volume, especially for extended periods of time, such as in a broadcast situation, can damage your hearing permanently.* Good production practice (and common sense) dictates moderate volumes for all headphone use.

7.11 HARDWIRING AND PATCHING

Audio equipment in the production studio is connected together by two methods: **hardwiring** and **patching**. Hardwired connections are somewhat permanent (such as the CD player directly connected to the audio console) and are usually soldered or wired by the engineer. Equipment that may, from time to time, be moved from one production area to another (such as an audio recorder) is often connected by male and female connectors known as plugs and jacks. More will be said about the typical audio connectors in the next few sections of this chapter.

Many pieces of audio equipment, and even two different production studios, are often connected together through the use of a **patch panel** or **patch bay**, as it is also called. Most patch panels are configured as two rows of 24 phone jacks in a one- or two-unit rack space as shown in Figure 7.9.

FIGURE 7.10 A portion of a patch panel that is "normalled" (A) and a portion of a patch panel that has been "patched" (B).

FIGURE 7.11 An audio routing switcher operates in a manner similar to a patch panel. (Image courtesy of Lectrosonics.)

The patch panel is located between the equipment and the audio console so that the input and output of each piece of equipment is wired to the patch panel.

There are often several modes that patch bays can be set to; however, in a typical setup, the top row of sockets on the panel is where the audio signal is coming from, and the bottom row of sockets is where the signal is going to. Putting a patch cord into the correct holes in the panel allows you to interconnect and reconfigure the various pieces of equipment or studios. Patch cords are available as either a single-plug cord or a double-plug cord. A double cord works well for stereo patch bays since it has two plugs at each end. One side of the plug casing will be marked (usually with a serrated or ribbed edge), so that you can keep left and right channels correctly aligned on both the input and output sockets of the patch panel. Of course, single cords work fine, too—just remember to always plug in one cord from the top row right channel of the patch panel to the bottom row right channel before plugging in the left channel. That way you won't cross channels, which is easy to do if you plugged both left and right channels of the top row before plugging in the bottom row.

Figure 7.10 shows a portion of a patch bay (A) in which two CD players are linked to two channels on an audio console. With no patch cord put into the panel, CD 1 is linked to Channel 3 and CD 2 is linked to Channel 4. In patch panels, the top row is internally wired to the bottom row, and the audio signal flows in that manner. When it is unpatched like this, it's known as a "normalled" condition. Figure 7.10 shows another portion of a patch panel (B) that links the output of the audio console to audio recorders. When normalled, the PGM (program) output goes to CD-R 1, and the AUD (audition) output goes to MiniDisc

1. The PGM signal could be sent to MiniDisc 1 (as shown) by putting a patch cord from the PGM position on the top row to the MiniDisc 1 position on the bottom row. Now the signal flow has been changed, and that's the purpose of a patch panel—to allow flexibility in configuring the audio studio. In this way, the audio signals from various pieces of equipment can be sent to the audio console, and the audio console output can be sent to various pieces of equipment.

An alternative to the patch panel is the **audio routing switcher**. The router (see Figure 7.11) operates just like a patch panel by allowing several input sources to be switched to a single output (or sometimes multiple outputs); however, the switching is done electronically by selecting the appropriate switches or buttons, rather than by using patch cords. Most audio routers are centered around a matrix of "x" number of inputs times "x" number of outputs. Any one input can be sent to all the outputs, or all the outputs can be sent to one single input, or any combination can be configured. In other words, any input can be sent to any output. Similar types of audio distribution equipment, using CAT5 computer cable, are being used today to feed audio signals to multiple locations around the production studio.

7.12 COMMON AUDIO CONNECTORS

In most situations, you'll be dealing with four types of audio connectors: RCA, XLR, phone, and miniphone. In general, the female, or receiving, connectors are called **jacks** and the male connectors are called **plugs**, but often the terms "plugs," "jacks," and "connectors" are all used interchangeably.

The **RCA connector** is also known by the old time name, **phono connector**. Notice that it is "phono," not "phone." Most home stereo equipment uses this type of connector and many professional-quality CD players also utilize RCA connectors. This connector is always a mono connector, so two of them are needed for a stereo signal. Because of this, RCA connectors are often bundled in pairs and color-coded—red (right channel) and black or white (left channel). The male plug consists of a thin outer sleeve and a short center shaft that plugs into the female jack (see Figure 7.12). Although there are female in-line jacks, the female end is most often enclosed in a piece of equipment (such as an audio recorder or preamp) so that the male end will just plug directly into the equipment. RCA connectors are used for unbalanced connections and are prone to picking up extraneous electrical noises, such as switch noise or hum.

The **XLR connector** is also known as the **Cannon connector** or **three-pin connector**. It's the most common microphone connector in audio production use and is also often used as the input–output connection on audio recorders. By convention, male XLR connectors are outputs and female XLR connectors are inputs. This connector attaches firmly and cannot be disconnected unless the latch lock is pressed. The three prongs of the male plug fit into the conductor inputs of the female jack. The guide pin on the female end fits into the slot for the guide pin on the male end so that the connector can't be put together improperly (see Figure 7.13). Like the RCA connector, the XLR connector is mono, so a stereo connection requires one XLR connector for the right channel and one for the left channel. The balanced three-conductor wiring of the XLR connector makes this a high-quality connection that is less likely to pick up noise through the cable.

The **phone connector** is also known as the ¼-inch **phone**. Notice that it is called "phone," not "phono." Most pro-quality headphones are connected to the audio console with a phone plug, and most patch bays consist of female phone jacks into which phone plugs are inserted. The **miniphone connector** (also called a **mini**) is most often required to connect portable audio recorders to other pieces of production equipment. The output of many portable recorders is a female minijack. As you would expect, the miniphone is a smaller version of the phone connector. Although there are various sizes of miniphone connectors, the ones used most in audio production are ⅛ inch or 3.5 millimeters. The phone and miniphone plug consist of a tip and a sleeve, which go into the female jack. Male mono plugs have one insulating ring that separates the tip from the sleeve, and stereo plugs have two insulating rings, which actually define the ring portion of the connector (see Figure 7.14). If the signal is stereo, both the female and male connectors should be stereo. Again, the female end is often enclosed in a piece of equipment, but you can get inline jacks if needed.

FIGURE 7.12 The RCA or phono plug is one of the common audio connectors. (Images courtesy of Switchcraft, Inc., a Raytheon Company; and Mackie Designs, Inc.)

FIGURE 7.13 XLR connectors feature a locking latch that prevents them from being accidentally disconnected. (Images courtesy of Switchcraft, Inc., a Raytheon Company; and Mackie Designs, Inc.)

FIGURE 7.14 Phone and miniphone connectors can be either stereo or mono. (Images courtesy of Switchcraft, Inc., a Raytheon Company; and Mackie Designs, Inc.)

7.13 OTHER CONNECTORS AND CONNECTOR ADAPTERS

Most of the connectors mentioned so far are intended for analog inputs or outputs; however, more and more of the equipment in the audio studio today has digital connections. Some digital connections utilize standard broadcast connectors—specifically the XLR and RCA plugs and jacks—and other digital inputs and outputs use different types of connectors. When XLR connectors are used for digital audio, you may see an input or output labeled **AES/EBU**. This denotes the digital standards set by the Audio Engineering Society and the European Broadcasting Union. Digital RCA connectors follow the **S/PDIF** (Sony-Philips Digital Interface Format) standards. If these regular audio connectors are used for a digital audio connection, the cable employed should be designed for digital audio.

Two others that are often used for digital hookups include the **BNC** and **Toslink** connectors. The Toslink connector was developed by Toshiba and is the most common optical connector for digital audio. The connectors are usually molded plastic with a fiber-optic glass cable and are more common in audiophile applications. BNC connectors (see Figure 7.15) feature a locking design along the lines of the XLR and are designed for use with 75-ohm cable. Used extensively for years in video applications, BNC connectors are now being developed specifically for audio use with radio's digital equipment.

The newest connectors found in audio studies and equipment come from the increased use of computer equipment in audio production. In fact, many production studios are being designed around **Ethernet** and **FireWire** cables and connectors (see Figure 7.16). The Ethernet or RJ-45 connector looks and operates like a larger version

FIGURE 7.15 Some digital connections require the use of connectors not normally associated with the wiring of audio equipment. (Image courtesy of Neutrik USA.)

of the standard modular telephone jack and is commonly wired with CAT-5 cable (explained later in this section). Many audio console control surfaces are now connected to their I/O frames with this connector, greatly decreasing the amount of wiring necessary for a typical audio studio. Apple Computer gave the IEEE 1394 digital interface the name "FireWire." This tiny four-pin jack or plug is capable of very high speed digital data transfer (400 Mbps) and is finding use in connecting audio editing systems with computers. There is also a larger, six-pin version that carries both data and power. Another connector being used is the **USB** (Universal Serial Bus) which can have either a rectangular (Type A) or square (Type B) jack. This connector

FIGURE 7.16 Connectors common to the computer industry are being used more and more in audio facilities and equipment: (A) Ethernet, (B) FireWire, (C) USB.

FIGURE 7.17 The multipin connector is one type of nonstandard audio connector.

can link audio I/O to computer recording and editing systems and, as mentioned earlier, has been used to directly connect a microphone to a computer.

Instead of using any of the connectors previously mentioned, some equipment manufacturers use a nonstandard connector for the input and output signals. For example, some audio recorders use a multipin connector, similar to the one shown in Figure 7.17, that includes input and output, as well as remote start and cue functions.

Something else in the connector realm that is very handy to have in any audio production studio is a supply of **connector adapters**. These enable you to change a connector from one form to another. Let's say, for example, that you need to connect an RCA output to a phone connector input, but the only cable you can find has an RCA connector at both ends. You can convert one of the RCA connectors to

a phone connector with an adapter. This is a single piece of metal, which in this case houses a female RCA input at one end and a male phone output at the other. When the male RCA connector is inserted into the female end of the adapter, the signal is transferred from the RCA connector to the phone connector, and from there it can go to the phone input. Adapters usually come in most handy in emergency situations when some connecting cable fails, so having a variety of them around is good production practice.

7.14 BALANCED AND UNBALANCED LINES

The standard cable most often used in analog audio production consists of two stranded-wire conductors that are encased

FIGURE 7.18 Typical audio cable is designed for a balanced wiring scheme. (Image courtesy of Cooper Industries, Belden Division.)

in plastic insulation plus a third uninsulated shield wire, all encased in a foil wrapping and another plastic sheathing, as shown in Figure 7.18. For most wiring practices, the inner wires are designated + (red) and − (black); the uninsulated wire is the shield or ground wire. The audio signal is carried on the positive and negative conductors. This type of cable is referred to as three-wire, or **balanced cable**, and often requires the XLR connector, because that is the one designed to connect three wires and is also utilized by many types of audio equipment.

Another type of cable is two-wire, or **unbalanced**. In this configuration, the negative wire also acts as a ground. An unbalanced cable is not as good as a balanced cable, because unwanted audio interference, such as that created by a nearby electric motor, can creep into the two-wire system. Also, balanced cables can be longer than unbalanced cables without encountering degradation of the signal. Finally, equipment that utilizes unbalanced cable generally outputs a lower level signal than equipment that employs balanced wiring. Ideally, balanced and unbalanced cable should not be mixed in the same audio setup, but sometimes this can't be avoided, because different pieces of equipment are built for different cabling.

Wiring digital equipment is going to bring some new cabling concerns. On one hand, because the digital signal carries both stereo channels on a single data stream, wiring digital equipment actually takes less cable than a normal installation. However, except for fairly short runs, ordinary audio cable should not be used for digital applications. As already noted, Toslink connectors are "wired" with fiber-optic cable that easily handles a digital signal. RCA cables used for digital should be 75-ohm impedance and coaxial in design; that is, the signal wire and shield wire are aligned along the same axis. This design usually means that the audio signal wire goes down the center of a surrounding shield. Cables following AES/EBU standards utilize normal XLR wiring configurations, but the actual wire should be 110-ohm impedance. Some digital studio setups today are connecting an audio console interface with an audio engine using CAT-5 wiring. Taken from the computer industry, CAT-5 consists of four twisted pairs of copper wire using an RJ-45 connector. As noted with the connectors, we will continue to see more nontraditional wiring in the audio production studio as digital becomes the standard.

7.15 MICROPHONE, LINE, AND SPEAKER LEVELS

Equipment inputs and outputs can be one of three audio levels: microphone, line, or speaker. You can think of these levels as very low for microphone level (which usually must be preamplified to be used further), normal for line level (most equipment will use line levels), and very high for **speaker levels** (designed to drive a speaker only). Problems arise when various levels are mismatched. For example, if you tried to feed an audio recorder from a speaker-level source, you would probably distort the recording, because the speaker-level source would be too loud, and there is no control to turn it down. Another problem would occur if you fed a microphone-level signal into a line-level input. In this case, the signal would be too low to be usable, because microphone levels must be preamplified to a usable level. Most audio equipment inputs and outputs are clearly designated as microphone, line, or speaker level, and good production practice dictates sending only the proper output to the proper input.

Fortunately, most of the cabling of audio studios and equipment will have been done by the engineer, and all the connections of various pieces of equipment will have been worked out so that everything matches.

7.16 STUDIO TIMERS

Timers have already been mentioned, because many audio consoles have them built-in, but it is not uncommon to find a separate studio timer in the audio production room (see Figure 7.19). Because the timing of production work is so important, an accurate timing device is crucial. Most studio timers are digital, showing minutes and seconds, and include at least start, stop, and reset controls. Many timers can be interfaced with other equipment (such as audio recorders and CD players) so that they automatically reset to zero when that piece of equipment is started. Shorter timers (10 minutes) are usually adequate for audio production work; however, 24-hour timers are often found in the studio.

7.17 TELEPHONE INTERFACE

A simple **telephone interface**, or **telephone coupler** (see Figure 7.20), is a piece of equipment designed to connect telephone lines to broadcast equipment. In a basic configuration, the telephone goes through the interface and comes into the audio console on its own channel (just like a CD player, for example). The caller volume is controlled with that channel's fader, in addition to a caller volume control on the interface. Once a call is taken by the announcer and the interface is switched on, the announcer talks to the caller through the studio microphone, not the telephone instrument (which can be hung up at this point)

FIGURE 7.19   An audio studio timer provides accurate timing for production work. (Image courtesy of Radio Systems.)

FIGURE 7.20   A telephone interface allows mixing an audio signal and a telephone signal. (Image courtesy of Comrex Corporation.)

FIGURE 7.21   This portable IP audio codec can interface with DSL, cable, Wi-Fi, 3G cellular, satellite, POTS, and other communication services. (Image courtesy of Comrex Corporation.)

and hears the caller through the headphones. The interface electronically maintains an isolation between the studio "send" signal and the caller "return" signal, providing a high-quality, clear telephone signal.

In addition, many audio facilities have installed high-quality digital services that give a clearer signal than the older analog systems. One such service is ISDN (Integrated Services Digital Network) which is a communications standard for sending voice or data over telephone line. With the appropriate interface equipment, the telephone becomes just another audio input: it can be easily recorded (and later edited), mixed with other sound sources, and otherwise manipulated for production use.

Another telephone interface is a compact, handheld unit that allows for connection to a number of different wired and wireless data circuits. Although units like the one in Figure 7.21 can connect to standard telephone lines or POTS (Plain Old Telephone Service), it also can send audio over DSL, cable, Wi-Fi, 3G cellular, the Internet, satellite, and other communication networks. This portable IP (Internet Protocol) audio codec makes possible field remotes in situations where setting up a rack of telephone interface equipment just isn't possible.

7.18 OTHER STUDIO ACCESSORIES

Cleaning supplies are common audio studio accessories, many of which have to do with the care of CDs. Simple CD-cleaning cloths and sprays are used to remove dirt, dust, and fingerprint smudges from the CD surface. Other CD accessories include a laser lens cleaner and CD repair kits to remove scratches.

With more and more computer equipment making its way into the audio production studio, cleaning supplies for the monitor screen and keyboard need to be included as another accessory.

In most studios you'll find a supply of empty plastic cases for CDs, known as **jewel boxes** or **jewel cases**. These are needed because many promotional CDs come in paper jackets rather than cases, recordable CDs come in bulk with no cases of any kind, and regular CD cases do break from time to time. Good production practice dictates keeping the CD in its case when not in use to prevent scratches or problems from dust and dirt. Audio production projects often entail burning a CD copy of the final production and having a jewel case for that CD will keep your production work in good playing condition.

PRODUCTION TIP 7A
Proper Vinyl Storage

Most production facilities still have a stack of vinyl LP records around, such as an old sound effects library or a production music bed library. Of course, some radio stations still have a collection of music on records. If you're looking to store your vinyl for the long term, do it the right way. Use a conventional wooden enclosure designed for record storage that is appropriate for the size of your collection. The most important point about vinyl storage is to keep the records absolutely vertical. If you do, the only weight at the edge of the record will be the record itself. If you allow the records to lean to one side or the other, then the weight will be unequal and it could cause the disc to warp. Also avoid storing records in either very dry locations, which will cause the paper record jackets to crumble, or very damp locations, which will cause mildew. A temperature between 65 and 70 degrees Fahrenheit with relative humidity between 30 and 40 percent offers the best environment for storing vinyl.

7.19 CONCLUSION

Often, monitor speakers and studio accessories are given little or no thought. Some production people are concerned only with making sure sound comes out of the speakers and that some accessory items are available. But, as you now understand, the role of the monitor speaker in audio production is not as minor as one might initially believe. And although not every accessory used by the professional has been mentioned in this chapter, you have been introduced to many common items used in the production studio, so you're less likely to run across something that makes you ask, "What's this for?"

Self-Study

1. What components make up a two-way speaker system?

   a) tweeter, woofer, and midrange speaker
   b) tweeter, woofer, and crossover
   c) tweeter and woofer
   d) tweeter, woofer, and two crossovers

2. What is the transducing element of a speaker called?

   a) a tweeter
   b) a crossover
   c) a woofer
   d) a driver

3. Which speaker enclosure design utilizes a tuned port to provide a highly efficient system with a full bass sound?

   a) acoustic suspension
   b) bass reflex
   c) bass boom
   d) sealed box

4. Which individual speaker is designed to reproduce higher frequencies?

   a) woofer
   b) crossover
   c) tweeter
   d) bass reflex

5. For proper stereo sound, the listening angle formed between the speakers and the listener should be 90 degrees.

   a) true
   b) false

6. Which broadcast connector has a guide pin?

   a) RCA
   b) phone
   c) XLR
   d) phono

7. Which is the most practical place to locate monitor speakers in a production room?

   a) near the upper corners, close to the wall
   b) on the counter
   c) not in the room at all, but in an adjoining room
   d) in the middle of the wall, close together

8. Which is true if two speakers are out of phase?

   a) The bass sounds will be generated at the rear of the cones.
   b) Both negative wires will be connected to negative terminals.
   c) Both positive wires will be connected to positive terminals.
   d) The cone of one speaker will be moving out while the cone of the other speaker is moving in.

9. Which broadcast connector is always mono?

    a) phone
    b) miniphone
    c) 1/4-inch phone
    d) RCA

10. Which type of monitor speaker will most likely be found in the audio production studio?

    a) ribbon speaker
    b) electrostatic speaker
    c) dynamic speaker
    d) condenser speaker

11. Which component of a speaker system divides the incoming audio signal into different frequencies and sends the proper frequencies to the appropriate driver?

    a) pigtail leads
    b) tweeter
    c) woofer
    d) crossover

12. Which type of headphone is designed with a porous muff that rests directly on the ear?

    a) closed-cushion headphone
    b) circumaural headphone
    c) earbud
    d) supra-aural headphone

13. Unbalanced audio cables are more susceptible to interference than balanced cables.

    a) true
    b) false

14. Having a high-power, external monitor amplifier in your production studio will allow you to record or broadcast a louder signal than using the internal monitor amp in the audio console.

    a) true
    b) false

15. Small speakers set on short stands, placed left and right of the audio console so the listener hears mostly direct sound at ear level, are known as which type of monitors?

    a) dynamic
    b) near-field
    c) acoustic suspension
    d) out-of-phase

16. When a patch panel is normalled, a patch cord is used to link broadcast equipment assigned to the top row of the panel to the equipment assigned to the bottom row.

    a) true
    b) false

17. Which broadcast connector has a sleeve, ring, and tip?

    a) RCA
    b) Cannon
    c) XLR
    d) phone

18. Which connector is most likely to be used for a patch bay?

    a) phone
    b) miniphone
    c) RCA
    d) multipin connector

19. What is a connector adapter used for?

    a) to transfer a signal in a patch bay
    b) to change a connector from one form to another
    c) to make a balanced line unbalanced
    d) to change a telephone signal to an audio signal

20. Which configuration describes a balanced cable?

    a) two wires
    b) three wires
    c) three ground wires
    d) two ground wires

21. The normal outputs of a CD player produce which level of audio signal?

    a) microphone
    b) line
    c) speaker
    d) none of the above

22. Which production room accessory is used to protect compact discs?

    a) disc wipes
    b) connector adapter
    c) jewel box
    d) timer

23. By convention, male XLR connectors are outputs and female XLR connectors are inputs.

    a) true
    b) false

24. Which production room accessory is used to connect telephone lines directly to broadcast equipment?

    a) audio routing switcher
    b) telephone coupler
    c) patch panel
    d) XLR connector

25. What would be the best type of monitor when you need to use a microphone in the production studio to record a voice over music?

    a) headphones
    b) a tweeter
    c) an acoustic suspension
    d) a bass reflex

ANSWERS

If you answered A to any of the questions:

1a. No. This speaker complement would be in a three-way system. (Reread 7.3.)

2a. No. A tweeter is a speaker designed to produce high frequencies. (Reread 7.2 and 7.3.)

3a. No. The acoustic suspension design is relatively inefficient. (Reread 7.4.)

4a. Wrong. The woofer is designed to reproduce the lower frequencies. (Reread 7.3.)

5a. No. This would put the listener directly in front of one of the speakers, and all the sound would appear to be coming out of that speaker. (Reread 7.6; check Figure 7.6.)

6a. No. (Review Figures 7.11 to 7.14; reread 7.12 and 7.13.)

7a. Correct. This gives the operator good sound and also leaves the counter clear for other equipment.

8a. No. You're confusing this with speaker enclosures. (Reread 7.4 and 7.7.)

9a. No. The phone connector can be either stereo or mono. (Review Figures 7.11 to 7.14; reread 7.12 and 7.13.)

10a. No. Ribbon speakers are generally too exotic in design and too expensive for broadcast use. (Reread 7.2.)

11a. Wrong. You may be confused because this is a part of an individual speaker that receives an input signal, but after it has been divided into the proper frequencies. (Reread 7.3.)

12a. No. This is a headphone with a ring-shaped ear cushion designed to encircle the ear and rest on the head. (Reread 7.10.)

13a. Right. This is a true statement because one wire conducts the signal and also acts as a ground, so unbalanced cables are more likely to pick up unwanted noise.

14a. Wrong. A monitor amp has no relation to the broadcast or recorded signal; it only controls the volume of the monitor speakers. (Reread 7.8.)

15a. Although they may be dynamic speakers, this term usually refers to the speaker driver. There is a better answer. (Reread 7.2 and 7.6.)

16a. Wrong. A normalled patch panel is actually unpatched, so no patch cords are used. (Reread 7.11.)

17a. No. The phono connector only has an outer sleeve and tip. (Review Figures 7.11 to 7.14; reread 7.12 and 7.13.)

18a. Right. A male phone plug is the most likely connector to use with a patch bay.

19a. No. You would be very unlikely to use an adapter with a patch bay. (Reread 7.11 and 7.13.)

20a. No. Two wires would be unbalanced. (Reread 7.14.)

21a. Wrong. Microphone level is a low output level, which must be preamplified to be usable, and is primarily produced by microphones, as the name implies. (Reread 7.15.)

22a. No. You're close, because a disc wipe can be used to clean a CD and dust and fingerprints off the disc, but there's a better answer. (Reread 7.18.)

23a. Correct. This is a true statement.

24a. Wrong. An audio router can be involved in selecting various inputs and outputs, but it can't connect a telephone line by itself. (Reread 7.11 and 7.17.)

25a. Yes. Headphones would prevent feedback and allow the operator to hear the music when the speakers are muted because the microphone is on.

If you answered B to any of the questions:

1b. Correct. These are the basic components of a two-way speaker system.

2b. Wrong. The crossover divides the electrical signals and sends them to the speaker drivers. (Reread 7.2 and 7.3.)

3b. Right. This answer is correct.

4b. No. The crossover is not a speaker but an electronic device for sending various frequencies to different speaker drivers. (Reread 7.3.)

5b. Correct. This is false because an angle of about 60 degrees should be formed between the listener and the speakers for the best stereo sound.

6b. No. (Review Figures 7.11 to 7.14; reread 7.12 and 7.13.)

7b. No. The sound can be good, but the speaker takes up counter space that could be used for something else. (Reread 7.6.)

8b. No. One negative wire connected to a positive terminal would put them out of phase. (Reread 7.7.)

9b. No. The miniphone connector can be either stereo or mono. (Review Figures 7.11 to 7.14; reread 7.12 and 7.13.)

10b. No. Electrostatic speakers are generally too exotic in design and too expensive for broadcast use. (Reread 7.2.)

11b. Wrong. This is a part of a speaker system that reproduces high frequencies. (Reread 7.3.)

12b. No. This is another name for the closed-cushion headphone, which has a ring-shaped ear cushion designed to encircle the ear and rest on the head. (Reread 7.10.)

13b. Wrong. This is a true statement. (Reread 7.14.)

14b. Correct. This is the right response, because monitor amps have no relation to the broadcast or recorded signal.

15b. Yes. Some production people think that the best sound is heard through near-field monitoring.

16b. Yes. When a patch cord is put into a patch panel, it is no longer normalled.

17b. Wrong. Cannon is just another name for the XLR connector. (Review Figures 7.11 to 7.14; reread 7.12 and 7.13.)

18b. No. You're warm but not correct. (Reread 7.11 and 7.12.)

19b. Correct. It transfers the signal so that another form of connector can be used.

20b. Right. There are three wires: positive, negative, and ground.

21b. Right. Line-level outputs are standard for most broadcast production equipment, such as CD players and audio recorders.

22b. No. This has nothing to do with compact discs. (Reread 7.18.)

23b. No. This is a true statement. (Reread 7.12.)

24b. Correct. This is the best answer.

25b. No. This is only part of a monitor speaker. (Reread 7.3 and 7.10.)

If you answered C to any of the questions:

1c. No. You're close though, but you've left out one component. (Reread 7.3.)

2c. No. A woofer is a speaker designed to reproduce low frequencies. (Reread 7.2 and 7.3.)

3c. Wrong. There's no such enclosure design. (Reread 7.4.)

4c. Correct. The tweeter is the speaker designed to reproduce high frequencies.

6c. Right. The XLR jack has a guide pin that prevents it from being connected incorrectly.

7c. No. You couldn't hear them if they were in another room. (Reread 7.6.)

8c. No. One positive wire connected to a negative terminal would put them out of phase. (Reread 7.7.)

9c. No. A 1/4-inch phone or phone connector can be either stereo or mono. (Review Figures 7.11 to 7.14 and reread 7.12 and 7.13.)

10c. Yes. The dynamic speaker is found most often in the production studio.

11c. Wrong. This is a part of a speaker system that reproduces low frequencies. (Reread 7.3.)

12c. No. This is a type of headphone that is designed to fit into the ear. (Reread 7.10.)

15c. Wrong. Although they may be acoustic suspension speakers, this term is usually associated with the speaker enclosure. There is a better answer. (Reread 7.4 and 7.6.)

17c. No. (Review Figures 7.11 to 7.14 and reread 7.12 and 7.13.)

18c. No. (Reread 7.11 and 7.12.)

19c. No. Adapters are not related to balance. (Reread 7.13 and 7.14.)

20c. No. Although there are three wires, they aren't all ground wires. (Reread 7.14.)

21c. No. Speaker level is quite high and is designed to drive a monitor speaker. Most production equipment, like a CD player, would have to have its output signal amplified to reach speaker level. (Reread 7.15.)

22c. Yes. Jewel boxes are plastic protective cases for compact discs.

24c. Wrong. A patch panel could be involved in wiring a telephone line to an audio console, but it can't connect a telephone line by itself. (Reread 7.11 and 7.17.)

25c. No. You're confusing monitors and enclosures. (Reread 7.4 and 7.10.)

If you answered D to any of the questions:

1d. Wrong. Only a single crossover is required in a speaker system. (Reread 7.3.)

2d. Yes. The driver transforms electrical signals into mechanical energy and thus audible sound.

3d. No. This is another name for an acoustic suspension speaker, which is relatively inefficient. (Reread 7.4.)

4d. No. Bass reflex describes a speaker enclosure design, not an individual speaker. (Reread 7.3 and 7.4.)

6d. No. Phono is just another name for the RCA connector. (Review Figures 7.11 to 7.14 and reread 7.12 and 7.13.)

7d. Wrong. This would really limit sound dispersion and any stereo imaging. (Reread 7.6.)

8d. Right. The sounds will be fighting each other when this happens.

9d. Correct. You must use two RCA connectors for stereo, one for each channel.

10d. No. You might be thinking of a microphone; there is no such speaker. (Reread 7.2.)

11d. Correct. A crossover is a network of filters that divides the audio signal into different frequencies and sends it to the proper individual speaker.

12d. Yes. Also known as open-air or hear-through cushion headphones, supra-aural headphones are designed to rest directly on the ear.

15d. No. Out-of-phase speakers are miswired, and this has nothing to do with speaker placement. (Reread 7.6 and 7.7.)

17d. Correct. The miniphone connectors also have them.

18d. No. (Reread 7.11 to 7.13.)

19d. No. There are devices to do this, but they are interfaces, not connector adapters. (Reread 7.13 and 7.17.)

20d. Wrong. (Reread 7.14.)

21d. No. There is a correct answer and this isn't it. (Reread 7.15.)

22d. No. This has nothing to do with a compact disc. (Reread 7.18.)

24d. Wrong. You're quite confused if you chose this answer. (Reread 7.12 and 7.17.)

25d. No. You're confusing monitors with speaker enclosure designs. (Reread 7.4 and 7.10.)

Projects

PROJECT 1

Compare speaker/listener placement.

Purpose

To make you aware of how sound can change as the relationship between speaker and listener changes.

Notes

1. If your studio is too small for you to hear any differences, just indicate that this is the case.
2. The most important thing for your drawings will be to show the relative dimensions of the studio and the position of the speakers.

How to Do the Project

1. Make three sketches of your control room, showing where the speakers are located.
2. On the first drawing, put an *X* where the production person usually sits. On the second drawing, put an *X* at another spot in the control room where you can stand and listen to the monitors. Do the same for the third drawing.
3. Play some music (you can use the music provided on the CD-ROM that accompanies this text) through the monitor speakers, and position yourself in each of the three places where you have placed *X*s. Listen for any differences in the way the music sounds at the three locations.
4. Write a short report detailing how the music sounded at each position.
5. Put your drawings and your report into a packet labeled with your name and the title, "Speaker/Listener Relationship." Give the packet to your instructor to receive credit for this project.

PROJECT 2

Identify common connectors found in the audio production studio.

Purpose

To familiarize yourself with audio connectors and how they are used in the production studio.

Notes

1. Figure 7.22 shows some of the connectors you'll use for this project.
2. If you have trouble identifying them, review Figures 7.12 to 7.14.

How to Do the Project

1. Draw four columns on a sheet of paper and label them "A," "B," "C," and "D." On another sheet of paper, draw three or four more unlabelled columns.
2. Write the correct name for each connector beneath the appropriate letter. If the connector is also often called by another name, include both names.
3. Indicate whether this connector is mono, stereo, or can be both.
4. Now look around your studio and see how many instances you can find where each connector is used and note this on your list. Provide specifics on how the connector is being used. For example, "the output of the CD player uses RCA connectors for the left and right channels."
5. Try to find at least one instance of use for each connecter, but be aware that some connectors may be used numerous times in the studio.
6. On the second sheet, list other types of connectors that you find in your audio studio.

FIGURE 7.22 Common audio connectors.

7. You should be able to identify them from descriptions in the text. Remember to note how they are being used in the studio.

8. Label your forms with your name and the title, "Audio Connectors." Turn it in to your instructor to receive credit for this project.

PROJECT 3

Record a 60-second "concert commercial."

Purpose

To develop your skill in creating a spot for a concert by a recording artist, a type of spot frequently heard on radio.

Notes

1. This project assumes that you have some type of digital audio editor in your studio; however, it can also be accomplished with other equipment.

2. The production incorporates two announcer voices, a music bed, and several "clips" from the artist's songs.

3. You can write the actual script as you want it, but follow the basic concept given here.

4. Exact production directions aren't given in this project, because there are many ways to accomplish the recording and editing.

How to Do the Project

1. Record four or five segments of songs from the artist's biggest hits. Each clip should be about 10 seconds long, but some may be longer and others shorter.

2. You should pick segments of the song that are readily identifiable—usually the chorus or "hook" of the song. Try to end the clip at the end of a phrase so that it isn't just cut off in the middle of a word. Make sure the last clip doesn't fade out, as you want to finish the spot with a strong, natural ending.

3. Start recording each segment a bit before the point you actually want and record a bit beyond the actual end. Mark the true start point and end point using your audio editor and then label and save each segment.

4. Record the announcer lines with both announcers "trading lines." However, the announcers should read the last line together. If your editor has effects capability, add some reverb or a flanging effect to the voices.

5. Your script should use lines similar to this:
Announcer 1: "Appearing live at the Rock Arena, (Artist Name)!"
Announcer 2: "Join (Artist Name) on June 25th for (his/her/their) first-ever concert in (Your City)!"
Announcer 1: "Here's the summer concert you've been waiting for!"
Announcer 2: "Tickets are just $50 and can be purchased at the Rock Arena Box Office or at www.rockarena.com!"
Announcer 1 & 2: "Don't miss this chance to see (Artist Name) in concert at the Rock Arena, June 25th!"

6. Using your audio editor, assemble the spot in a sequence that alternates between announcer tracks and song clips, beginning with Announcer 1's first line.

7. Add a background music bed that will pull the whole spot together. You might edit an instrumental segment from one of the artist's songs to do this, or you might find a music bed from the CD-ROM that fits the style of the other music used in the spot.

8. When you mix the music bed in, you should start with the bed at full volume for a couple of seconds and then fade it under the announcer segments. When the music clips are playing, the music bed should be faded out entirely.

9. Listen to the finished commercial. If it's good enough, prepare it for the instructor.

10. Write your name and "Concert Commercial" on the recording, and turn it in to your instructor to receive credit for this project.

8

SIGNAL PROCESSING EQUIPMENT

8.1 INTRODUCTION

Signal processing, or audio processing, is nothing more than altering the sound of audio—such as an announcer's voice or a CD. We've already seen a few forms of audio processing in the equalization capabilities of some audio consoles and the bass roll-off feature of some microphones, but most signal processing is accomplished either by the use of separate audio components or software. Modern audio equipment, especially audio editing software and digital audio workstations, includes features that allow for **digital signal processing (DSP)** of the sound signal and in many of today's audio production situations, any audio processing is accomplished in a postproduction environment.

Several signal processing devices will refer to the terms "wet" and "dry." The incoming, or unprocessed, audio signal is considered a dry signal, and the outgoing audio signal that has been processed is considered the wet signal.

This chapter focuses on the capability of audio editing software to signal process and also looks at other commonly used electronic audio processors. However, be aware that the amount of equipment available for signal processing in any production facility can vary widely, from essentially none to a veritable smorgasbord of electronic black boxes or software effects to choose from.

8.2 WHY USE SIGNAL PROCESSING EFFECTS?

Signal processing usually involves the manipulation of the frequency response (tonal balance), stereo imaging, or dynamic range of the sound signal. As noted earlier in the text, frequency response refers to the range of all frequencies (pitches) that an audio component can reproduce and we can hear, that is, around 20 Hz (low bass) to 20 kHz (high

treble). Imaging refers to the perceived space between, behind, and in front of monitor speakers and how we hear individual sounds within that plane. Dynamic range refers to the audible distance between the softest sounds that can be heard over noise and the loudest sounds that can be produced before distortion is heard. Most audio processing used in the production studio is to accomplish one of three effects: to alter recordings to suit individual taste, to create special audio effects, or to cut down on various forms of audio noise.

Audio processing can be used to alter the sound of a CD (or any music) or an announcer's voice to suit an individual's taste, and changing the tone with an equalizer is one of the most common kinds of audio processing. For some production work, you may need to accentuate the bass of an announcer's vocal track. Boosting frequency settings between 50 and 100 Hz certainly would help to do so. Perhaps a background music bed seems overly "bright," so you attenuate frequencies in the 10- to 18-kHz range to lessen their impact. As another example, reverb is sometimes added to an announcer's microphone to give it a more "live" sound or to simulate a different acoustic environment. Remember, however, that audio processing is a subjective process and what sounds great to one person may not sound so great to another. However, some specific adjustments like those just mentioned would usually be noticed as a positive improvement. The key to good signal processing is to use any effect moderately and to experiment to find just the right sound you're looking for.

Another reason for using signal processing is to achieve a special audio effect. For example, cutting down most of the lower frequencies below 1 kHz leaves a very tinny-sounding vocal that might be perfect as a robot voice. You could create an effect that approximates an old-fashioned, poor-quality telephone sound by boosting the frequency bands at 640 and 800 Hz and cutting the frequency bands on either side of this range. Many such effects are achieved by experimenting with various settings for the equalizer.

Using a flanger effect (where one audio signal is mixed with an identical signal that is slightly delayed a continuously changing amount of time) can give a voice an otherworldly sound, and a chorusing effect can easily make one voice appear to be several.

Audio processing is also used to deal with unwanted noise such as hiss, one of the common forms of noise in production work. **Hiss** describes a high-frequency noise problem inherent in the analog recording process. Hiss sounds exactly as you would imagine and is heard by the human ear within the frequency range of 2 to 8 kHz. Using an equalizer to cut or turn down the frequency settings closest to this range can attenuate hiss to a less noticeable level. An audio filter is sometimes used to combat hum, which is another form of noise in production work. **Hum** is a low-frequency problem associated with leakage of the 60-hertz AC electrical current into the audio signal. A poor or broken ground in any part of the electrical circuit can cause hum, and it, too, sounds exactly as you would imagine. Attenuating frequencies right around 60 Hz would lessen the problem.

However, even with careful adjustment, it's often impossible to eliminate noise entirely. Remember, you also affect the program signal as you equalize, so any audio processing is usually a compromise between less noise and a still-discernible signal. Digital recording technique has lessened hiss and hum problems, but in audio production you are often working with prerecorded audio that may already have such inherent problems.

More audio processing uses will become apparent later in this chapter as we look at the various signal processing devices.

8.3 SOFTWARE OR BLACK BOX SIGNAL PROCESSING

As mentioned previously, probably the majority of audio processing today is accomplished with software programs. Computer-based recording and mixing programs, like Adobe Audition or Digidesign Pro Tools, feature the ability to utilize a multitude of audio processing effects, including equalization, echo chamber, hiss reduction, chorusing, pitch shifting, reverb, flanging, and noise reduction, to mention only a few.

The basic process with most audio editing programs is to select the audio you wish to process and then select the effect you wish to apply. Usually, you are able to preview the effect to make sure it is doing what you wish and, in most cases, you will be able to adjust numerous parameters about the effect to fine-tune and get the precise sound you're trying to achieve.

Originally, signal processing was accomplished with electronic black boxes or individual units designed to produce one particular effect. So if you wanted to add reverb, you needed a reverb unit, and if you wanted to change the tone of a voice, you needed to have a graphic or parametric

equalizer. The audio signal was routed through the device and then to a recorder, public address system, or to be broadcast over the air. Each device was generally housed in a single rack unit, and most featured a number of controls that would allow the operator to adjust the effect and achieve the exact sound desired. Studios might employ a whole rack of various boxes to have available the audio processing that might be required; however, eventually, multi-effects boxes were developed to offer, as the name implies, several effects in one unit.

Software and black box devices continue to coexist, and there is no real agreement over which approach is better. In fact, you'll find proponents of both who will argue long and hard that their systems work best.

8.4 EQUALIZERS

One of the most commonly used signal processors is the equalizer. The term **EQ** refers to the general process of equalization when an equalizer is used to cut or boost the signal level of specific frequencies; essentially, it is just **tone control**. You're familiar with bass and treble tone controls, because most stereo systems have them. When you turn up the treble, you increase the volume of the higher frequencies. Unfortunately, a treble control turns up *all* the higher frequencies. An equalizer, on the other hand, offers greater flexibility and allows the operator to differentiate, for example, between lower high frequencies and upper high frequencies, and to make different adjustments to each.

Most equalizers found in the audio production studio are passive or **unity-gain** devices. The sound signal that has passed through the equalizer's circuits is no stronger or weaker overall than the input sound signal was. In other words, if the processor's controls are set at zero, they should have no processing effect on the incoming audio signal. Of course, if the signal is processed by increasing the level of several different frequencies, then the overall volume of the outgoing signal will be louder than the unprocessed signal. The two main kinds of equalizers found in audio production are the graphic equalizer and the parametric equalizer.

8.5 THE GRAPHIC EQUALIZER

The **graphic equalizer** is more common and derives its name from the rough graph of a sound's altered **frequency response** formed by the slider control settings on the equalizer's front faceplate (see Figures 8.1 and 8.2). A digital graphic equalizer may have a "select" button for each band and "raise" and "lower" buttons to adjust the volume of each band. As shown in Figure 8.1, you'll still see the frequency response curve formed by your settings, but on multiple LED bar-graph meters instead of the positions of the slide controls.

FIGURE 8.1 The graphic equalizer, whether digital or analog, can boost or cut the volume at various frequencies and provide a visual representation of the EQ being provided. (Image courtesy of Alesis.)

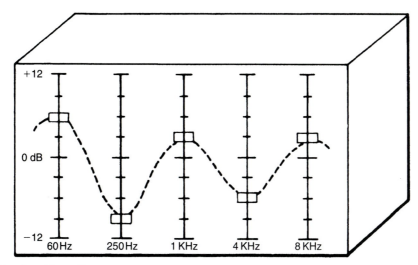

FIGURE 8.2 A simple 5-band graphic equalizer.

Graphic equalizers come in different designs, but all of them divide the frequency response range into separate frequency bands, arranged left to right in order of increasing frequency. A complex design would be a stereo 13-octave equalizer with 31 controls; a simple mono 10-band octave equalizer would feature ten controls on 1-octave intervals. If the first band of a full-octave equalizer was at 31 hertz, the second would be at or near 62 hertz, the third at 125 hertz, and so on. Obviously, the more bands you have to work with, the greater tone control you have, but it also becomes harder to correctly manipulate the equalizer. Most broadcast-quality graphic equalizers feature 15 or 31 band channels. Each band has a volume control that's "off" in a middle or flat position and can move up to increase ("boost") or down to attenuate ("cut") the volume at that particular frequency. This volume range varies, but +12 to −12, or 12 decibels of boost or cut, is a common configuration.

To understand equalization techniques, look at the simple 5-band equalizer shown in Figure 8.2. Note how the slider setting would demark a frequency response graph, indicating how the original sound was being manipulated. Typical equalizing procedure starts with all bands set "flat" or at the mid-position. Then each band is adjusted by increasing or decreasing the volume of various frequencies. If we were playing rock music through this equalizer, the boost at 60 hertz would give the drums extra punch; cutting back at 250 hertz would help minimize bass boom. The increase at 1 kilohertz would add brilliance to the voices, and the slight decrease at 4 kilohertz would

minimize the harshness of the sound. Finally, the boost at 8 kilohertz would add presence to the highs. There is no one correct setting for an equalizer, and we could just as easily have had all different settings and yet produced an excellent sound. There are, however, settings that could make the sound very poor, and the production operator needs to beware of altering any sound too much. By adding a little here and taking away a little there, you can usually improve any poor-sounding audio.

As previously noted, audio editing software often includes signal processing capability. Figure 8.3 shows the screen for Adobe Audition's graphic equalizer, which allows you to select a 10-, 20-, or 30-band unit. Clicking on the virtual slider control lets you cut or boost the volume of the specific frequency. The position of the sliders and the top portion of the screen give a visual representation of what is happening to the audio signal. Equalization procedures are exactly the same as with any other graphic equalizer. Clicking on the Preview button lets you hear the equalized or "wet" signal and actually change settings as it is playing back. When you have the sound you're looking for, click on the OK button and the original audio will be changed according to the EQ settings.

8.6 THE PARAMETRIC EQUALIZER

The **parametric equalizer** gives the operator more flexibility with three basic controls: one to choose the actual center frequency to work on, one to control the bandwidth of frequencies selected, and one to control the volume of the specified frequencies. In other words, the parametric equalizer is used for finer control of the frequencies within a sound than the broad control offered by graphic equalizers. For example, the 5-band graphic equalizer mentioned previously had fixed frequency bands at 60, 250, 1,000, 4,000, and 8,000 hertz, but a parametric equalizer allows the operator to select an exact frequency. For example, instead of a set band at 1,000 hertz, you might choose a band at 925 hertz or 1,200 hertz. If the graphic equalizer were increased at 1 kilohertz, not only would that frequency get a boost, but so would the adjacent frequencies according to a preset bandwidth determined by the manufacturer (perhaps from 500 to 1,500 hertz).

Parametric equalizers allow the operator to adjust that bandwidth. For example, still using the 1-kilohertz center frequency, the parametric equalizer operator could select a bandwidth of 800 to 1,200 hertz or a narrower bandwidth of 950 to 1,050 hertz to be equalized. Most equalizers also have a bypass switch that allows the sound signal to pass through the equalizer unaffected, or not equalized at all, so you can compare the original sound with the equalized sound. Figure 8.4 shows one type of parametric equalizer.

8.7 AUDIO FILTERS

An audio filter is a simple type of equalizer which affects a whole range of the audio signal. For example, a **low cut filter** cuts, or eliminates, frequencies below a certain point, say 500 hertz. Instead of a normal frequency response of 20 to 20,000 hertz, once the signal goes through this filter, its response is 500 to 20,000 hertz. A **low pass filter** allows frequencies below a certain point to pass or remain unaffected. In other words, a cut filter and a pass filter are opposites in their actions. A **band pass filter** eliminates frequencies except for a specified band. It has a low cut point (maybe 1,000 hertz) and a high cut point (maybe 3,000 hertz). When a signal is sent through this filter, only that portion of the signal between the two cut points is heard. A **band reject filter** is just the opposite of the band pass filter in that it allows frequencies to pass except for a specified frequency range. A **notch filter** is a special filter that completely eliminates an extremely narrow range of frequencies or one individual frequency, such as AC hum at 60 Hz.

Usually filters are used to correct a specific problem. Of course, filters eliminate both the problem *and* the actual program signal, so careful use is necessary to maintain a good audio signal after filtering has taken place. Figure 8.5 shows

FIGURE 8.3 The graphic equalizer screen from an audio editing program. (Adobe screenshot reprinted with permission from Adobe Systems Incorporated.)

FIGURE 8.5 Digital editing software can replicate an analog filter. (Adobe screenshot reprinted with permission from Adobe Systems Incorporated.)

FIGURE 8.4 A parametric equalizer offers greater control of various frequencies within a sound than the graphic equalizer. (Image courtesy of Rane Corporation.)

a digital audio editing program that has a filtering function. This screen illustrates the use of a low pass filter so that low frequencies are allowed to pass through the filter unaltered. The cutoff point has been set at 661.5 hertz, so the high frequencies above this point are rejected or removed from the original audio. The graph gives a visual representation of what is happening to the audio.

8.8 NOISE REDUCTION

We've mentioned the problem of noise inherent in the production process, especially with recording. Signal processing devices, known as **noise-reduction** systems, have been devised to help prevent noise. Note that these electronic devices can't get rid of noise that already exists; their job is to prevent noise from being *added* to a recording. Digital recording does not need to use noise-reduction devices because the noises they are meant to eliminate are ones inherent in the analog recording process. There are two systems commonly used with analog recording: Dolby and dbx®. Dolby noise-reduction is commonly built into cassette and reel-to-reel recorders and you'll find the dbx® Type III noise-reduction circuitry in some of their EQ products. Both systems are **companders**—their general operation is to compress (reduce the dynamic range of) an audio signal during recording and then expand the signal during playback—but they are not compatible systems.

There are several **Dolby** noise-reduction systems in use in recording studios, broadcast stations, home stereo equipment, and movie theaters, but the Dolby B, C, S, and SR noise-reduction systems are most likely to be found in production equipment. The two-part Dolby process consists of encoding the program signal before recording begins and noise can be introduced into the recording. In the second part of the process, during playback decoding, levels that were increased are decreased to their original levels, and any noise introduced during the recording process is also reduced so it now seems much lower in relation to the program level. Depending on the system employed, up to 25 decibels of noise reduction can be attained using the Dolby process. As with all other signal processing equipment, careful use is required to achieve the results the operator wants. Dolby SR (for spectral recording) and Dolby S are more sophisticated noise-reduction systems from Dolby Laboratories. Dolby S (derived from the SR system) is designed to be an improved version of the Dolby B and Dolby C systems.

Unlike Dolby, the **dbx®** system compresses the signal over the entire frequency range during recording. Noise buildup usually introduced in the recording process is dramatically reduced (noise reduction of 40 decibels can be attained); however, as with all noise-reduction systems, any noise present in the original audio signal is not reduced.

Although digital audio recording will not generally introduce noise, most software programs have features for noise reduction so that audio recorded outside the system and then brought into it can be improved. For example, a sound effect or piece of music from a vinyl record may contain pops and clicks from excessive use. Some software programs include a feature that would eliminate this noise by first analyzing the audio to determine where the pops are and then repairing or reconstructing the audio at that point. There may be several parameters to set, and a bit of trial and error is usually required to get the correct settings, but salvaging just the right piece of music may be critical to a specific production project. Other noise-reduction features may help eliminate or reduce tape hiss, 60-cycle AC hum, microphone background noise, or other noise problems heard in the audio.

Generally speaking, the more consistent the noise you want to remove is, the easier it will be to dispose of. For example, the consistent hum of a refrigerator is easier to remove than the sound of traffic going by, as each car engine will have its own frequency. Some noise-reduction software allows you to sample a short section of unwanted background noise, and then remove the sound from a longer section of audio. Using this process, the hum of a refrigerator behind a conversation can virtually be eliminated very simply, automatically, and without having to experiment with frequencies. But there is always the chance that parts of the desired signal will be mistaken for refrigerator noise and be eradicated as well.

However, as the noise is embedded in the audio you want to keep, noise reduction is a trade-off between how much noise level you can decrease and how much loss of audio quality you can afford. Still, depending upon the sophistication of the software program you may have available, there is a great deal that can be done to improve a noisy audio signal.

8.9 REVERB AND DIGITAL DELAY

A signal processor that affects the **imaging** of sound is the reverberation unit, probably the second most common type of processor. It manipulates the sound signal to artificially produce the sound of different acoustic environments. As we've mentioned, reverb is reflected sound that has bounced off two or more surfaces. Sound heard (or produced) in a small studio "sounds" different than sound produced in a large hall or auditorium, and reverb is the main characteristic that audibly creates the difference.

The modern production studio is likely to have a **digital reverb** unit that is either an electronic device (see Figure 8.6) or a feature of an audio editing program. The original signal is fed into the unit and electronically processed to achieve the reverb effect; then the altered signal is sent out of the unit. Besides a black box digital reverb, audio editing software may also have reverb, echo, or delay functions. Figure 8.7 shows a reverb screen from one audio editing program. In addition to building your own reverb sound by

FIGURE 8.6 A digital reverb unit can simulate various acoustic environments by altering the "image" of the sound. (Image courtesy of Yamaha Corporation.)

FIGURE 8.7 A digital reverb program, within audio editing software, can have various preset acoustic environments, ranging from a coat closet to a concert hall. (Adobe screenshot reprinted with permission from Adobe Systems Incorporated.)

setting various parameters, note that several preset acoustic environments can be chosen, such as a medium-sized auditorium or a tiled bathroom shower. Merely selecting the appropriate preset and clicking on the OK button will transform the original audio so that it sounds as if it had been recorded in that environment with the corresponding reverb effect.

A **digital delay** unit can be used in both the production studio and the on-air control room. As its name implies, this signal processor actually takes the audio signal, holds it, and then releases it to allow the signal to be used further. The time the signal is held or delayed can be varied from fractions of a second to several seconds. Although there are analog delay units, most systems are digital, and if the incoming signal is analog, it is converted from its analog form to digital for processing and back to analog after processing. In a radio station on-air studio, a delay unit (see Figure 8.8) is often used in conjunction with phone-in talk shows. The program signal is sent through the delay unit to provide approximately a 7-second delay before it is sent to the transmitter. If something is said by a caller that should not be broadcast, the operator has time to "kill" the offending utterance before it is actually broadcast. The delay system will dump the delayed signal and revert to the live signal to do this. Listeners who call a program using a delay system are asked to turn their home radio down if they're talking to an announcer on-air, because the sound they hear on the radio is the delayed sound and not the words they are actually saying into the telephone. It's extremely

difficult to carry on a conversation when you can hear both the live and delayed sounds.

In the audio production studio, delay units are used to create special effects similar to reverb. Set for an extremely short delay, the units can create an effect that sounds like a doubled voice or even a chorus of voices. These types of effects are most commonly included in a multi-effects processor, which will be mentioned shortly, but also may be available as one of the special effects of digital audio software programs.

PRODUCTION TIP 8A
World Wide Web Effects

The Internet can be a source for some interesting DSP effects. This isn't pirated software, but legitimate programs that are available for free or nominal cost. Most are plug-ins that you can add to your digital audio software program, but some you can just install on your computer on their own.

One free program you might want to check out is Izotope's Vinyl. It's a DirectX plug-in that works fine with Adobe Audition, but it's also available in a few other Windows-based formats. Best of all, it's free. You'll need to go to their web site at www.izotope.com and click on the "Vinyl" icon. Then you'll have to supply some registration information that will allow them to email you back the necessary install information. Once you've completed the download, you'll need the install information the first time you use the plug-in with your audio software.

Vinyl is a vinyl record simulation. It lets you take an audio file and process it so it sounds like it is being played back on a record player. There are several presets, and you can also make a number of parameter adjustments, including adding hum (electrical noise) or turntable rumble (mechanical noise). You can add dust and scratches to your recording, as well as warp to give you that great off-speed or off-center "wow" sound. As with most signal processing devices, you'll have to experiment to find the right sound you're looking for, but Izotope provides a handy "10 Steps to Lo-Fi" help screen to get you started. There are, no doubt, other programs on the Web, so some search time might be beneficial. However, remember that one small effect used as part of a production can be very effective, but too many special effects take away from their uniqueness.

FIGURE 8.8 A delay unit is often used in conjunction with radio talk shows to prevent material that should not be broadcast from going out over the air. (Image courtesy of Eventide, Inc.)

8.10 DYNAMIC RANGE

When we mention **dynamic range** in an audio production context, we're referring to the range of volumes of sound that equipment can handle. This intensity of a sound is measured in decibels (dB). One **decibel** represents the minimum difference in volume that we can hear, but a change of 3 decibels is often necessary before we actually do perceive a difference in volume. The dynamic range goes from 0 decibels at the **threshold of hearing** to 120+ decibels at the **threshold of pain**. A whisper is around 20 decibels, normal conversation is near 60 decibels, and shouting is about 80 decibels. Average music-listening levels are between 30 and 80 decibels, but some rock concerts have been measured above 110 decibels. Dynamic range also relates the volume of one signal to another, such as signal to noise or input to output.

We should note that dynamic range is measured on a logarithmic scale. For example, to hear one audio signal twice as loudly as another, you would have to increase the volume of one by 10 decibels in relation to the other. A 60-decibel dynamic range was once considered quite adequate for high-quality production equipment; today's digital equipment, however, offers an increased dynamic range and a 90-plus decibel range is now common.

Why would you want to reduce dynamic range? Even modern equipment can have trouble handling extremes in dynamic range. If equipment is set to handle typical volume levels, when extremely loud levels are encountered the equipment overloads. If everything is set to handle extremely loud levels, when you hit a quiet section nobody can hear it.

8.11 COMPRESSORS, EXPANDERS, AND NOISE GATES

The compressor is one of the two most common signal processing devices used to affect the dynamic range of the audio signal; the limiter is the other. Although they are most often used to process an audio signal between the studio and the transmitter, they are also used in the production room to process the signal before it's sent to an audio recorder.

The **compressor** operates as an automatic volume control and reduces the dynamic range of an audio signal put through this unit. In the contemporary production studio, the compressor is used if the audio signal is too loud to automatically lower it. Several adjustments on the compressor determine its actual operation. The threshold of compression is the setting of the level of signal needed to turn on the compressor. As long as the audio signal stays below this point, the compressor doesn't do anything, so the compressor really needs to work only some of the time. If the input is too low, the threshold of compression will never be reached, and if the input is too high, the compressor will severely restrict the dynamic range. The compression ratio determines how hard the compressor works or how much it will turn down audio above the threshold. A ratio of 5 to 1 means that if the level of the incoming signal increases to 10 times its current level, the output of that signal from the compressor will only double.

Compressors also have settings for attack time (how quickly volume is reduced once it exceeds the threshold) and release time (how quickly a compressed signal is allowed to return to its original volume). The release time adjustment is very important because too fast a setting can create an audible pumping sound as the compressor releases, especially if there is a loud sound immediately followed by a soft sound or a period of silence.

An **expander** is essentially the opposite of a compressor and is used to expand the dynamic range of an audio signal. Today's expanders are set to operate only below a threshold level on low-volume audio so they make quiet passages quieter. As was noted earlier, the process of noise reduction uses compressor and expander technology. A **noise gate** is a type of expander used to reduce noise by turning the level of an audio signal that falls below a set threshold point way down. For example, it could be set so that pauses in a piece of music would be attenuated to "zero" volume so that background noise would not be recorded. Audio editing software often includes some type of dynamics processor that can emulate stand-alone compressors, limiters, expanders, and noise gates.

8.12 LIMITERS

A **limiter** is a form of compressor with a large compression ratio of 10 to 1 or more. Once a threshold level is reached, a limiter doesn't allow the signal to increase anymore. Regardless of how high the input signal becomes, the output

FIGURE 8.9 The compressor/limiter is used to process the dynamic range of an audio signal. (Image courtesy of Symetrix, Inc.)

FIGURE 8.10 Flanging—a psychedelic, swooshing sound—is a phase-shifted, time-delay effect easily created with audio editing software. (Adobe screenshot reprinted with permission from Adobe Systems Incorporated.)

remains at its preset level. If they're adjustable, attack and release times on limiters should be quite short. Both the limiter and the compressor can be rather complicated to adjust properly. Too much compression of the dynamic range makes an audio signal that can be tiresome to listen to, and pauses or quiet passages in the audio signal are subject to the pumping problem mentioned earlier.

Because they're often associated with the transmitter only, compressors and limiters are usually the domain of the engineer. If you do have access to them in the production facility, it may take some experimenting to get the kind of processing that you're looking for because there are no standard settings for signal processing devices. Figure 8.9 shows a system that combines both a compressor and limiter in a single unit.

8.13 OTHER SIGNAL PROCESSORS

A **flanger** is another processor for producing a specific special effect. This unit electronically combines an original signal with a slightly delayed signal in such a way as to cause an out-of-phase frequency response that creates a filtered swishing sound. Flanging, also called phasing, was originally accomplished by sending an audio signal to two reel-to-reel tape recorders and then physically slowing down one of the reels by holding a hand on the flange, or hub, of the reel. As the two signals went in and out of sync with each other, the audio would cancel and reinforce, creating a psychedelic phase-shift effect. Figure 8.10 shows the flanger screen from an audio editing software program. The Original–Delayed slider on the top left side of the screen controls the mix between the dry (original) audio and the wet (flanged) signal. Portions of both must be mixed to achieve the effect of slightly delaying and phasing the signals. Like with many of the other signal processing effects using audio software, there are several other adjustments that can be made to create just the effect you're looking for, or you can just choose a preset effect by clicking on one of the descriptive names on the right side of the screen.

A **de-esser** is an electronic processor designed to control the sibilant sounds without affecting other parts of the sound signal. Many microphone processor units include a section that is essentially a de-esser. A **stereo synthesizer**, as the name implies, is a processor that takes a mono audio signal (input) and simulates a stereo signal (output).

Some processors use a form of delay to provide separation between the left and right channel outputs; others use a form of filtering to send certain frequencies to one channel and other frequencies to the other channel to provide a synthetic stereo effect.

8.14 MULTI-EFFECTS PROCESSORS

Rather than using several individual signal processor "boxes," many signal processing devices are designed so that they perform more than one function—that is, more digital effects can be created from a single black box. For example, Eventide, Yamaha, and Lexicon all provide popular signal processing tools for the production studio (see Figure 8.11). These devices offer a variety of audio effects in one unit, including the ability to alter the pitch of an incoming audio signal, time compression and expansion, delay, natural reverb effects, flanging, time reversal, and repeat capabilities. Any production person should find it enjoyable to experiment with the variety of creative effects that can be produced with a multi-effects processor.

As we've noted throughout this chapter, another form of multi-effects processor is the digital audio workstation or audio editing software. In addition to offering improved editing capabilities, most workstations or software programs have provisions for adding special effects to the audio signal. Often you can add an effect to the audio by mouse-clicking on a preset effects button. Otherwise, you may have to set various parameters to create the signal processing effect that you desire, and that can range from being fairly easy to extremely complex. Regardless of this fact, editing software or workstation systems are still, in many cases, simpler to set up and operate than their black box counterparts.

FIGURE 8.11 This multi-effects processor, an Eventide Harmonizer, puts several signal processing effects in a single "black box." (Image courtesy of Eventide, Inc.)

8.15 CONCLUSION

This chapter is not intended to be a complete guide to signal processing equipment. There are other units in use in production facilities, and there are other effects available through audio editing software programs. Neither is this chapter designed to make you a professional operator of such equipment. What is intended is that you become aware of a number of the more common processors and that you have an understanding of their basic purpose. The actual operation of most of this equipment will take some trial-and-error work in your production facility. Use signal processing in moderation, and bear in mind that a lot of great production has been produced using no signal processing equipment at all.

Self-Study

1. The equalizer processes an audio signal by altering which of the following?

    a) volume
    b) imaging
    c) dynamic range
    d) frequency response

2. An audio signal that has been equalized would be called a "dry" signal.

    a) true
    b) false

3. Which type of equalizer can select an exact center frequency and bandwidth as well as alter the volume at that frequency and bandwidth?

    a) graphic
    b) parametric
    c) dielectric
    d) full-octave, 10-band

4. What type of filter would most likely be used to attenuate or eliminate a 60-hertz hum in a recording?

    a) low pass filter
    b) band pass filter
    c) notch filter
    d) low cut filter

5. The 60-hertz hum mentioned in Question 4 could also have been eliminated by the use of either Dolby or dbx® noise reduction.

    a) true
    b) false

6. Which signal processor affects the imaging of a sound?

    a) equalizer
    b) noise-reduction unit
    c) de-esser
    d) reverb unit

7. How could you create a tinny voice using signal processing equipment?

    a) Cut out most of the lower frequencies.
    b) Cut out most of the higher frequencies.
    c) Eliminate the EQ.
    d) Increase compression.

8. Which noise-reduction system is most likely to be found in the audio production studio?

    a) Dolby A
    b) Dolby S
    c) Type I
    d) Flanger

9. Which is a true statement about the Dolby system of noise reduction?

    a) Volumes of certain frequencies are increased during recording and decreased during playback.
    b) The dbx® is increased with a calibrated tone so that it attains the level of 30 decibels.
    c) All frequencies pass through, except ones that have been preset by the notch filter.
    d) Once a threshold level is reached, the signal isn't allowed to increase any more.

10. A noise gate is which type of signal processing equipment?

    a) limiter
    b) equalizer
    c) expander
    d) imager

11. Which is true about a compressor?

    a) usually has a compression ratio of 10 to 1
    b) lowers a signal that's too loud and raises one that's too soft
    c) doesn't operate unless it's connected to a digital delay unit
    d) produces an out-of-phase, filtered, swishing sound

12. Any signal processing equipment that's labeled a unity-gain device would amplify all frequencies of the signal going through that equipment an equal amount.

    a) true
    b) false

13. Which of the following is *not* a type of Dolby noise reduction?

    a) Dolby S
    b) Dolby B
    c) Dolby C
    d) Dolby D

14. Which signal processing device is most likely to offer a variety of effects, such as pitch change, time compression, reverb, and flanging?

    a) dbx® Graphic Equalizer
    b) Eventide Broadcast Delay
    c) dbx® Compressor/Limiter
    d) Eventide Harmonizer

15. Which signal processing device inputs a mono signal and outputs a simulated stereo signal?

    a) digital delay
    b) band cut filter
    c) flanger
    d) stereo synthesizer

16. Today's digital equipment offers an increased dynamic range, and a range of how many decibels is now common?

    a) 153
    b) 90
    c) 60
    d) 3

17. A digital audio workstation usually includes digital reverb and delay effects but rarely any other type of signal processing capability.

    a) true
    b) false

18. Which graphic equalizer setting would most likely be used to add "brilliance" to an announcer's voice?

   a) boost at 60 Hz
   b) cut at 250 Hz
   c) boost at 1 kHz
   d) cut at 8 kHz

19. Which signal processor is designed to help control sibilance in an announcer's voice?

   a) compressor
   b) limiter
   c) de-esser
   d) digital reverb

20. Which of the following is the opposite of a compressor?

   a) equalizer
   b) expander
   c) flanger
   d) limiter

ANSWERS

If you answered A to any of the questions:

1a.   No. You're headed in the right direction. Equalizers do increase or attenuate volumes at specific frequencies, but they do this to alter another sound characteristic. (Reread 8.1, 8.2, and 8.4.)

2a.   No. A dry audio signal is an unprocessed signal. (Reread 8.1.)

3a.   No. Center frequencies and bandwidths are usually preset on graphic equalizers. (Reread 8.5 and 8.6.)

4a.   No. This type of filter allows lower frequencies to pass and would not eliminate noise at 60 hertz. (Reread 8.7.)

5a.   No. Noise-reduction units, regardless of brand name, can't eliminate noise that already exists in a recording. They only prevent noise during the recording process. (Reread 8.8.)

6a.   No. Equalizers affect frequency response. (Reread 8.2, 8.4, and 8.9.)

7a.   Correct. Cutting the bass will give a tinny sound.

8a.   No. (Reread 8.8.)

9a.   Correct. It's a two-step process.

10a.   No. In a way it is the opposite. (Reread 8.11 and 8.12.)

11a.   Wrong. That's a limiter. (Reread 8.11 and 8.12.)

12a.   No. A unity-gain device doesn't amplify the overall level of the incoming signal at all. (Reread 8.4.)

13a.   Wrong. This is one of the Dolby noise-reduction systems. (Reread 8.8.)

14a.   No. This doesn't really exist. It's a mixture of signal processing. (Reread 8.5, 8.8, and 8.13.)

15a.   No. You may be thinking about a stereo synthesizer that uses a form of delay. (Reread 8.9 and 8.14.)

16a.   No. You may be getting this confused with the threshold of pain. (Reread 8.10.)

17a.   No. Most digital audio workstations have multi-effect capability. (Reread 8.1 and 8.13.)

18a.   No. This would punch up the bass. (Reread 8.5.)

19a.   Wrong. This is a form of automatic volume control used to affect dynamic range. (Reread 8.11 and 8.14.)

20a.   No. You might be confusing frequency response and dynamic range. (Reread 8.2 to 8.6, 8.10, and 8.11.)

If you answered B to any of the questions:

1b. No. Imaging can be affected by other signal processors. (Reread 8.1, 8.2, and 8.4.)

2b. Correct. This is the right response.

3b. Yes. The parametric equalizer gives the operator the greatest control over the EQ process.

4b. No. This type of filter is usually used to allow a range of frequencies to pass, not to eliminate a single frequency. (Reread 8.7.)

5b. Yes, because you can't eliminate existing noise with noise-reduction units.

6b. No. Noise-reduction units affect dynamic range. (Reread 8.8 and 8.9.)

7b. No. That is where the tinny sound would be. (Reread 8.2.)

8b. Correct. It's one of the newer common ones.

9b. No. (Reread 8.8.)

10b. No. A noise gate has nothing to do with frequencies. (Reread 8.4 and 8.11.)

11b. Yes. It lowers and raises signals in that manner.

12b. Yes. Unity-gain devices don't amplify the overall level of the incoming signal.

13b. Wrong. Dolby B is a common noise-reduction system found on cassette recorders. (Reread 8.8.)

14b. No. This isn't correct. Delay is a single type of audio processing, often used with radio talkshows. (Reread 8.9 and 8.13.)

15b. No. You may be thinking about a stereo synthesizer, which uses a form of filtering. (Reread 8.7 and 8.14.)

16b. Correct. This is the right response.

17b. Yes. Most digital audio workstations have multi-effect capability.

18b. No. This would minimize bass boominess. (Reread 8.5.)

19b. Wrong. This is a form of automatic volume control used to affect dynamic range. (Reread 8.12 and 8.14.)

20b. Correct. Because the expander increases dynamic range, it is the opposite of a compressor.

If you answered C to any of the questions:

1c. No. Dynamic range can be affected by other signal processors. (Reread 8.1, 8.2, and 8.4.)

3c. Wrong. There's no such thing. (Reread 8.5 and 8.6.)

4c. Correct. This type of filter allows all frequencies to pass except a specified one, which we could specify at 60 hertz to eliminate the hum.

6c. Wrong. A de-esser is an electronic processor designed to control sibilant sounds. (Reread 8.9 and 8.14.)

7c. Wrong. That wouldn't really be possible. (Reread 8.2.)

8c. No. (Reread 8.8.)

9c. No. You are confusing this with filters. (Reread 8.7 and 8.8.)

10c. Correct. A noise gate is a type of expander.

11c. No. They have nothing to do with each other. (Reread 8.9 and 8.11.)

13c. Wrong. Dolby C is a common noise-reduction system found on cassette recorders. (Reread 8.8.)

14c. No. This isn't correct. (Reread 8.8 and 8.11 to 8.13.)

15c. No. You're thinking about another signal processing device. (Reread 8.14.)

16c. Wrong. You may be getting this confused with the level of normal conversation. (Reread 8.10.)

18c. Yes. This would add brilliance to a voice.

19c. Right. This is the correct answer.

20c. No. Flanging concerns phase-shift and time delay, but not dynamic range. (Reread 8.10, 8.11, and 8.13.)

If you answered D to any of the questions:

1d. Correct. Equalizers allow you to adjust selected frequency volumes and thus alter the audio signal's frequency response.

3d. No. This would be a type of graphic equalizer. (Reread 8.5 and 8.6.)

4d. Although it could eliminate a 60-hertz hum, low cut filters normally are designed to eliminate all frequencies below a certain point. There's a better response. (Reread 8.7.)

6d. Yes. This is what reverb units do by electronically changing the apparent acoustic environment in which we hear the sound.

7d. No. A compressor acts as an automatic volume control affecting the dynamic range of an audio signal. (Reread 8.2 and 8.11.)

8d. No. This is not a noise-reduction unit. (Reread 8.8 and 8.13.)

9d. Wrong. This happens in a limiter, but not during noise reduction. (Reread 8.8 and 8.12.)

10d. No. A noise gate does not deal with imaging. (Reread 8.2 and 8.11.)

11d. No. You're thinking of a "flange" effect. (Reread 8.11 and 8.14.)

13d. Right. This is not a current Dolby noise-reduction system.

14d. Yes. This is a multi-effect processor.

15d. Correct. As the name implies, a stereo synthesizer makes a mono signal into a "fake" stereo signal.

16d. Wrong. You're thinking about the amount of change in volume that's usually necessary before we actually hear a difference in level. (Reread 8.10.)

18d. No. This would decrease the highs, if anything. (Reread 8.5.)

19d. Wrong. This is a type of processor used to affect imaging of an audio signal. (Reread 8.9 and 8.14.)

20d. Wrong. A limiter is a type of compressor, not the opposite of it. (Reread 8.10 to 8.12.)

Projects

PROJECT 1

Record a commercial spot that uses a signal processing effect.

Purpose

To develop skill in incorporating a signal processing effect into an audio production.

Notes

1. This project assumes that you have enough familiarity with your studio equipment to accomplish basic recording and production techniques.
2. The production incorporates a single announcer voice, a music bed, and some type of signal processing technique.
3. You will need to write a simple script that can be read in about 20 seconds. Write the copy about a store and use the phrase "One Day Sale!" several times in the script.
4. There are many ways to accomplish this project, so don't feel like you must follow the production directions exactly.

How to Do the Project

1. Record the script (voice only) onto an audio recorder. Each time the "sale" phrase is read, add some type of signal processing effect (reverb, flanging, echo, EQ, and so on). Depending on your studio, you may be using a "black box" processor or a signal processing effect available in your audio editing software.
2. Select a music bed that is appropriate for the style of the spot. You might find one on the CD-ROM that came with this text.
3. You can play back the music bed directly from a CD, or you may have to record it on another recorder from the CD-ROM.
4. Set correct playback levels for both the vocal track and the music bed. Both will start at full volume. Then cue both to the beginning sound.
5. Mix the vocal track and music bed to complete the spot.
6. Start the music bed at full volume. Start the vocal track and simultaneously fade the music bed slightly so the vocal track is dominant.
7. As the vocal ends, bring the music bed back to full volume and then quickly fade it out as you approach 30 seconds.
8. It may take you several attempts to get the spot to come out correctly. If you need to "do it over," just cue everything and try again.
9. On the completed project, write your name and "Signal Processing Spot," and turn it in to your instructor to receive credit.

PROJECT 2

Use multitrack recording to create a chorusing effect.

Purpose

To practice the multitrack techniques of chorusing and bouncing while keeping a track sheet.

Notes

1. This project assumes you have a multitrack recorder or an editing software system with at least four tracks.
2. Your system should be set up so that you can record from a microphone as well as a source (such as a CD player) that can play music.

3. You can use any dialogue you want, but the first line of "Mary Had a Little Lamb" works well.
4. You may find music appropriate for this project on the CD-ROM that came with this text.

How to Do the Project

1. Record your selected dialogue on Track 1.
2. While playing back Track 1, overdub the dialogue again on Track 2.
3. As you're doing your recording, keep a track sheet similar to the one shown in Chapter 3.
4. Bounce Tracks 1 and 2 onto Track 3.
5. While listening to Track 3, overdub the dialogue again on Track 1.
6. Bounce Tracks 3 and 1 onto Track 4.
7. Listen to Track 4. It should sound like a chorus of four voices.
8. Record a music bed on Track 1.
9. Mix down Track 1 and Track 4 so that you have a spot with a vocal track over a music bed.
10. Dub the finished project, and turn in the recording to your instructor to receive credit for this project. Make sure you include the track sheet with your name and label it "Chorusing Production."

PROJECT 3

Restore an audio clip using noise-reduction software.

Purpose

To make you aware of some of the characteristics of noise-reduction signal processing.

Notes

1. You'll need audio editing software that includes noise-reduction capability to complete this project.
2. Adobe Audition is being used as an example; however, you should be able to complete the project with other similar programs.
3. The audio clip which you can "restore" is on the CD-ROM that came with this text or your instructor may provide a different clip for your use.

How to Do the Project

1. Using Adobe Audition in "edit view," select "file" (from the top menu bar) and then "extract audio from CD." You could also record the audio clip from a CD player into Audition.
2. With the audio clip waveform on the screen, select and highlight a small section of "noise." Usually there is something just before the music or voice starts that can be grabbed.
3. Select "edit" (from the top menu bar), then "restoration," and then "capture noise-reduction profile." (If you get a pop-up window, just click "OK.")
4. Select "edit" (from the top menu bar), then "select entire wave."
5. Next, from the top menu bar, select "effects," then "restoration," and then "noise-reduction (process)."
6. In the pop up window, select "preview."
7. Listen to the processed audio. If you don't like how it sounds, you can try changing some of the various adjustments, but usually the presets will give you very good results.
8. Click "OK" to have the noise reduction applied to the audio clip.
9. Record both the original audio clip and processed audio clip onto a CD-R or other medium.
10. Listen to both clips several times.
11. Write a short paper that describes the differences you noted. Label the paper "Noise-Reduction Differences."
12. Turn in this paper and the recording you made to your instructor to receive credit for this project.

9

PRODUCTION SITUATIONS

9.1 INTRODUCTION

The equipment that has been discussed in previous chapters can be used for many types of studio audio productions, including commercials, image enhancers, disc jockey shows, music recording, news, sports, traffic, weather, talk shows, drama, and variety. Although many of these program forms relate to radio, some can be used for other audio-based material, such as music CDs, club disc jockeying, and demo recordings for job applications. Entire books have been written about each of these types of material; this chapter will not give you the in-depth knowledge you need to perfect any of the program forms. It will, however, get you started in the right direction. Experience and advanced training can then provide you with more specialized skills.

9.2 PRODUCING COMMERCIALS

People who work for advertising agencies and radio stations are likely to be involved with producing commercials. At some stations, dealing with commercials is a full-time position, and at many stations the disc jockeys spend a portion of their workday doing commercial production work. At their simplest level, commercials consist of straight copy that the announcer reads over the air. At their most complex level, they are highly produced vignettes that include several voices, sound effects, and music. In between are commercials such as those that feature celebrity testimonials, dialogue between two announcers, or an announcer reading over a **music bed**.

Commercials, because they are inserted within other programming, are usually an exact length such as 15 seconds, 30 seconds, or 60 seconds. Otherwise part of the commercial might be cut off if it runs long, or yield **dead air** if it runs short. At many stations, commercials are brought in and taken off by computers, which are very unsympathetic to anything that's too long or too short.

Anyone reading commercial copy should use a natural, sincere style. Reading commercials in a condescending manner is definitely uncalled for. Commercials pay station salaries and should be treated with respect. If you're to read commercial copy live, you should read it over ahead of time to avoid stumbling on words. If the commercial involves both reading live and playing a prerecorded segment, make sure you rehearse the transition between the two. Sometimes a prerecorded spot sounds like it's ending, but it actually contains additional information—perhaps new store hours or a bargain price. If you're to read material after the recording ends, you want to make sure you don't read on top of the recorded information.

Probably the most basic form of commercial you'll produce involves an announcer reading over a music bed or sound effects. The usual format for a commercial with music is that the music bed fades in or begins at full volume for a few seconds and then fades under and holds as the announcer begins reading the spot. The **voice-over** is read on top of the music bed, and then the music bed is brought up to full volume at the end of the voice-over for a few seconds until it fades out or ends cold (see Figure 9.1). Although this seems simple enough, it may not come easily until you've practiced. Not only must you be concerned with timing, you also have to determine how much music to use to establish the spot, balance the levels between voice and music bed, and correctly manipulate

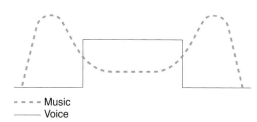

FIGURE 9.1 A drawing that illustrates a commercial that consists of an announcer reading over a music bed that fades in and out.

the broadcast equipment. Often you do all this at the same time, although it is possible to record the voice-over and mix it with music at a later time.

Reading over sound effects is similar to reading over music, in that the sound should fade up and down. Sound effects are usually short; they often need to be **looped** (recorded over several times) in order to cover the length of the commercial. This task is easy to accomplish with computer editing. The sound can simply be copied and laid on the **time line** as many times as needed.

Highly produced spots usually take a relatively long time to prepare. **Minidramas**, which often start with music and involve several people bantering to the accompaniment of sound effects, involve a great deal of preproduction, rehearsing, mixing, and editing. They are among the most challenging, creative products that an audio production person handles. Often different parts of them are recorded at different times. The talent record their parts and then leaves, especially if they're high-paid talent. Then the production person mixes the talent skit with music and sound effects.

PRODUCTION TIP 9A
Music Punctuators

For radio spots that consist of a mixture of the announcer's voice and a background music bed, the voice should be dominant, because it conveys the important information of the spot. The music is in the background and helps convey the mood of the spot. You can make this basic radio production more interesting for the listener by raising the volume level of the background music slightly during natural pauses in the vocal track. This step will move the music from the background to the foreground momentarily. The listener will pay attention to this change, because our ears "follow" movement and will focus on the subtle shift. Make sure that you turn down the background music when the voice starts again. You can punctuate key phrases or concepts in your spot with this technique, and your production work will sound more lively than just keeping the music constantly in the background.

9.3 ENHANCING IMAGE

Imaging (sometimes called **branding**) defines the station as a product so that the listeners know what to expect when they tune in. It involves many elements, some of which are printed material such as posters or billboard ads. But imaging is also heavily incorporated between program elements such as music, commercials, or news stories. People who can produce short, catchy material to help establish the brand are valuable to the station.

There are many types of imaging materials. They have been given names, some of which are:

Bumper: A prerecorded audio element that consists of voice-over music that acts as a transition from a **stop set** (commercials) to or from other content. It might, for example, consist of music and the disc jockey saying his/her name in an unusual manner.

Jingle: A produced programming element that includes the singing of call letters, a station slogan, disc jockey names, or other imaging elements.

Liner: A sentence or sentences that a disc jockey says over the intro to a song or during a break between songs. An example might be "It's always golden here at KAAA."

Promo: Short for promotional spot, this is an announcement, usually the length of a commercial, that promotes an upcoming station event such as a concert or a contest. A promo for a contest, for example, might include excited reactions of past contest winners, the contest rules, the prize, and how this contest relates to the station programming.

Slogan: A short pithy group of words that help listeners remember the main image a station wants to convey (see Figure 9.2). An example is "All news all the time."

Station ID: An identification of the station. The FCC requires that all stations identify themselves by call letters, frequency, and city of license at least once an hour. Many stations also include how the station is known within their ID—for example, "KLUV, your spot for love songs." Also many stations do station IDs more often than once an hour, but they do not need to include all the required elements when they do so.

Stinger: A sound effect or musical effect that punctuates so that it will capture attention. A station might, for example, play four chimes accompanied by its call letters at the top of every hour.

Sweeper: A recorded element of voice, voice-over music, or a sound effect that bridges two songs together or creates a transition from commercials back to music or vice versa.

Teaser: A short segment, usually broadcast before a commercial break, the intent of which is to keep the listener turned to the station. And example would be "Coming up—how you can win two free tickets to the Pistons game."

As you can tell, many of these concepts are similar or overlapping. In addition, the terms are not uniform. What

---

RADIO STATION SLOGANS
B1 with the Music
Goodtime Oldies
More Stimulating Talk Radio
Radio Jalapeno
Timeless Classics
Today's New Country
The Voice of Pittsburgh
Where Ministry Blesses Many
The World's Greatest Radio Station
Your Peace and Justice Community Radio Station

FIGURE 9.2 Here are ten slogans. Which do you think are most creative? Most effective? Most descriptive?

one station calls a bumper, another might call a sweeper. The exact definitions are not nearly as important as the need for all these elements to convey something to the listener that will distinguish the station from all the other stations on the air and attract the **target audience** that the station wants to attract.

All these imaging elements are short. Although a station cares a great deal about how it is perceived, it cannot devote too much of airtime to establishing itself or it will lose its audience. If you are producing something to enhance a station's image, you must make it compact, memorable, and unique.

9.4 ANNOUNCING MUSIC

Music constitutes the largest percentage of radio station programming and is usually introduced and coordinated by a **disc jockey (DJ)**. If you become a disc jockey, you'll probably be spending most of your time in the on-air studio doing your production work live (see Figure 9.3). On-air broadcasting is fast-paced, pressure-packed, and, for most people, a lot of fun.

Although the main element of the programming is music, the main duty of the disc jockey is talking. Much of this talk involves introducing music. For this, your announcing style must fit the format of the radio station. For example, fast-paced, high-energy, rapid-fire speech is not appropriate for a classical music or big band format but may be required at a contemporary hit or rock radio

station. Develop a variety of ways of getting into and out of the music. Many beginning announcers latch onto one introduction and use it over and over ("Here's a classic from the Beatles . . ."; "Here's a classic from Bob Dylan . . ."; "Here's a classic from . . ."). If you have trouble thinking of clever material, read the **liner notes** on the CD or research the artist on the Internet. This will often give you ideas for something to say that's unusual or informative.

Your station may have certain policies regarding what you say and how you say it. For example, some stations require you to talk over the beginning and ending of every record (so that listeners cannot record a clean copy of the entire song). Other stations may require you to say the station call letters every time you open the microphone.

As a disc jockey, you'll also be talking about things other than music. For example, you may need to give the time, temperature, commercials, weather, news, or traffic reports. Or you may introduce other people, such as the newscaster, who will give some of this information. Station policy will probably dictate whether you must be formal about these introductions or have the latitude to banter with the other person.

Regardless of what's going on within the live production situation, always assume that the microphone is open. Don't say anything that you wouldn't want to go out over the air. This includes personal conversations and, of course, indecent language. Many studios have an on-air light inside the studio as well as the one outside the door. This inside light is to alert the announcer to the fact that the mic is live, but the best rule is to assume that the microphone is always on.

FIGURE 9.3 The radio disc jockey manipulates all the broadcast equipment and adds the element of live announcing within the style of the radio station's format. (Image courtesy of iStockphoto, Lisa Kyle Young, Image #2286303.)

Obviously, as a disc jockey, you need to be proficient at operating the equipment so that you can cue up and play the music. You need to think ahead, because you are normally operating equipment and talking. For example, if you have to bring in a feed from a network, you must know exactly when and how to do it. It's also good practice to have an alternative if something goes wrong. If the CD player you want to play doesn't start, have a backup plan prepared in advance. A good announcer can overcome most miscues so that the listening audience doesn't even know that anything went wrong.

Make sure you have previewed your music, especially to know how songs begin and end. This will ensure that you avoid **walking over** (beginning to "outro" a song before it's really over) a false ending. Previewing also helps you know how much instrumentation there is at the beginning of the record before the vocal starts so that you can talk over the instrumental but not the vocal. There is no excuse for a disc jockey playing music on the air that he or she isn't completely familiar with.

Plan how you'll get from one piece of music to the next if you play them consecutively. You might want to review the sound transitions mentioned in Chapter 5, "The Audio Console." Remember to use a variety of ways rather than the same method time after time. Listen to the on-air monitor frequently, if not continuously. Most audio consoles allow the DJ to hear the program line, the audition line, or the on-air signal; however, only the on-air signal allows you to hear exactly what the listener hears.

Sometimes disc jockeys are not in an on-air studio announcing music live. Instead, they are **voice tracking**. Voice tracking is simply when an announcer prerecords the vocal portion of his or her air shift—such as song introductions, time checks, and so on—that will be mixed with the music, commercials, and other programming elements later. Often computer software that allows a station to automate its programming also facilitates voice tracking. In this way, rather than doing a 4-hour air shift in real time, the DJ can record in a much shorter period of time—often about one-quarter of the time. In addition, voice tracking allows announcers to record several shifts both for the local station and for stations in other markets. It is not uncommon for an air personality to voice track a number of different formats for stations in several markets in one session.

Voice tracking has been around for quite a while; the **countdown** shows heard on radio have long been voice tracked. But technology and radio consolidation of the last several decades has made it more prevalent and more controversial because the jocks who create this "virtual radio" have replaced live and local DJs. Using "cheat sheets" listing local names, places, and events, a voice-tracking announcer can sound like he or she is in Portland, Maine, when the announcer is really in Dallas, Texas. Many listeners may not even realize their favorite "local" announcer has never been to their market. One result of voice tracking

is that DJ jobs are being lost because one announcer can cover several air shifts. On the other hand, top-quality DJs from larger markets can be heard on smaller-market stations, and stations can save money through voice tracking. There are pros and cons to this method of creating radio content, but it is a practice that anyone wishing to become a radio announcer should be familiar with and become proficient at.

9.5 RECORDING MUSIC

Another type of job open to people with audio skills is that of recording musical groups. Most of these jobs involve recording and mixing songs to be distributed on CDs or over the Internet. Sometimes groups are recorded (or aired live) in radio station studios where the disc jockey interviews the group and then has them perform.

Recording music is a fairly complicated form of audio production that often involves numerous microphones and long hours of recording. You can record the whole musical group at once or you can record individual instruments and mix them at a later time. (Obviously, if the performance is live, you must send out the whole group at once.)

When you record a whole group, you must place microphones very carefully so that you achieve the proper balance. If the group is fairly small, you can place a mic by the sound hole of each instrument and, of course, mic the vocalists (see Figure 9.4). But if you place a mic the same distance from a trumpet sound hole as from a violin sound hole, the trumpet will drown out the violin—and probably everything else. There are no set rules on how to position the mics; it takes experimentation and experience. In general, for recording music, you want **cardioid condenser** mics with a large **frequency response** and **dynamic range**, and you want to position them on stands (see Chapter 4, "Microphones"). It helps if the output of each mic is recorded on a separate track into an audio board. Then several audio technicians working at the console can make minor changes in the volume of various instruments as the sound is on its way to the recorder.

Better yet, in terms of quality and control, is to record each instrument separately. You might, for example, start by recording the guitar player performing the entire song. Then, the singer, while listening to a playback of the guitar, would perform. The singer would be recorded on a different track than the guitar and you would not need to adjust for the differing volume levels because you will be mixing them together later. But you do need to make sure you have good sound quality in terms of being **distortion**-free, **on-mic**, rich in frequencies, and so forth. By the same manner, you could lay down a drum track, a clarinet track, and so on. Later you could mix the sounds together starting and stopping and adjusting as needed to obtain the best recording possible. You can also add effects, such as

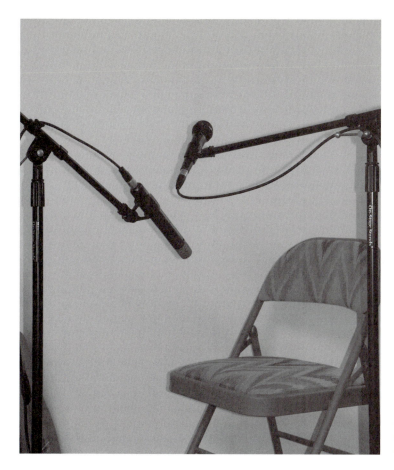

FIGURE 9.4 This is an effective setup for a person who plays guitar and sings. One mic is by the person's mouth and the other is by the guitar sound hole.

reverberation and equalization (see Chapter 8, "Signal Processing Equipment").

Recording each instrument at a different time, however, may not allow for the energy and flow that musicians in a band, for example, might exchange during a performance. This is especially true in the case of jazz music, where riffing off of and interacting between the various musicians is a hallmark of the form. However, the different musicians can be sonically isolated from each other, allowing for each instrument to be recorded separately, while the musicians can, by way of headsets, be fed the live mix of all the performers so as to be able to interact and react to the composition as it ebbs and flows among the musicians. Many studios are equipped so as to allow sonically isolated musicians to see each other through glass walls.

If you are recording a large group, such as a symphony orchestra, you cannot mic each instrument. Instead, you mic various sections of the orchestra (violins, drums, trombones) usually with mics that are hung from overhead. As with a smaller group, technicians at an audio console set and adjust volume levels, but it is also wise to record each mic on a separate track so that changes can be made in the recording after the fact.

There are many other possible steps related to recording music. Sometimes music recorded from real instruments is mixed with computer-created music. Sometimes several versions made from the same recording session are released. In general, the recording process is a very important aspect of the music business.

PRODUCTION TIP 9B
Miking a Guitar

If you are into guitar music, you might like to try this guitar-miking method used by professional sound engineer Bil VornDick. It is for someone who is just playing the guitar and not singing, but it uses two microphones. Bil uses different microphones, depending who the artist is, but one of his favorites is the Neumann KM84, a condenser cardioid mic that operates on **phantom power**. It has a switch that allows it to be used close to loud instruments, handling 130 db without distortion.

Bil places one mic toward the right side where the neck joins the body, pointed between the hole, arch, and neck—the area where the higher transients are. The other mic looks down from where the musician's right shoulder is, because most guitar players play to the right ear. This mic is pointed toward the sound hole and covers the area between the wrist and shoulder. It emulates what the guitarist is hearing and has a deeper tonal **timbre** than the first mic. He has to be careful about **multiple-microphone interference**, or keeping the mics far enough apart that they do not cancel each other's sound.

9.6 PREPARING AND ANNOUNCING NEWS

If you're involved with radio production, you're likely to do news work at some point. In some instances, the disc jockey may just **rip and read** from the news service on the hour or half hour. Of course, most radio news is now read directly off a computer screen so "rip 'n' read" just refers to the practice of reading a newscast cold or with no rewriting or preparation. As we'll note in a moment, this is not good broadcast practice. At the other extreme are all-news stations, which have many people involved with the news, often including two on-air anchors at any one time (see Figure 9.5). Whatever situation you find yourself in, some knowledge about newscasting will prove useful.

Even if you're expected to simply read a short newscast each hour, you should give some time and thought to your presentation. First, you must decide which news to present. You probably have a station news format to follow, but you should also try to select those items that are most likely to be of interest to your listeners.

You may find that you need to do some rewriting of the wire service news and write some transitions to take the listener from one story to the next. Timing is important on a newsbreak. Beginning newscasters sometimes run out of news to read before the newscast time is up. To prevent this, you should pad your newscast with some extra stories that you can cut if you have to, but that also provide a cushion if you need extra material. You'll usually need to get commercials in at an appropriate time during a newscast, so make sure that you know when this happens and be prepared for it. Don't read a newscast cold. Read it over first so that you're familiar with the material. Rewrite anything that isn't natural for you, such as tongue-twisting phrases that you might trip over or long sentences that make you run out of breath. Avoid too many numbers or facts jammed into a single sentence. Whenever something is unclear, rewrite to make it simple and easy to understand. Remember, broadcast news should be conversational and written for the ear, not the eye.

When a news story includes the actual voice of the person in the news, such as the mayor commenting on the new city budget, that segment is called an **actuality**. Most radio news operations strive to include many actualities within a newscast, because these bring life to the news. It's more interesting to hear the mayor's comments than the voice of an announcer telling what the mayor said. Many of these actualities are gathered by field reporters (see Chapter 10, "Location Sound Recording"); however, you can also make use of the phone to gather them. Many small radio stations have one-person news departments, and in these cases the phone actuality is especially crucial. At some stations, a **telephone interface** is used to semipermanently hook up phones to an audio recorder or audio console. But you can

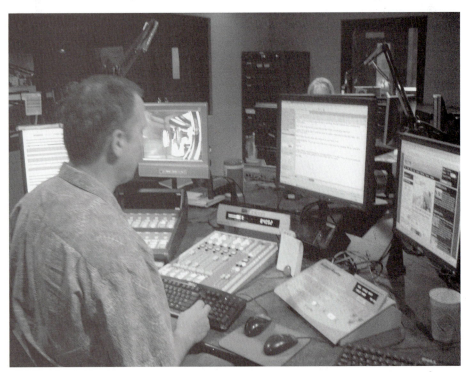

FIGURE 9.5 This setup at an all-news stations is made for two anchors. Each has his/her own audio board, monitors, and other equipment. By positioning their monitors appropriately, they are able to maintain eye contact.

also use a microphone that's specifically made to attach to the phone. You must obtain permission to record someone for broadcast use, and your station newsroom probably has specific guidelines to follow for doing this.

Actualities generally need to be edited. For this, you should use all the editing techniques presented in Chapter 3, "Digital Audio Production," and include one very important rule: Make sure that when you edit, you don't change the meaning of what someone has said. Ethical news procedures dictate that a great deal of care be taken in this area because the elimination of a single word can significantly alter a news report. When you're editing and need to eliminate part of what a person said, either because it's too long or it's irrelevant, try to match voice expressions where the statement leaves off and where a new one begins. For example, don't make an edit that jumps from a fast-paced explanation a speaker was making to a measured response he or she was formulating. Edits are usually best if made at the end of thoughts, because a person's voice drops into a concluding mode at that point. Be careful not to edit out all the breaths the person takes, because doing this will destroy the natural rhythm. Try to maintain a constant background level throughout the actuality. To do this, you may have to mix in background noise from one part of the recording to another.

9.7 REPORTING SPORTS, TRAFFIC, AND WEATHER

At some radio stations, the same person who reads the news also reports on other related elements such as sports, traffic, and weather. At other stations, especially all-news stations, there are separate reporters to cover these topics.

Sports announcers need to know sports in general as well as the particulars of the sports for the area in which they are reporting. Unlike other reporters, they are allowed to show a bias for the home team and are expected to have an upbeat, hyper vocal presentation. At some stations the same people who report sports on a regular basis from the studio also cover play-by-play at various sports venues. The equipment setup at a sports box at a stadium is similar to that in a studio, in that there are microphones and a small audio board, but there are also differences, which will be covered in Chapter 10.

In cities with heavy congestion, traffic reports have increased in importance. But traffic reporting can be very expensive if it involves a helicopter and reporters driving the streets to report on conditions (see Chapter 10). In some cities, specialized companies handle traffic reports for a number of stations. Reporters change their tone and banter as they switch from reporting for a rock station to an all-news station to an easy listening station. In addition to obtaining details from reporters in the field, employees of traffic companies or radio stations can obtain traffic information by listening to police radios, by encouraging listeners to call in with traffic jam information, and by looking at Internet site maps that are tied to sensors in the highways that indicate how fast cars are progressing on the road. Someone involved with traffic reporting needs a knowledge of the area in order to know which traffic jams are most likely to impact listeners.

Weather is an important subject in most communities; particularly so in the morning, as people prepare to leave

FIGURE 9.6   This is one of many maps that the National Oceanic and Atmospheric Administration (NOAA) provides on the Internet.

for the day and in the evening as they are heading home. Some stations require their forecasters to have meteorology degrees so that they can explain weather conditions and the weather forecast to the listeners. Other stations have someone who calls the weather service or checks one of the government or private web sites that constantly update local and national weather (see Figure 9.6). At the simplest level, the person giving the weather report can simply look out the window.

Some stations also have a person who deals with business news, regularly reporting on the stock market and related items. There are specialists who report on other topics such as art shows, fashion, education, health, or movies, and there are people who give commentaries on current events. Often these people work on a contract basis for syndication companies who supply audio material to a host of stations nationwide.

9.8 HOSTING TALK SHOWS

There are many types of talk shows—**shock jock** morning shows, public affairs programs that deal with local or national issues, sports talk programs, psychology and self-help programs, religious talk, right-wing and left-wing political talkers, and on and on. Some talk shows consist of one person talking, others involve a host and a knowledgeable guest, and many include call-ins from listeners (see Figure 9.7).

Not everyone is cut out to handle hosting a call-in talk show. You must be fast on your feet and able to ad lib in an entertaining and effective manner. For many programs, you're expected to have more than broadcast production knowledge. For example, a sports program or radio psychology show requires a host with some expertise in those areas. Sometimes the call-in talk show host has an engineer handling the equipment and a producer screening the calls so that the host can concentrate on dealing with the callers, but this is not always the case, especially in smaller-market radio. A call-in show host has to be able to handle people tactfully (or, in some cases, abrasively, if that's the style of the program).

The host must remain in charge of the program. You should keep the program moving, trying not to give too much time to any one caller. If you have a guest to whom people are posing questions, you should give information about the guest and redirect questions if they're not understandable.

Research is crucial to talk shows. Even if the show is one host spouting his or her opinions, the audience will sense when the host doesn't know what he or she is talking about. A good host will research the subject and the guest before doing a program that involves a guest. Not only will this provide background, but it should also enable the host to generate a list of questions to ask.

Asking the right questions really means asking good questions. For example, ask questions that require more than a simple yes or no answer. Rather than asking, "Do you agree

FIGURE 9.7 This public affairs talk show involves a discussion between the program host and a studio guest. (Image courtesy of Alan R. Stephenson.)

with the mayor's new policy regarding the police?" ask, "What do you think of the mayor's new policy regarding the police?" Ask short, simple, and direct questions. The question, "Given the salaries of employees and the possible raises they will receive, what do you think the effects will be on the social security system and the GNP?" will most likely get a response of "Huh?" Break complex questions down into a number of questions such as, "How do you think increasing salaries 5 percent will affect the GNP?" Ask questions that don't require very long answers. Don't ask, "What would you do to improve the city?" Instead ask, "What is the first thing you would do to improve the city?" Don't bias your questions, such as "You do believe that the mayor's new policy is correct, don't you?"

Asking good questions also means knowing how to handle the answers, whether they come from a guest or a listener. For example, if the answer is too wordy, ask the person to summarize the response. If the answer is muddy or unclear, ask the question over again in smaller parts. If the answer is evasive, come back to it later, or ask it again from a different angle. If the response gets off track, redirect. And if the response goes on and on, interrupt politely and redirect.

Listen carefully to what the guest or call-in person says so that you can ask appropriate follow-up questions. Sometimes interviewers become so engrossed in thinking about the next question that they miss an important point that could lead to something significant. Although you should organize your program ahead of time and jot down some questions or points you want to cover, don't slavishly stick to your questions. In all probability, when you ask question one, the guest will also answer questions three and seven, for example, so you must constantly flow with the conversation. The more you can lead off what the guest or a listener says, the more natural the whole show will appear. But make sure you do get the information you want. Most talk shows are aired live, but if the material is recorded, it may be necessary to edit. As with news, be certain that you do not change the meaning of what someone said.

When you have a number of different guests, identify them frequently, because the listener may have difficulty keeping track of the various voices. Even a single guest should be reintroduced during a 30-minute program. Not only does this remind listeners who your guest is, but it introduces him or her to those listeners who joined the program while it was in progress.

9.9 PERFORMING DRAMA AND VARIETY

Drama isn't produced very often on radio anymore. Sometimes there are comedic skits within variety shows that also include music, jokes, quizzes, and other elements. But variety shows, too, are rather rare, occurring primarily on public radio (see Figure 9.8). When drama or variety shows are performed in a studio, they require some unique production skills. Usually actors perform several parts, so

FIGURE 9.8 *Prairie Home Companion* starring Garrison Keillor (right) involves many production elements, including sound effects performed live by Tom Keith (left). (Copyright Prairie Home Productions. Used with permission. All rights reserved.)

an actor needs to be able to create a number of distinct voices. Otherwise audience members will not be able to distinguish one character from another.

Sometimes sound effects are performed live or at the same time that the drama or variety show is being recorded. The people performing them are skilled in using their bodies, voices, and various implements to create a wide variety of sounds. Along with music, these sound effects establish locale, tell the time, create mood, indicate entries and exits, establish transitions, and add humor. Sound effects and music can also be prerecorded or taken from a CD and edited into the production at a later time. Dramas and variety shows are fun to produce, but they do not have the broad audience appeal they had during the 1930s and 1940s before television was available.

9.10 CONCLUSION

This chapter has been devoted mainly to audio productions that occur within the studio environment. But there are many times when sound is gathered at a field location, broadcast from a helicopter, played at a club, used in conjunction with video, or connected to a variety of media forms such as the Internet and podcasting. The following chapters will explore these varieties of sound recording. When you finish the book you should have a well-rounded view of a large number of audio recording possibilities and an appreciation for the fact that audio production can be an exciting career. It is certainly possible to have a great deal of variety in your day-to-day occupation and you will have numerous opportunities to be creative and innovative.

Self-Study

QUESTIONS

1. How would a radio DJ "walk over" a false ending of a song?

   a) by leaving the microphone open when it should be off
   b) by beginning the outro of a song before it is really over
   c) by recueing a CD
   d) by researching an artist on the Internet

2. What is the reason sound effects sometimes need to be looped?

   a) They are too short.
   b) They need to be recorded after the talent is recorded.
   c) Then need to punctuate a minidrama.
   d) They need to be created live for a variety show.

3. Which of the following might be used before a commercial break?

   a) a sweeper
   b) a teaser
   c) a bumper
   d) any of the above

4. Which of the following describes good radio talk show technique?

   a) Give each caller all the time he or she wants.
   b) Ask all your questions in the order you have them written down.
   c) Ask complex questions so that you cover the topic thoroughly.
   d) Ask follow-up questions based on the interviewee's response.

5. A fast-paced announcing style would be most appropriate for a disc jockey working at which type of radio station?

   a) classical music format
   b) big band format
   c) all-news format
   d) contemporary hit radio format

6. Which of the following best describes what should occur for a commercial that consists of an announcer reading over a music bed?

   a) The announcer will read with a condescending tone.
   b) The commercial will always be cut off because it is not the prescribed length.
   c) The music bed will begin at full volume then fade under as the announcer begins talking.
   d) The balance between the voice and music bed will favor the music bed.

7. Approximately how long should it take an announcer to record a 4-hour air shift by voice tracking?

   a) one-quarter hour
   b) 1 hour
   c) 2 hours
   d) 4 hours

8. Which of the following are you least likely to do when you record each instrument of a band separately rather than recording them all together?

   a) adjust the volume of each instrument so it is at a different level
   b) record the guitar and then record the drums
   c) make sure your recording is not distorted
   d) mix the sounds together when you are finished recording and then add reverb

9. What does the term "actuality" refer to?

   a) the voice of the news announcer
   b) a pad for a newscast
   c) wire service copy
   d) the voice of a person in the news

10. Which of the following is true about the content of radio news copy?

    a) It should contain as many facts and numbers as possible.
    b) It should be written in simple, easy-to-understand sentences.
    c) It should be sonically isolated.
    d) It should be written using long, explanatory sentences.

11. Which of the following are you more likely to do if you are recording an orchestra than if you are recording a string quartet?

    a) place mics by the sound hole of each instrument
    b) place mics by sections rather than individual instruments
    c) place mics carefully to achieve proper balance
    d) record each mic on a separate track

12. Which of the following would not be a good reason for editing a news actuality?

    a) to cut out a cough
    b) to cut out material that is irrelevant
    c) to change the meaning of the story
    d) to shorten the length of the story

13. Which type of announcer has the most latitude to be hyper and biased?

    a) a sportscaster
    b) a traffic reporter
    c) a stock market reporter
    d) a news anchor

14. Which of the following is the best definition of a jingle?

    a) a sentence that a disc jockey says over the intro to a song
    b) a short imaging element that includes singing
    c) a promotional spot that explains a contest
    d) a sound effect that punctuates

15. Which of the following would be the best radio interview question?

    a) Do you favor capital punishment?
    b) What do you think will happen regarding an amendment against capital punishment being added to the Constitution after it has been discussed by the state legislature in light of the case pending in Florida at the present time and the one recently decided in Illinois?
    c) What do you think will be the outcome of the present attempt to outlaw capital punishment?
    d) You favor capital punishment, don't you?

ANSWERS

If you answered A to any of the questions:

1a. No. This is something that shouldn't be done. (Reread 9.4.)

2a. Yes, this is the correct answer. They need to be recorded over and over to cover the length of something, such as a commercial.

3a. This answer is correct, but it's not the best answer. (Reread 9.3.)

4a. No. This could get very boring. (Reread 9.8.)

5a. Definitely not. (Reread 9.4.)

6a. No. This should never happen. (Reread 9.2.)

7a. No. This is too short. (Reread 9.4.)

8a. Correct. You would adjust the volumes later.

9a. No. You have the wrong voice. (Reread 9.6.)

10a. Wrong. Audience members won't be able to comprehend all of them as they go by quickly. (Reread 9.6.)

11a. No. That would take way too many microphones. (Reread 9.5.)

12a. Wrong. This would be a legitimate reason to edit. (Reread 9.6.)

13a. Correct.

14a. Wrong. This is more likely to be the definition for a liner. (Reread 9.3.)

15a. Wrong. This question could be answered "yes" or "no." (Reread 9.8.)

If you answered B to any of the questions:

1b. Correct. That's the definition of "walk over."

2b. No. It wouldn't make any difference. (Reread 9.2.)

3b. This answer is correct, but it's not the best answer. (Reread 9.3.)

4b. No. You don't want to stick slavishly to your questions. (Reread 9.8.)

5b. No, that wouldn't be appropriate. (Reread 9.4.)

6b. Wrong. You can certainly make it the prescribed length. (Reread 9.2.)

7b. Yes. Usually an announcer can produce an air shift in about one-quarter of the actual time by voice tracking.

8b. Wrong. You would be likely to record one instrument and then another when recording separately. (Reread 9.5.)

9b. Wrong. (Reread 9.6.)

10b. Definitely correct.

11b. Yes. When there are that many instruments you place the mics by sections.

12b. No. That is one of the main reasons for editing. (Reread 9.6.)

13b. Wrong. Traffic reporters aren't biased. (Reread 9.7.)

14b. This is correct.

15b. Wrong. This question is much too convoluted. (Reread 9.8.)

If you answered C to any of the questions:

1c. No. This has nothing to do with cueing. (Reread 9.4.)

2c. No. This would have nothing to do with looping. (Reread 9.2.)

3c. This answer is correct, but there is a better answer. (Reread 9.3.)

4c. Wrong. Complex questions are not called for. (Reread 9.8.)

5c. Wrong. There aren't even disc jockeys for this format. (Reread 9.4.)

6c. This is the correct answer.

7c. No. This is too long. (Reread 9.4.)

8c. Wrong. You want to check distortion regardless how you are recording. (Reread 9.5.)

9c. No. It has nothing to do with wire service copy. (Reread 9.6.)

10c. No. Sonically isolated refers to recording music. (Reread 9.5 and 9.6.)

11c. No. You always want to place mics carefully. (Reread 9.5.)

12c. This is correct. You definitely don't want to change the meaning of the story.

13c. No. A stock market reporter should be serious. (Reread 9.7.)

14c. No. This is more likely to refer to a promo. (Reread 9.3.)

15c. Yes. This is the best-stated question.

If you answered D to any of the questions:

1d. Wrong. This has nothing to do with "walking over." (Reread 9.4.)

2d. Wrong. If they are live, they definitely don't need to be looped. (Reread 9.2.)

3d. Yes. Many of these imaging terms have interchangeable uses.

4d. Correct.

5d. Right. This format is fast-paced.

6d. No. If anything, it's the other way around. (Reread 9.2.)

7d. Wrong. This is as long as the shift. (Reread 9.4.)

8d. No. This would be something you do when you record separately. (Reread 9.5.)

9d. This is the correct answer.

10d. No. The audience needs shorter sentences. (Reread 9.6.)

11d. Wrong. You'd be more likely to do this with a string quartet. (Reread 9.5.)

12d. No. Shortening is a legitimate reason to edit. (Reread 9.6.)

13d. Wrong. News anchors should not be hyper or biased. (Reread 9.7.)

14d. No. This is the definition for a stinger. (Reread 9.3.)

15d. Wrong. This is a biased question. (Reread 9.8.)

Projects

PROJECT 1

Record an air-check tape.

Purpose

To instruct those interested in doing on-air broadcasting in how to make an audition or demo recording, something required when applying for a job.

Notes

1. To apply for on-air jobs in broadcasting, you may send your resume and an air-check recording to many stations. An air-check is a recording of less than 5 minutes that shows how you handle on-air broadcast situations.
2. Ideally, an air-check is an edited-down sample of your actual on-air work, but if you aren't on the air on a regular basis, a simulated air-check can be put together in the production studio.
3. Try to make the recording as general as possible so that it could be sent to several different types of stations.
4. Put those things you do best at the beginning. Many potential employers don't have time to listen past the first 30 seconds and will rule you out if they don't like the beginning. Don't structure the recording so that it builds to a climax, because probably no one will listen that far.
5. Feel free to use things that you've done for other projects for this assignment.
6. Keep the pace moving. Don't do any one thing for too long.
7. The CD-ROM contains a sample air-check. You may want to listen to it before starting your own.

How to Do the Project

1. Plan what you intend to include in your recording. An air-check format might include ad lib introductions to a few songs (either fade out the music after a few seconds, or edit to the end of the songs so that the listener doesn't have to hear the whole song), some production work (commercials, station promos, and so on), and a short newscast. If you can do play-by-play sports, you might want to include that. There is no standard format, so do whatever showcases your talent best.
2. Plan the order of your recording. Make it sound like a continuous radio show as much as possible.
3. Record the project and listen to it. Redo it if it doesn't present good broadcasting skills.
4. On the recording, write your name and "Air-Check Project." Turn in the completed recording to the instructor to receive credit for this project.

PROJECT 2

Record a 5-minute radio interview show in which you are the interviewer.

Purpose

To prepare you for this common type of broadcasting situation.

Notes

1. Your interview must be exactly 5 minutes. Meeting the exact time without having an awkward ending will probably be the hardest part of the project, but it's a lesson worth learning because broadcasting is built around time sequences.
2. Don't underprepare. Don't fall into the trap of feeling that you can wing this. In 5 minutes you must come up with the essence of something interesting, and you can't do this unless you are

organized. You'll also only be able to record the interview once. You can't redo this project, so you need to get it right the first time.

3. Don't overprepare. Don't write out the interview word for word. It will sound stilted and canned if you do.

4. Five minutes is actually a long time; you'll be amazed at how much you can cover in this time.

5. As the interviewer, don't talk too much. Remember, the purpose is to convey the ideas of your guest to the audience, not your own ideas.

How to Do the Project

1. Select someone to interview. If you're taking a course, it will probably be easier to do this project with someone in class.

2. Decide what the interview will be about. You may select any subject you wish. You could talk about some facet of a person's life or his or her views on a current subject, or you could pretend the interviewee is a famous person.

3. Work up a list of questions. Generate more than you think you'll actually need, just in case you run short.

4. Think of a structured beginning and ending for the show, because those will probably be the most awkward parts.

5. Discuss the interview organization with your guest so that you are in accord as to what is to be discussed, but don't go over the actual questions you're going to ask.

6. Record the interview, making sure you stop at 5 minutes. Listen to it, and check that it has recorded before your guest leaves. You are finished with the project once the interview is recorded. Even if it didn't come out as you had hoped, do not redo this project.

7. On the recording write "Interview Project" and your name. Give the interview to your instructor to receive credit for this project.

10

LOCATION SOUND RECORDING

10.1 INTRODUCTION

Sometimes you need to undertake audio production beyond the confines and comforts of a studio. You lose some control when you enter the "real world," because you no longer have a room designed to maximize proper acoustics and you do not have sophisticated equipment to aid your production. But what you lack in control, you often make up in adventure once you are out in the field.

10.2 TYPES OF FIELD PRODUCTION

One very common type of field production involves gathering news. Radio networks, news agencies, all-news radio stations, and many other radio stations have reporters out in the field interviewing newsmakers and members of the public and reporting on what is happening locally, nationally, and internationally. In a similar manner producers of public affairs programs often venture into the field to obtain **actualities** and other audio for their programs (see Figure 10.1).

Traffic reporters travel surface streets or ride in helicopters to report traffic conditions. They have become increasingly important as cities become more congested and are often the reason people turn to a particular station. They must respond quickly to changing conditions.

Play-by-play sportscasters, by definition, need to be at the location where the sports event is taking place. They must keep up the chatter to avoid **dead air**, and they must

FIGURE 10.1   An example of recording an interview in the field. (Image courtesy of iStockphoto, Bonnie Jacobs, Image #5803709.)

FIGURE 10.2   This live location event featuring a mariachi band needed a fair amount of audio equipment so that it could be heard by the people in attendance and also recorded.

convey visual information that the audience cannot see. They must be aware of crowd noises and sounds from the game itself that will enhance (or detract from) the broadcast. Sports announcers often work as a team, with one announcer providing the play-by-play while another offers color commentary, along with game statistics.

Concerts and other live events are often recorded in the field at the same time they are being performed in front of an audience. Miking such events so that everyone in the audience can hear the material in a properly balanced fashion can be a challenge (see Figure 10.2). On a smaller scale, audio technicians are often asked to set up sound equipment for company activities, such as sales or promotion events, which involve people speaking and also using various audio/visual equipment.

There are many other types of location situations. Sometimes you may need to record background noises, such as monkeys chattering for a feature about a zoo or incoherent sounds of people talking to use as background for a commercial. Disc jockeys who play at clubs (see Figure 10.3) need to project their voices into the crowd. They also make use of "play" audio equipment, such as turntables, in novel ways more akin to a musician playing an instrument than a sound technician capturing, editing, or outputting audio.

10.3 COMMON LOCATION SOUND PROBLEMS

The main sound problems you are likely to encounter when you are on location are those that come from everything else that is happening at the location. You are likely to hear people talking in the background, air conditioners operating, lawn mowers cutting grass, airplanes flying overhead (or nearby if you are in a helicopter), sports fans cheering a home run, or jackhammers digging up streets. You can use these sounds to your advantage if they are elements that fit with your production and if they are not so loud that they drown out your voice, but it is more likely that they are going to be a nuisance.

Microphones do not pick up in the same manner as people's ears and brains. When you are talking to a friend you are often not aware of airplanes flying overhead or birds chirping in the trees; you are able to concentrate on your friend's words—a phenomenon known as **selective attention principle**. Microphones and recording equipment do not abide by this principle. If your recording includes an airplane sound that you didn't notice, the sound will come through loud and clear on playback.

Other sound problems on location are related to the recording process. Talent and crew members who are

FIGURE 10.3 This club disc jockey uses a turntable as part of her performance. (Image courtesy of iStockphoto, Lise Gagne, Image #5512525.)

out in the field are often not as disciplined about keeping quiet as when they are in the silent environment of a studio. If you are covering a news story, there will probably be other reporters there who aren't going to stand around quietly while you record your material. Recording equipment is usually close to the microphone and it can itself be a source of noise. Sensitive microphones pick up wind noises, sometimes even ones that are too gentle to be heard with the ear. Your equipment can also be in conflict with other electronic equipment resulting in a **hum**.

PRODUCTION TIP 10A
How to Get Rid of a Hum

Hum is a low rumble, usually at a frequency of 60 hertz, that can be picked up by recording equipment even though you do not hear it. It is usually caused by electric equipment such as fluorescent lights, vacuum cleaners, or power saws. The easiest way to get rid

of it is to find the offending equipment and turn it off. But that may not be possible—a factory owner is not going to shut down the factory because you are getting hum.

Another option is to make sure your equipment cables are not running parallel to the power cables of the offending equipment. Cables that run parallel are more likely to pick up hum than those that run perpendicular. If that doesn't work, try moving to a different location.

If you absolutely have to live with the hum then try not to record anything else at the same frequency—anything that sounds like it is at the same pitch as the hum. When you go back to the studio, you may be able to use signal processing to filter out the 60-hertz frequency where the hum is and leave the rest of the recording undisturbed.

Weather is another problem that causes location sound problems. Thunder and lightning can cause static or just plain noise. Some equipment won't work in very cold or very hot conditions. Some locks up if there is too much humidity. If there is rain, you must have some means for keeping the equipment covered.

Other problems relate to the way that people treat you. If someone makes the effort to come to a studio, they are, in all probability, going to talk to you. But if you are on location, especially if you are reporting news, people may refuse to talk to you because they don't want to be part of the story—they may not want to be associated with something they feel could reflect on them negatively. On the other hand, people may talk too much, trying to break in to your coverage or production with opinions of their own. Disc jockeys who work at clubs often have problems with people drowning them out.

And then, of course, you may be at least partially responsible for loud noise that annoys the neighbors who call the police. This is particularly likely if you are setting up sound for a rock band.

10.4 SITE PLANNING FOR LOCATION RECORDING

Some of the problems common to location sound recording can be solved by surveying the location ahead of time. (Figure 10.4 lists elements you might want to consider when you scout a location.) If you know that the air conditioning is loud and intermittent, you may be able to secure permission to turn it off for the period of time you will be recording. If the site is near an airport, try to determine how often the planes take off, so you can plan to stop recording occasionally. If there are fluorescent lights, ask whether you can turn them off. If you are miking a band or performing in a club, check out the acoustics ahead of time and think

---

LOCATION SURVEY CHECKLIST

Type of material being recorded:
Potential location of shooting:
Principal contact person:
Address:
Phone number:
Email address:

Sound:

    Are there background noises, such as air conditioning, phones ringing, airplanes, lawn mowers,
    that may interfere with audio? If so, how can they be corrected?
    Where can the microphones and cable be placed?
    Are any particular microphone holders or stands needed?
    What types of microphones should be used?
    Will microphone cable be needed? If so, how much?
    Will it be necessary to plug equipment into wall outlets? If so, where are they located?
    How many, if any, extension cords will be needed?

General:

    Where is parking available?
    If passes are needed to enter the premises, how can they be obtained?
    Where are the nearest places to eat?
    Where are the nearest washrooms?

FIGURE 10.4   A location survey form.

through microphone needs. Determine how much crowd noise wafts up to the sports announcers' booth; you may want to enhance it by placing an omnidirectional mic over a section of the crowd or you may want to mitigate it by using a more directional announcer's mic.

Of course, you cannot always survey a location ahead of time, especially if you are covering news. But even then, you can survey places where news occurs frequently—city hall, a police station, a community center—and determine the best places to position microphones. Occasionally producers hire guards to keep people away from sites where material is being recorded. That keeps down the people noises, but the guards cannot keep birds from singing in the trees.

Sometimes you need a permit from a city government in order to record, especially if music is involved. Even if you don't need a permit, it is a good idea to have owners of facilities (such as restaurants) sign a permission form (see Figure 10.5) just in case someone tries to stop your audio recording.

Parking is another consideration; make sure there is enough parking for all people involved. Reporters have special permits that enable them to park close to the scene of stories, but these have exceptions. For example, they are not allowed to park in spaces reserved for the handicapped. Carry along a good map in case you get lost; have a radio so you can listen to weather reports (and your radio station, if you work for one).

Even if you haven't been able to check a site ahead of time, make sure you check your equipment carefully before

you leave the studio area. Students are well advised to actually record and play back some material before leaving for a location so that they know the equipment is working properly.

10.5 USING MICROPHONES

Out in the field you will probably want to use a **dynamic mic**, because it is more rugged than a **condenser mic** and will not require a battery. **Cardioid** is better than **omnidirectional** for interviewing, and if you are recording sounds in the distance—an animal in a tree, a fire in the forest—you may want to use a **super-cardioid**. If you are going to be recording crowd noises, you will want an omnidirectional mic. A hand mic is best for news and interviews (see Figure 10.6); you position it near your mouth when you are talking and near the interviewee when he/she is talking. Except in unusual circumstances, don't let people you are interviewing hold the mic; they probably won't hold it correctly and you will lose control of the interview. If you need to record moving talent, you should use a **wireless lavaliere mic** (see Chapter 4). In any case, if at all possible, carry at least one more mic than you will need, just in case.

When you are outside, it is a good idea to have a **windscreen** on your mic (see Figure 10.7). Mics pick up even gentle breezes as a hissing sound and windscreens cut down on this noise.

LOCATION PERMISSION FORM

Note: This is not intended as an authentic legal document. It is just a representation of a location release.
Check with your organization's lawyer before using.

The undersigned Owner or authorized representative of the Premises located at:

_____
_____
_____

hereby grants to the Production Company:

_____

its licensees, successors, assigns, and designees, an irrevocable license to enter upon and record at the Premises in connection with the production and distribution of the audio production tentatively entitled:

_____

This permission includes, but is not limited to, the right to bring cast, crew, and equipment onto the Premises. All things brought onto the Premises will be removed at the end of the production period. The Production Company shall leave the Premises in as good order and condition as when entered, reasonable wear and tear excepted. The Production Company shall indemnify the Owner for any loss and liability incurred as a direct result of any property damage or personal injury occurring on the Premises caused in connection with the Production Company's use of the Premises.

The Production Company shall own all rights in and to recordings made on or about the Premises forever and for all purposes. The Production Company shall have no obligations to pay any fee or other consideration for the exercise of the rights granted.

This Agreement may not be modified except by another writing signed by the parties.

Signature _____

Printed Name_____

Phone Number_____

Email Address _____

Date_____

FIGURE 10.5   A sample permission form.

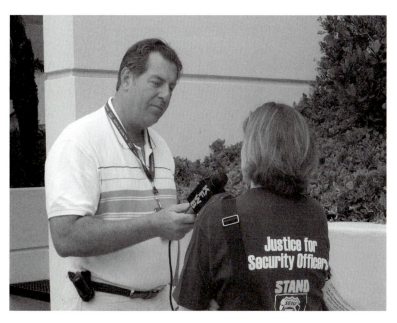

FIGURE 10.6   Reporter Pete Demetriou of Los Angeles station KFWB using a Sennheiser MD40 cardioid hand mic to interview a woman leading a group of picketers.

Miking musical groups is particularly interesting and can be complex. If the performance is just for people in the vicinity, sometimes you need to mic only the vocalist because the instruments will carry well enough (see Figure 10.8). Other times, especially if you are recording, you should mic the vocalist and the sound holes of the instruments. Refer to Figure 10.2 and notice how the mics are pointed at the string instrument sound holes, how the singer is miked, and how the trumpets, which are louder than other instruments, are not miked. If you have a large band or orchestra, you can mic individual sections (the violins, the trombones) and send each mic to a separate audio **channel**. Technicians at an audio board then mix the sounds so that they are at the desired volumes.

FIGURE 10.7   A windscreen. (Image courtesy of iStockphoto, Kryzysztof Kwiatkowski, Image #3428747.)

10.6 USING RECORDERS

The main recorders used for location work are the small portable ones that record on **hard drive** or **memory cards** (see Chapter 6, "Digital Audio Players/Recorders"). However, **MiniDisc** recorders, **digital audio tape (DAT)** recorders, and even analog cassette recorders are sometimes used. The most valuable recorders are those that can be used to undertake at least minimal editing. News reporters, in particular, need to edit interviews and other sounds so that they can send their stories back to the stations from the field. It is also helpful if the recording medium is compatible with the studio editing system—in other words, if the memory card or hard drive can be inserted into the studio equipment so that the material on it can be edited into a production without a great deal of downloading and complicated transfer of data. You might, for example, record cars buzzing by on a freeway, then go back to the studio and give the memory card to a person editing a feature on the history of transportation. The easier it is for that person to incorporate the car sounds into the feature, the better.

Batteries are the main potential problem related to portable recorders. You should make sure that a recorder's battery is fully charged before you take it out, and you should bring along extra batteries. Most vehicles that are used regularly for audio recording (such as news vans) have built in charging capabilities and reporters should charge batteries that have run down. You should replace the battery when it registers 25 percent full; if you don't, it is bound to go dead

FIGURE 10.8   In this situation, where the band is performing live, only the vocalist has a mic. (Image courtesy of iStockphoto, A-Digit, Image #4693200.)

just as you are recording your most important interview. At the end of your recording session, make sure you charge the battery for the next user. About once a week, take the battery all the way to empty and then recharge it in order to maximize its performance. At some colleges technicians handle recharging batteries, but in other situations students check out battery chargers and are expected to return the batteries fully charged.

FIGURE 10.9   A portable mixer being used in a location situation.

10.7 USING MIXERS

Most audio **mixers** used in the field are simple ones that allow you to adjust the volume for several inputs (see Figure 10.9). News vans often have small audio boards built into them so the reporter can mix together recorded sounds and his/her voice to build a story.

More complicated mixers are used for club performances and mixing band or orchestra music. These have more inputs and possibilities for **signal processing** (see Chapter 8). If the band is performing live, but someone also wants to record it, that person might connect a recorder to **house sound**—the sound generated for the people at the venue where the band is performing (see Figure 10.10).

If you record house sound, you must pay careful attention to the quality and volume of the sound entering your recorder. Concerts are often loud and the mix going to the crowd gathered at the venue will result in distortion when recorded. Don't trust your **VU meters**; they may not be set to take into account the loudness of the music. See whether someone at the venue can send you tone from a **tone generator** so that you can calibrate your sound. Listen

FIGURE 10.10   This reporter is plugging a portable Morantz recorder into a mixer. This mixer is used to amplify and combine the sounds from microphones picking up the announcer, singers, and musical instruments.

to the output from your recorder on **headphones** and lower your volume input controls if it is distorted.

10.8 USING HEADPHONES

When you are on location it is important to have high-quality headphones, preferably **circumaural** (see Chapter 7, "Monitor Speakers and Studio Accessories"). You want something that shuts out external noises so that you can hear clearly what you are recording and be aware of unwanted sound. Headphones can be used when you are recording, while you are listening to material to edit it, and after you have it in the finished form. You can also use them to **cue** up material when you have an audience and don't want them to hear the cueing sound. When it is inappropriate to wear headphones (such as when you are interviewing someone), make sure ahead of time that you have your recorder levels set properly so that the interview will not be too loud or too soft.

Sportscasters and helicopter traffic reporters wear headphones in part so they can hear instructions from the station ("time for a commercial break," "head over to Route 58"). Usually there is a microphone attached to the headphone assembly so that they can operate hands-free—a necessity for someone flying a helicopter and a convenience for sportscasters who are often juggling statistics while they report (see Figure 10.11). Headphone-microphone combinations are usually referred to as a **headset**.

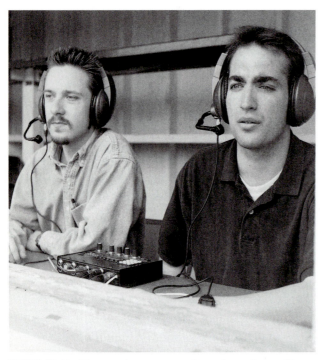

FIGURE 10.11 These sports announcers who work as a team, with one announcer providing the play-by-play, while another offers color commentary and game statistics, wear headphones with microphones attached so they can work hands-free. (Image courtesy of Alan R. Stephenson.)

10.9 GETTING THE SIGNAL BACK TO THE STUDIO

Sometimes you record material in the field and carry it by hand back to the studio where you or others edit it and prepare it for broadcast. But in many instances, it is necessary or desirable to send the material to the station so that it can be edited or broadcast immediately. The most obvious example is on-the-spot news. A radio news facility would not want a reporter to cover a fire by driving back to the studio with each update. People want the news as it is happening. In the same manner, play-by-play needs to get from the venue to the airwaves as the game is in progress.

Audio facilities use various methods to transmit a signal from a location to the station and from there to the station transmitter. One of the oldest methods, still in use to some degree, is a plain old telephone line. A microphone or a recorder is attached to a phone jack and the sound is sent through the phone switching system in the same manner that your voice is sent when you call a friend on a landline phone. There are phone systems, such as **ISDN** and **ATM**, that yield higher sound quality than your home phone, but they operate through wires in much the same manner as a home phone. **Telex** is another system that has been around for awhile. It is basically a telegraph system that was adapted for shortwave radio. It uses airwaves rather than wires.

Another system called a **remote pickup unit** (**RPU**) uses a band of frequencies that the FCC set aside for electronic news gathering and other remote broadcasting. This system uses special equipment often referred to as "Marti," because that is the name of the main company that provides the gear (see Figure 10.12). For this method, a small transmitter at the field location must line up with an antenna that a station has placed somewhere in the local vicinity, usually on a high hill. In order for the transmission to work it must be in "**line of sight**." That means the transmitter must be able to "see" the antenna—not literally, but in such a way that the signal can get from the location to the antenna without being cut off by buildings or hills.

FIGURE 10.12 A Marti RPU. (Image courtesy of Broadcast Electronics.)

When sound needs to be sent longer distances, satellites are brought into play. There are two types of satellites, geosynchronous and low-earth orbit. **Geosynchronous** ones are approximately 22,000 miles above the earth, moving at the same speed as the earth, so they appear to hang above a particular position on earth. Because they are so far away, there is a great deal of lag time between when the audio signal is sent to them and when it is returned to earth. They are more likely to be used for the transport of completed television programs than for radio news gathering. **Low-earth orbit (LEO) satellites** are 200 to 700 miles above earth, so although there is still a delay of sound when they are used, the delay is not as great as that with geosynchronous satellites. They do not hang above a particular spot, but there are many of them, so there is always at least one over every area. **Satellite phones** (see Figure 10.13) that deliver audio from remote locations use these LEO satellites.

Wireless **broadband** (see Figure 10.14) is another way that audio facilities receive information from the field. Companies such as Sprint sell to stations and networks secure transmission services that travel to and over the Internet. In addition, with special equipment, reports from the field can be sent through cell phones (see Figure 10.15), and there are also ways to send an audio report as an attachment to an email.

If you are sending audio back to a station, it is important to know the characteristics of the particular system you are using. If it is essential that the audio feed actually gets to its destination (as is the case in news reporting), then the station should provide redundancy so that if one system doesn't work, another can. For example, if your primary system involves a Marti, you should know where in your town there are "**dead spots**"—places where the signal will be obstructed. In those places you may need to use a cell phone or an ISDN line instead.

People at locations also need a way to talk to people at the home base, so that they can find out when they need to

FIGURE 10.13 A satellite phone. (Image courtesy of iStockphoto, Alberto Pomares, Image #5297098.)

FIGURE 10.14 Equipment needed for wireless broadband transmission.

FIGURE 10.15   Equipment that can be used to send audio with a cell phone.

send a feed, where they should go next for breaking news, and other logistical information. Through the years, two-way radios and walkie-talkies have been used for this purpose, but now cell phones are the main way that people communicate.

Whenever possible, conduct a trial feed to make sure that the people at the station or network can receive your field report before you send it. A feed that cuts off in the middle is annoying to listeners. Also, all the transmission equipment runs on batteries, so you must make sure they are properly charged in the same manner as your recording equipment batteries. Reporters sometimes go out to cover stories by themselves, and so they are responsible for operating all the equipment. The best story in the world will be useless if it cannot get from the location to the listener.

10.10 HANDLING VEHICLES

If you are going to a location, you obviously need to have some way to get there. As a student, this probably means that you will drive your own car, although for some location recording it is possible to use public transportation and carry your equipment with you. **Stringers** (people who search for news stories that they can cover and then sell the reports to stations, networks, or news agencies) also use their own transportation.

Most radio stations and other news gathering organizations provide vehicles for reporters, commonly a news van that is outfitted with equipment for editing and transmitting. Sometimes the vans have **scanners** so that reporters can listen to police and fire department radios. Reporters are often issued laptops so they can write their stories (see

Figure 10.16) and also search the Internet if they are in an area where they can access it. Having paper around to make notes and to use as a backup when the computer inevitably crashes is still a must. Laptops, too, have batteries that need to be checked and charged.

A vehicle serves as a mobile office/studio—the place where the audio person writes, records, mixes, and transmits. It is the responsibility of the person using it to keep it in good condition. If you are a reporter, keep the gas tank three quarters full (see Figure 10.17), because you never know when you will need to suddenly travel a long distance to cover a story. Fill up at the end of your shift so the next person using the van will have a full tank. Check the vital signs—oil level, tire pressure, and, of course, batteries. Most news gathering organizations have a mechanic who keeps the various vehicles operating, but the reporter needs to undertake routine maintenance and report any malfunctions to the mechanic.

There also are news and traffic helicopters (see Figure 10.18) that people reporting from the air operate. Obviously, these are very expensive vehicles that require special training. Although it is somewhat dangerous, usually one person flies the helicopter and also reports the traffic or news. Stations with helicopters often hire a person who is first and foremost a helicopter pilot and then train that person to be a reporter. Sometimes several news agencies will share one helicopter reporter.

10.11 PROVIDING FOR YOUR OWN NEEDS

When you are recording on location, you may not have the comforts of a studio, so you need to make sure that you will

FIGURE 10.16   A reporter writing a story in his "studio." Notice the mixer and editing system that are next to him. The transmitting equipment is farther to the right.

FIGURE 10.17   The same reporter taking care of his studio's vehicle by keeping the tank three quarters full.

be safe and able to carry out your duties. If you are only going out for an hour or two to record someone in an office building, you probably do not need to take any extra precautions. But if you are going to be out in the sun for several hours, you may at least want to take along some water and suntan lotion and find out where the nearest food and washroom facilities are located.

If you are a news reporter, you should have more supplies with you, because you never know where you might wind up during the course of a day (see Figure 10.19).

FIGURE 10.18   A news helicopter. (Image courtesy of iStockphoto, Dan Barnes, Image #5288449.)

You might be covering a fire or bank robbery where you can accidentally find yourself in harm's way. You should think through all the possibilities in your part of the country and plan your supplies accordingly.

PRODUCTION TIP 10B
How to Pack a Survival Bag

What are some of the items in Pete's bag and why might he need to use them?

- Jacket with many pockets: This item allows him to place equipment and supplies in the jacket and operate hands-free.
- Bulletproof vest: Issued by his radio station, he wears this whenever he is covering a story, such as a bank robbery or a hostage-taking, where there might be firearm action that results in stray bullets.
- First-aid kit: Similar to any first-aid kit, this is something that all car owners would be well-advised to carry in their vehicles.
- Solution for cleaning out eyes: If covering a fire or chemical spill, this is beneficial in order to keep eyes from being damaged. The main ingredient is Johnson's baby shampoo.
- Hard hat: This, too, is issued by the radio station and is needed for any construction area or any situation where there could be danger to the head.

- Fireproof clothing: Because Pete reports in an area that has numerous fires, his station issues all reporters a fireproof shirt and pants and a fireproof covering for the head.
- Gas mask: Another station-issued item, a gas mask is needed if there are toxic chemicals or gases.
- Boots: Keeping a pair of old boots in the bag comes in handy for covering stories in rugged terrain.
- Flares: Like flares that people should carry in their automobiles, these can be lit to warn of danger.
- Binoculars: These come in handy for covering stories where reporters are not allowed near the scene. He can look through the binoculars to get a better idea of the situation and then report more thoroughly.
- Food and water: Energy bars come in handy when it is not possible to go to a restaurant, and water can be used for drinking and for washing off anything that may need it.
- Flashlight: For covering stories at night, a flashlight is indispensable.

Protect yourself in other ways, too. Keep in shape, because gathering news can, on occasion, be physically rigorous and require long hours. Make sure to eat at regular intervals whenever you can. Keep your own "gas tank" three quarters full, in case you need to cover a story where you will not be able to eat a regular meal. If someone relieves you when you are on an extended story, make sure that you convey to them not only the latest events related to the story but also the possibilities of danger and the status

A

B

FIGURE 10.19 Reporter Pete Demetriou holds the bag (A) of supplies that he keeps with him when reporting. In (B), he shows some of the contents of the bag. (Note: The big cases are not part of the bag's contents; they are there just to help display the contents.)

of the equipment. Expect someone to do the same for you and ask specific questions if they don't.

10.12 POSTPRODUCTION CONCERNS FOR LOCATION RECORDING

As already mentioned, it is possible that you will do a little editing at the location, especially for short items. But if you are going to be recording material that will become part of a lengthy feature or documentary that is highly edited, there are some special considerations you may wish to think about.

You should try to record everything **flat**—that is, everything should be recorded at the same volume level. During editing, you or someone else will no doubt raise and lower the volume of different elements, but if they were all recorded at the same level, this will be an easier task than trying to compensate for a variety of levels.

You may need extra audio referred to as **ambient sounds** or **wild track**. Sometimes ambient sounds are broken into atmosphere sounds, room tone, and walla walla. **Atmosphere sounds** add authenticity and interest to your production. For example, you might record sounds of a brook for a feature about the environment. You can often find atmosphere sounds on sound effects CDs, but sometimes you need to record them before you begin editing.

Room tone involves recording about 30 seconds of "silence" in the location (a city park, a concert hall) where you have been recording your program material (an interview, a musical group). Cast and crew remain silent while you record but you pick up the general sound of the location, using the same mic that you used for your main audio. Each location has a particular sound because of its acoustics and elements within it, such as air conditioning or the whir of a computer fan. Room tone is used during editing to smooth edits. For example if you cut from a recording

where a person was talking in a machine room full of operating equipment to a recording of that same person talking in the studio, you may find that the cut is too abrupt, because the machine noise disappears too quickly. To solve the problem, you mix some room tone from the machine room with the studio audio.

For **walla walla**, you record people's voices so that you cannot understand actual words that they are saying. Walla walla is useful when you have important foreground noise but you want to fill it in with background noise. For example, if you are producing a commercial for a restaurant where you record the restaurant owner in a studio, you might want to mix in walla walla to give the impression of a crowded restaurant. Walla walla got its name because sometimes the best way to record it is to have a group of people say "walla walla" over and over at different speeds and with different emphasis.

Anytime you are engaged in postproduction, you should keep ethics uppermost in your mind. During editing, it is very easy to change the meaning and intent of what someone said. Don't succumb to this temptation just because it makes your editing easier. Always aim to make something sound as close as possible to what actually occurred.

10.13 CONCLUSION

As you can see, location recording can be quite different from studio recording. When you are on location, you have more technical responsibility. You must also be more flexible. As a reporter, you may be pulled off one story and sent to another. Even though you have undertaken careful preplanning for an audio documentary, you may find when you arrive that crucial elements have changed in the last few hours. You need to do the best job you can under the circumstances and, whenever possible, enjoy the experience.

Self-Study

QUESTIONS

1. Which of the following is most likely to use a helicopter?

   a) a play-by-play sportscaster
   b) a traffic reporter
   c) a disc jockey working in a club
   d) a rock band

2. Why should a reporter keep a station news van gas tank three quarters full?

   a) to conserve gasoline
   b) to make sure that he/she will have enough gas to leave quickly to cover a story that is at some distance
   c) to keep the battery chargers in the van from discharging
   d) to keep the scanner operating

3. Which of the following should you do when you are scouting a location that you plan to use for recording?

   a) Park in a handicapped parking space to see if you get a ticket.
   b) Give your location survey form to a musician so he or she can arrange to record a song about it.
   c) Bring along some malfunctioning equipment and try to get someone at the location to fix it.
   d) Have the owner of the location facility sign a form that gives you permission to record there.

4. Which of the following should you be sure to do if you are using house sound?

   a) Listen with your headphones to the output of your recorder so you can tell whether your sound is distorted.
   b) Cue up the sound carefully so the audience cannot hear it.
   c) Always use a DAT recorder.
   d) Bring your own audio mixer.

5. Which of the following is most likely to have a problem caused by low battery power?

   a) a microphone
   b) a memory card
   c) a recorder
   d) headphones

6. When should you replace batteries in your equipment?

   a) when they are 25 percent empty
   b) when they are 25 percent full
   c) once a week
   d) when they are totally drained

7. Which is the most common microphone for interviewing in the field?

   a) a dynamic cardioid handheld mic
   b) a condenser super-cardioid wireless mic
   c) a dynamic omnidirectional lavaliere mic
   d) a condenser cardioid windscreen mic

8. Which person is most likely to have his/her microphone attached to the headphone assembly?

    a) a news reporter doing an interview
    b) a guitar player
    c) a helicopter traffic reporter
    d) a circumaural public affairs producer

9. Which system for getting sound from a location back to the studio uses frequencies set aside by the FCC specifically for this purpose?

    a) ISDN
    b) Telex
    c) cell phone
    d) RPU

10. Which of the following refers to people's incoherent voices in the background of an audio recording?

    a) walla walla
    b) atmosphere sound
    c) flat sound
    d) room tone

11. What are "dead spots"?

    a) a recording that is flat
    b) places where stringers find news
    c) places from which a transmitted signal will not reach its destination
    d) places at clubs where disc jockeys can place their turntables

12. Which of these does the selective attention principle enable you to do?

    a) Concentrate on having a conversation with someone even though there are many other noises nearby.
    b) Keep your equipment from locking up in high humidity.
    c) Hire a security guard to keep people away from your recording equipment.
    d) Scoop other reporters because interviewees will be talking to you, not them.

13. Which of the following would be most important if you, as a news reporter, are covering a man barricaded in a house who occasionally shoots from a house window?

    a) suntan lotion
    b) energy bars
    c) a bulletproof vest
    d) fireproof clothing

14. Which of the following is true of LEO satellites?

    a) They orbit about 22,000 miles above the earth.
    b) They are used for satellite phone transmission.
    c) They appear to be stationary in the sky.
    d) They are an outgrowth of the telegraph.

15. Which of the following would you be most likely to use to adjust the volume for several inputs, such as an announcer's voice and background noise from a busy street?

    a) a channel
    b) a mixer
    c) a hum
    d) circumaural headphones

ANSWERS

If you answered A to any of the questions:

1a. No. The sportscaster would be in an announce booth. (Reread 10.2.)

2a. No. You will use the same amount of gas regardless. (Reread 10.10.)

3a. Absolutely not. You should never park in a handicapped spot unless you have a sticker to park there. (Reread 10.4.)

4a. Correct. House sound can lead to distortion.

5a. This is not the best answer. Some condenser microphones have batteries that will discharge, but in the field you generally use a dynamic mic. (Reread 10.6.)

6a. No. You are confusing empty and full. (Reread 10.6.)

7a. Yes. This is the best choice. A dynamic mic is rugged and both the cardioid pickup pattern and hand holding are best for an interview.

8a. Wrong. When you are doing an interview you need to place the mic close to the interviewee, which you can't do if it's attached to your headphones. (Reread 10.8.)

9a. Wrong. ISDN is a wired service that does not use the airwaves. (Reread 10.9.)

10a. Right. Walla walla is the correct answer.

11a. Wrong. These are two entirely different concepts (Reread 10.9 and 10.12.)

12a. This is correct. Human beings, unlike microphones, can decide what is most important to hear.

13a. No. You might want suntan lotion if you are outside, but it is not the most important thing on the list. (Reread 10.11.)

14a. No. That describes a geosynchronous satellite. (Reread 10.9.)

15a. Wrong. The sound might be on a channel, but that is not what you would use to adjust it. (Reread 10.5 and 10.7.)

If you answered B to any of the questions:

1b. Correct. Of all the options given, the traffic reporter would be most likely to use a helicopter.

2b. Correct. You may need to get somewhere quickly and you need the gas to get there.

3b. Wrong. This is a nonsensical answer. (Reread 10.4.)

4b. This is not the best answer. You are not really in charge of cueing up the sound. (Reread 10.7 and 10.8.)

5b. Incorrect. Memory cards don't use batteries. (Reread 10.6.)

6b. Yes. This is the correct answer.

7b. Incorrect. None of the parts of this answer are correct. (Reread 10.5.)

8b. Wrong. A guitar player usually needs a mic by the mouth and one at the sound hole. (Reread 10.8.)

9b. Wrong. Telex does not use those frequencies. (Reread 10.9.)

10b. Incorrect. This is not the purpose of atmosphere sound. (Reread 10.12.)

11b. Wrong. These two subjects are unrelated. (Reread 10.9 and 10.10.)

12b. Wrong. The selective attention principle has nothing to do with humidity. (Reread 10.3.)

13b. No. This is probably the least important thing. (Reread 10.11.)

14b. You are right. This is the correct answer.

15b. This is correct. You would use a mixer.

If you answered C to any of the questions:

1c. Absolutely not. (Reread 10.2.)

2c. Incorrect. Gas and battery chargers are not related in this case. (Reread 10.10.)

3c. Wrong. This is a somewhat nonsensical answer. (Reread 10.4.)

4c. Wrong. Any type of recorder will work. (Reread 10.6 and 10.7.)

5c. Yes. You must carefully monitor your recorder's batteries.

6c. No. It is more dependent on their use than any particular time frame. (Reread 10.6.)

7c. No. One part of this answer is right, but the rest isn't. (Reread 10.5.)

8c. Right. Traffic reporter is the correct answer.

9c. No. Cell phones have their own general use frequencies. (Reread 10.9.)

10c. Incorrect. Flat sound would not refer just to people's voices. (Reread 10.12.)

11c. Yes. This is the correct answer.

12c. No. Security and selective attention principle have nothing to do with each other. (Reread 10.3.)

13c. Yes. This would be most important.

14c. Wrong. This is more attributable to geosynchronous satellites. (Reread 10.9.)

15c. No. This is totally off base. (Reread 10.7.)

If you answered D to any of the questions:

1d. No. Maybe for publicity purposes, but this is certainly not the best answer. (Reread 10.2.)

2d. Wrong. Gas does not operate the scanner. (Reread 10.10.)

3d. Correct. This is by far the best answer.

4d. No. House sound assumes the house has a mixer. (Reread 10.7.)

5d. No. Headphones is not correct. (Reread 10.6 and 10.8.)

6d. No. You don't want to wait this long as they may keep you from recording something important. (Reread 10.6.)

7d. Incorrect. All parts of this answer are wrong. (Reread 10.5.)

8d. Incorrect. This answer doesn't even make sense. (Reread 10.8.)

9d. Yes. RPU is the correct answer.

10d. Wrong. There is a much better answer. (Reread 10.12.)

11d. No. These two concepts are not related. (Reread 10.9.)

12d. Wrong. Selective attention principle has nothing to do with scooping reporters. (Reread 10.3.)

13d. No. There is a better answer. This would only be needed if the house catches on fire. (Reread 10.11.)

14d. Wrong. These are two different technologies. (Reread 10.9.)

15d. No, you might use these to listen to the sounds but not to adjust them. (Reread 10.7 and 10.8.)

Projects

PROJECT 1

Listen and plan for sounds.

Purpose

To make you aware of various sounds in a location environment and to help you figure out ways to keep sounds you want and eliminate sounds you do not want.

Notes

1. You do not need to use the exact locations mentioned for this project or to use the exact recording ideas. Feel free to improvise, but keep within the spirit of the assignment.
2. You do not need to go to the locations in the order given; you can mix them up.
3. You may want to use a recorder with a built-in mic. Generally, you record with the same mic you used for your main recording, but in this case you do not have a main recording.

How to Do the Project

1. Secure a recorder (and a mic if the recorder does not have one built in).
2. Go to a noisy outdoor location, such as a corner on the main street of your town. Stand there for about 10 minutes. Turn the recorder on and also make a list of all the sounds that you hear. Pretend that you are preparing a news story about the number of cars that are parked illegally. Consider the following questions:
   a. Which of the sounds that you heard would you like to keep and why?
   b. Which would you like to get rid of and how might you get rid of them?
   c. Are there any sounds you would like to add?
3. Go to a quiet outdoor location such as a residential street. Again turn your recorder on and also make a list of all the sounds you hear in 10 minutes. Pretend you are preparing a documentary about the history of this particular street. Consider the three questions listed in Steps 2a, b, and c.
4. Go to a noisy indoor location, such as a restaurant at dinner time. As with Steps 1 and 2, record and make a list of sounds you hear. Then pretend that you are preparing a commercial for the restaurant. Think through the questions in Steps 2a, b, and c.
5. Go to a quiet indoor location such as your bedroom and record and list the sounds you hear. Pretend you are preparing to record an argument between a mother and a son in this room and again think about Steps 2a, b, and c.
6. Listen to the your recordings and note any ways you might change your answers to questions based on Steps 2a, b, and c.
7. Write a report about your experience. Include your lists of sounds and your answers (and revised answers) to the questions above. Give any other observations you might have by answering such questions as:
   a. Is it easier to change the nature of sound inside or outside? In a noisy location or a quiet one?
   b. Does the type of program you are producing (news, documentary, commercial, drama) affect the need to alter sounds?
   c. Did your ability to hear all the sounds improve as you went from the first location to the last location?
   d. Were there any sounds you heard on the recorded material that you did not note on the list you made?
6. Turn your paper in to your instructor to get credit for this assignment.

Record atmosphere sound, room tone, and walla walla.

Purpose

To give you practice recording these three types of ambient sounds and to familiarize yourself with location recording.

Notes

1. You may have to experiment and record some of these (particularly walla walla) several times until they sound authentic.
2. Try to do all of these within a small geographic area so that you do not need to spend a great deal of time traveling.
3. Make sure that you know how to check out and use your facility's portable audio equipment. Check to make sure it is working before you leave the facility and report any problems when you bring it back.
4. If you can't check out an omnidirectional mic, a cardioid will do, but omnis are better for gathering general sound.

How to Do the Project

1. Think of some sound that you feel would make a good atmosphere sound—a river, cars on a busy highway, pots and pans banging. Secure an omnidirectional mic and a recorder. Hold the mic near where the sound is generated and record it. Listen to it and decide whether or not it sounds appropriate. If not, experiment by holding the mic closer or farther away until you achieve the sound that you want.
2. Find a room that has at least some noise factors in it—a fan, air conditioning, electronic equipment. Hold your mic in the middle of the room and record the room tone. Play it back and see if you can discern sound.
3. Gather a few of your friends together and have them say "walla, walla" at different speeds and with different emphasis. They should definitely not say "walla, walla" as a chorus; each person should say it with different timing and quality. They will probably feel pretty silly, but record them and see how they sound. If you don't think their recording could be used as background talking noise, record them again.
4. Turn in all three recordings to your instructor so you get credit for this assignment.

11

SOUND PRODUCTION FOR VIDEO

11.1 INTRODUCTION

Most of what has been covered in this book deals with audio-only material, such as a disc-jockeyed show or a radio newscast. Frequently, however, audio is used in conjunction with video—a TV documentary, a music video, a talk show, an animated cartoon, a dramatic movie, a video game, and so on.

To some extent, dealing with audio joined with video is no different than dealing with audio alone. Microphones used for a TV game show have the same directionality and construction options as those used for a radio interview. The audio board used to record a cooking show has many of the same controls as one used by a disc jockey. If the video is shot outside the studio, wind noises will be a problem, just as they are for audio recording. However, there are also differences in the audio techniques needed when video is an element—differences that this chapter will address.

11.2 THE IMPORTANCE OF SOUND TO A VIDEO PRODUCTION

Audio adds a great deal to any video production. Some have estimated that audio supplies 80 percent of the information and that video supplies only 20 percent. This does not mean that audio gets as much respect as video, however. On a video shoot, much more time is usually consumed by the needs of the picture than the needs of the sound. If an audio operator encounters a problem recording sound, the director is often less sympathetic than that director would be to a cinematographer's problem. One audio operator who regularly works on television productions has confessed to a method he uses to handle this situation. If he needs time to fix an audio problem he will say, "I think I saw a shadow on the actor's face." While crew members are scurrying trying to find what might be a source of a shadow, he has time to rectify his audio problem.

The good news is that as audience members build home theaters with surround sound, they demand the best in audio. Their demands are trickling down to the production

process and audio is gaining more respect. There are exciting, challenging jobs available for those who want to work with the sound of video production.

11.3 THE NEED TO ACCOMMODATE THE PICTURE

Audio recordists who are preparing material to be used with video need to take the picture into account. For example, for some forms of programming, such as television news or music shows, it is perfectly acceptable for the microphone to show in the picture. But for fictional forms (dramas, sitcoms), the presence of a mic will break the illusion, because in real life, people who are having an argument or embracing each other do not wear microphones.

Audio must also be recorded in such a way that it fits the needs of the overall program. It the material is fictional, then the sound must serve the needs of the story; if the scene is tense, the music and sound effects must be intense. For productions with complicated audio, such as movies, a **sound designer** is often hired to plan the overall strategy for sounds and to consider the purpose of sound in relation to the video. Throughout the remainder of this chapter we will cover various types of sound common to video production, how these sounds are recorded, and how they are incorporated in the final product.

11.4 RECORDING SPEECH

Recording the spoken word is very important in any type of video program. If the audience members cannot understand the **dialogue** of a drama or the conversation of a talk show, they will not be able to follow the story or learn from the information. As with any form of recording, you must decide the directionality of the microphone(s) that you plan to use. **Cardioid** mics are the workhorses of video recording, because they do not pick up sounds well from one side, the side where the video equipment usually is. For example, in a studio shoot, the video cameras rolling over the floor to capture shots might be heard through an **omnidirectional** microphone. Also, as with audio recording, you must decide on the construction of the mic. If the mic is likely to be moved often, you probably want the more rugged **dynamic** mic. If the mic is going to be recording a wide range of frequencies, you may opt for a **condenser** mic.

The positioning of the mic is usually much more complex when video is involved than when only audio is being recorded. For an interview situation, a television reporter might use a handheld mic in a fashion similar to how a radio reporter would hold it, but for dramas, sitcoms, and similar material, the microphone must not be obvious in the picture.

11.5 THE FISHPOLE

The most common type of microphone holder used for video production is one that is hardly ever used for radio or other audio-only productions. It is called a **fishpole** because it is a long pole with a mic at the end. The operator holds the fishpole (also referred to as a **boom**) and moves it above the heads of the performers, pointing the end of the mic toward the actor's mouth. The best position is 1 to 3 feet above the performer and 1 to 4 feet in front. It is particularly effective for recording dialogue, because the person holding the fishpole can move the mic quickly to capture dialogue of different people (see Figure 11.1).

But the fishpole has disadvantages. If the camera shot is at all wide, the mic is likely to show in the picture. Directors often like to use two cameras at the same time, one showing a long shot and another a close-up (see Figure 11.2). Therefore, audio operators have to be creative in the placement of the boom. Sometimes the solution is to place the pole at the talent's feet with the mic pointing up toward the mouth. Some audio operators place a piece of white tape on the end of the mic. That way the camera operator

FIGURE 11.1 A boom operator (right) readying a fishpole for use. It is best to position the fishpole so the mic is 1 to 4 feet in front of the mouth of the person speaking and 1 to 3 feet above it.

FIGURE 11.2 In this situation, two cameras are recording the same shot. The camera on the left has a wide shot and the camera on the right has a close-up. Therefore, the audio person needs to hold the mic a little higher than would be proper if only the close-up camera were shooting.

can easily spot it if it dips into the picture, and the camera operator and audio operator, working cooperatively, can determine just how low the mic can come.

Another problem with the fishpole is that it is likely to cast a shadow on the characters or the set. There usually is no way to prevent a shadow, but you can minimize it by positioning the fishpole in such a way that the shadow falls onto the floor or onto a flowerpot or other piece of scenery where it will not be noticed. If that doesn't work, someone can stand by the microphone and look to see what light is causing the problem (see Figure 11.3). Moving that light slightly to the left or right can often redirect the shadow to a harmless area. Because a boom mic is often used to record several people talking, there is always the possibility that one person will talk more quietly than another. Usually this can be overcome by placing the mic closer to one person than to the other, but this involves skill and experience on the part of the fishpole holder.

PRODUCTION TIP 11A
Holding a Fishpole

Holding a fishpole can be tiring. If you do not have a great deal of upper-body strength, you would be well-advised to visit a gym and do a little body building before attempting a long day of

shooting. Before you actually hold the fishpole for a long time, experiment with it to find several positions that are comfortable for you and then occasionally switch from one to the other. You will probably find that having your arms stretched out at far as possible is one of the better positions because that way you can balance the weight equally on both arms as opposed to having most of the weight on the arm nearest to the mic. During shooting, take every opportunity you can to put the fishpole down, even for a few seconds between shots. This will relax your arms and make it easier for you to hold the fishpole for the next shot.

11.6 THE LAVALIERE

As already mentioned in Chapter 4, "Microphones," another way to record speech is with a **lavaliere (lav)**, a small mic (see Figure 11.4) that can be clipped to a person's clothing. The best way to position it is 8 to 10 inches below the talent's mouth, attached to a tie or blouse, making sure that it is not in a position where it will pick up the rustle of clothing. Lav mics are often wireless so that they give the person wearing it more freedom (for example, the cooking show chef can move about the studio kitchen or the drama actor can run down the street), but they can also be totally wired. In either case, they usually include

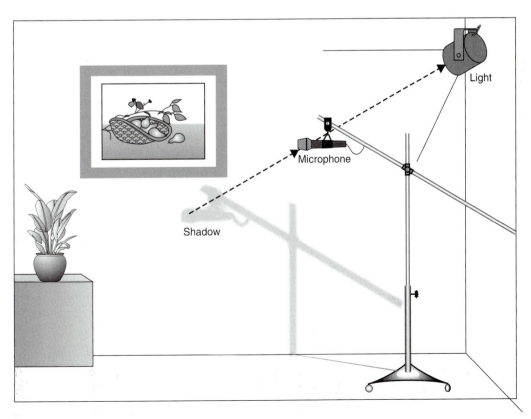

FIGURE 11.3 You can see what light is causing the microphone shadow if you stand in the shadow and look at the microphone. The offending light will be the one you see behind the mic.

FIGURE 11.5   A boom stand.

FIGURE 11.4 A lavaliere microphone. (Image courtesy of Bosch Communications Systems.)

a power supply/transmitter antenna that can be worn on a belt or waistband or buried in a set. If the mic is wireless, the antenna transmits the signal to a receiver that is then attached by wire to a recording device. If it is wired, a connection from the power supply goes to an audio board or recorder. Each person has his or her individual lav, so it is easy to record each person's speech on a different track of an audio recorder.

A disadvantage of lavalieres is that they are sometimes visible in a close-up. Also, the cables that are part of the lav assembly should be strung under the person's clothes because, even if it is all right for the mic to show, a cable draped down the front of a shirt or blouse looks sloppy. Depending on what the person is wearing, the stringing of the cables can be difficult. Also, because each person must be miked separately, if the people get too close together, there is the danger of **multiple-microphone interference** (see Chapter 4).

11.7 OTHER FORMS OF MICROPHONE POSITIONING

Some large-scale video productions, such as musical reviews, use **perambulator booms**, which are movable platforms that can move the mic in, out, up, down, and various other directions. More modest **boom stands** (see Figure 11.5) consist of a long horizontal pipe with a standard thread for a microphone on one end and a weight on the other end to balance the microphone. This pipe is attached to a vertical stand that is attached to wheels. The boom stand can be moved around to record different people in much the same way as the fishpole. It is easier on the arms of its operator than a fishpole, but not as maneuverable as a human body.

Mics can also be hidden on the set. Frequently microphones are placed in recesses of a news sets directly in front of where the anchors sit. For dramas, they can be hidden in flowerpots or other props. For a TV studio shoot, they can hang from the **grid** in the ceiling. Hidden locations free the talent of the need to deal with mics or even look at them, and as long as they pick up the sound well, they represent a valid way to mic. The main problem with them is that they do not move and, for most video productions, the performers move. The mic in the flowerpot might pick up the actress well while she is sitting on the sofa, but loses her sound as she walks to the door. Worse yet is hiding the mic in something that moves during the course of a shot—when the uncle picks up an umbrella to exit and the sound goes out the door with him.

There are times when **desk stand** mics are used for guests on public affairs TV shows, when **floor stands** are used for music videos, when hand mics are used by talk show hosts who converse with people in the audience, when **headsets** are used by TV sports announcers, and when **shotgun mics** are used to record distant sounds for a video documentary. The use of these devices has the same advantages and disadvantages as have already been discussed in Chapters 4 and 10.

11.8 CONTINUITY AND PERSPECTIVE

Continuity and perspective are two concepts that play a larger role in video productions than in audio-only productions. **Continuity** refers to shooting in such a way that there will be a consistent progression from one shot to another when the final product is assembled. On a movie set, continuity is almost an obsession, mainly because scenes are shot out of order. One of the crew positions is a **script supervisor** who has as a main part of her/his job making sure shots will work together. Is the actor wearing the same tie as he enters his car in a scene shot on Monday

FIGURE 11.6 To sync picture shot on film and sound recorded on a separate recorder so that they could ride together for editing purposes, filmmakers used (and still use) a clapper, such as the one shown here. At the beginning of each shot, a crew member holds the clapper in front of the film camera and claps the sticks together. In the editing suite, the frame where the clapper closes is lined up with the sound of it closing. Then the rest of the shot that follows is in sync. (Image courtesy of iStockphoto, Tomasz Rymkiewicz, Image #5540076.)

as he is wearing when he gets out of his car in a scene shot on Thursday? In a documentary about an author, was the author holding the book in her right hand both for the long shot and for the close-up that was shot after the interview?

Script supervisors are supposed to check for audio continuity also, but in reality, that job often falls to the audio recordist. If the air conditioning is operating during a long shot of a couple arguing, it should also be on during the close-ups of the couple, so that when the editor cuts from a long shot to a close-up, the background noise level will not change. When everyone breaks for lunch, you should note how far away the mic was from the performers so that when shooting starts again after lunch, the mic can be in the same position. To the extent possible, you should use the same mic for the same person throughout a production. Because each mic has its particular sound, switching mics can change the sound. Sometimes this is not possible, however. You may be using a boom for the bulk of the shooting but need to switch to a wireless lav for a long shot of a person running. In such circumstances, you should listen to recordings of various available mics and choose ones that sound fairly similar.

Perspective relates to distance. If a dog is barking in the background of a shot, the dog's sound should be different than if it is in the foreground of the shot. In this way, the viewers will feel closer to or farther from the dog and the sound will reinforce what they are seeing on the screen and help give the two-dimensional frame more of a three-dimensional feel. The easiest way to achieve proper perspective is to move a mic farther away or closer to the sound. If the mic is on a fishpole, it usually needs to be farther away for a long shot because it will show if it is right above the actor's head. Lav mics present a problem with perspective. They are always the same distance from the person's mouth so should not be used when perspective changes are needed. Hidden mics can be good for perspective if the picture relates to where the mic is placed. If

the shot widens as the actress moves back from the hidden mic, perspective will be accurate. But if the camera follows the actress with a close-up while she is moving farther from the mic, the perspective will be incorrect.

11.9 THE RECORDING PROCEDURE

The simplest way to record sound for video is to plug the end of the microphone cable into the camera and record the sound on the tape or hard drive that is part of the camera assembly. This works well for a single sound, such as a news reporter doing a stand-up. But if the sound is more complex, involving a number of different voices or a number of different microphones, it is a good idea to have additional equipment that can control sound. If a program is being shot in a TV studio, the mics run through an audio board and the sound is adjusted just as it is for any production that involves studio audio. In the field, many audio recordists use a portable mixer so that they can manipulate sounds—for example, record a soft-spoken person at a high volume level on one track while recording a person with a louder voice at a lower level on another track.

The output from this mixer can be sent directly to the camera (either through a wire or in a wireless manner) or it can be recorded separately on an audio recorder. Recording separately is referred to as **double-system sound** and recording onto the same source as the video is called **single-system sound**. Double-system recording was historically used for movies shot on film, because the sound couldn't be recorded on the film in an effective manner that allowed for editing. Sound and picture were recorded on separate pieces of equipment and later synched by lining up the picture and sound of a **clapper** (see Figure 11.6).

Video is edited electronically, so there is no technical reason to record sound separately. However, double-system

FIGURE 11.7 This audio operator is sitting in a corner of a studio where a scene for the TV show *Family Affair* is being shot. He has all his equipment on a portable cart.

sound recording is often used with video recording for a number of reasons. Not having an audio cable or a wireless receiver attached to the camera allows the camera operator more flexibility of movement. If sound is recorded using both single- and double-system recording, the editor has more flexibility once the project is in the editing suite. Perhaps more important is that the camera operator is busy framing the picture and often doesn't have time (or the inclination) to make sure the sound is being recorded properly. A person who devotes his or her entire attention to audio recording will produce a better product. In fact, big-budget productions usually have at least two audio people—one to hold the fishpole and another to operate the recording equipment.

PRODUCTION TIP 11B
Recording with Your Eyes Shut

There is a great deal happening during a video shoot: people moving props, makeup artists powdering actors' foreheads, technicians rearranging lights. It is easy to get distracted. If you are in charge of recording audio, try to arrange to sit off to the side with your mixer and/or recorder (see Figure 11.7). Wear high-quality headphones so that you can hear the sound you are recording distinctly and then close your eyes. This approach will allow you to concentrate on the sound and ignore the other hubbub. You will find it much easier to identify audio problems, such as extraneous noises that should not be part of the recording.

11.10 RECORDING SOUND EFFECTS

Many sound effects for video productions are obtained from CDs or the Internet, in the same manner as for audio productions (see Chapter 1, "Production Planning"). But there is a different concept that must be considered for video: **sync sound** versus **non-sync sound**. Synched sounds are those that are tied to the picture—when a dog that is onscreen barks, the audience expects to hear the bark and they expect it to coordinate with the picture. Barks that occur out of sync with the opening and closing of the dog's mouth are unacceptable. However, if the dog is offscreen, the bark does not need to be synched to the picture. In fact, you can use a standard sound effect, eliminating the need to record the sound at all.

Most commonly, onscreen synched sound effects are recorded during video production; in fact, it is almost impossible not to record them. For that reason, they need to be carefully miked. If the person talking is petting the dog, the boom mic picking up the voice is adequate for picking up the barks. If the dog is by itself but onscreen, it may need to be separately miked—not necessarily an easy chore. You need to experiment with different mics and different positions to see what works well. You might be able to hide or hang the mic or use a fishpole or shotgun mic. If the dog's barking occurs when the actor is not talking, you can, in a pinch, rely on sound effects of a dog barking that can be synched in postproduction. But if the man is talking while the dog is barking and they are therefore on the same track of audio, you need to make sure that you are picking up both sounds adequately. If the sound effect is non-sync, the process is much easier. You can place the mic wherever it sounds best, because there is no chance of it showing in the finalized production.

Video games have presented interesting challenges in terms of sound effects. For starters, the types of sounds used in video games often need to be "manufactured." They are not sounds that can be found in everyday life or on sound effects sources. Many of them are created by manipulating normal sounds in computers—raising the **pitch**, changing the **timbre**, stretching the vowels. Others are ingeniously constructed by such methods as running a razor over a bell or hitting a pillow with a wrench. Microphone selection and placement is varied until the proper effect is achieved. Even sounds based on real ones such as gunfire need to be manipulated, because they change as the dynamics of the game change. For example, if a player is too close to a cannon when it fires, this action might trigger an automatic change in loudness that brings about a realistic ringing in the player's ears. Sometimes sounds are "placed" on tires or windshields and triggered only when the player hits one of those areas. Everything needs to work together. If the player does hit the windshield, there needs to be the additional sound of glass falling to the ground. All of this organization takes a great deal of foresight and enables many creative recording sessions.

11.11 RECORDING AMBIENT SOUNDS

Ambient sounds, as discussed in Chapter 10, "Location Sound Recording," are general background noises, such as room tone, atmosphere sounds, and walla walla. They are just as important for video programs as for audio productions. It is often harder to record **room tone** on a video shoot, however, because there are more crew members. Getting everyone to be quiet for 30 seconds so that you can record the ambience of the place where you are shooting can be a difficult task. Camera operators, grips, and lighting technicians are usually eager to pack up the equipment, but you should record the room tone with all the equipment still in place. Otherwise, the room will have more of a hollow sound. The best mic to use is the one that you used to record whatever was happening in the room—an interview, dialogue for a drama, and so on. Doing so will further help ensure a similar sound quality that can be used later in postproduction.

Atmosphere sounds are usually recorded at a different time than the main portions of a production or they are obtained from prerecorded sources. As with audio only, these sounds, such as a bubbling brook or a noisy highway, add to the feel of the final product. With video, they must also coordinate with the picture. Although they do not need to be in sync with the picture, they must portray reality. If the highway in the picture shows a traffic jam, the atmosphere sound should not be that of traffic whizzing by. Most video cameras have a built-in microphone that should not be used in most video production circumstances, because it picks up noises close to the camera much better than it picks up dialogue from someone 5 feet away. However, for atmosphere sounds, the **camera mic** is often the best one to use, because you are trying to record general sounds of

FIGURE 11.8 On this camera, the camera mic is mounted right above the lens. (Image courtesy of iStockphoto, Oktay Ortakcioglu, Image #4892147.)

a particular area (see Figure 11.8). Of course, you don't really need a camera to record atmosphere sounds; you can just use an audio recorder, but video people usually record everything through a camera so that it is all in one place.

Walla walla (the sound of people talking in the background) is more likely to be needed for video productions than audio productions, because video productions are more likely to be fictional, with a highly produced sound track. Often scenes such as those in a bar are filmed with only the main characters talking and everyone in the background moving their mouths but not making any sounds. This gives a clean dialogue track to which other sounds can be added in postproduction. Walla walla is best recorded with an omnidirectional mic (which can be a camera mic) either by hiring people to say "walla walla" or by going to an actual location, such as a bar, and taping the sound of people talking (see Chapter 10).

11.12 RECORDING MUSIC

Music for a video project is usually recorded after the project has been edited, so that the music can fit precisely where it is needed. Some music, such as opening theme music, can be recorded ahead of time, and music that is

FIGURE 11.9   TV composer Ray Colcord (*Family Affair, Touched by an Angel, The Simpsons*) works out of a studio in his home, where he has a full array of software and hardware to aid his composing.

TIMING SHEET

Title: A Thrill a Minute
Director: Adrian Jones
Scene: 15

Code	Time	Description
00:48:40:12		Phil and Shorty enter the bar, look around and sit at a table.
00:49:10:00	00:00:00:00	Music starts as Mitzi moves toward the two men. The camera follows her as she sits and gives them the eye.
00:49:15:23	00:00:05:23	Cut to CU of Shorty.
00:49:17:21	00:00:07:21	Shorty: We didn't come in here looking for trouble. So if you're trouble, you can get lost.
00:49:24:03	00:00:14:03	Cut to CU of Mitzi. Mitzi: Actually, I have some information for you.
00:49:29:25	00:00:19:25	Cut to MS of Phil and Shorty looking at each other.
00:49:31:50	00:00:21:50	Phil: Well, I guess we might be interested in that. You got a private spot around here where we can talk?
00:50:40:40	00:00:30:40	Music swells then fades out as Phil, Shorty, and Mitzi head toward a hallway in the bar.

FIGURE 11.10   A timing sheet.

part of the plot, such as a rock band song that the leading actor and some of his buddies play, is recorded during the course of the main production, but generally music recording is one of the final stages.

Music can come from a variety of sources. There are many companies that supply stock music for a modest fee (see Chapter 1), but it is hard to find prerecorded music that fits the exact mood and timing required by most video productions.

A great deal of music for video is supplied by composers who work at their computers laying down various tracks of synthesized instruments (see Figure 11.9). They may never meet anyone involved with the production; in fact, a composer can live in France and compose music for a movie made in Hollywood. Often the video director or someone aligned with the production makes a **timing sheet** (see Figure 11.10) for the composer. It lists the **time code** numbers for places where the director feels that music should be added, and the composer is, of course, given a time-coded copy of the movie to use as a guide. The composer records music of the right mood and length and sends it over high-quality phone lines or the Internet to the director, who may ask for some changes or accept it as is and incorporate it within the movie. All the "recording" is undertaken in the composer's computer.

Other times, the composer might write a musical score designed to be played by an orchestra or band hired by the video production company. The composer (often acting as the conductor) leads the group of musicians through the music. The portions of the video that require music are projected onto a screen in front of the composer so that he/she can make sure the recording fits the length and needs of the video. This is undertaken in a studio environment with technicians working at a large audio console to fade-in and mix various groups of instruments. The miking and recording process is similar to that for the musical recordings discussed in Chapter 10.

When music is the mainstay of a program that is live or recorded as though it were live, a large audio crew is needed. *American Idol*, for example, has one group of audio technicians attending to the band and another attending to the singers. In addition, there are audio technicians handling the sound for the audience, the host, and the judges. All of these people need to work in close coordination with each other so that the sounds blend properly. They also must work cooperatively with the crew members handling the light cues, the camera work, and the scenery in order for the program to reach the audience as a seamless whole.

11.13 RECORDING ADR

ADR stands for **automatic dialogue replacement** (sometimes also called **looping**). There really is nothing automatic about it. It is a rather tedious process of rerecording dialogue that for some reason was recorded improperly during production. The reasons for needing ADR are usually legitimate—such as noises from a busy airstrip that were impossible to eliminate, or an actor who was too out of breath from physical activity to record useable dialogue.

If the director knows that the sound is going to need to be rerecorded, the audio crew does not need to try to record

FIGURE 11.11 An ADR facility. Actors undertaking ADR look at the screen to sync the sound. They can stand or sit on the stool and that way they can move if they need to change perspective. Having a podium where they can place a script or notes also helps the process. (Image courtesy of Sony Pictures Entertainment.)

FIGURE 11.12 This Foley walker is in a Foley pit moving branches in relation to what he sees on the TV screen. The mic on a boom stand is pointed toward the branches. (Image courtesy of Henninger Media Services.)

it properly. Instead they can record a **scratch track**—audio that is clear enough to be used as a guide during ADR but not good enough for the final production. During the ADR process, actors come to a soundproof room where they watch short segments (loops) of themselves on screen and listen through earphones to the scratch track for that loop. They rehearse lines until they feel they can say them in sync with their lips on the screen. Then they record the lines into a mic—usually a cardioid mic on a boom stand (see Figure 11.11). When they finish they go on to the next loop. A sound technician sits in a separate room by an audio console, playing back the loops and recording the new dialogue.

Of course, one problem with ADR is that it is recorded in pristine conditions, whereas the original audio (including parts of the dialogue that were perfectly fine) was recorded in a location with background noise. Here is where recorded room tone is a necessity. What is recorded in ADR will need to be mixed with room tone for the final product. ADR is expensive, so it is always preferable to record the sound properly on location, but sometimes looping is unavoidable.

A similar process to ADR is used for dubbing video productions into foreign languages or recording voices for an animated film. Although no faulty dialogue is being replaced, a technician plays short loops of video to actors who rehearse and then record the appropriate words.

sounds like footsteps on concrete, the thud of a falling book, the clink of water glasses. **Foley walkers**, agile people who are often dancers, watch the video on a screen and perform the acts needed to provide synchronous sound for the various movements. The room where they record is equipped with various surfaces—sand, cement, tile, gravel—and various materials that they need to perform—high-heeled shoes, tree branches, water, utensils. They rustle cloth if a woman on screen walks close to the sofa, they don tennis shoes and run on cement if a man is jogging, they fall during fight scenes, scream in terror, and do whatever else is needed to enhance the sounds for the movie (see Figure 11.12).

A technician sits in an adjoining room recording all the sounds through an audio board onto a server or tape recorder. This technician or the Foley walkers make sure a microphone (usually cardioid) is properly placed to pick up the sound. If a Foley walker is trudging through sand, the mic will be by his or her feet. If he or she is pouring water from one pitcher to another, the mic will be at table height. Because the mic needs to be moved a great deal, it is usually mounted on a **boom arm**. Foley walkers often work in pairs with a man performing the acts related to men and a woman imitating women's movements, but sometimes one Foley walker undertakes all the actions. Foley is completed after the video is edited so that the Foley walkers are recording sounds as they will be needed for the final version of the project.

11.14 RECORDING FOLEY

Most **Foley** work involves recording sounds that relate to actions in a movie or video production—for example,

11.15 RECORDING VOICE-OVERS

Voice-overs (VO) (also called **narration**) are easier to record than ADR or Foley, because they do not involve synced sound. Depending on the type of production, they can explain complicated processes, indicate what a person is thinking, or comment on what is occurring in the picture.

They are often recorded in soundproofed rooms with a setup similar to that of ADR, but they can be recorded from beginning to end without the looping. The person doing voice-over usually needs to watch the video so that the pace of reading matches what is on the screen. Sometimes, however, the VO is recorded before the video is put together and then the video is edited to match the narration.

A cardioid mic attached to a desk stand or boom arm is generally used for voice-overs. Readers usually have scripts, and these are best displayed on a computer screen behind the mic. If the script is on paper, its pages should not be stapled together, because when they are turned they will make a shuffling noise. Rather readers should have loose script pages that they can lift off and gently place to the side.

11.16 POSTPRODUCTION CONSIDERATIONS

Before a video production is complete, the sounds need to be edited and mixed together. This can be a simple operation such as making sure the musical interludes for an interview show are the correct length and do not overpower the speech. Or it can be a complex task that involves mixing dialogue, sound effects, ambient sounds, music, ADR, Foley, and voice-over. If there are many sound sources, they are often initially dealt with separately from the picture. While an editor is putting together the picture and dialogue, the sound designer or a **sound editor** is collecting and organizing the sound effects and ambient sounds and making sure that any ADR, Foley, or VO is under way.

Some of the sounds undergo **sweetening** at this point. Sweetening refers to making changes in the audio, usually to make everything sound better. For example, a door slam recorded during production might not sound realistic enough so the audio technician would sweeten it by adding some **reverb**. Audio technicians replace poorly recorded dialogue with ADR. They **filter** out an electrical hum accidentally recorded during a documentary interview. If there are continuity errors, they try to fix them, perhaps by adding walla walla to cover a gaff.

Once the editor has completed a rough cut of the picture, the sound editor can view it and create a **spotting sheet**, which indicates where in the production each effect should be placed (see Figure 11.13). The timing sheet for the composer also comes at this point.

Sound technicians place the various sound effects and other sounds on audio tracks, usually within a computer program (see Chapter 3, "Digital Audio Production"). Once the picture and dialogue are complete, the sounds (with the aid of time code) are positioned where they are needed—the gunshot when the trigger is pulled, the chirping birds throughout a bucolic scene. Sometimes, such as for a music video or a documentary with elaborate voice-over, the picture is edited to the sound, so the audio track is built first. Usually, however, the sounds are matched to the picture. They are initially laid down without taking volume into account; they are simply placed where they are needed in the production.

11.17 FINAL MIX

The **final mix** is the time when the relative volumes are adjusted to fit the needs of the story. It can be undertaken

SPOTTING SHEET

Project: A Day in the Field
Spotter: Alicia Fong

Page Number: 2
Director: George Walters

Item	Sync/Non-Sync	In-Time	Out-Time	Description
20	NS	01:42:15:10	01:43:12:09	Airplanes landing
21	NS	01:45:26:29	01:46:15:12	Muddled voices
22	S	01:49:52:12		Suitcase hits floor
23	NS	01:49:52:12	01:53:05:05	Traffic noises
24	NS	01:54:03:27	01:56:22:17	Restaurant noises
25	S	01:56:13:25		Door slam
26	NS	02:03:14:23	02:04:03:10	Cell phone ringing
27	NS	02:10:52:12	02:11:01:24	Glass breaking
28	NS	02:11:27:03	02:12:04:19	Dog barking
29	S	02:12:46:18		Glass breaking
30	NS	02:15:33:16		Thunder
31	NS	02:16:12:15	02:19:22:04	Rain, wind, and thunder
32	S	02:21:45:23		Car backfire
33	NS	02:21:50:20	02:23:47:04	Children playing
34	NS	02:23:47:04	02:26:33:12	Traffic noises
35	NS	02:24:55:23		Thunder
36	NS	02:26:10:10		Thunder
37	S	02:30:12:14		Hit glass
38	NS	02:33:05:06	02:34:55:07	Dogs barking

FIGURE 11.13 A spotting sheet.

CUE SHEET

Title: The Next Episode   Sound Designer: Susan King
Director: Philip Acosta   Page: 3

Min.: Sec.	Track No. 1 Dialogue	Min.: Sec.	Track No. 3 Music A	Min.: Sec.	Track No. 4 Music B	Min.: Sec.	Track No. 6 Effects A	Min.: Sec.	Track No. 7 Effects B
		02:15	/ Fade-in Guitars			02:15	Wind blows		
02:31	Henry: Try to see							02:41	Tree branch falls
02:47	(last word) obvious								
02:49	Marcia: No, never again								
03:15	(last word) yesterday								
		03:21	Cross-fade\	03:21	/Cross-Fade Drums	03:21		03:21	Rain
03:25	Henry: Someday								
04:02	(last word) gun			04:03	Fade-out\				
						04:06	Gun shot		

FIGURE 11.14   A cue sheet.

within a computer program or in a room with a large screen, an audio board, and excellent speakers. Several technicians sit at the audio board, perhaps with one concentrating on dialogue, one on music, and one on sound effects. They watch the production in small increments, altering the volume of various elements so that the sounds have the proper **balance**—music does not overpower the sound of a car engine starting or one person's dialogue is not noticeably louder than another. They double-check perspective to make sure that sounds in the distance are fainter than sounds in the foreground.

They **fade-in** and **fade-out** music, **cross-fade** Foley sounds, **segue** sound effects, mix room tone with ADR, and so on. Sometimes they **upmix** dialogue or other sounds that were recorded in **mono** so that they become **stereo** or **surround sound**. They do this by using the **pan** control on the audio board to place the sound to the left or right of one of surround sound's 5.1 positions. They create the enveloping sound effects sounds, such as that of an airplane that sounds like it is flying behind you from left to right.

They usually have a **cue sheet** (see Figure 11.14) to work from so that they know what the director has in mind. The technicians must work cooperatively so that all of the sounds will work together harmoniously.

If the final mix is completed using a computer program, one person does the whole thing. Under these circumstances, sweetening and the final mix can be one in the same—the audio operator alters and fixes sounds while mixing them, one small section at a time. If a production is simple (for example, adding opening and closing music and two sound effects), using a computer editing program is adequate. However, for complicated audio that needs extensive mixing and a large number of cross-fades, having several people work on sound together is faster and more likely to yield a better result.

If sound is going to be used on a computer for web-based material or video games, it is best to mix it within computer software. Video games present particular challenges when the games try to create different sounds depending on what the player is doing. For example, in first-person shooter games, if the player is holding the weapon steady, the audio focus may be on heartbeat and music intensity. If the player seems less confident, the sound track might consist of many distracting ambient noises.

11.18 CONCLUSIONS

Sound production for video productions is more complex than sound production for audio-only productions. It requires a knowledge of the principles related to all audio recording plus an ability to record and postproduce audio so that it enhances the overall production. Those that can effectively manipulate audio in the service of the story are valued in video production.

Self-Study

1. What is the name of a sheet given to a composer that includes time code numbers of where the director thinks that music is needed?

   a) a cue sheet
   b) a spotting sheet
   c) a timing sheet
   d) a segue

2. Which of the following would be a perspective problem?

   a) A person is seen in a close-up, but the person's voice sounds like it is coming from a distance.
   b) The rumble of a train is heard when a man is talking to a woman but is not heard when the woman replies to the man.
   c) The sound cuts in and out because the microphones are too close together.
   d) The script supervisor neglected to note where the mic was positioned when the crew broke for lunch.

3. Why is a fishpole effective for recording audio for video?

   a) It is also known as a boom.
   b) It is likely to cast a shadow.
   c) It needs to be held four feet in front of the talent.
   d) It can move above the heads of several performers.

4. What is a disadvantage of using a lavaliere mic to capture sound for a movie?

   a) It does not fit well on a desk stand and desk stands are the most common mic holders for movies.
   b) It might be visible in a close-up.
   c) It can be wireless.
   d) It is hard for the script supervisor to see.

5. Which of the following is a movable platform that can be used to move a microphone in various directions?

   a) grid
   b) shotgun
   c) table stand
   d) perambulator boom

6. Why are cardioid mics appropriate for recording dialogue for video?

   a) They generally don't pick up sounds from the area where the video equipment is operating.
   b) They are rugged.
   c) They are less likely to cast a shadow than omnidirectional mics.
   d) They are large microphones.

7. Which of the following would be an example of double-system sound?

   a) recording some material in sync and some out of sync
   b) recording to an audio recorder rather than the camera
   c) recording without using a mixer
   d) recording for a video game by using a clapper to ensure correct pitch

8. Which of the following is most likely to need various walking surfaces such as brick, tile, and cement?

   a) Foley
   b) ADR
   c) single-system sound
   d) VO

9. For which type of television show is there the most need for the microphone to be invisible?

   a) news report
   b) drama
   c) music video
   d) talk show

10. What is another name for automatic dialogue replacement?

   a) ATM
   b) looping
   c) scratch track
   d) narration

11. Which of the following is least likely to be an ambient sound?

   a) atmosphere sound
   b) walla walla
   c) room tone
   d) music

12. Which of the following is most likely to involve filtering out a hum from an audio track?

   a) transferring audio to multitrack tape
   b) cross-fading
   c) sweetening
   d) recording with a boom stand

13. What is one way that dealing with audio joined with video is different from dealing with audio only?

   a) Wind noises are more of a problem for video, because it is usually shot in a studio.
   b) Cardioid microphones are never used for video shoots.
   c) Audio uses only digital audio consoles and video uses analog audio consoles.
   d) Microphone placement can be more difficult for video, because the microphone should not show in the picture.

14. What is the title of the person who plans the overall strategy of sounds for a video production?

   a) sound designer
   b) script supervisor
   c) Foley walker
   d) composer

15. What might a microphone that is put in a vase of flowers that is on the set be called?

   a) a floor mic
   b) an omnidirectional mic
   c) a hidden mic
   d) a flower mic

If you answered A to any of the questions:

1a. Wrong. This is used for the final mix. (Reread 11.12 and 11.17.)

2a. You are right.

3a. Although a fishpole is also known as a boom, that doesn't have anything to do with its effectiveness. (Reread 11.5.)

4a. No. Desk stands aren't used often. (Reread 11.6 and 11.7.)

5a. No. This is not the correct term. (Reread 11.7.)

6a. Correct. Cardioids are less likely to pick up unwanted equipment noise.

7a. Wrong. Sync has nothing to do with double-system recording. (Reread 11.9 and 11.10.)

8a. This is the correct answer. These would be part of the Foley stage.

9a. No. In news reporting it is acceptable to hold a mic. (Reread 11.3.)

10a. Incorrect. This is where you get your money. (Reread 11.13.)

11a. No. Atmosphere sound is considered ambient sound. (Reread 11.11.)

12a. Wrong. Transferring to tape won't filter out unwanted sound. (Reread 11.16.)

13a. No. Wind would be the same for both types of productions and there wouldn't be wind in a studio. (Reread 11.1)

14a. Yes, sound designer is the correct answer.

15a. Wrong. This is not a name for a microphone. (Reread 11.7.)

If you answered B to any of the questions:

1b. Wrong. A spotting sheet is for other kinds of sounds. (Reread 11.12 and 11.16.)

2b. No. This would be a continuity problem. (Reread 11.8.)

3b. No. This would be a reason it is undesirable. (Reread 11.5.)

4b. Yes. This could be a disadvantage.

5b. Wrong. A shotgun isn't a platform. (Reread 11.7.)

6b. Not the best answer. Cardioids might be rugged and they might not depending on their structure. (Reread 11.4.)

7b. Yes. This is the correct answer for double-system sound.

8b. No. There is a better answer. (Reread 11.13 and 11.14.)

9b. Correct. You would not want a mic to be seen in a drama.

10b. Right. Looping is the correct answer.

11b. No. Walla walla is considered ambient sound. (Reread 11.11.)

12b. Incorrect. Cross-fading has nothing to do with filtering. (Reread 11.16 and 11.17.)

13b. Absolutely not. Cardioid mics are used for both, but are particularly useful for video shoots. (Reread 11.1 and 11.4.)

14b. No, the script supervisor deals with continuity. (Reread 11.3 and 11.8.)

15b. No. It might be omnidirectional, but pickup pattern doesn't have anything to do with its placement. (Reread 11.7.)

If you answered C to any of the questions:

1c. Yes. A timing sheet is the correct answer.

2c. This describes an entirely different phenomenon. (Reread 11.6 and 11.8.)

3c. No. That is a proper position, but that doesn't determine effectiveness. (Reread 11.5.)

4c. No. This is more likely to be an advantage. (Reread 11.6.)

5c. Incorrect. This is not a platform. (Reread 11.7.)

6c. Not the best answer. The type of mic is not what causes a shadow. (Reread 11.4 and 11.5.)

7c. Wrong. A mixer can be useful, but it's not the answer. (Reread 11.9.)

8c. Incorrect. This answer is unrelated. (Reread 11.9 and 11.14.)

9c. No. Singers often hold mics when they are performing. (Reread 11.3.)

10c. Wrong. Although a scratch track can be part of the process, it is not the other name. (Reread 11.13.)

11c. No. Room tone is considered to be ambient sound. (Reread 11.11.)

12c. Right. Sweetening is the correct answer.

13c. No. This wouldn't make any sense. (Reread 11.1)

14c. Wrong. This person only deals with Foley, not other aspects of sound. (Reread 11.3 and 11.14.)

15c. Correct. It could be called a hidden mic.

If you answered D to any of the questions:

1d. Wrong. This isn't even a sheet. (Reread 11.12 and 11.17.)

2d. Wrong. This could lead to a continuity but not a perspective problem. (Reread 11.8.)

3d. Yes. In this way, people can move.

4d. This is not the best answer. It may be a true statement but it is not a disadvantage. (Reread 11.6 and 11.8.)

5d. Yes. This is the correct term.

6d. Wrong. Size depends on construction. (Reread 11.4.)

7d. Very wrong. These elements have little to do with each other. (Reread 11.9 and 11.10.)

8d. Incorrect. (Reread 11.14 and 11.15.)

9d. No. A mic doesn't need to be invisible for a talk show. (Reread 11.3 and 11.7.)

10d. No. This isn't the right term. (Reread 11.13 and 11.15.)

11d. Yes. This is the correct answer.

12d. Wrong. A boom stand would not help. (Reread 11.17 and 11.16.)

13d. Yes, this is the correct answer.

14d. No. A composer only deals with music. (Reread 11.3 and 11.12.)

15d. No, there is no such thing. (Reread 11.7.)

Projects

PROJECT 1

Determine the importance of sound and picture.

Purpose

To help you decide whether you agree that audio provides more information than video.

Notes

1. Different genres of programs have different emphasis on video and audio. A talk show, for example, places a great deal of dependence on audio, and a western with many action scenes emphasizes video. Therefore, you may wish to use several shows for this project and mention the differences in your report.
2. If it is possible to record the programs at the same time you are undertaking this project, you will then be able to look at them afterwards to see what was really happening.

How to Do the Project

1. Sit in front of your TV set and mute the sound. Watch for about 15 minutes and see how much of what is going on you understand.
2. Jot down your reactions—what you think you understand and what you don't and what degree of frustration you think someone might have if there really were no sound.
3. Turn the sound back on and sit with your back to the TV set so you cannot see the picture. Listen for about 15 minutes and consider how much of what is going on you understand.
4. Jot down your reactions—what you think you understand and what you don't and what degree of frustration you think someone might have if there really were no picture.
5. Using your notes, write a report about your experience. If possible, try to figure out what percent of the material you understood when you only watched the picture and what percent you understood when you only listened to the sound.
6. Give your report to your instructor.

PROJECT 2

Record sound for a video project.

Purpose

To give you experience coordinating sound elements with the needs of the picture.

Notes

1. The CD-ROM that accompanies this book contains some video material that you can use for this exercise, but you can also create something of your own.
2. If you are enrolled in a video production class, offer to be the sound designer for a group project and use that experience rather than what is on the CD-ROM.
3. Don't bite off more than you can chew. Be realistic about what types of sounds you can actually obtain. Don't spend a lot of money buying sound effects or traveling to exotic locations to record something. Use your ingenuity rather than your pocketbook.

How to Do the Project

1. View the video material on the CD-ROM and plan the sounds you would like to add to it in terms of voice-over, sound effects, atmosphere sounds, music, and so on.
2. Gather all these sounds from CDs, from the Internet, or by recording them yourself.
3. Use whatever editing program you have access to for inputting the audio and video and editing it. You might want to reread some of the material in Chapter 3 that is related to editing.
4. Turn your project in to your instructor to receive credit.

12

INTERNET RADIO AND OTHER DISTRIBUTION PLATFORMS

12.1 INTRODUCTION

Digital technology has changed not only audio production techniques but also the very nature of how audio content is delivered. Radio stations, program syndication companies, and other content providers have found that in order to keep up with the times, they must align themselves with the Internet and other nontraditional distribution outlets. For many, this means building **web pages** that tie to programming by promoting contests, concerts, and other special events. Nearly all stations now also **netcast** their broadcast signal over the Internet, broadening their audience from a local area to potentially the whole world, as well as allowing office workers to listen to the radio on their computers throughout the work day. As access to the Internet spreads—from the desktop computer at home or in the office, to the laptop at a growing number of cafes and businesses, entire cities being blanketed with wireless Internet signals, and cell phones that can process broadband data in a pocket—audio content creation and delivery options become nearly limitless.

The Internet has allowed nearly anyone to start a radio station. College radio stations that had existed as over-the-air FM stations now are streaming over the Internet as well and can reach an international audience. Many colleges lacking the resources or available frequencies in their particular area to broadcast over the air now have radio stations and radio training programs where they could not before, via Internet radio. The proliferation of Internet radio in colleges has been a particular benefit to broadcasting students who go away to college because their friends and relatives back home can now hear their radio programs. Alumni can use Internet radio to stay informed about their school, perhaps listening to the sports events.

In fact, any group or individual with the proper equipment can now program a "radio station" that can be heard throughout the world (see Production Tip 12A). A 2007 study from Bridge Ratings & Research shows that 57 million people are listening to Internet radio on a weekly basis.

Existing radio broadcasters and neophytes alike are hoping to attract these listeners to their programming and increasing advertising revenue.

This chapter looks at the techniques for creating an Internet radio station as well as other radio distribution methods, new as well as tried and true.

PRODUCTION TIP 12A
From Internship to Internet

I started my radio career through a high school internship program and was hired at the end of my first semester for the 7 p.m. to midnight position. I was pretty pleased with myself, even if I hated most of the music that I played—top 40 adult contemporary. But I had caught the radio bug and picked a college that specialized in multimedia broadcasting.

I was in college all of 3 months when the magic of radio disappeared, to be replaced by the business of radio. Advertising, marketing, public relations, communication skills, and broadcasting history all reared their ugly heads and made for dreary days. All I wanted was to be in front of the microphone, be funny, and play music that I liked. Reality bites—and I lost my taste for radio.

It wasn't until years later in 1994 during a move to British Columbia in Canada that I came across a few of my demo tapes, which I played for my wife. We had a good laugh, talked about the good old days, put the tapes away, and went to bed. But all night I found myself lying there with my eyes wide open, thinking about what I wanted to do when I grew up . . . again. The next day the tapes came out again, we had one more listen, and then they went into the garbage.

Flash forward to my early thirties and another move, during which one last tape was found. It had somehow survived the Great Demo Tape Culling of 1994. It was never played, because at that point we didn't have a tape deck anymore. We did have a budding family, though, and the tape initiated a discussion with my daughters—stories of when daddy was a radio host. They giggled and, as I looked at my wife and kids, I realized I actually felt excited about something again. Everything I had told my kids about living out your dreams came back to slap me in the face. I think my wife saw the look on my face, but we never said anything to each other. The next day I bought a new computer and started changing my home office into a studio.

Slowly but surely, equipment was added to the studio as I researched how to create a streaming radio station. I knew I wouldn't get back into mainstream radio, but I also knew that I would be much happier as an independent station. I was playing mainstream rock until I learned of Canada's changing copyright laws—nothing to mess around with. With the help of my oldest daughter, I wired a computer with a soundboard, two monitors, a sound relay mixer, a telephone system, four microphones, VOIP, surround sound, and all the free software I could find. The list of what I had to learn in order to get this off the ground was staggering, in hindsight. From learning how to build a web site, to running a web server and being my own IT department took a lot of work. But it was actually fun.

The irony of it all is that I have had to rely heavily on my "dreary" postsecondary education to sell advertising, program the station, and find the proper content and topics to talk about. I am the General Manager, Program Director, News Director, Sales Manager, Copy Department, Producer, Office Assistant, Engineer, and Announcer, all wrapped up in one. I guess my resistance to finishing things in school got me 20 years off course from a truly fulfilling career.

After my copyright scare, I decided to play only unsigned bands and solo musicians. Like me and my radio station, I know they are doing what they do because they love it. My family is taking up the love too; they have each started shows of their own.

My wife has a daily show about current events and pop culture. She is the official queen of all streaming media . . . to me anyway. My oldest daughter, now nine, likes to DJ and wants to set up a special program for her elementary school for extra credit—and to look cool, too, I would imagine. As I set things up for her in the studio, she puts her coolest clothes on as a preshow ritual. I let her know that people can't see her, but she insists that if people can hear her, they can see her too. I'm pretty sure I have the wisest nine-year-old in history. My youngest daughter, now six, likes to sit on my lap and strum away at the guitars we have in the studio for our infrequent musical guests.

I don't know where this will all end, but I know that I *am* what I wanted to be when I grew up. I also know that my family and I will have something we enjoy to do together for years to come. At times the number of our listener streams passes the 10,000 mark, and we're exploring getting a broadcast frequency. I'm looking forward to the journey as much as I am proud of what has already been accomplished.

Mike Huffman

FreeRocker.com

FIGURE 12.1 Photo by Paisley Town.

12.2 WEB PAGES

While many listeners to web radio programs access them directly through a media player, such as RealPlayer, Microsoft's Media Player, or Apple's iTunes, or download content to their iPods, MP3 players, or phones, chances are that at some point or another they will want to visit a station's web page in a browser. The web page can provide information about the station's content, as well as have links to additional content.

The **home page** (see Figure 12.2) will, of course, contain a hyperlink that will allow listeners to hear a station live. Many stations, rather than relying on third-party media players, as they have in the past, have developed their own proprietary players on which they can communicate their brands and display revenue-generating advertising. However, in addition to live content, many stations or on-air personalities provide previously recorded **on-demand** content of program material from the past or even program material that was never broadcast live. For example, one file might contain last night's basketball game, another file might be a talk show from a week ago, and another might contain an unedited version of an interview that was broadcast only in its abridged form. When listeners click on those files, they hear the programming from the past, not what is currently being programmed. In commercial radio, this recorded content often requires a paid subscription to access. Many stations and on-air talent direct listeners from the web site of the station to Audible.com, where they will have to pay a monthly fee to access archived audio content. Public radio stations typically have a much more generous offering of free on-demand content on their web sites, though, with proprietary players, they can require listeners to first hear a pitch for the station's latest fund-raising campaign. However, today, even on public radio, many popular syndicated programs are now available on-demand at Audible.com for a fee. NPR's "Car Talk" and Garrison Keillor's "News from Lake Wobegone" are examples.

A web site, in addition to allowing listeners to listen live or play or download on-demand content, may also include

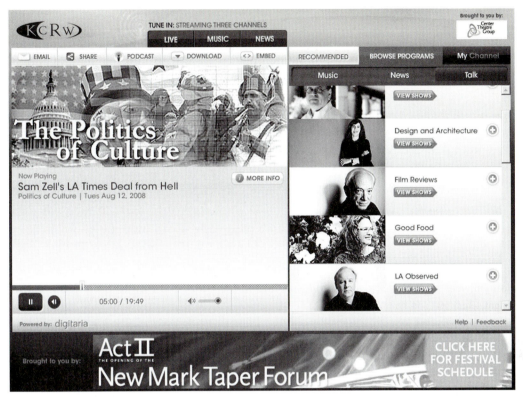

FIGURE 12.2 KCRW's proprietary media player bypasses third-party players like RealPlayer, QuickTime, and Windows Media Player, allowing the station to brand its player as it likes, advertise other shows, sponsors, and even offer built-in links to purchase products. (Image courtesy of Santa Monica College-Based National Public Radio station KCRW; 89.9FM; KCRW.com.)

FIGURE 12.3 This block diagram shows how sound goes from the on-air console of a radio station through the encoder, server, and player to the listener's computer speakers.

written information about disc jockeys, contests, program schedules, text-based news stories, and other features. How exactly web pages are organized is largely up to each individual station and is beyond the purview of this book. There are many programs (Microsoft FrontPage, Adobe DreamWeaver, and Adobe Flash) that can be used to build eye-catching web pages. This text concentrates on what you need to create the audio portion of an Internet radio station.

12.3 OVERVIEW OF THE AUDIO PROCESS FOR STREAMING

To undertake real-time **streaming audio** of a live broadcast, the output of the on-air console needs to get to the **sound card** (also called an **audio card**) of a computer that contains encoding software. This **encoder** system translates the analog audio from the sound card into a digital

streaming format and sends it to a **server**, which is a much larger computer. The server sends the audio data stream over the Internet to the **player** software on the listener's computer, where it is decoded and played out over the analog speakers attached to the listener's computer (see Figure 12.3). The sound must be changed from analog to digital, because analog audio cannot stream. It must be converted back to analog because the human ear cannot hear digital.

Connecting the output of the audio console to the computer sound card is fairly simple. As discussed in Chapter 5, "The Audio Console," most consoles have several outputs, so one can be designated for the Internet. The signal can still go out over the airwaves. The input to consumer-grade sound cards is usually a **miniphone connector**, and the input on professional-grade sound cards is either **RCA**, **XLR**, or a digital connection that can be made from a digital mixer. There are also FM radio sound cards that can pick up an on-air FM signal and bring it into the computer.

To place files on the Internet that can be accessed on-demand, you can simply create a **soundfile**, such as MP3 or WMA, using audio editing and encoding software. The size and quality of the soundfile must be considered carefully to ensure that listeners can play it easily and that your server will have the bandwidth capacity necessary to serve it to listeners. Although broadband connections are becoming de rigueur, there are still some people in the United States and many more abroad who access the Internet via low bandwidth—dial-up telephone connections of 56 kilobytes per second or less. These potential listeners will be turned off if files that they try to listen to cannot download fast enough to be heard uninterrupted.

Different types of audio content require different settings to maximize quality and minimize size. For example, a soundfile that contains only talk may be encoded at much lower quality (and size) than a musical soundfile, where a broader frequency range is desired. Some sites choose to offer several different-sized files of the same material. This way, people who are connecting via dial-up can select a smaller file, and those connected through broadband can listen to a higher-quality file. As the algorithms used to compress file sizes of audio have improved over the past decade, encoding has utilized **variable bit rates (VBR)** more and more effectively—automatically reducing the amount of data when there is little or no signal (such as if there is silence or a single, constant tone), and increasing it when more data is required to produce complex soundscapes (such as multi-instrumental, polyphonic music from a band or orchestra). The process of creating VBR content, however, takes time and therefore is only appropriate for on-demand files, not live streaming. In live streaming a **constant bit rate (CBR)** is used, which, depending on the bandwidth, can result in more complex sounds being washed out and silence that is just as bandwidth-intensive to download as when there is sound.

There are two different ways to listen to on-demand sound files—streaming and nonstreaming. Streaming begins to play sound on the listener's computer soon after the listener clicks on the link to it. Streaming provides near-instant access to material, but playback may be interrupted if the speed of the listener's Internet connection cannot consistently keep up with the amount of information that needs to be transmitted per second to keep sound playing.

With nonstreaming listening, the file must be completely downloaded before it begins to play. This allows even listeners on dial-up connections to listen to uninterrupted, high-quality audio files, if they are patient enough to wait through long download times.

12.4 ENCODERS

The sound card in the computer that encodes is used to translate an analog signal into a digital format. The signal is sampled and then compressed so it can be sent efficiently over the Internet and be received by people who are using DSL, cable, or dial-up **modems** that can operate anywhere from 28 to 300 kilobytes per second or even higher. (A T1 or T3 1,540 or 45,000 kilobyte connection using fiber-optic cable is available, but still very expensive, and is usually used only by commercial entities with large computer networks. This high bandwidth is more appropriate to transmit simultaneous streams of Internet radio than to receive it.)

Many audio operations strive to have their Internet files be CD-quality. As you learned in Chapter 3, "Digital Audio Production," CDs are encoded using a **sampling** rate of 44.1 kHz. In other words, they are sampled at 44,100 times per second. In addition, each sample has a **bit depth** of 16 bits. One way to look at bit depth is to relate it to **signal-to-noise ratio** (see Chapter 2, "The Studio Environment"). The higher the number of bits, the higher the signal-to-noise ratio, and hence the better the signal. You get approximately 6 **decibels (dB)** of signal to noise for each bit, so 8-bit audio is about 48 dB of signal to 1 dB of noise, and 16-bit audio is a very respectable 96 dB. A 44.1, 16-bit signal uses a lot of bandwidth—roughly 1.4 megabits per stereo second (44,100 samples per second, times 16 bits per sample, times 2 for stereo, equals 1,411,200 bits).

When data is sent over the Internet, it needs **overhead** (more bandwidth) so that the packets it is sent in arrive at their destination properly. What all this means is that in order to receive pure CD-quality sound, a listener might need a connection to the Internet that operates at approximately 1.7 **megabytes** per second. Most people have modems that operate from 56 to 300 **kilobytes** per second. Another way to look at this is that it could take as long as 2 hours to download a 3-minute piece of CD-quality music using a 56K modem. Somehow the bandwidth used by an audio signal being sent over the Internet must be reduced.

There are several ways to handle this reduction. One solution is to send a monaural signal instead of a stereo one. That cuts the bandwidth needed in half. Another method is to employ **compression**, which is the method used by most of the encoding systems. It does degrade the quality of the signal somewhat, but it gets the bandwidth down to about one-tenth of what is needed for pure CD-quality sound. Most compression systems use some form of **perceptual coding** that is based on characteristics of the human ear. For example, there are certain sounds humans cannot hear (such as those below 20 Hz or above 20,000 Hz). These can be eliminated. Similarly, there are also sounds that human ears hear better than others. If two sounds are playing at the same time, we hear the louder one but not the softer one. By taking human hearing into account, a great deal of what is in a normal sound signal can be eliminated without much damage to the quality. Some compression systems also deal with silence. They take out the silent places within the audio and insert a code that places the silence back in when the sound is **decompressed** before it gets to the listener's audio speakers.

There are many encoding programs on the market, such as the Windows Media Encoder and Nullsoft's SHOUTcast. Most have the capability to encode both for live streams and on-demand content and have various settings to allow for limits on file size, audio degradation, and the amount of time it takes to encode. There are always trade-offs. The concept of having to choose any two for the options of "cheap, fast, and good" applies when it comes to audio encoding, too. If you have the time and computer resources to allow your computer to do several passes at compressing a file, the result can be cheap (in terms of the amount of bandwidth it costs) and good, but cheap and fast will result in poorer quality.

FIGURE 12.4 This Wi-Fi radio and media player can receive Internet radio stations, podcasts, and other audio streams, as well as streaming music stored on your PC through the radio. (Image courtesy of Roberts Radio.)

12.5 SERVERS

Computers used as **servers** must run audio software that is specially designed to handle sending out multiple audio data streams simultaneously. Bandwidth again comes into play. Unlike over-the-air radio service, where one signal can reach an infinite number of listeners, for Internet service you must provide a separate audio stream from the streaming server for each listener. This setup can take up large amounts of bandwidth, especially if audio is encoded at high quality (and size); therefore, Internet radio stations must limit the number of listeners who can tune in at any one time. Sometimes this number is as small as 10, but other stations choose to incorporate multiple servers with high bandwidth connections to the Internet that can handle 1,000 or more listeners simultaneously.

Most colleges, universities, and other educational institutions now have servers that connect to the Internet. The most common procedure for a college Internet radio station is to use part of the space on the university server. It is possible (although expensive) for a station to have its own server, or it can contract to use part of a server from an Internet Service Provider (ISP) or some other source. ISPs usually charge based on the amount of bandwidth a station occupies, so this is another reason to pay careful attention to bandwidth needs.

12.6 PLAYERS

The player software resides on the listener's computer. It receives the audio data stream from the server and decodes and decompresses it into analog sound that can be heard from the computer speakers. Most streaming audio does not stay on the listener's hard drive; it streams in and is then discarded.

What actually happens is that the initial compressed audio data is placed into a buffer area, analogous to a small storage tank. Once a certain amount of data has partially filled the "tank," the soundfile begins to play. Streamed audio is poured into the top of the tank while the playback

audio is being drained from the bottom of the tank. The filling of the tank is slightly faster than the draining of the tank, so there is always enough in reserve to continue playing the audio if the input stream is momentarily interrupted.

The player software is available to listeners for free or at a low price. They simply download it from the web site of the company providing it or, in many cases, it comes preinstalled on store-bought computers. Additionally, as noted, some radio stations now build their own proprietary players, so a third-party player isn't required. Most of these players are created using Adobe's Flash Player (the same player behind most of today's Internet video, including YouTube), so the Flash Player plug-in is required for your web browser.

A few companies have developed stand-alone radios designed to receive Internet radio stations, podcasts, and other audio streams without a desktop or laptop computer. The unit shown in Figure 12.4 is a portable Wi-Fi Internet radio.

12.7 SOFTWARE OPTIONS

Usually the company that provides the encoder and server software to a station is the same company that provides the listener with software. This arrangement can present a problem, especially for the listener who needs one brand of software to listen to one station and another to listen to a different station. Although both brands of software can be downloaded for free or for a minimal cost, the two may compete to be the dominant (default) software on the consumer's computer. This can create incompatibility problems.

In addition, the players and software are always being updated. The major manufacturers in the market want to keep providing a better, more dependable product—thus

FIGURE 12.5 RealNetworks' web page allows you to download its player and to access other RealNetworks' services. (Image courtesy of RealNetworks, copyright 1995–2004, RealNetworks, Inc., all rights reserved.)

siphoning off customers from the competition. The newest encoding software or file type might be very appealing for content providers, in terms of providing better-quality sound with smaller file sizes, thus allowing more simultaneous outgoing streams, but if visitors haven't upgraded or don't know how to upgrade to the latest version of software that can play the file type, they will only be frustrated by this jump to the cutting edge.

The major software players at present are Real from RealNetworks (www.real.com), Windows Media from Microsoft (www.microsoft.com), and iTunes/QuickTime from Apple (www.apple.com/quicktime). Others providing software are Nullsoft's Winamp (www.winamp.com) and MusicMatch (www.musicmatch.com).

RealNetworks (see Figure 12.5), being the first audio player to enter the market in 1995, continued to dominate the streaming content market in the mid- to late 1990s, but started to lose significant market share when Microsoft bundled its own player, Windows Media Player, with its nearly ubiquitous operating system, Windows (see Figure 12.6). With the introduction of the iPod in October 2001, Apple's iTunes began capturing significant market share, even in the PC market.

The number of audio file formats can cause headaches for consumers of audio. The grand-daddy of compressed audio files, the .mp3, has been joined by Microsoft's

proprietary .wma (Windows Media Audio) format and the .mp4 format (used more by Apple), which is capable of transmitting audio, video, and subtitles, but is often renamed as a .m4a file to denote that it contains audio, or a .m4v to denote video. To confuse things further, although the .wma format can be played on Apple's iTunes (though only with a third-party plug-in installed), .mp4 (or .m4a) files are not supported by Microsoft's Windows Media Player, though they can be played on Microsoft's Zune portable player. Real Media has its .rm file format, which likewise has compatibility issue that, along with the other file/player issues, will probably all be out of date by the time this book goes to print.

Apple's QuickTime player (see Figure 12.7), though supported by both PC and Mac computers, has always remained a distant third in the audio game (though it has more adherents for video). Many users claim, however, that the Windows Media Player, and especially Real's media players, have become too big for their britches. Some complain that, for the user who just wants to listen to an audio clip, the offerings from Real and Microsoft have confusing and overly complicated navigation schemes—some that seem designed to trick users into accidentally signing up for "premium" services that require payment. QuickTime, its adherents claim, provides a more no-nonsense and straightforward interface. The most bare bones of the players

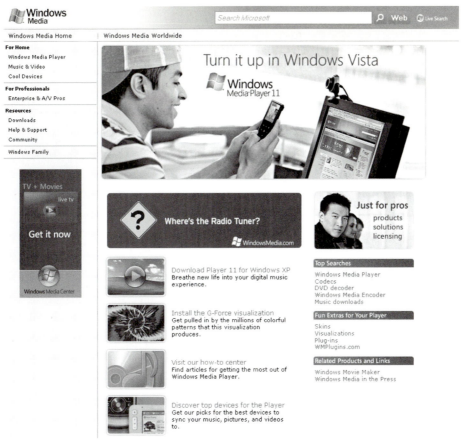

FIGURE 12.6   Microsoft provides a great deal of information to anyone interested in getting an Internet radio station up and running. (Image courtesy of Microsoft.)

FIGURE 12.7   QuickTime's web page emphasizes both video and audio features. (Image courtesy of Apple.)

(and the one with the least compatibility issues—at least at this printing) is Nullsoft's Winamp.

Many Internet radio sites now offer streams in all three of the proprietary formats: Windows, Real, and QuickTime. Others limit themselves to two formats or only one, usually either Real or Microsoft. Some sites have even made well-publicized switches from one format to another after users complained of being duped into paying for players because the link to the free version of the player was squirreled away several obscure clicks into the provider's web site.

PRODUCTION TIP 12B
Internet Audience and On-Air Talent Interaction

The Internet, as a very flexible tool for exchanging information and communication, can be used to expand the product of any business—radio included. Allowing listeners to feel that they are a part of a radio station or show is a good way to assure they keep coming back, though it can backfire as well, so care must be taken in the introduction of such technologies and add-ons.

The Internet and a good webmaster can offer countless cheap and easy ways to invite listeners to get involved in a station: chat rooms, instant messaging, and message boards with more threads than an unraveling sweater. Audience members can communicate directly with on-air talent, management, and other audience members—either in real time or through archived posts. But it is important for users of such services to feel that the service is active, if they are to be encouraged to come back. If you set up a station message board with 20 different subcategories, and if many of the categories see little use or new postings, it will look to visitors like the whole site is dead and they will move on to greener pastures. Better to start out with just one category and then break it up after the site is already populated and when the main topics that visitors are interested in discussing become evident.

Another concern is that Internet sites that allow users to interact with the site run the risk of being "flamed" by mischievous or malicious individuals who may post incendiary content to your site that could set off a "flame war," with different visitors trying to get in their last rancorous word. It is often a good idea to have a "moderator" for your site—someone who reviews posts for unwanted content before the content is posted to the site. However, if you plan to moderate your site, make sure that you have the personnel to do so. Nothing will so quickly turn off a visitor as posting to a site, only to see the post lingering in moderator purgatory for days before actually being added to the site.

12.8 ON-DEMAND FILES AND PODCASTING

As mentioned previously, one of the advantages of Internet radio is that you can place programs on a server that listeners can access at any time. Thus, your listeners can hear your programming at times that are convenient for them, but it also means the listener can determine exactly what they want to listen to.

When you record material that you want to place in an on-demand mode, you should take special care to make a high-quality recording because these files, too, go through encoding, compression, and other processes. The more useful audio information the system has to analyze, the better. You should try to record with minimal background noise and high-quality equipment.

In order to prepare on-demand material, you create soundfiles and then place these on your server so that your listeners can access them through their players. Most soundfiles end with .wav, .avi, .rm, .wma, or .mp3.

MP3 has received particular attention because of its use in downloading music files from the Internet. It is an audio file format that is supported by a large number of shareware applications that convert music from CDs. MP3 is one compression system for audio. Its full name is MPEG-2, Layer 3. MPEG stands for Moving Picture Experts Group, the group that developed compression systems for video data. This MPEG system encompasses a subsystem for audio compression that is referred to as Layer 3; it is based on the "perceptual coding" discussed earlier.

The three major streaming providers (RealNetworks, Microsoft, and Apple) now support this format in addition to their own proprietary systems. Some of the lesser-known players use MP3 as their streaming technology and do not have their own proprietary systems.

Podcasting is also sending digital files (mostly MP3) over the Internet, but is different from regular on-demand downloadable files, in that it relies on RSS (Really Simple Syndication) feeds with the audio file in the enclosure tag for playback on a media player or computer. "Podcast" generally refers to both the audio content and the method of delivery. The term originated from iPod and broadcasting, but has come to be short for a more generic "personal on-demand broadcasting." Podcasts can cover almost any topic, but many have been music shows, verbal journals, political essays, lectures, or talk shows. Podcasts can be syndicated or subscribed to, and new content can be downloaded automatically through an aggregator that is capable of reading RSS feeds. The listener can search for podcasts using key words and a feed management program that constantly searches servers for new material and then automatically notifies the listener when it finds something. Apple's iTunes is one popular source for finding and subscribing to podcasts and offers several tutorials on developing and posting podcasts on the Web.

The basic process for creating a podcast is not that difficult. First, you have to create the audio file or content of your program. The next section describes how you can build a home studio for creating audio files. Regardless of what audio format you use to create your files, you will need to convert them into MP3 files before you can podcast them. Next you need to create an RSS feed file. This file will tell what the content of your program is and allows aggregators or readers to find and access your podcast. While there are templates and tutorials on the Internet to manually write a RSS file, you can also find software that will simplify the process. Next upload both the audio file and RSS file to your web site or to the site of a firm that specializes in hosting podcasts. Make sure that your MP3 audio file and the RSS file are located in the same directory. You also want to validate your RSS feed file. You can do so by going to feedvalidator.org and typing in the URL of the RSS file. Finally, you need to publicize your podcast, on your own site and by listing it in various podcast directories. Listeners will receive your podcast on their home computers and many will then download to their iPod or other MP3 player and listen at a time convenient for them.

12.9 BUILDING A HOME STUDIO FOR INTERNET AUDIO PRODUCTION

Building a mini production studio in your own home is not difficult at all. In fact, with merely a computer microphone, and appropriate audio editing software, you could record productions for Internet radio stations, podcasting, and other Internet applications. Add a few additional pieces of audio equipment and your home studio becomes even more "professional" and offers more flexibility in use. However, before assembling any equipment, consider where you'll locate the studio. Although it's not likely that you can dedicate a whole room to a studio and turn it into an actual acoustically correct studio environment, consider finding a quieter spot—perhaps a corner of a room away from windows and doors that can allow exterior noise to leak in. Also avoid any room that might have an air conditioner or other background noise source that occurs on a regular basis.

The computer should have a fairly fast CPU of at least 2 GHz, a minimum hard drive size of 120 GB, and at least 512 MB of RAM. Any upgrading beyond these specifications will make your system work even better. Your computer will also need a CD/DVD reader/writer and a good sound card. Instead of a computer, you could consider a multitrack digital workstation, but, in most cases, a computer will be less expensive and easier to work with, and you may already have the equipment in your home.

Although many computers include an adequate sound card, you probably should invest in one of better quality or consider using an external audio interface. For one thing, most computer sound cards will have tiny 1/8-inch input and output jacks, which are difficult to work with; better-quality ones offer 1/4-inch or XLR I/O. Lynx, Digital Audio Labs, and Digigram offer sound cards with digital and analog inputs, as well as other desirable features that make them popular for home studios. Another approach is to use

FIGURE 12.8 M-Audio's FastTrackPro is a 4-input, 24-bit/96 kHz USB audio recording interface designed to let you record with professional results. (Image courtesy of M-Audio.)

an external interface, such as an M-Audio USB recording interface (see Figure 12.8) or a small audio mixer from Mackie or Behringer. Often this setup will give you more inputs, better mixing control, and direct connectivity to your computer.

The microphone used in your system should be of good quality, but a nice general-purpose microphone, like the Shure SM57, can be found for about $100; most other manufacturers also have microphones in this range. You may also consider a USB microphone designed to plug directly into your computer. Remember, if you plan to do interviews, record group discussions or a band, you will need more than one microphone to get good, high-quality recordings.

A home recording studio also needs monitor speakers or headphones. You can get by with the speakers that came with your computer, but better-quality speakers will allow you to judge the quality of your productions better. If you are using an external interface or mixer, it probably has an output to drive a pair of speakers. Of course, headphones will also work, but again, look for some that are fairly good quality.

The final piece of "equipment" needed for a home studio is the editing/recording software. At least one basic stereo editing software program, Audacity, can be downloaded from the Internet at no charge (see Chapter 3). Other programs—like Adobe Soundbooth, Digidesign Pro Tools, or Cakewalk SONAR—offer multitrack capability, sound processing, and additional editing features, and are fairly inexpensive. Put these pieces of equipment together and you'll be ready to record in the privacy of your own home studio.

12.10 COPYRIGHT

Copyright in relation to the Internet has become a major concern. Because it is so easy to copy digital material, the

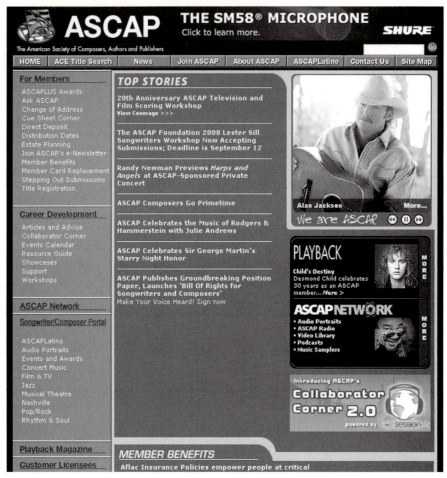

FIGURE 12.9 Each of the three music licensing companies have license agreements for new media or Internet broadcasting. (Image courtesy of ASCAP, copyright © 2004 ASCAP. Reproduced with permission of the American Society of Composers, Authors, and Publishers from www.ascap.com.)

copyright laws (written in the 1970s) either do not cover the concept or are ineffective in stemming the tide of illegal copying. An Internet radio station must remain aware of the latest in copyright legislation and enforcement or it can find itself in major legal trouble.

There are three agencies that license music to radio stations—ASCAP, BMI, and SESAC. These organizations (see Figure 12.9) have been in business for many years and have negotiated license agreements that enable regular radio stations to play music without having to negotiate for each song. The agencies collect a set fee from each station and then have stations submit logs of what they play. They then distribute the money collected to composers and music publishers based on an approximation of how often each selection was played. There are three agencies, because each of them handles different music, but a station that subscribes to all three can feel confident that it is playing music without violating copyright laws. These organizations have determined minimum annual fees for Internet broadcasting—$288 for ASCAP, $299 for BMI,

and $220 for SESAC. Additional fees apply when your site turns a profit, and special arrangements are in place for stations broadcasting religious music. If you are starting an Internet radio station and you are planning to use prerecorded music of any kind, you should make sure you contact these agencies (www.ascap.com, www.bmi.com, www.sesac.com).

Another web site to consult regarding copyright is that of the Recording Industry Association of America (RIAA). Its web address is www.riaa.org; it constantly updates information about copyright procedures (see Figure 12.10). This site will help you determine what licenses you need and how to obtain them. Other licensing requirements are administrated by the SoundExchange, which is an independent, nonprofit performance rights organization designated by the U.S. Copyright Office to collect and distribute digital performance royalties for recording artists and sound recording copyright owners when their sound recordings are performed on digital cable or satellite television music channels, or Internet and satellite radio.

FIGURE 12.10 The Recording Industry Association of America provides copything information. (Image courtesy of RIAA.)

12.11 INTERNET RADIO STATION LISTING SITES

Once you have established an Internet radio station, you want people to know about it. With all the material on the Internet, it would be hard for any but the most avid fans to find your station. To help solve this problem, there are Internet sites that list radio stations (see Figure 12.11). They list by format type, geographic area, and various other parameters, and simply link to all the radio stations they list. Some charge for listing and some don't. You would be well advised to contact as many of these as possible to see whether they will list your station.

Most computer audio players now have a built-in radio station listing service, so that potential listeners no longer need to go through a browser or search engine to find radio stations. This feature can be both good and bad for radio stations. It allows listeners to easily find their station, but though it provides a link, it does not require listeners to visit the stations' web sites, where additional advertising, appeals for support, and branding can occur.

So, for starters, it would be best to contact the companies that provide the encoder/server/player software. Other sites that list radio stations that you may want to check out are:

www.radiolocator.com
www.live365.com
www.radiotower.com
www.shoutcast.com
www.live-radio.net
www.vtuner.com
www.wikipedia.org

Establishing and operating an Internet radio station can be a rewarding activity and a very good learning experience for anyone interested in a career in either traditional radio or new media technologies.

12.12 OTHER DISTRIBUTION MEANS

New distribution techniques, such as the Internet, are not unusual in radio programming. As each new form takes

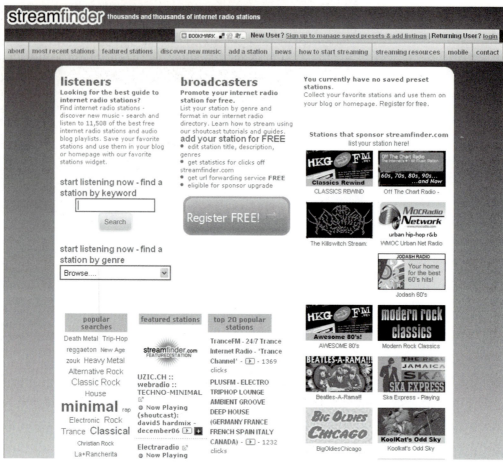

FIGURE 12.11   This site allows you to find Internet radio stations by searching genre, featured stations, popular stations, or keywords. (Image courtesy of www.streamfinder.com.)

hold, the old ones undergo change, but the need for programming remains. Regardless of how the material is distributed, content must be produced in such a way that meets the entertainment and information needs of the public.

AM over-the-air entertainment broadcasting started in the 1920s and was the dominant form of radio distribution for many years. FM was developed during the 1930s but did not come to fruition until the 1960s, and it later overtook AM as the favored listening form. When cable TV went through a growth spurt in the 1980s, it added audio-only services to its menu, but although many cable subscribers elect to utilize the service, it has never achieved the cachet of AM or FM radio, being mostly a background music provider without disc jockeys or special events. However, another form of broadcasting that distributes in a digital form directly from satellites to radio receivers has created serious competition for traditional over-the-air AM and FM. Their response has been to create their own digital radio (HD or high-definition radio).

12.13 SATELLITE RADIO

Satellite radio beams radio programming directly from a satellite to a home, car receiver, or portable receiver. The signals are distributed nationally with no need for local stations that broadcast to a local area. Programming is uplinked from earth-based studios to satellites designed to transmit the signal back to earth and provide coast-to-coast coverage. If the satellite signal may be interrupted, such as in some urban areas, ground repeaters are used to beam the signal to listeners. Because satellite radio is a digital service, its signals are of higher quality than traditional, nondigital AM or FM broadcasting.

In 1997, the FCC granted two companies, Sirius Satellite Radio and XM Satellite Radio, the right to broadcast satellite radio; however, in July 2008, the FCC allowed these two companies to merge into a single satellite radio service (Sirius XM Radio). Consumers are charged a monthly fee for access to hundreds of channels of music, news/talk, sports, and entertainment programming. Many channels are narrowly focused to particular interests such as *The Grateful Dead Channel*, *Bluegrass Junction*, *The Howard Stern Show*, *Laugh USA*, and many others. Some of the offerings are commercial free (usually the music channels); others carry nominal commercials; still others mirror the amount of advertisement time that terrestrial commercial radio has. In fact, some of the stations provided by the service, such as Los Angeles KIIS-FM, are just simultaneous broadcasts of terrestrial broadcasts with commercial breaks included. Some programming that was once available on traditional radio stations has now moved to satellite radio, such as *The Howard Stern Show*. Satellite radio occupies different frequencies from current radio broadcasting, so anyone wanting to hear them needs a satellite radio receiver. There are radios for auto, home, and mobile use, and most are relatively inexpensive. Most auto manufacturers offer satellite radios as standard or optional equipment in new cars. You can also subscribe and listen to satellite radio through your computer.

Although satellite radio has not been a training ground for students, this type of service is something students should prepare for if they wish for a career in radio. The multitude of channels and their narrow focus will provide an opportunity for creativity in both programming and production.

12.14 DIGITAL DISTRIBUTION NETWORKS

Another way digital technology and the Internet have affected radio and audio production is the ability to deliver CD-quality audio to radio stations using **digital distribution networks**. DG Systems is one company that provides such a service (DG Fast Channel) by linking radio stations with ad agencies, production houses, and record companies through an Internet-based network.

Under traditional analog techniques, radio spots were recorded onto audiotape masters, then dubbed to tape copies, and finally delivered by mail or courier to individual stations. A digital distribution network features PC-based servers in the ad agency, production house, or record company onto which audio files are loaded. This audio is sent via satellite or Internet to network headquarters, and then, with appropriate instructions, to receivers at client stations.

Because they employ digital technology, these networks offer fast or even instantaneous delivery of digital quality audio to stations around the country. They have been used to send out commercials, newly released singles, and other production material. Digital distribution networks have also been used to facilitate simultaneous recording from two different locations.

12.15 CABLE RADIO

Many cable TV systems provide digital CD-quality audio services that are piped into the home along with the cable

TV service. Obviously, these **cable radio** signals cannot be heard in an automobile, so they are limited to in-home listening. In some instances the cable systems charge extra for these services, and in other instances the services are part of the basic package. There are both commercial-free programs and ones that contain advertisements. Sometimes the audio is used as background for text channels listing local events or program schedules. Some of the companies providing these audio services also make them available to broadcast networks or commercial establishments such as doctors' offices. Sometimes a cable company will provide only one channel of audio services, whereas other companies provide multiple channels. The offerings are varied, such as news programs from around the world, classical music, religious programming, and foreign language programming.

Many colleges operate public access cable channels and place student-produced audio on the channel, often behind a layer of character-generated announcements about the school. This is frequently the same programming that is going out over the Internet radio station or the on-air station, thus giving the student work a broader audience.

12.16 OVER-THE-AIR BROADCASTING

The most traditional way that radio programming is delivered is over the airwaves by local stations. The sound goes from the station's studio to the **transmitter**. Here it is **modulated**, which means the signal is superimposed onto a **carrier wave** that represents a particular station's frequency. Some stations operate in the **AM** band, where the frequencies are 535 to 1,705 kilohertz, and others are in the **FM** band of 88 to 108 megahertz. These frequencies are much higher than sound frequencies (20 to 20,000 hertz) and can travel much farther than sound. Once the sounds have been modulated, they are sent out of the station antenna into the air. The carrier wave can be picked up by a radio receiver that demodulates the signal and turns it back into sound that the ear can hear.

Technically, the difference between AM and FM involves how the on-air signal is modulated. AM stands for **amplitude modulation** and involves a method that varies the amplitude, or height, of the carrier wave in order to represent the sound. FM stands for **frequency modulation** and is a process that changes the frequency of the carrier wave in order to represent the sound. Figure 12.12 shows a representation of the two types of modulation.

FM signals are of better quality than AM signals, in part because of the modulation techniques. For example, AM is more subject to static, because static is most likely to occur at the bottom and top of the carrier wave. For FM, that part of the wave can just be cut off to eliminate static, but for AM the top and bottom must remain because they are the key to how the modulation occurs. There are many other reasons why FM is of better quality. One is that FM signals occupy more bandwidth than AM, because bandwidth

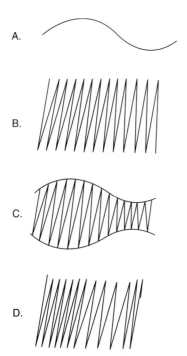

FIGURE 12.12 (A) An electrical wave that represents original sound. (B) The carrier wave of a radio station that is of a much higher frequency. (C) How the carrier wave is changed for amplitude modulation. Note that the height of the carrier wave is varied to take into account the characteristic of the sound wave. (D) How the carrier wave is altered for frequency modulation. Note that the frequency or distance between the waves is varied and related to the original sound wave—the frequency is decreased where the sound wave is lowest.

FIGURE 12.13 An HD radio receiver. (Image courtesy of Radiosophy.)

FIGURE 12.14 How HD radio works. (Image courtesy of iBiquity Digital Corporation.)

was not given a great deal of consideration when AM was developed in the 1920s.

Fortunately for colleges, most student-operated radio stations are in the FM band. This has nothing to do with modulation or bandwidth; it has more to do with politics. Many early AM stations were operated by educational institutions, but as radio's popularity grew and frequencies were in short demand, the universities lost out to commercial interests. When FM was established, the educators convinced the FCC to reserve some of the frequencies (88.1 to 91.9) for noncommercial use so that commercial stations could not operate in that band. Today, many of these frequencies are licensed to colleges and universities that use them for public radio programming or as student stations. As previously mentioned, sometimes the programming going out to the community from the FM antenna also goes over the Internet or over a cable TV system.

12.17 HD RADIO

In 2002, the FCC approved "in-band, on-channel" (IBOC) technology to permit existing AM and FM radio stations to transmit a digital signal. The sole developer of the technology is iBiquity Digital Corporation. **HD radio**, as **digital radio** is known, provides FM radio that is

CD-quality and AM radio that rivals the quality of current FM radio, making traditional radio broadcasting more competitive with satellite-delivered radio. Figure 12.13 shows a radio set capable of receiving HD radio signals. HD radio technology offers the ability to multicast, so in addition to a digital main channel, two secondary channels can provide different programming. In mid-2008, over 2,000 HD stations were licensed, with 1,775 on-the-air and about half that many providing multicasts. HD radio receivers are offered by several electronics manufacturers and continue to become available at a lower price with some units below the $100 price mark. HD radio is also an option or standard equipment for many auto manufacturers.

Figure 12.14 shows how HD radio works. The analog signal is sandwiched between digital information (1) and along with the audio program, text (such as artist and song information) can be transmitted. Once the digital signal layer is compressed (2) using iBiquity's HDC compression technology, the combined signal is transmitted (3) on the station's regular frequency. HD radio receivers pick up the digital signal and older, analog radios still receive the regular AM or FM signal (5). Multipath distortion (common radio interference) can occur when part of a signal bounces off an object (4) and arrives at the receiver at a different time than the main signal. HD radio receivers are designed to sort through reflected signals and reduce static, hiss, pops, and fading.

12.18 CONCLUSION

At present there is a wealth of outlets for student audio work. In addition to stations operated by colleges and universities, there are Internet sites, cable services, and broadcast stations that accept individual programs produced by students. Anyone wishing to get experience and exposure while a student can certainly find a distribution outlet for quality audio work.

Self-Study

1. How has the Internet been important to college radio?

   a) Stations can have an international audience.
   b) Alumni can keep in touch by listening to the college radio station over the Internet.
   c) Colleges that could not have a station because of lack of available frequencies can now have one.
   d) All of the above.

2. Which of the following defines on-demand programming?

   a) programming that is streamed live over the Internet
   b) files of programmed material that can be accessed over the Internet
   c) the icon that listeners click on to receive live streaming
   d) a home page as opposed to a web page

3. Which of the following aspects of Internet radio is on the listener's computer?

   a) encoder
   b) server
   c) player
   d) overhead

4. Which type of soundfile allows listeners with low-bandwidth connections to the Internet to still listen to high-quality, on-demand soundfiles?

   a) streaming
   b) nonstreaming
   c) FM
   d) Flash

5. Someone with a modem operating at 56 kilobytes per second can easily receive uncompressed, analog audio signals from the Internet.

   a) true
   b) false

6. As an audio signal requires more and more bandwidth, which of the following will occur?

   a) the faster the system will operate
   b) the lower the signal-to-noise ratio will be
   c) the greater the frequency of the sound will be
   d) the higher the quality of the sound will be

7. Approximately how much does the signal-to-noise ratio improve with each additional bit when you are dealing with bit depth?

   a) 44.1 kilohertz
   b) 48 dB
   c) 6 dB
   d) 1,411,200 bits

8. Which is true about perceptual coding?

   a) It takes into account what sounds the human ear can't hear.
   b) It involves sending a mono signal instead of a stereo one.

c) It is a compression system that increases the amount of bandwidth a signal uses.

d) It places more silence in a signal so it can be easily decompressed.

9. Computers that serve Internet radio stations do not need to have as much bandwidth as those that receive the signal.

a) true

b) false

10. What is one difference between Internet radio and over-the-air radio?

a) Internet radio stations do not need to pay license fees to play music.

b) Internet radio covers a smaller geographic area than over-the-air radio, enabling only people who are close to its server to receive its signal.

c) Each listener is served individually for Internet radio, but an over-the-air signal can be picked up by anyone who has a radio within the service area.

d) Internet radio was developed earlier than over-the-air radio.

11. Streamed audio stays on a listener's computer in a large buffer area that acts like a storage tank.

a) true

b) false

12. Which two audio streaming formats are currently used by the most stations?

a) QuickTime and Real

b) Windows Media and QuickTime

c) Real and Winamp

d) Real and Windows Media

13. Which of the following software audio players has a simple interface and few compatibility issues?

a) Winamp

b) Windows Media Player

c) QuickTime

d) RealPlayer

14. What is the audio compression system based on the one developed by the Moving Picture Experts Group known as?

a) WAV

b) MP3

c) QuickTime

d) AVI

15. Which of the following is a music licensing agency?

a) ISP

b) RIAA

c) ASCAP

d) MPEG

16. Which of the following delivers CD-quality radio content, such as commercials, to radio stations around the country?

a) digital audio workstation

b) digital distribution network

c) digital audio card

d) digital audio editor

17. Which of the following was developed the earliest?

   a) AM radio
   b) FM radio
   c) cable radio
   d) satellite radio

18. Which mobile form of radio requires a subscription and a special receiver?

   a) cable radio
   b) Internet radio
   c) FM radio
   d) satellite radio

19. Which company was one of two designated by the FCC to establish a satellite radio service?

   a) Apple
   b) RealNetworks
   c) Sirius
   d) Microsoft

20. What is one difference between AM and FM?

   a) AM stations have greater bandwidth than FM stations.
   b) AM stations modulate by varying the height of the carrier wave, whereas FM stations modulate by varying the frequency of the carrier wave.
   c) FM stations are more subject to static than AM stations.
   d) More college radio stations are on the AM band than are on the FM band.

ANSWERS

If you answered A to any of the questions:

1a. This is basically correct, but there is a better answer. (Reread 12.1.)
2a. No. By definition, on-demand is not streamed live. (Reread 12.2.)
3a. No. An encoder would be used by the station. (Reread 12.3, 12.4, and 12.6.)
4a. Wrong. A quality streaming soundfile will not play easily on a computer with low bandwidth. (Reread 12.3.)
5a. Wrong. (Reread 12.4.)
6a. No. It would be just the opposite. (Reread 12.4.)
7a. No. This relates to sampling, not bit depth. (Reread 12.4.)
8a. You are right. Perceptual coding takes into account what a human can hear.
9a. No. It is the opposite. (Reread 12.4 and 12.5.)
10a. Wrong. They must both pay. (Reread 12.5 and 12.10.)
11a. No, not on the listener's computer. (Reread 12.6.)
12a. No. These are not the top two. (Reread 12.7.)
13a. This is the best response. Nullsoft's Winamp is a bare-bones player and one with few compatibility issues.
14a. No. This can indicate a soundfile, but not a compressed one. (Reread 12.8.)
15a. No. (Reread 12.5 and 12.10.)
16a. No. A DAW could be utilized to produce a commercial, but it is not used to send spots around the country. (Reread 12.14.)
17a. Yes, in the 1920s.
18a. No. The cable TV system is not mobile. (Reread 12.13 and 12.15.)
19a. Wrong. This is not a satellite radio company. (Reread 12.7 and 12.13.)
20a. Wrong. It is the other way around. (Reread 12.16.)

If you answered B to any of the questions:

   1b.   This is basically correct, but there is a better answer. (Reread 12.1.)

   2b.   Correct. A listener can click on a file on a web page.

   3b.   No. A server would be used by the station. (Reread 12.3, 12.5, and 12.6.)

   4b.   Correct. Nonstreaming files can be downloaded and then listened to.

   5b.   Right. Data must be compressed or else the information would take forever to download.

   6b.   Wrong. This has more to do with bit depth. (Reread 12.4.)

   7b.   No. This number was used in reference to 8-bit sound. (Reread 12.4.)

   8b.   No. That is a form of bandwidth reduction, but it is not related to perceptual coding. (Reread 12.4.)

   9b.   Yes. You are correct.

 10b.   Wrong. It would be the opposite. (Reread 12.5 and 12.16.)

 11b.   Correct. It does not stay on the listener's computer.

 12b.   No. These are not the top two. (Reread 12.7.)

 13b.   No. This is considered a more complicated player and has compatibility problems. (Reread 12.7.)

 14b.   Yes. This stands for MPEG-2, Layer 3.

 15b.   No. This organization has been involved with copyright disputes, but it doesn't license music. (Reread 12.10.)

 16b.   Yes. This is the correct response.

 17b.   No. There is a better answer. (Reread 12.12.)

 18b.   No. Internet radio sometimes requires a subscription, but it is not mobile. (Reread 12.13.)

 19b.   Wrong. This is not a satellite radio company. (Reread 12.7 and 12.13.)

 20b.   Correct. You understand the modulation well.

If you answered C to any of the questions:

   1c.   This is basically correct, but there is a better answer. (Reread 12.1.)

   2c.   No. The program is not an icon, and they would not click to stream. (Reread 12.2.)

   3c.   Yes. The listener's computer has the player.

   4c.   No. FM is not a soundfile. (Reread 12.3 and 12.16.)

   6c.   Wrong. Bandwidth and frequency are not related here. (Reread 12.4.)

   7c.   Yes. This answer is the correct choice.

   8c.   No. This is wrong for a lot of reasons, one of which is that compression does not call for an increase in bandwidth. (Reread 12.4.)

 10c.   Right. Internet radio requires a separate stream for each listener.

 12c.   No. Winamp is not a file format. (Reread 12.7.)

 13c.   No. This is considered a more complicated player and has compatibility problems. (Reread 12.7.)

 14c.   No. This is Apple based. (Reread 12.7 and 12.8.)

 15c.   Correct. ASCAP is one of the music licensing agencies.

 16c.   No. A digital audio card is part of a desktop radio system. (Reread 12.14.)

 17c.   Wrong. This didn't come along until much later than some of the other choices. (Reread 12.12.)

 18c.   No. FM radio, though mobile, does not require a subscription. (Reread 12.13 and 12.16.)

 19c.   Yes. XM Satellite Radio was the other company.

 20c.   No. It is the other way around. (Reread 12.16.)

If you answered D to any of the questions:

   1d.   Yes, this is the correct answer. All of the answers apply.

   2d.   No. On-demand programming could be placed on a home page or web page, but it is not either of them. (Reread 12.2.)

   3d.   Wrong. Overhead is not a relevant term here. (Reread 12.3, 12.4, and 12.6.)

   4d.   Wrong. Although Flash is capable of transmitting sound, it does not allow users to download files onto their computers for later use. (Reread 12.2 and 12.3.)

6d. Correct. More bandwidth equals higher quality.

7d. No. This huge number was used in relation to a minute of stereo sound. (Reread 12.4.)

8d. No. This answer does not relate to perceptual coding. (Reread 12.4.)

10d. No. (Reread 12.5 and 12.12.)

12d. Correct. Real and Windows Media are the top two.

13d. Wrong. Real's player is considered more complex with its numerous options and has compatibility issues. (Reread 12.7.)

14d. No. This can indicate a soundfile, but not the right one. (Reread 12.8.)

15d. Wrong. This is an organization dealing with compression. (Reread 12.8 and 12.10.)

16d. No. A digital audio editor could be used to produce a commercial, but it's not used to send spots around the country. (Reread 12.14.)

17d. No. This is very new. (Reread 12.12.)

18d. Correct. Satellite radio is a subscription service.

19d. No. Microsoft, though it seems to have its fingers in most businesses, is not directly in charge of a satellite radio company. (Reread 12.13.)

20d. Wrong. That is not the band where college radio is located. (Reread 12.16.)

Projects

PROJECT 1

Report on the differences and similarities among six radio station web sites.

Purpose

To give you a feel for how stations are currently utilizing the Internet.

Notes

1. Try to select different types of stations—for example, ones that are Internet only, ones that are both broadcast and Internet, AM stations, and FM stations.
2. Consider both the audio and visual elements as you do your analysis.

How to Do the Project

1. Find six different stations that have web pages on the Internet. Feel free to use the Internet sites that list radio stations, as mentioned in Section 12.11.
2. Go to one of the web sites and click on a soundfile or on the live streaming. If necessary, download the player software.
3. Make notes about the appearance of the site and about the type of audio material that is available. Look at the various pages and see the types of materials that are included. You might want to consider such facets as how much material is on the home page; whether the site contains live streaming and on-demand files and, if so, what types of on-demand files are included; the color scheme of the pages; the organizational principles around which the pages are presented; the extent to which on-air personalities are featured; and so on.
4. Do the same for five additional sites.
5. Write a report that compares and contrasts the radio station presentations. See if you can find trends or recurring features. For example, do music stations tend to use the Internet in different ways than talk stations? Are there things that Internet-only stations include that broadcast stations do not? Do most of the station sites include daily schedules?
6. Put your name on your report and label it "Web Site Analysis." Give the report to your instructor to receive credit for this project.

PROJECT 2

Tour a broadcast radio station transmitting facility.

Purpose

To enable you to see a broadcast transmitter firsthand and better understand the broadcast process.

Notes

1. Although you may have toured a radio station already, you may not have seen the transmitter facility, because many broadcast studios are physically separated from the transmitter site.
2. Try to arrange to talk with an engineer, who is the person that can give you the most information.
3. Make sure that before you go you have some ideas about what you want to find out.
4. Your instructor may have set up a tour for the entire class, or the engineer at your college FM station may offer a tour of your own station. Either case is fine for completing the project.

How to Do the Project

1. Select a station. (If the instructor has arranged a station tour for the whole class, skip ahead to Step 4.)
2. Call someone at the station, tell him or her that you would like to see the station's transmitter site and talk with someone about it so you can write a report for a radio production class, and ask if you may visit.
3. If the answer is yes, set a date; if not, call a different station.
4. Think of things you want to find out for your report. For example:
    a. How does the line out of the audio console get to the transmitter?
    b. Is there any signal processing equipment at the transmitter site?
    c. Does the station use amplitude modulation or frequency modulation, and exactly where is this modulation equipment located?
    d. What is the physical layout of the transmitter site?
    e. How does the signal get from the transmitter to the antenna?
5. Go to the station transmitter site. Tour to the extent the station personnel will let you and ask as many questions as you can.
6. Write a report about what you found out.
7. Put your name and "Transmitter Site Report" on your report, and hand it in to your instructor to get credit for this assignment.

GLOSSARY

A-B miking   A method of stereo miking where one microphone feeds the right channel and another microphone feeds the left channel.

Absorption   The process of sound going into the walls, ceilings, and floors of a studio.

Absorption coefficient   The proportion of sound that a material can absorb in relation to the sound it will reflect back. A coefficient of 1.00 means that all sound is absorbed in the material.

Acoustics   The science of how sound behaves in an enclosed space.

Acoustic suspension   A speaker enclosure design that consists of a tightly sealed box that prevents rear sounds from disrupting main speaker sounds.

Actuality   A voice report from a person in the news rather than from the reporter.

Actual malice   As relates to libel, something that was known to be harmful and incorrect but which was reported anyway.

Adaptive Transform Acoustic Coding (ATRAC)   A data compression system used for MiniDiscs.

ADR   See *Automatic dialogue replacement.*

AES/EBU   A digital connector standard set by the Audio Engineering Society and the European Broadcasting Union.

Aliased   The shifting of frequencies that are not within the range of hearing into the audible range.

AM   See *Amplitude modulation.*

Ambient sounds   Background noises that are desirable for an audio or video production and that are often recorded and added to the production.

Amplifier   A piece of equipment that boosts the strength of a signal, often as it goes from one audio element to another.

Amplify   To make louder.

Amplitude   The strength or height of a sound wave or radio wave.

Amplitude modulation   A form of radio transmission in which the amplitude (height) of a carrier wave is varied according to the characteristics of the sound signal being broadcast.

AMS   See *Automatic music sensor.*

Analog   A recording, circuit, or piece of equipment that produces an output that varies as a continuous function of the input, resulting in degradation of the signal as material is copied from one source to another.

Announce booth   See *Performance studio.*

Anti-aliasing   Filtering the input signal during the digital process to prevent the creation of unwanted frequencies, usually ones not within the audible range.

ATM   Asynchronous transfer mode; a high-speed telephone system capable of transmitting audio.

Atmosphere sounds   Recorded sounds that give a sense of location or a particular feeling.

ATRAC   See *Adaptive Transform Acoustic Coding.*

Attack   The time it takes an initial sound to build up to full volume.

Audio board   See *Audio console.*

Audio card   A connection between a computer-based audio workstation and other audio equipment; also known as a "sound card."

Audio chain   The route through various pieces of equipment that sound takes in order to be broadcast or recorded.

Audio console   The piece of equipment that mixes, amplifies, and routes sound; also known as a "mixer."

Audio routing switcher   A type of patch panel that allows audio inputs to be switched to various outputs electronically.

Audio signal   A sound signal that has been processed into an electromagnetic form.

Audio tape recorder   A device that rearranges particles on magnetic tape in order to store sound.

Audition   An output channel of an audio console.

Automatic dialogue replacement (ADR)   Rerecording dialogue in a studio situation that for some reason was not recorded properly during production; also known as "looping."

Automatic music sensor (AMS) A button on a digital audio tape recorder that allows the operator to skip forward or backward to the start of a new song.

Aux See *Auxiliary*.

Auxiliary An output channel of an audio console.

Backing layer The back side of audio tape—the side that does not have a magnetic coating.

Balance Recording or mixing sound in such a way that the proper elements are emphasized and one sound does not drown out another that is more important.

Balance control A knob on stereo input channels used to determine how much sound goes to the right channel and how much sound goes to the left channel.

Balanced cable A cable with three wires—plus, minus, and ground.

Band cut filter See *Band reject filter*.

Band pass filter A filter that cuts all frequencies outside a specified range.

Band reject filter A filter that allows all frequencies to pass except a specified frequency range.

Bass reflex A speaker enclosure design that has a vented port to allow rear sounds to reinforce main speaker sounds.

Bass roll-off switch A switch that turns down bass frequencies to counter the proximity effect.

Bidirectional Picking up sound from two directions; usually refers to a microphone pickup pattern.

Binary A number system that uses two digits: 1 and 0.

Bit depth Number of data bits used to encode a digital sample.

Blast filter See *Windscreen*.

BNC connector A bayonet type connector with a twist lock that is used for digital audio and for video.

Boom A microphone stand that sits on top of a base or is held by a person in a fishpole style.

Boom arm A microphone stand for use in the radio studio, consisting of metal rods designed somewhat like a human arm; one end goes into a base that can be mounted on a counter near the audio console, and the other end supports the microphone.

Boom stand A stand that can be placed away from an announcer; usually consists of one vertical pipe with a horizontal pipe at the top of it.

Bouncing A multitrack recording technique that combines two or more tracks and transfers them to a vacant track; also known as "ping-ponging."

Boundary microphone See *Pressure zone microphone*.

Branding The act of defining a station so listeners know what to expect when they tune in.

Broadband A high-speed data transmission system that can accommodate audio and video and connect to the Internet faster than dial-up telephones.

Bumper A prerecorded audio element, which usually consists of voice and music, that is used as a transition between different forms of content.

Cable Wire that carries audio signals.

Cable radio Music services offered by cable TV systems.

Camera microphone A mic that is built into a camera or permanently mounted on it.

Cannon connector See *XLR connector*.

Capacitor microphone Another name for a condenser microphone.

Capstan A metal shaft that controls the speed of a tape recorder.

Cardioid Picking up sound in a heart-shaped pattern; usually refers to a microphone pickup pattern.

Carrier wave A radio wave that is constant in amplitude or frequency but can be modulated by some other audio signal; used to deliver a radio broadcast signal.

Cartridge A device that converts the vibrations from the turntable stylus into variations in voltage; also, the endless-loop tape container used in a tape recorder.

Cartridge recorder A tape recorder that uses tape that is in an endless loop.

Cassette A plastic case containing ⅛-inch audio tape.

Cassette recorder A tape recorder that records and plays back ⅛-inch tape housed in a plastic case.

CBR See *Constant bit rate*.

CD See *Compact disc*.

CD player See *Compact disc player*.

CD-R See *CD recorder*.

CD recorder A type of CD machine that can record as well as play back compact discs.

CD-RW A CD format that can be recorded on more than once.

CF See *Compact Flash*.

Channel The route an audio signal follows; also, a grouping of controls on an audio console associated with one input.

Chorusing A multitrack overdubbing technique in which an announcer reads the same script on several different tracks to give a "chorus" effect.

Circumaural See *Closed-cushion headphones*.

Clapper A wooden palette with a hinged piece of wood across the top that is used to sync sound, because the sound of wood hitting wood can be matched up with the picture of the two hitting each other.

Closed-cushion headphones A ring-shaped muff that rests on the head, not the ear, through which a person can hear sound.

Close proximity monitoring See *Near-field monitoring*.

Coding In digital technology, assigning a 16-bit binary "word" to the values measured during quantizing.

Cold ending A natural, full-volume ending of music or a song.

Combo The working procedure in which the radio announcer is also the equipment operator.

Compact disc (CD) A round, shiny disc onto which sound is recorded digitally so that it can be read by a laser.

Compact disc (CD) player The piece of equipment that uses a laser to play back compact discs.

Compact Flash (CF) One of the many formats of portable digital memory upon which large quantities of broadcast-quality audio can be recorded.

Companders Signal processing equipment that compresses dynamic range during recording and expands it during playback.

Compression A sound wave characteristic that occurs when the air molecules are pushed close together; also, a system for encoding digital data bits so fewer can be placed on a recording medium yet still represent the original data.

Compressor A volume control usually associated with the transmitter that boosts signals that are too soft and lowers signals that are too loud.

Condenser microphone A microphone that uses a capacitor, usually powered by a battery, to respond to sound.

Connector adapters Freestanding connector parts that allow one connector form to be changed to another.

Connectors Metal devices to attach one piece of audio equipment to another.

Constant bit rate (CBR) A technology used for live streaming, wherein data—complex or simple—has the same bit rate.

Continuity Consistent and unobtrusive progression from one shot to another without distractions in terms of audio or video elements that are present in one shot and absent in the other.

Control board See *Audio console*.

Convergence The amalgamation of various media, such as radio and television, so that they share common traits.

Copyright The exclusive right to publish or sell certain literary, dramatic, musical, or artistic works.

Countdown A type of music show in which the most popular songs are played in reverse order of their popularity, for example, a Top 10 countdown would start with the tenth most popular song and end with the most popular.

Cross-fade To bring up one sound and take down another in such a way that both are heard for a short period of time.

Crossover An electronic device that sends low frequencies to the speaker woofer and high frequencies to the tweeter.

Cross-pair miking See *X-Y miking*.

Cross-talk The picking up on a tape track of the signal from another track.

Cue To preview an input (such as a CD or audiotape) before it goes over the air; also, to set up an audio source at the point where it is to start.

Cue sheet Lists used during the final mix that indicate when each sound of a production should be brought in and taken out.

Cue talent A signal given to talent that means, "You're on"; it is given by pointing the index finger at the talent.

Cue wheel Part of a CD player that allows the operator to find the exact starting point of the music.

Cut A hand signal given to talent at the end of a production; it is given by "slicing your throat" with your index finger.

Cut 'n' splice A form of editing used during the analog era wherein audio tape was cut with a razor blade and put back together with splicing tape.

DAT See *Digital audio tape*.

Data compression See *Compression*.

DAW See *Digital audio workstation*.

dB See *Decibel*.

dbx® A noise-reduction system that compresses both loud and soft parts of a signal during recording and then expands them during playback.

Dead air A long pause on a broadcast when no sound is heard.

Dead spot A place from which a remote unit cannot send a signal to a studio or other destination, usually because buildings or hills are in the way of a line-of-sight transmission.

Dead studio A studio with very little echo or reverberation, caused by a great deal of absorption of the sound.

Decay The time it takes a sound to go from full volume to sustain level.

Decibel (dB) A measurement to indicate the loudness of sound.

Decompressed The process of restoring an audio signal that has been encoded with some type of data compression system.

De-esser A processor that gets rid of sibilant sounds without affecting other parts of the signal.

Demographics Information related to specific statistics about a population such as sex, age, occupation, and education.

Desk stand A microphone stand for a person in a seated position.

Dialogue Words that are spoken by a person in a radio or television production.

Diffusion Breaking up sound reflections by using irregular room surfaces.

Digital A recording, circuit, or piece of equipment in which the output varies in discrete on/off steps in such a way that it can be reproduced without degradation of the signal.

Digital audio tape (DAT) High-quality cassette tape that can be dubbed many times without degradation because of the sampling process of its recording method.

Digital audio workstation (DAW) A computer-based system that can create, store, edit, mix, and send out sound in a variety of ways, all within one basic unit.

Digital cart recorder A piece of equipment that operates similarly to an analog cart machine but stores sound on a computer disk.

Digital delay A unit that holds a signal temporarily and then allows it to leave the unit.

Digital distribution network A network that links ad agencies, production houses, or record companies with radio stations to deliver CD-quality audio via PC-based servers and phone lines.

Digital radio In-band, on-channel radio that AM and FM stations use to provide high-quality digital sound.

Digital reverb A unit that produces reverberation electronically.

Digital signal processor (DSP) A type of electronic audio card used for computer editing.

Digital Versatile Disc (DVD) A data storage format that has the capacity to hold a feature-length movie on a compact disc–styled medium. It can also be used for music and computer data.

Direct sound Sound that goes straight from a source to a microphone.

Disc jockey (DJ) A person who introduces and plays music for a radio station. The term arose because the person plays recorded discs and "rides gain" on the audio board.

Distortion A blurring of sound caused by overamplification or other inaccurate reproduction of sound.

DJ See *Disc jockey.*

Dolby A noise-reduction system that raises the volume of the program signal most likely to be affected by noise during production, then lowers it again during playback so that the noise seems lower in relation to the program level.

Double-system sound A sound recording method wherein sound is recorded on one piece of equipment and picture on another.

Dovetailing A multitrack overdubbing technique in which a single announcer appears to have a dialogue with himself or herself by recording different parts of a script on different tracks.

Dramatic pause Giving a little extra silence before making an important point.

Drop-out A flaking off of oxide coating from audio tape so that the total signal is not recorded.

DSP See *Digital signal processor.*

DSP audio card A necessary component in order to use standard computers to edit audio.

Dubbing Electronically copying material from one tape to another.

Duration The time during which a sound builds up, remains at full volume, and dies out.

DVD See *Digital versatile disc.*

Dynamic microphone A microphone that consists of a diaphragm, a magnet, and coils. It is extremely rugged and has good frequency response, so it is used often in audio recording.

Dynamic range The volume changes from loud to soft within a series of sounds; also, the amount of volume change a piece of equipment can handle effectively.

Dynamic speaker A speaker with a cone attached to a voice coil. Electrical current in the voice coil creates a magnetic force that moves the cone.

Earbud A headphone that fits in the ear.

Echo Sound that bounces off one surface.

Electret microphone A type of condenser microphone with a permanently charged capacitor.

Electromagnetic speaker Another name for a dynamic speaker.

Electrostatic headphones Headphones that require external amplification.

Electrostatic speaker A rarely used type of monitor speaker.

Encoder In streaming audio, a computer or software that converts the analog signal into a digital format.

Envelope The stages that sound goes through during its duration from full volume to silence.

EQ See *Equalization.*

Equalization (EQ) The adjustment of the amplification given to various frequencies such as high frequencies or low frequencies.

Equalized Audio sound that has had the amplification of its various frequencies adjusted.

Equalizer The unit that adjusts the amount of amplification given to particular frequencies such as high or low frequencies.

Ergonomics Design factors within a facility that reduce operator fatigue and discomfort.

Ethernet An international standard for local area network transmission technology.

Expander Signal processing equipment that increases the dynamic range of sound, for example, making low-volume passages even lower in volume.

Fade To gradually increase or decrease the volume of music to or from silence.

Fade-in To bring sound up from silence to full volume.

Fade-out To take sound from full volume to silence.

Fader Part of an audio console that moves up and down to control volume. Also known as a slider.

Feedback A howling noise created when the output of a sound (usually from a speaker) is returned to the input (usually a microphone).

Filter A unit or part of a computer audio program that cuts out a particular frequency range of the audio signal.

Final mix The last sound work in an audio or video project where the volume levels of the various tracks are set and made to coordinate with the picture.

FireWire A connection that enables digital signals to go from one piece of equipment to another; also known as 1394.

Fishpole A type of mic holder that consists of a pole held by an operator.

Flanger A device that electronically combines an original signal with a slightly delayed one.

Flat A method of recording wherein everything is recorded at approximately the same volume.

Flat frequency response The quality of a frequency curve wherein all frequencies are produced equally well.

Floor stand A microphone stand for a person in a standing position.

FM See *Frequency modulation.*

FM microphone A microphone that does not need a cable, because it consists of a small transmitter and receiver.

Foley To record sounds, such as footsteps and branches moving, in sync with the picture.

Foley walker A person who creates sounds within a facility where sounds are recorded in sync with the picture.

Frequency The number of cycles a sound wave or radio wave completes in one second.

Frequency modulation (FM) A form of radio transmission in which the frequency (wavelength) of a carrier wave is varied according to the characteristics of the sound signal being broadcast.

Frequency response The range of highs and lows that a piece of audio equipment reproduces.

Full-track A recording method that uses the whole tape for one monophonic signal.

Fundamental A basic tone and frequency that each sound has.

Gain control A knob or fader that makes sound louder or softer.

Gain trim Controls on an audio board that are used to fine-tune the volume of each input.

Geosynchronous satellite A satellite positioned approximately 22,233 miles above the earth that travels the same orbit as the earth thereby appearing to hang indefinitely above a certain earth position.

Give mic level A signal given to talent to tell them to talk into the microphone so the audio engineer can set controls properly. It is given by "chattering" one hand, with the palm down and the thumb under the second and third fingers.

Graphic equalizer An equalizer that divides frequency responses into bands that can then be raised or lowered in volume.

Grease pencil A crayon-like substance used to mark edit points on an analog tape.

Grid In a television studio, pipes close to the ceiling from which lights are hung.

Half-track mono The recording of two separate mono signals on a tape—one going to the left and one going to the right.

Hand signals Method of communication that radio production people use when a live microphone prohibits talk or when they are in separate rooms.

Hard drive A large storage medium either built into a computer or offered in a portable mode.

Hardwiring Connecting equipment in a fairly permanent manner, usually by soldering.

Harmonics Exact frequency multiples of a fundamental tone.

HD radio A name for in-band, on-channel digital radio that AM and FM stations use to provide high-quality digital signals.

Head An electromagnet that rearranges iron particles on tape; also, the beginning of an audio tape.

Headphones Tiny speakers encased in something that can be placed in, or close to, the ear.

Headset A combination headphone and microphone in one unit, usually used by sportscasters and helicopter traffic reporters.

Hear-through cushion headphones See *Open-air headphones*.

Hemispherical A microphone pickup pattern that captures sound well within a 180-degree angle.

Hertz (Hz) A measurement of frequency based on cycles of sound waves per second.

Hiss A high-frequency noise problem inherent in the recording process.

Hoax A deceptive trick, often done just for the sake of mischief.

Home page The initial or index page for an Internet web site.

House sound Sounds generated and mixed by technicians at a venue such as an auditorium that can then be picked up by someone else plugging into the final output of the venue equipment, usually so that they can record the sound.

Hum A low-frequency noise problem caused by leaking of the 60-cycle AC power current into the audio signal.

Hyper-cardioid Picking up sound well from the front, but not the sides; usually refers to a microphone pickup pattern.

Hz See *Hertz*.

IBOC See *In-band, on-channel*.

Idler arm A tension part of a reel-to-reel tape recorder that will stop the recorder if the tape breaks.

Imaging The apparent space between speakers and how sounds are heard within the plane of the speakers; the act of defining a station so listeners know what to expect when they tune in.

Impedance The total opposition a circuit offers to the flow of alternating current.

In-band, on-channel (IBOC) A method of digital audio broadcasting used by terrestrial radio stations.

Indecency Language that, in context, depicts or describes, in terms patently offensive as measured by contemporary community standards for the broadcast medium, sexual or excretory activities or organs.

Indirect sound See *Reflected sound*.

In phase A combination of two sound waves such that their crests and troughs exactly align.

Input selectors Switches that are used to choose microphone or line positions on an audio board.

Insert edit See *Punch in*.

In the mud Operating volume consistently below 20 percent on the VU meter.

Invasion of privacy The act of not leaving someone alone who wants to be left alone, especially a celebrity.

ISDN Integrated Services Digital Network; a type of digital phone line for audio and data transmissions.

Jacks Female connectors.

Jewel box A plastic case for a CD.

Jewel case   See *Jewel box*.

Jingle   A short audio piece that includes the singing of such elements as the station call letters or slogan.

kHz   See *Kilohertz*.

Kilobyte (kB)   A unit of computer memory or data storage capacity that is approximately 1,000 bytes.

Kilohertz (kHz)   1,000 cycles per second.

Laser   An acronym for "light amplification by simulated emission of radiation"; a narrow, intense beam in a compact disc that reads encoded audio data.

Laser diode   A semiconductor with positive and negative electrons that converts an electrical input into an optical output.

Latency   The short amount of time required to convert analog audio into digital audio, add a digital effect to audio, or move audio from one location to another.

Lavaliere microphone (lav)   A small microphone that can be attached unobtrusively to a person's clothing.

Leader tape   Plastic tape that does not contain iron particles to record; it is used primarily before and after the recording tape so that the tape can be threaded.

LEDE   See *Live end/dead end*.

LEO   See *Low-earth orbit satellite*.

Libel   Broadcasting or printing something about a person that is both harmful and false.

Limiter   A compressor with a large compression ratio that won't allow a signal to increase beyond a specified point.

Line level   An input that has already been preamplified.

Line of sight   A method of transmitting a signal wherein the transmitter and the receiver are lined up in such a way that there could be a visual communication between them.

Liner   A sentence or two that a disc jockey says over the opening of a song or between songs.

Liner notes   Information found on the back of vinyl albums or inside compact discs about the songs, artists, writers, and so forth; often used by announcers to provide ad-lib information.

Live bouncing   A multitrack recording technique that combines two or more tracks plus a live recording and transfers them to a vacant track.

Live end/dead end (LEDE)   A studio where one end of the studio absorbs sound and the other end reflects sound.

Live studio   A studio with a hard, brilliant sound caused by a great deal of reverberation.

Long play (LP)   A record that can hold at least an hour of music.

Loop   To record something such as a sound effect over and over in order to make it longer.

Looping   See *Automatic dialogue replacement*.

Low-earth orbit (LEO) satellite   A satellite positioned approximately 200 to 400 miles above the earth that is often used for satellite phones.

Low cut filter   A filter that eliminates all frequencies below a certain point.

Low pass filter   A filter that allows all frequencies below a certain point to go through unaffected.

LP   See *Long play*.

Magnetic layer   The part of the tape that contains the iron oxide coating.

Magneto-optical design   A recordable CD that records on a magnetic alloy and uses laser light to play back.

Master fader   The control that determines the volume of the signal being sent from the audio console.

MD   See *MiniDisc*.

Megabyte (MB)   A unit of computer memory or data storage capacity that is approximately one million bytes.

Memory card   A chip that can retain information without a power source and can be recorded on and then erased and recorded on again.

Microphone   A transducer that changes sound energy into electrical energy.

Microphone level   An input that has not been preamplified.

MIDI   See *Musical Instrument Digital Interface*.

Mid-side miking (M-S miking)   A method of stereo miking where three microphones are arranged in an upside-down T pattern.

Mini   See *Miniphone connector*.

MiniDisc (MD)   A 2½-inch computer-type disk that can hold 74 minutes of digital music.

Minidrama   A short episode or story line such as is often found in commercials.

Miniphone connector   A small connector with a sleeve and a tip.

Mixer   See *Audio console*.

Modem   A device used for communication of computer data over standard telephone lines that converts digital signals to analog and vice versa.

Modulated   A radio wave whose frequency or amplitude has been changed according to the characteristics of another audio signal to broadcast that signal.

Monaural   One channel of sound coming from one direction.

Monitor amplifier   A piece of equipment that raises the volume level of sound going to a speaker.

Monitor speaker   A piece of equipment from which sound can be heard.

Motor   The part of a turntable that makes the platter turn.

Moving-coil microphone   Another name for a dynamic microphone.

MP3   A compression system for audio that is a subsystem of the video MPEG compression format.

M-S miking   See *Mid-side miking*.

Multidirectional microphone   A microphone that has switchable internal elements that allow it to employ more than one pickup pattern.

Multiplay   A type of CD player that can hold up to 200 CDs and access material on them according to a prescribed pattern.

Multiple-microphone interference Uneven frequency response caused when microphones that are too close together are fed into the same mixer.

Multitrack recorder A machine or computer software program that can record four or more tracks, all going in the same direction.

Musical Instrument Digital Interface (MIDI) A communication system that allows musical instruments, other electronic gear, and computers to communicate with and control each other.

Music bed Background music used in commercial production to convey the tone or mood of the commercial.

Music library A CD or Internet site that has numerous selections of music that are copyright cleared.

Mute switch A control on an audio console that prevents the audio signal from going through a channel; similar to an on/off button.

Narration A non-sync voice track that accompanies a picture.

Near-field monitoring Placement of monitor speakers on a counter on each side of an audio console so that they are extremely close to the announcer.

Netcast To "broadcast" radio programming or similar material using audio streaming on the Internet.

Noise Unwanted sound in electronic equipment.

Noise gate A signal processing device that reduces noise by suddenly turning way down any audio signal below a set threshold point.

Noise reduction Methods of eliminating unwanted sound from a signal.

Nondirectional Another word for omnidirectional; usually refers to a microphone pickup pattern.

Non-sync sound Audio that does not need to match the picture, either because it is a general sound or it is offscreen.

Notch filter A filter that eliminates a narrow range of frequencies or one individual frequency.

Obscenity Material that contains the depiction of sexual acts in an offensive manner; appeals to prurient interests of the average person; and lacks serious artistic, literary, political, or scientific value.

Omnidirectional Picking up sound from all directions; usually refers to a microphone pickup pattern.

On-air lights A signal that comes on to indicate that a live microphone is on in the studio.

On-air studio The studio from where programming is broadcast.

On-demand Programming that can be accessed at any time.

On-mic When a sound has good presence because it is recorded directly into the mic as opposed to at the side or back of it.

On/off switch A control to stop or start an electronic device.

Open-air headphones Devices to hear sound that fit onto the ear.

Out of phase A phenomenon that occurs when the sound wave from one microphone or speaker is up and the sound wave from a second microphone or speaker is down; the combined result is diminished or canceled sound.

Output selectors Buttons that determine where a sound goes as it leaves the audio console.

Overdubbing Adding new tracks to something that is already recorded; usually a multitrack recording technique.

Overhead Additional bandwidth that is available if necessary for audio streaming on the Internet.

Overmodulated Too loud for the equipment to handle.

Overtones Pitches that are not exact frequency multiples of a fundamental tone.

Pan Using controls to send part of a stereo signal to the left channel and part to the right channel.

Pan knob The part of an audio board that controls how much sound goes to the right channel of a stereo system and how much goes to the left channel; also known as "pan pot."

Pan pot See *Pan knob*.

Parametric equalizer An equalizer that can control the center frequency and the bandwidth that will have its volume raised or lowered.

Patch bay See *Patch panel*.

Patching Connecting equipment together through the use of jacks and plugs.

Patch panel A board that contains jacks that can be used to make connections with plugs. Also known as Patch bay.

Payola Accepting money under the table from a record producer in return for playing a particular piece of music on the air.

Peaking in the red Modulating a signal so that it reads above 100 percent on the VU meter.

Pegging the meter Operating sound so loudly that the needle of the VU meter hits the metal peg beyond the red area; also known as "pinning the needle."

Penetration Sound going through a surface and being transmitted into the space on the other side of the surface.

Perambulator boom A large three-wheeled movable platform that holds a mic operator and a mic in such a way that the mic can move in various directions to capture sound.

Perceptual coding Data compression based on characteristics of human hearing.

Performance release A form that gives a producer the right to include words and actions from a person in a media program.

Performance studio A studio used primarily by actors or musicians that has microphones but no other production equipment.

Personal audio editor A compact portable digital editor that records onto a hard drive.

Perspective The spatial relationship of sound; for example, sounds that are supposed to be distant should sound distant.

Phantom power Power that comes from a recorder or an audio board through a microphone cable to a condenser microphone.

Phase   The up and down position of one sound or radio wave in relation to another.

Phone connector   A connector with a sleeve and a tip.

Phono connector   See *RCA connector.*

Photodiode   The part of a CD player that provides the data signal that will be converted to an audio signal.

Pickup pattern   The area around a microphone where it "hears" best.

Pinch roller   A rubber wheel that holds tape against the capstan.

Pin connector   See *RCA connector.*

Ping-ponging   See *Bouncing.*

Pinning the needle   See *Pegging the meter.*

Pitch   Highness or lowness of a sound determined by how fast its sound wave goes up or down.

Planar-magnetic   A rarely used type of monitor speaker.

Plastic base   The middle part of audio tape, usually made of polyester.

Plate microphone   See *Pressure zone microphone.*

Platter   The part of the turntable on which the record rests.

Play-by-play   A term designating sports broadcasting from the scene.

Player   In relation to audio streaming, the software or computer used to decode and play back audio on the listener's computer.

Plugs   Male connectors.

Podcasting   Transmitting material so it can be viewed or heard on portable devices such as iPods.

Polar pattern   A two-dimensional drawing of a microphone's pickup pattern.

Pop filters   A ball-shaped accessory placed over the microphone to reduce plosive sounds.

Pot   See *Potentiometer.*

Potentiometer (Pot)   A round knob that controls volume.

Preamplification   The initial stage at which volume is boosted.

Pressure microphone   Another name for a dynamic microphone. See *Dynamic Microphone.*

Pressure zone microphone (PZM)   A flat microphone that, when set on a table or other flat surface, uses that surface to collect the sound waves and therefore can pick up audio levels from a fairly widespread area.

Print-through   The bleeding through of the magnetic signal of one layer of tape to an adjacent layer of tape.

Prism system   The part of a CD player that directs the laser to the disc surface.

Production studio   The place where material for radio is produced before it is aired.

Program   An output channel of an audio console.

Promo   An announcement that is usually 30 or 60 seconds long that promotes an upcoming station event.

Proximity effect   A boosting of bass frequencies as a sound source gets closer to a microphone.

PSA   See *Public service announcement.*

Public figures   Well-known people—ones who have to prove actual malice in a libel suit.

Public service announcement (PSA)   A commercial-like announcement, usually 30 or 60 seconds long, that extols a charity or other nonprofit organization that does not pay for the airtime.

Punch in   Editing by recording over one section of a track but leaving what was before and after the edited section intact.

PZM   See *Pressure zone microphone.*

Quantizing   In digital technology, determining how many levels or values each sample will be broken down into; the standard for most digital recording is 65,536 quantizing levels (16-bit).

Quarter-inch phone   See *Phone connector.*

Quarter-track stereo   The recording of two stereo signals on one tape in which two signals go to the left and two go to the right.

Radio microphone   Another name for an FM microphone.

Rarefaction   A sound wave characteristic that occurs when the air molecules are pulled apart.

Rate   The number of words spoken in a given time period.

Razor blade   What was used to cut analog tape in order to edit it.

RCA connector   A connector with an outer sleeve and a center shaft; also known as a "pin connector" and a "phono connector."

R-DAT   See *Rotary head digital audio tape.*

Reel-to-reel recorder   A tape recorder that uses open reels of tape placed on a supply reel and a take-up reel.

Reflected sound   Sound that bounces back to the original source.

Region   In digital audio editing, a common designation for a section of audio that is to be edited or saved for later use.

Regulated phase microphone   A microphone that consists of a wire coil impressed into the surface of a circular diaphragm that is suspended within a magnetic structure.

Reinforced sound   Sound that causes objects to vibrate at the same frequency as the original sound.

Release   The time it takes a sound to die out from a sustained level to silence.

Remote pickup unit (RPU)   A piece of equipment used to send a location feed back to a destination such as a radio station; it operates by using frequencies assigned by the FCC for electronic news transmission.

Remote start switches   Buttons that enable a piece of equipment to be operated from a distance.

Reverb   See *Reverberation.*

Reverberation (Reverb)   Sound that bounces off two or more surfaces.

Reverb ring   The time it takes for a sound to go from full volume to silence.

Reverb route   The path a sound takes from a source to a reflective surface and back again.

Reverb time   See *Reverb ring*.

Revolutions per minute (RPM)   The number of times a record on a turntable makes a complete rotation within a minute.

RF microphone   Another name for an FM microphone.

Ribbon microphone   A microphone that consists of a metallic ribbon, a magnet, and a coil. Because it is bulky, heavy, and fragile, it is rarely used in radio anymore.

Riding levels   See *Riding the gain*.

Riding the gain   Adjusting volume during production. Also known as "riding levels."

Rip and read   To read news copy from the wire service machine with very little editing.

Room tone   The general ambient noise of a particular location that is often recorded so that it can be mixed with sound during postproduction.

Rotary head digital audio tape (R-DAT)   Another name for digital audio tape.

RPM   See *Revolutions per minute*.

RPU   See *Remote pickup unit*.

Rundown sheet   A list of segments that will be included in a program and the approximate time each will run.

SACD   Super audio compact disc; a higher-quality compact disc format.

Sampling   In digital technology, the process of taking readings from the original sound source to convert to binary data.

Sampling rate   The number of times per second that a reading of the sound source is taken in order to convert it to binary data.

Satellite phone   A special telephone that transmits to satellites in low-earth orbit, allowing audio to be transmitted from distant outlying areas.

Satellite radio   Beaming radio programming from a satellite directly to home or automobile receivers.

Scanner   A piece of equipment that can be used to listen to frequencies used by police and fire departments.

Scratch track   Dialogue that is recorded during the shooting of a video production with the knowledge that it will not be used during editing but will serve as a guide for automatic dialogue replacement.

Script   A written guideline from which to produce a media-related program.

Script supervisor   The person whose job it is to make sure that there are no potential continuity problems while a production is being shot.

SD   See *Secure digital*.

Sealed box   See *Acoustic suspension*.

Secure digital (SD)   A small audio recorder that records on a removable media card.

Segue   To cut from one sound at full volume to another sound at full volume.

Selective attention principle   The ability of humans to ignore some sounds in their surroundings and concentrate on sounds they want to hear.

Sel sync   Selective synchronization; a tape recorder feature that makes a record head act as a play head.

Sensitivity   A microphone's efficiency in terms of its ability to pick up various volumes.

Server   A powerful master computer used to store and distribute files on demand.

Shellac   A combination of a resin excreted by a beetle and alcohol that was once used to make records.

Shock jock   A disc jockey or who intentionally makes off-the-wall or titillating comments with the intent of shocking audience members.

Shock mount   A microphone holder that isolates the microphone from mechanical vibrations.

Shotgun microphone   A highly directional microphone that consists of a microphone capsule at one end of a tube or barrel that is aimed toward the sound source.

Signal processing   Manipulating elements of sound, such as frequency response and dynamic range, so that the resulting sound is different from the original sound.

Signal-to-noise ratio (S/N)   The relationship of desired sound to inherent, unwanted electronic sound. The higher the ratio, the purer the sound.

Single-system sound   Recording both sound and picture on the same recording medium.

Slapback echo   A unique echo effect created by dubbing one audio track over another without synchronization.

Slider   See *Fader*.

Slip cueing   Preparing a record to play by having the turntable motor on and holding the edge of the record until it should be played.

Slogan   A short, pithy group of words used to describe a radio station.

Slug   A part of a news script that gives the title or general content of a story.

SMPTE time code   An electronic language developed for video by the Society of Motion Picture and Television Engineers that identifies each picture frame.

S/N   See *Signal-to-noise ratio*.

Solid-state recorder   An audio recorder that uses compact flash or other solid-state storage devices as its recording medium.

Solo switch   A button that allows one particular audio board sound to be heard on the monitor.

Sound bite   A short audio statement in which a person gives information or comments on some topic.

Sound card   See *Audio card*.

Sound designer   A person who develops the overall approach to sound for a video production.

Sound editor   The person who spots for and acquires the various sounds needed to accompany a video production.

Soundfile   A segment of audio recorded on a hard disk; usually associated with digital audio editors.

Soundproofing   Methods of keeping wanted sound in the studio and unwanted sound out of it.

Sound signal   A noise that has not been processed into an electromagnetic form.

Source/tape switch   A switch that allows someone to monitor either the input or the output of a tape recorder.

Spaced-pair miking   See *A-B miking*.

S/PDIF   A Sony-Philips Interface Format standard for RCA connectors.

Speaker   A transducer that converts electrical energy into sound energy.

Speaker level   An input that has been amplified several times in order to drive a speaker.

Speed selector switch   On a turntable, the control that determines whether the record plays at 33$\frac{1}{3}$ RPM or 45 RPM.

Splicing block   The device that held audio tape during analog editing.

Splicing tape   Special tape used for holding together audio tape in the analog editing process.

Split-pair miking   See *A-B miking*.

Spotting sheet   A paper that indicates what sounds are needed and when they are needed for a video production.

Stacking   A multitrack overdubbing technique in which an announcer "sings harmony" to a previously recorded track.

Standby   A signal given to talent just prior to going on-air by holding one hand above the head with the palm forward.

Standing wave   A combination of a sound wave going in one direction and an identical sound wave going in the opposite direction.

Station ID   A short over-the-air identification of a station usually giving its call letters and perhaps its slogan; the FCC requires station identification at least once an hour.

Stereo   Sound recording and reproduction that uses two channels, one coming from the right and the other from the left, to imitate live sound as closely as possible.

Stereo microphone   A microphone that incorporates small, multiple sound-generating elements as part of a single microphone housing that can record sound in such a way that when it is played back, it sounds like it is coming from two areas.

Stereo synthesizer   A device that inputs a monophonic audio signal and simulates a stereo output signal.

Stinger   Individual, short, sharp sound effects designed to capture immediate attention.

Stop set   A series of commercials played over the air at one time.

Streaming audio   Using the Internet to transfer audio data from one computer to another so that it can be heard in real time.

Stringer   A person who is paid for news stories he or she gathers if some news organization uses them.

Stylus   A small, compliant strip of metal that vibrates in record grooves.

Super-cardioid   Picking up sound well from the front but not the sides; usually refers to a microphone pickup pattern.

Supply reel   The reel on the lefthand side of a reel-to-reel or cassette tape recorder that holds the tape before it is recorded or played.

Supra-aural   See *Open-air headphones*.

Surface-mount microphone   See *Pressure zone microphone*.

Surround sound   A multichannel audio format that refers to five full-bandwidth channels (right, left, center, right rear, left rear) and one limited-bandwidth channel (bass subwoofer).

Sustain   The amount of time a sound holds its volume.

Sustain ending   Music or songs that end with the last notes held for a period of time, then gradually faded out.

Sweeper   A recorded element usually consisting of voice, music, and/or sound effects that creates a transition between songs or commercials and music.

Sweetening   The act of improving sound during the post-production stage of audio or video production.

Sync sound   Audio that must match the video, such as spoken words that need to match lip movement.

Take-up reel   The reel on the right-hand side of a reel-to-reel or cassette tape recorder that holds the tape after it is recorded or played.

Talk-back switch   A simple intercom on an audio console that allows the operator to talk with someone in another studio.

Tape guide   A stationary pin that leads tape through the transport system of a reel-to-reel recorder.

Tape transport   The part of a tape recorder that moves the tape from the supply reel to the take-up reel.

Target audience   The group of people, usually defined by demographics, that a radio station particularly wants to attract.

Teaser   A short segment, usually broadcast before a commercial break, to keep the listeners tuned to the station.

Telephone coupler   See *Telephone interface*.

Telephone interface   A piece of equipment that connects telephone lines to broadcast equipment.

Telex   A location to station transmission system based on telegraph technology but adapted for short wave radio.

Tension arm   A moveable guide for tape on a reel-to-reel recorder.

Three-pin connecter   See *XLR connector*.

Three-way system   A monitor speaker that divides sound not just to a woofer and tweeter, but also to another driver such as a midrange.

Threshold of hearing   The softest sound the human ear can hear, noted as 0 decibels.

Threshold of pain   The loudness level at which the ear begins to hurt, usually about 120 decibels.

Timbre   The distinctive quality of tone that each voice or musical instrument has, composed of the fundamental tone, plus overtones and harmonics.

Time code A system of marking frames of audio and video that indicates hours, minutes, seconds, and frames and that can be used to place audio in sync with video because they both have the same time code.

Timing sheet A list given to a music composer that gives time code numbers where music should be written for a video project.

Time line The part of an editing program that shows a graphical display of the sound so that it can be edited.

Tone The quality of a particular sound.

Tone arm The device that holds the turntable cartridge and stylus.

Tone control A control that increases the volume of the high frequencies or the low frequencies.

Tone generator An element in an audio board or other piece or equipment that produces a tone that can be set to 100 percent to calibrate equipment.

Toslink A connector developed by Toshiba that is used for digital audio.

Track sheet A format for keeping notes of what material is recorded on what tracks of a multitrack recording.

Transducer A device that converts one form of energy into another.

Transmitter Equipment used to broadcast a radio signal.

Transport button Mechanisms, such as play and fast forward, that move audio through a system, be it a tape recorder, an editing system, or another form of audio.

Tray The area where the CD sits so that it can spin and be read by the laser.

Trim control See *Gain trim*.

Trimmed Cut down or edited, usually only a small amount.

Tube microphone Condenser microphones that incorporate a vacuum tube.

Turntable A device for spinning a record and converting its vibrations into electrical energy.

Tweeter The part of a speaker that produces high frequencies.

Two-column script Scripts that have video elements in the left-hand column and audio elements in the right-hand column.

Two-track stereo The recording of two tracks on one tape, both going in the same direction to produce stereo sound.

Two-way speaker system A speaker that has a woofer, a tweeter, and a crossover to send the sound to each.

Ultra-cardioid Picking up sound well from the front, but not the back or sides; usually refers to a microphone pickup pattern.

Unbalanced cable Cable with two wires, of which one is positive and the other is combined negative and ground.

Undermodulated An audio signal or recording in which the volume of the signal is too low, causing noise to be more noticeable.

Unidirectional Picking up sound from one direction; usually refers to a microphone pickup pattern.

Unity-gain A device whose circuits do not make the output signal louder or softer than the input signal.

Upmix To take a monaural sound and make it into stereo or surround sound.

USB A Universal Serial Bus connector used to link audio (and other things) to computers.

User interface A device, such as a keyboard or mouse, that allows a person to interact with a computer.

Utility See *Auxiliary*.

Variable bit rate (VBR) A compression technology used with on-demand files that automatically reduces the amount of data where there is little or no signal, such as during silence.

Variable resistor A device that controls the amount of signal that gets through the audio console, and thereby controls the volume.

VBR See *Variable bit rate*.

Vented box See *Bass reflex*.

Vinyl A durable synthetic resin used to make records.

Voice doubling A multitrack overdubbing technique in which an announcer reads the same script on two different tracks to give a double voice effect.

Voice-over Speech over something else, such as music.

Voice tracking The practice of a radio announcer recording various vocal elements that will later be incorporated into a regular on-air shift, either locally or in a different city.

Volume Loudness.

Volume control See *Gain control*.

VU meter A unit that gives a visual indication of the level of volume.

Walking over Talking over the vocal portion of a song, such as when an announcer is introducing a record; normally, an announcer talks over only the instrumental portion.

Walla walla A background sound created by recording people's voices in a manner in which you cannot hear the actual words they are saying.

Waveform The shape of an electromagnetic wave.

Wavelength The distance between two crests of a radio or sound wave.

Web page A screen that can be called up on the Internet using a computer browser.

Well See *Tray*.

Wild track Background noises that are desirable for an audio or video production and that are often recorded and added to the production; they are also called ambient sounds and the name "wild track" comes from the fact that they are recorded "wild," as in separate from the video or main audio.

Windscreen A ball-shaped accessory placed over the microphone to reduce unwanted sound coming from wind or breezes.

Wireless headphone A device to hear sound that transmits an RF or an infrared audio signal from the source to the headphone.

Wireless microphone Another name for an FM microphone.

Woofer The part of the speaker that produces low frequencies.

Wow Slow variations in sound speed.

XLR connector A connector with three prongs. Also known as Cannon.

X-Y miking A method of stereo miking in which two microphones are placed like crossed swords.

APPENDIX

ANALOG AUDIO EQUIPMENT

A.1 INTRODUCTION

Analog technology served the audio world well for approximately a century. Now, however, a person entering the field of audio production will encounter primarily **digital** equipment. As a result, analog equipment has lost its importance—and we have relegated it to the back of the book! It is highly unlikely that you will ever work in an analog-dominated environment, but many facilities still have analog equipment that they use on occasion or for specialized purposes. In this appendix, we will discuss many of these pieces of equipment, giving you the information you will need to know if you are in a position where you are operating the equipment.

We will not discuss microphones or speakers in this appendix. Although they can contain digital elements, they are still basically analog and probably always will be. The human voice box and the human ear operate in an analog fashion. Barring some major genetic breakthrough, people are not going to spew forth 0s and 1s from their mouths or hear them with their ears. At the beginning and end of the audio process, analog will remain with us. Therefore, what was discussed in Chapters 4 and 7 about microphones and speakers covers the analog aspects of these pieces of equipment.

Even if you have no contact with the analog equipment discussed in this chapter, you may find it interesting or perhaps just quaint. A knowledge of history is always advantageous. Some of the capabilities and quirks of modern digital equipment are there because people wanted to keep the best of the analog characteristics and make it easy for people who were experienced in analog to make the transition to digital. You may wind up marveling at what audio practitioners were able to do in the past, given some of the limitations of the equipment.

A.2 TURNTABLES

The **turntable** (see Figure A.1) was the first piece of analog equipment to succumb to digital replacement when the **compact disc (CD)** player became popular in the early 1980s. Because a turntable cannot record, its functions relate only to playing back sound material. The two basic functions are to spin a record at the precise speed at which it was recorded, and to convert the variations in the grooves of the record to electrical energy. The main parts of most professional turntables include a platter, an on/off switch, a motor, a speed selector switch, a tone arm, a cartridge/stylus, and a preamplifier.

The **platter** is a metal plate about 12 inches across covered by a felt or rubber mat. It spins the record that is placed on top of it. The **on/off switch** turns on the **motor** and the motor turns the platter. The **speed selector switch** is needed because during the reign of turntables several types and sizes of records were developed. The first were 10-inch discs invented around 1900 that operated at 78 **revolutions per minute (RPM)**. They had very large grooves

FIGURE A.1 A turntable showing the on/off switch, speed selector buttons, platter, tone arm with the cartridge and stylus at the end, and volume control. (Image courtesy of Denon Electronics.)

and held only 3 minutes of music per side. Also, they were made of **shellac** and so were thick and heavy, and broke easily. In the late 1940s, two different formats that were made of less breakable **vinyl** and had smaller grooves started to replace the 78s. One was 7 inches in diameter, played at 45 RPM, and held about 5 minutes per side. The other was the **long-play (LP)** record, which was 12 inches, operated at 33-1/3 RPM, and could hold about 30 minutes per side. Because these various formats existed, turntables were developed with a speed selector switch that controlled the speed of the motor.

The **tone arm** is usually a metal tube attached to a pivot assembly near the back of the turntable. Its purpose is to house the **cartridge** and **stylus** and allow them to move freely across the record as it is played. The stylus (sometimes referred to as the needle) is a small, highly compliant strip of metal with a diamond end that touches the record groove. It picks up the vibrations from the record and sends them to the cartridge where they are converted into variations in voltage and then sent to the **preamplifier** to increase the level of the signal. From there, the signal can be sent to another piece of equipment, such as a speaker or an audio board. Some turntables have a volume control to adjust the loudness of the sound leaving the turntable.

A.3 TURNTABLE USE

Today, turntables are used as performance instruments, an application that early audio technicians never envisioned, and a use that is possible because of the way that turntables cue (see Production Tip A.A). Club disc jockeys and others utilize turntables to create unusual sounds that they incorporate within their performances. Turntables are also used to play vinyl recordings that are in someone's record collection and were never remastered for compact disc. In fact, some new turntables have a digital output to facilitate transferring vinyl discs to some form of digital media.

If you are working with a turntable, you should handle the tone arm gently. Most tone arms have small handles by the cartridge/stylus assemble that you should use to pick up the arm and place it on the record. Do not touch the stylus with your fingers. If it's necessary to remove dust, do this by blowing lightly on it, or use a fine-hair brush. If you are using a turntable made after 1960, it probably only has a two-speed speed selector switch of 45 or 33-1/3 RPM, because by then, those formats had replaced the 78s. One other thing to watch for is that the 45 RPM records have a larger center hole than the 33s, so turntables include a separate adapter to fill the hole. If that adapter has been misplaced (and many of them have), you will not be able to play the 45 RPM records.

Care of the records is also very important. Dust can be a big problem, because it can cause permanent pops in the record grooves and scratches on the record. The static electricity produced by playing a record compounds the

problem by attracting more dust. Use a good-quality record cleaner before playing records to help minimize the dust problem. Unlike CDs, records can be wiped clean with a cloth and record-cleaning fluid, using a circular motion following the record grooves. Records should be handled by the edges to avoid getting fingerprints on the grooved surface. Unless they're being played, keep records in their paper/plastic inner sleeve and cardboard jacket and stored them in a vertical position to prevent them from warping.

PRODUCTION TIP A.A
Cueing Records

If you are going to be playing a record on a turntable or using a turntable as a musical instrument, you will need to use its ability to **cue**. When radio disc jockeys used turntables, their cueing process was fairly complicated by today's standards. Because the motor does not get up to speed instantly, the record has to start turning slightly before its sound is needed. If the motor isn't up to speed when the music starts, the record produces a **wow** sound—a change in pitch caused by slow variations in the playback speed. (You can hear this sound on the book's accompanying CD-ROM.) This was an undesirable sound on early radio, but is often used to advantage by today's club disc jockeys to create unusual audio effects.

There are several techniques for cueing records. For the conventional one, you place the stylus in the outer groove and then rotate the turntable platter clockwise until the first sound is heard. Then, if you do not want the "wow," you back-track the platter (turn it in reverse) about a quarter turn. Then you turn the on/off switch to "on" just before you want the sound to begin. Of course, if you want a "wow," you can start a record at any point and also rotate it while it is playing.

Another way to cue a record is known as **slip cueing**, because you hold the edge of the record with your finger, using enough force to keep it from spinning when the on/off switch is turned to "on" (the turntable platter is spinning below the record). Then you release the record when the actual sound is to begin. You can attempt to slip cue only if the turntable platter has a felt mat: a rubber mat does not allow the platter to continue to spin as you hold the record edge. Both methods of cueing records take practice and skill and can produce interesting effects.

A.4 REEL-TO-REEL AUDIO TAPE RECORDERS

Prior to the advent of digital recorders, analog **audio tape recorders** were the workhorses of the production room. The **reel-to-reel tape recorder** first surfaced in the 1940s and was the most-used recorder for several decades. All tape recorders are devices that rearrange particles on magnetic tape so that sound impulses can be stored on the tape and played back later. The physical makeup of the tape consists of three basic layers: a **plastic base** sandwiched between a **backing layer** and a **magnetic layer** (see Figure A.2). The top layer is composed of tiny slivers of magnetic oxides that are capable of storing an electromagnetic signal. Another type of tape, called **leader tape**, is made of colored paper or plastic and is not capable of recording because it does not have a magnetic layer. Its main use is at the beginning and end of a tape so that it undergoes the wear and tear of threading the tape through the recorder, not the magnetic tape. It can also be written on, so it can be used to identify what is on the tape. Reel-to-reel recorders use magnetic tape and leader tape that is 1/4-inch wide, but other types of recorders use different widths.

The rearranging of particles on the magnetic tape is undertaken by the recorder's **heads**, which are small electromagnets. When a tape is unrecorded, it consists of magnetic particles that are on the tape in a random pattern (see Figure A.3). The heads arrange these particles to represent sounds. Usually, professional-quality recorders have three heads: erase, record, and play. The erase head is always before the record head so that old material can be erased and new material recorded at the same time. With the play head behind the record head, it's possible to monitor what you've just recorded. When the machine is just in play, the erase and record heads are disengaged.

An important part of a reel-to-reel tape recorder is its **tape transport**, which is clearly shown in Figure A.4. It is the part of the recorder that is involved with the actual motion of the audio tape. The audio tape is threaded manually from left to right, so the left reel is the **supply reel** (the reel that has audio tape on it as you begin to use the recorder) and the right reel is the **take-up reel**, which starts out empty. Behind each reel (inside the tape recorder) are motors that help drive the tape from one reel to the other and help maintain proper tape tension. The standard reel sizes used in audio production for many years were 5-inch, 7-inch, and 10½-inch reels.

The audio tape is kept in line with various **tape guides** and **tension arms** so that it properly passes the heads (which are under the little box in the middle of the recorder). The tape guides are sometimes just stationary pins that provide a track or groove the width of the audio tape. The tension arms are generally movable. As the audio tape threads through them, they provide some spring, or tension, against the tape. One of these tension arms is usually an **idler arm**; if the tape breaks, this arm drops down into an "off" position, and the reel-to-reel recorder stops running. The heart of the tape transport is the capstan and pinch roller. Normally located just to the right of the tape heads, the **capstan** is a metal shaft, and the **pinch roller** is a

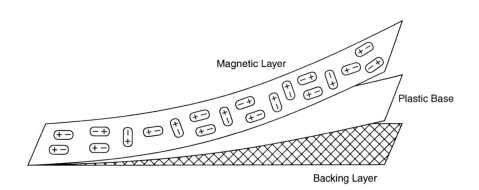

FIGURE A.2 The basic "layers" of audio tape are the magnetic layer, the plastic base, and the backing layer.

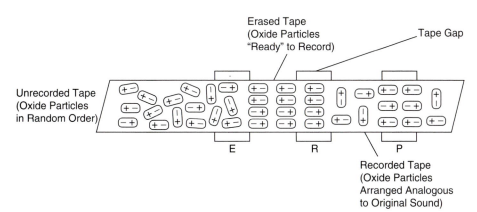

FIGURE A.3 Tape recorder heads align the metallic particles of audio tape in a pattern analogous to the original sound.

FIGURE A.4 The top part of this reel-to-reel recorder includes the supply and take-up reel, tension arm, tape guides, heads under the box with "Tascam" on it, capstan, pinch roller, and idler arm. The bottom section contains VU meters, pots, controls for playing, pausing, and so on, and various function switches to route the sound. (Image courtesy of Tascam.)

rubber wheel. The audio tape must pass between these two components. When the recorder is running, the pinch roller holds the tape against the revolving capstan. The capstan controls the speed of the tape as it passes the heads.

Other components of a reel-to-reel recorder are its controls. Typically, recorders have buttons for on/off, rewind, fast-forward, play, stop, pause, and record. Often professional recorders also have a cue button that allows the tape to stay in contact with the tape heads during rewind and fast forward or even in the stop position, so you can aurally find a certain spot on the tape. The electronics of the audio recorder include record-level and play-level **potentiometers**, VU meters, and a source/tape switch. The **record-level pots** adjust the volume or level of the incoming sound signal while **play-level pots** control the volume of the sound signal as it's being played from the audio tape. What signal you see on the audio tape recorder **VU meter** is dependent on where the **source/tape switch** is set. In the "source" position, the VU meter shows the volume of the incoming signal while in the "tape" position, the VU meter shows the output level of the reproduced signal at the playback head. Later-model reel-to-reel recorders have counters that show minutes and seconds. Reel-to-reel tape recorders had speed selection because they were able to record and play back at varying speeds such as 7½ IPS (inches per second) and 15 IPS.

A.5 REEL-TO-REEL RECORDER USE

Today, reel-to-reel recorders are used primarily to play back archived materials. Many important programs were stored on reel-to-reel tapes, especially the 10½-inch reels, because they could hold a great deal of information. Today the content of those reels, like the content of vinyl records, is being transferred to digital media. One aspect of the 10½-inch reels is that they had a larger hole in the middle than other size reels and therefore needed special hubs to hold them on the supply and take-up reels. These hubs, like the 45 RPM adapters, may have strayed from their recorders.

If you are playing something back on a reel-to-reel recorder and it sounds groggy or like Donald Duck, you probably need to change the speed control. If the sound is not consistent or fades in and out, you may have dirty heads. Normal use of a tape recorder leaves some oxide material on or near the heads. It's good production practice to clean the tape heads gently with cotton swabs and head cleaner or denatured alcohol before you begin any production work. If there is one dominant sound but little bits of other sound creep in that probably means there is **cross-talk**—the signal from the dominant track is picking up sound from an adjacent track. You can check to make

FIGURE A.5 Drop-out is an audio tape problem that results in flaking of the oxide coating.

sure that the tape is properly aligned as it passes the heads, but the problem might not be correctable.

Another reason that you might hear garbled sound is that the recorder you are listening on has a different track configuration than the recorder used to record the material. Although all reel-to-reel recorders used tape that was 1/4-inch wide, they used the tape space in different ways. There were **full-track** recorders that used the whole 1/4-inch space to record one mono signal. There was also **half-track mono**, in which one signal could be recorded on the top half of the tape and then the tape was turned over and another signal was recorded on the other part of the tape going the opposite direction. When stereo came along, two signals were recorded on the tape, both going the same way, a configuration known as **two-track stereo**. Later on, reel-to-reel recorders were configured to record two stereo signals or a total of four tracks (**quarter-track stereo**) with each occupying one quarter of the tape: two going one way and two going the other way.

This was all well and good, except that tapes recorded on one type of machine might sound incoherent on another. For example, a tape recorded on a quarter-track stereo machine can be played on a full-track mono recorder. All the tracks will be heard; however, there will be recorded material going both forward and backward, and the resulting sound will be a garble. If you run into this problem when you are trying to listen to a tape, there is little you can do except try to find a different, compatible reel-to-reel recorder.

Print-through is another problem you may experience, especially if you are dealing with older tapes. It is the transfer of the magnetic signal on one layer of tape to the magnetic signal on the next layer of tape, either above it or below it on the reel. Visualize a jelly sandwich stacked on top of a peanut butter sandwich. If the jelly soaks through the bottom piece of bread and onto the peanut butter, print-through has occurred. It's most audible when one of the tape layers contains a very loud sound and the adjacent layer contains a soft sound. If you are recording something, you can prevent later print-through by making sure you don't overmodulate the signal and by using tape that is at least 1.5 mils (thousandths of an inch) thick.

Perhaps the biggest problem with audio tape is signal loss due to drop-out. **Drop-out** (see Figure A.5) is a defect in the oxide coating that prevents the signal at that point from being recorded. Drop-out can be a problem that occurred during the manufacturing of the tape, but it can also be caused by flaking of the oxide coating due to heavy use or improper storage. The results of these problems

(incorrect speed, cross-talk, tracking incompatibility, print-through, and drop-out) can be heard on the CD-ROM that accompanies this book. To some extent these problems can be overcome with digital technologies. For example, sound can be artificially created to fill in where drop-out has occurred. Although important material is restored that way, the process is tedious and expensive.

PRODUCTION TIP A.B
Sel Sync

If you are recording using a reel-to-reel recorder, you may need **sel sync** (selective synchronization). As already mentioned, the erase head is first followed by the record head, followed by the play head. Because of this head arrangement, you can't easily record one track in synchronization with a previously recorded track. For example, if you record one voice on one track and want to record another voice on another track on the same tape, you run into the following problem. As the previously recorded voice is playing, the sound signal is coming from the play head, but the second voice is recording at the record head. Because of the small distance between these two heads, you hear the previously recorded material a split second before you can record the second voice and therefore the two tracks will be out of sync when played back. To overcome this problem, some recorders have sel sync, which makes the record head also act as the play head. Now you're hearing the previously recorded material at the same time as you're recording the new material, so there is no time difference between them, and you can easily synchronize the two recordings.

A.6 CASSETTE TAPE RECORDERS

The **cassette recorder** found its way into the broadcast facility in the 1960s mainly because of its portability and ease of use, but also because a professional-quality cassette recorder could offer high-quality recordings. There are units, such as the one shown in Figure A.6 that mount into a rack in the studio, and there are also small portable cassette recorders that reporters and others can take into the field. (Prior to the rise of digital equipment, the portable recorders were also popular with consumers.)

One of the reasons (in addition to improved electronics) the recorder could be made in a portable configuration was that the cassette tape is narrower (1/8-inch) as compared to the 1/4-inch reel-to-reel tape. The tape also moves at a little less than 2 inches per second, so not as much tape is needed to obtain a quality recording. This tape is housed in a plastic case (see Figure A.7) that slips into the recorder—a definite time saver, because no one needs to thread it manually.

FIGURE A.6 A cassette recorder that mounts in a studio rack. (Image courtesy of Tascam.)

FIGURE A.7 The internal structure of an audio cassette tape.

A.7 CASSETTE RECORDER USE

Of all the analog tape recorder equipment, this is the one most likely to still be used in a production facility. If you do use one to record, you need to be aware of several potential issues. The portable recorders have a built-in microphone, but you should avoid using this microphone for broadcast work, because it often picks up as much internal noise (tape recorder motor, for example) as the sound you want. Use a good-quality microphone like those mentioned in Chapter 4.

Also, the tape that is in the cassette housing has a short leader tape attached at each end, and both ends of the tape are permanently attached to the reels. When recording onto cassettes, it's important to remember the leader tape, because if you're at the very beginning of the cassette, the actual recording will not begin for a few seconds, until you are past the leader tape.

Another feature of the cassette is the knock-out tab on the back edge of the cassette shell. There are two of these little plastic tabs (one for each side of the cassette), which allow the recorder to go into record mode. If someone has previously recorded on the tape and knocked out the tabs in order to be sure to save what was recorded, you won't be able to record over the cassette. To solve this problem, you

can put a small piece of cellophane tape over where the tab was, and it will record just as if the tab were still there.

You may also run into track problems, although they are not as confusing or severe as those related to reel-to-reel recorders. There are two basic cassette tape-recording methods. One is half-track mono and the other is quarter-track stereo. However, unlike reel-to-reel configurations, the tracks are laid out in such a way that the mono configuration and stereo configuration are compatible. In other words, you can hear a tape recorded using half-track mono on a stereo recorder and you can hear a cassette recorded in stereo on a mono recorder, but of course it will be heard as mono, not stereo.

A.8 CARTRIDGE TAPE RECORDERS

The **cartridge recorder** (shown in Figure A.8) became predominant in radio facilities during the 1960s and was used to play commercials, public service announcements, station promos, and jingles. For some radio stations, even the music was transferred from records to cartridge. The audio tape cartridge is constructed as a plastic container with a continuous loop of tape inside. The tape pulls from the inside and winds on the outside of the spool.

Audio carts put an inaudible cue tone just in front of the recorded information so that when music or a spot is played, the tone signals the machine to stop before it repeats itself. This automatic recueing also allows several different spots to be put on one cartridge and played one at a time without fear of playing another before stopping the machine. As cart machines became more sophisticated, they were able to put secondary and tertiary cue tones on the cartridge that could be used to indicate the end of a spot, to start another cart machine, and to activate other programming features often found in automated situations.

A.9 CARTRIDGE RECORDER USE

You are not likely to use analog cart machines, as they have been replaced by a variety of digital equipment. Most carts

Record/Play Unit   Play Only Unit

FIGURE A.8 The cartridge recorder and player once played a major role in delivering the commercials, PSAs, promos, jingles, and music heard on the radio. (Image courtesy of International Tapetronics Corporation.)

did not hold more than 5 minutes of tape, so they were not used for archival purposes. It you do need to operate one, however, they are simple. Some are play only, and because they cue themselves and stop themselves, all you really need to do is push the play button. Ones that record have a meter for setting levels and a record button.

FIGURE A.9   A splicing block. (Image courtesy of Xedit Corporation.)

A.10 AUDIO TAPE EDITING TOOLS

The tools used to edit during most of the analog days were not electronic—they consisted of a grease pencil, a splicing block, a razor blade, and splicing tape. The editing process was **cut 'n' splice** and has all but been replaced by computer editing. But if you have a need to undertake cut 'n' splice editing, you will use a white or yellow **grease pencil** to physically mark on the back or unrecorded side of the tape the points where you're going to cut. You do this utilizing a reel-to-reel recorder, where the tape is totally exposed. It is difficult to impossible to edit with a cassette or cartridge. The **splicing block** is a small metal or plastic block (see Figure A.9) with a channel to hold the audio tape and two grooves to guide the razor blade when cutting the tape. The grooves are usually at 45-degree and 90-degree angles to the audio tape. For almost all production work, you'll use the diagonal cut, because it provides more surface for contact with the splicing tape at the point of the edit and it provides a smoother sound transition. Any standard single-edged **razor blade** will work for cutting audio tape. **Splicing tape** is commercially available, although a bit hard to find these days, and is specially designed so that its adhesive material does not soak through the audio tape and gum up the heads of the tape recorder. Do not use cellophane tape to do editing work. Splicing tape is slightly narrower than audio tape so that any excess adhesive material does not protrude beyond the edge of the audio tape.

Audio was sometimes edited using a **dubbing** method, and some facilities still use this method for digital as well as analog editing. It requires the use of two tape recorders. You simply dub or copy from one to the other with the "master" tape recorder in the play mode, and the "slave" tape recorder in the record mode. You cannot do the precise types of editing that computer editing allows, but through careful manipulation you can transfer the material you want and eliminate material you do not want. Usually dubbing produces a glitch at the edit point that can range from barely noticeable to terrible, depending on the tape recorders used. Dubbing works very well if you simply want to make duplicate copies of any existing tape.

A.11 MAKING EDITS

If you are editing with the cut 'n' splice method, you will find that this involves a two-step process: marking the edit points and then splicing. Because audio tape passes through the recorder from left to right, sounds are recorded on the tape in the same manner. For example, the phrase "editing is really a two-step process" would be recorded on audio tape in this manner: "ssecorp pets-owt a yllaer si gnitide"—the rightmost word ("editing") would be recorded first. If you want to edit out the word "really" in this phrase, you would make two edit points, one on each side of the word. To do this, you find the playback head on the reel-to-reel recorder then play the tape, stopping it right before the word "really." By rocking the tape reels back and forth in the stop position, you can hear (with some practice) the beginning and end of the word "really." Make your mark at those two places in line with the middle of the play head, being careful not to get grease pencil on the head because it will cause head clog. If you are making more edits, you can proceed to mark them, too.

Once you have marked the edit points, it's time to perform the actual cut 'n' splice (see Figure A.10). Normal splicing technique follows these steps:

A. *Position the tape at the first edit mark in the splicing block.* You can do this by placing the splicing block below the recorder play head and pulling the tape down to it. The unrecorded side of the tape should be facing up in the splicing block, and the edit mark should be at the 45-degree cutting groove.

B. *Cut the tape at your first mark.* A simple slicing motion with the blade through the groove should cut the tape cleanly. Be careful! Razor blades are sharp and will cut your fingers as easily as they cut audio tape.

C. *Repeat Steps A and B at the second edit mark.* Remove the unwanted piece of audio tape, but don't discard it yet. It's good production practice to hang on to cut-out tape until after you're sure the splice has been accomplished as you want it. It's possible (although difficult) to splice the cut-out piece of tape back in and try the splice again if you've made a mistake.

D. *Butt the remaining tape ends together.* Move both pieces of the tape slightly left or right so that you don't butt them together directly over the cutting groove.

E. *Apply the splicing tape on the edit.* About 3/4 inch of tape is the proper amount. The splicing tape should be centered at the edit. Because the splicing tape is narrower than the audio tape, it should not protrude over either edge of the audio tape.

F. *Smooth out the splicing tape.* Be sure to get air bubbles out from under the splicing tape for a strong bond. Rubbing your fingernail over the splice will usually take care of this.

G. *Remove the audio tape from the splicing block.* Never do this by grasping one end and lifting; the edges of the channel in the splicer can damage the audio tape. The proper procedure is to grasp both ends of the tape just beyond the splicing block, apply slight pressure to the tape by pulling your hands in opposite directions, and lift straight up. The tape will pop right out of the block, and you will have completed your splice.

It's best not to fast rewind the tape until you've played it, to help secure the splice, so manually wind the tape on the feed reel until you're past the splice. Then, thread the tape on your recorder, and listen to the edited tape. If it came out as you wanted, you can discard the unwanted tape section. Sometimes you may find it necessary to shave a piece of the edit by splicing off one edge of the tape. If you've made a good edit mark, however, you'll rarely have to do this.

Editors often encounter problems with their first few splices. These are usually overcome with practice and experience. One of the most common problems with splicing-tape manipulation is simply using too much; a piece of splicing tape that's too long is difficult to position properly on the audio tape and makes the tape too stiff at the edit, which prevents proper contact with the tape recorder heads. On the other hand, a piece of splicing tape that's too short may not hold the audio tape together during normal use. Other problems arise when the splicing tape is put on crooked; a portion of the splicing tape will hang over the edges of the audio tape, making it impossible for the tape to glide through the tape recorder transport properly. Another problem is leaving a gap as you butt the two tape ends together. Obviously, a gap at the edit point will be heard as an interruption of sound or too long a pause. On the other hand, if you overlap the two tape ends as you butt them together, the splice won't occur where you thought it would. By now, you may be glad you were not editing during the analog era.

A.12 ANALOG AUDIO CONSOLES

It is not uncommon to find an analog **audio console** in the production facility. In fact, unlike most of the other pieces of analog equipment, analog audio consoles are still being manufactured (see Figure A.11). They are built so that they can handle digital inputs (such as CD players) and output to digital sources (such as a server), but the electronics of the console itself are analog. Some people feel that going through an analog process gives audio a more mellow, pleasing sound.

A.13 ANALOG AUDIO CONSOLE USE

The functions of an analog audio console, whether one from the past or one that is new, are essentially the same as those discussed in Chapter 5, "The Audio Console," for digital consoles. They have **input selectors** and **output selectors**, **VU meters**, **headphone jacks**, and so on. This is due in part to the fact that digital consoles were made to imitate analog consoles so that the operators switching from analog to digital would not have a steep learning curve. In addition, the functions that you need from a mixer (the ability to adjust **volume**, **equalize**, **pan**, and so on) are the same for the digital realm as for analog.

The main difference is the interface and the size. With a digital console, you may call up and execute functions by operating a mouse or touching a screen, and you can place on a computer screen only those functions that you need. With an analog board, you physically manipulate levers, buttons, and knobs. If these are numerous, then the console is going to be very large, whereas the digital console, regardless of the number of functions, can be the size of a computer screen.

A.14 SIGNAL PROCESSING EQUIPMENT

Analog **signal processing** often involved some ingenuity. For example, the equivalent of **digital delay** was sometimes accomplished by stringing audio tape from one recorder to

FIGURE A.10 To edit audio tape: (A) position tape at first edit mark; (B) cut tape at first mark; (C) position and cut tape at second edit mark; (D) butt tape ends together; (E) apply splicing tape; (F) smooth out splicing tape; (G) remove audio tape from splicing block.

FIGURE A.11   An analog audio console. (Image Courtesy of Toft Audio Designs.)

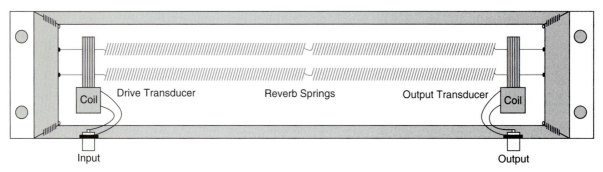

FIGURE A.12   The structure of analog spring reverberation.

another. An operator could listen to what was being said as the tape passed the first recorder's play head but the words would not be broadcast until the tape passed the second recorder's play head. If something inappropriate was said, the operator could shut off the second tape recorder before the nasty words got there.

Reverb was sometimes created by a spring (see Figure A.12). A transducer at one end of the spring caused the spring to vibrate when a signal was sent through it. A microphone at the other end picked up the altered signal from the spring. Those days are gone, having given way to digital signal processing, but there were also analog stand-alone black boxes, such as **equalizers**, **filters**, **compressors**, and **limiters**, and some of those are still in use. As with analog audio consoles, some people like the sound that they produce better than that from digital equipment or software programs.

A.15 SIGNAL PROCESSING USE

You won't find people stringing tape around the studio anymore, but you may need to operate analog stand-alone signal processing equipment. Each manufacturer has different configurations of controls for its signal processing equipment, so it helps if the instruction manuals are still available. Also, by using the information provided in Chapter 8, "Signal Processing Equipment," you should be able to get the equipment to operate effectively.

A.16 CONCLUSION

For years, turntables and audio tape recorders were the primary workhorses in most radio production studios and cut 'n' splice was the only way to edit audio tape. With the advent of digital equipment and the quality and convenience it offers, the use of older analog equipment and production techniques has all but disappeared. Analog has had an illustrious past and deserves occasional use and a revered position in the history of sound.

INDEX

257